Jock Dom

Russia

Revolution and
Counter-Revolution
1905-1924

A View from the Communist Left

Prometheus Publications

Published by
Prometheus Publications

BM CWO
LONDON
WC1N 3XX

email: uk@leftcom.org
http://www.leftcom.org

ISBN: 978-0-9935805-3-6

For Joyce

Contents

Introduction   5
Chapter 1: Prelude to Revolution   11
Chapter 2: Against Imperialist War   23
Chapter 3: The February Revolution   36
Chapter 4: Dual Power or Class War?   50
Chapter 5: The July Days   61
Chapter 6: The Kornilov Affair Mobilises the Masses   70
Chapter 7: The Proletariat Takes Power   79
Chapter 8: The "Honeymoon" of the Revolution   90
Chapter 9: The Treaty of Brest-Litovsk   102
Chapter 10: Soviet Power and the Bolshevik Party   111
Chapter 11: Red Army and Civil War in the International Context   124
Chapter 12: Proletarian Justice and Red Terror in the Civil War   142
Chapter 13: The Road to Kronstadt   158
Chapter 14: Kronstadt and Beyond   177
Chapter 15: Revolution is an Affair of the Masses   199
Chapter 16: Aftermath: Party, Class and Soviets   219
A Brief Chronological Guide   232
Selected Reading List of Works Cited   241
Endnotes   245
Index of Names   273

Introduction

The Russian Revolution of 1917 remains unique. It was the only time in history when workers themselves overturned the existing state in a conscious attempt to build socialism. The fact that the attempt eventually failed, and even gave rise to a monstrous new regime, does not diminish its significance, even after more than a century. For those who can see that capitalism is not the finally discovered form of human existence, but, on the contrary now threatens the very survival of our species, then the question of revolution will not go away. And any understanding of revolutionary experience has to take the Russian Revolution as its starting point. We say this in the full knowledge that there will be no repeat of the conditions which produced that revolution. There is nothing more ridiculous than revolutionaries today dressing themselves up in the clothes of the past. By "starting point", we mean looking at the broad outlines of the factors that produced that revolution and trying to identify what elements in it still have some validity for today. Undoubtedly much of what we draw from this analysis will be about "what is not to be done", since not only did the revolution fail in the longer run, but even in the way it developed in its earliest years, it was not flawless. This is unsurprising since revolutions tend not to stick to the clean paths of historical schemes dreamed up in the abstract. But the events of 1917-18 were not only more heroic, and promising, than the lies of Cold War hack historians would have us believe, they also offer rich lessons for the future.

There are already hundreds of books on the Russian Revolution in the English language alone. There have also been millions of words written about it by those who identify with the Communist Left. Most of these are about what lessons we can draw from the experience and are usually highly theoretical and highly valued as such. This book began life as a pamphlet in a similar vein. However, it soon became clear that we also needed to synthesise the more recent massive research into the revolution as a grassroots movement, in order to grasp its full story.

Not only do these take us deeper into the actual struggles of the time, but they also take us away from the stale Cold War analysis that some of the older generation were brought up with. The many works that have assisted in this respect are in the Reading List at the end but they all have their origins in the period after the current capitalist crisis made itself felt in the early 1970s, particularly following the collapse of the USSR, and which have gone on appearing right up to the present day. Using such sources, this book aims to furnish a new generation of the Communist Left with a balanced account of the successes and failures of the revolution itself, to enable them to make their own judgements.

At the same time these more recent works enable us to look at some issues in a fresh light. The most striking of which is to see the events of 1917, not as two separate revolutions, but as essentially part of the same process. Even though many of the participants themselves did not recognise it, the only way to understand the events of February 1917 is as a proletarian and not a "democratic" revolution. It is not surprising that contemporaries did not grasp this at first. It is always easier to study an event at a distance of time, than understand what is going on right in front of you. It is even harder when the action is taking a course that no-one really expected. The 1905 revolution had already shown what the Russian working class was capable of. In its wake both Trotsky and Lenin came up with formulae to try to explain how a feeble bourgeoisie tied to the apron strings of Tsarism could carry out a "democratic revolution". Both concluded in different fashion that the proletariat would first of all have to carry out the democratic revolution, but soon follow it up with a proletarian one. In 1917 history moved even faster than either of them had envisaged, and it certainly confounded everyone else. It was a perfect illustration of Marx's famous analysis in *The Eighteenth Brumaire of Louis Napoleon.* Just as human beings:

> *... seem to be occupied with revolutionising themselves and things, creating something that did not exist before, precisely in such epochs of revolutionary crisis they anxiously conjure up the spirits of the past to their service, borrowing from them names, battle slogans, and costumes in order to present this new scene in world history in time-honoured disguise and borrowed language.*

What made it even more difficult for the participants to see what was really going on was the fact that the bourgeoisie, aided and abetted by "socialists" like the Mensheviks and Right SRs, attempted to recuperate the revolutionary urge of the mass of the working class by setting up soviets whilst the most militant workers and the genuine supporters of soviets were still on the streets. The whole myth of "Dual Power" was built on this deceit. It was only Lenin's *April Theses* which recognised the new reality and gave expression to what was already happening – the continuous revolutionary events of 1917 were simply the playing out of the class war.

This work is divided into two parts.

The first demonstrates that in its historically-discovered form of government: the soviets, the Russian Revolution provided a lasting gain for the working class everywhere. We also demonstrate how, despite its inevitable subjective errors (much magnified by our class enemy), the Bolshevik Party became a genuinely revolutionary weapon of the Russian proletariat. On the way we debunk the myth that the October Revolution was a carefully planned coup by a bunch of professional conspirators, and demonstrate the profoundly mass character of October 1917.

The second half analyses how the revolution that began with so much promise of working class emancipation slid step by step into the creation of a one party state. The decline of working class initiative began as a result of an economic and social cataclysm which led to the working class abandoning their factories in hundreds of thousands, and was compounded by the civil war. In order to fight this war against Russian reactionaries aided by numerous imperialist powers, the Russian Communist Party (Bolshevik) created a standing army and a secret police. Neither of these were directly controlled by the soviets and they became the main agents of the new state that would be erected over the defeat of the workers. A defeat that would be confirmed by the events of 1921 at Kronstadt and elsewhere. This is an analysis from the viewpoint of the Communist Left but it is not a history of the various oppositions which could be broadly classed as the Russian Communist Left, even though they make an appearance. Their defeat in the face of the continuing isolation of the revolution to Russia will be the subject of another book which is already in preparation.

The counter-revolution in the USSR did not create state capitalism. That was already an increasing feature of capitalism everywhere, as it developed in the imperialist epoch. What a new class of *nomenklatura* did create though was a new, more extreme version of state capitalism. It was a command economy based on the continuing exploitation of the working class who were excluded from power. It was certainly not the socialism that the working class seemed to be fighting towards in 1917 and what we will need to once again fight for in the period to come. This study has been carried out with no other aim than to re-establish the communist programme of the next revolution on the original revolutionary premises of Marx.

It has been written for the new generation of working class militants, who may be more educated than in the past, but are less able to find a half-decent job in the declining capitalist system. They are no longer so hung up about the legacy of the counter-revolution that was the USSR (which vanished before they were born) but looking in increasing numbers at the social experiments of 1917-18, and the prospects of a saner and more rational society that could come out of them once we have absorbed the lessons. We hope that the research we have done will fire them to action against a system which has long lived on borrowed time. And for the rest of us time is running out. We have a world to save, but we can only win this battle by making capitalism history.

Acknowledgements

This is "a view" not "the view" from the Communist Left. The day we stop debating working class history is the day we have lost the fight for a working class future. It is the product of many years of discussion and debate within the Communist Left camp. For now, there are too many who have contributed to the formation of the ideas expressed here, but thanks in particular go to Joyce, Phil, Marcel, Nina, Miki, Ross, Emma, Mark, Saifi, Johan, Steve, Brennan, Andrew and Robert Mair who have proofread, made suggestions, questioned daft formulations, and generally made it a whole lot better than it would have been. Not all are members of the Communist Workers' Organisation, but all are certainly "*tovarishchi*".

Conventions Used in this Work

Dates: Tsarism, in line with the Russian Orthodox Church, continued to use the Julian Calendar which had been abandoned in the West for the Gregorian calendar centuries before. By the beginning of the Twentieth Century there were 13 days difference between them, which meant for example that the October Revolution took place on 25 October 1917 in Russia, but 7 November in Western Europe. The Provisional Government had announced a plan to abandon the Julian Calendar but the change did not occur until the Bolsheviks did it on 1/14 February 1918. Thus for dates before that both are given, dates after that refer only to the modern calendar.

Transliteration: The Russian language has more varied sounds than the English and the Cyrillic alphabet has more characters than the Roman so transliterations in different sources can vary. There are various "systems" (e.g. Library of Congress) employed by academic authors, but here the simplest and most common usage will be followed, unless quoting another author.

Petersburg: The city was founded by Peter the Great who named it after his patron saint but, due to his admiration for Dutch culture, it was originally St Petersburg (Sankt Pieter burkh) on its foundation in 1703. During World War One, on 1/14 September 1914 the German-sounding "sankt" and "burg" were dropped for the Russian name "Petrograd" (Peter's City). On the death of Lenin in 1924, despite his widow's objections, it was renamed Leningrad until, with the fall of the USSR, it reverted to St Petersburg in 1991. The Bolshevik Petersburg Committee, rejecting Russian nationalism, never used any other name in Lenin's lifetime. Workers in the city simply called it "Piter" whatever the official title. We have used only "Petersburg" throughout unless quoting a source (e.g. S.A.Smith's *Red Petrograd*).

The Bolsheviks: The Russian Social Democratic Labour Party (Bolsheviks or majority faction) formally separated from the Russian Social Democratic Labour Party Menshevik (or minority) faction in 1912. It changed its name to the Russian Communist Party (Bolshevik) in March 1918, a name it retained until 1925. Here we refer to them as "Bolsheviks" before March 1918 and as the "RCP(B)" or "Communists" or "Communist Party" thereafter unless quoting other sources.

Lenin's Collected Works: Unless stated otherwise all quotations from Lenin are taken from the 1963 English language version of V. I. Lenin's *Collected Works* printed by the Foreign Languages Publishing House in Moscow.

Spelling: The text of the book is written in UK English but where quoting from sources in US English the original spellings are retained.

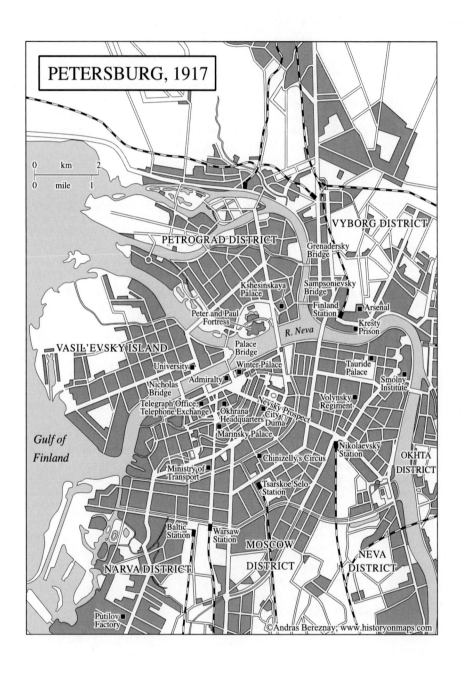

PETERSBURG, 1917

0 km 2
0 mile 1

VYBORG DISTRICT

PETROGRAD DISTRICT

Grenadersky
Bridge

Kshesinskaya
Palace

Sampsonievsky
Bridge

Peter and Paul
Fortress

Finland
Station

Arsenal

Kresty
Prison

R. Neva

VASIL'EVSKY ISLAND

Palace
Bridge

University

Winter Palace

Tauride
Palace

Nicholas
Bridge

Admiralty

Smolny
Institute

Telegraph Office;
Telephone Exchange

Okhrana
Headquarters

Nevsky Prospect

City
Duma

Volynsky
Regiment

Marinsky Palace

Gulf of
Finland

Chinizelly's Circus

Nikolaevsky
Station

OKHTA
DISTRICT

Ministry of
Transport

Tsarskoe Selo
Station

Baltic
Station

Warsaw
Station

MOSCOW
DISTRICT

NEVA
DISTRICT

NARVA DISTRICT

Putilov
Factory

©Andras Bereznay; www.historyonmaps.com

Chapter 1
Prelude to Revolution

Russian Society and State before 1914

In the vast literature on Tsarist Russia there is wide disagreement on the nature of the regime and the direction it was heading during the final years before the First World War. There are three main reasons for this. The first two lie in the notoriously unreliable statistical methods of the Tsarist government[1], and the vastness of an empire in which quite different social conditions existed alongside each other in the different regions.[2] Both factors make drawing a clear general picture difficult. However the third, and most significant, factor is the ideological aim of those writing Russian history. No-one can be neutral on an event so dramatic in class terms as the Russian Revolution. With the right selective use of the material evidence it is possible to argue many different things. Some argue that pre-revolutionary Russia was still mainly feudal, others that it was just becoming capitalist but its social backwardness ruled it out as cradle of proletarian revolution and still others that there would have been no revolution but for the "historical accident" of the First World War. These views are often direct or indirect ripostes to Lenin's 1899 work *The Development of Capitalism in Russia*. Although Lenin undoubtedly exaggerated in some areas (such as the extent of the disintegration of the peasant *obschina* or commune[3]) the one undeniable fact is that Russia after the mid 1880s was above all a society and economy in dramatic transition. This was because it was increasingly and rapidly becoming integrated into a world capitalist system which was as a whole experiencing dramatic changes. Russia may have remained under the political sway of an autocracy but it was one which was losing control of events. This contradiction between a dynamic economic development[4] and a reactionary regime that was trying to avoid any political change is the main reason why it was ripe for revolution. The precise nature of that revolution was however a subject of much debate amongst both Populists and Marxists at the time.

The autocratic state which this society in transition confronted had developed from the historical need for a strong central authority to hold it together in the face of threats to its existence from outside. Autocracy grew out of this external military threat and throughout its history only undertook social and political reforms in response to such threats. Ivan IV "Grozny" (usually translated as "the Terrible") did not institute serfdom but made it more central to his attempt to bolster his absolutism against both recalcitrant boyars (nobles) and the threat of Mongol or Tartar invasion. In addition, there was a need to prevent peasants fleeing from Muscovy to avoid taxation and thus weakening the state's revenues. The final motive came from a Tartar invasion of the Crimea in 1571 which led to the consequent abduction of thousands of peasants into slavery. The state needed a standing army to prevent this drain on its resources. Those who did military service for the Tsar were awarded *pomestie* land, along with the serfs to work it. The peasants were initially free to seek new masters but by a *ukase* (decree) of 1597 Boris Godunov took away even this limited freedom. The *pomeschiki* were not supposed to be able to pass on "their" land but in practice they became a hereditary landed class, although always beholden to the Tsar and exercising authority only as servants of the state. By the late Eighteenth century many *pomeschiki* had simply become parasitic landlords whilst the peasants were reduced to the condition of virtual slaves.

The debilitating consequences of this feudal regime in the era of rising capitalism was, once again, revealed by military failure. This time it was in the Crimean War (1854-6). Despite fighting a war on its own soil, despite the military incompetence of the enemy (this is the war of the Charge of the Light Brigade after all) and despite the enormous self-sacrifice of its serf army, Russia still lost. Alexander II (1855-81), inherited the war from his father, and quickly realised that drastic reform of the autocracy was needed. His famous epithet that "Better to abolish serfdom from above rather than await the time when it begins to abolish itself from below" spelled out the precise purpose of his reform – to save the autocracy. For this reason the reform which initiated the end of feudalism was a botched compromise. He would have invited revolution by simply freeing the serfs without offering land (especially since the serfs recognised that they might be owned by the nobility but "the land was God's"). At the same time Alexander did not want to undermine the social backbone of the regime amongst the aristocracy. The result was that the serfs were freed and given land but less[5] than they had worked before. For this privilege they had to repay the state over the next 57 years. These "redemption dues" were to be collected by the *starosti* (village elders) who ran the village commune, the *mir*[6] or *obschina*.

Peasants were still not free to leave the commune without the permission of the elders who replaced the former landlords as the agents of Tsarism in every commune. Indeed the peasantry could still be said to be without rights or access to any form of justice other than that of the *starosti* (who in fact dominated the village assembly (*skhod*) and usually only acted in the interests of the leading families in the village). The *mir* was responsible for the collection and payment of the taxes (the poll tax continued for 30 years after Emancipation[7]) for the whole village to Tsarist officials. It also decided on the periodic repartition of the land. This in itself became a problem since, in many areas, the villages were still farmed in strips like the three field system of medieval England. Every new family that was formed was allocated strips but as rural Russia experienced a population boom towards the end of the nineteenth century (twice as fast as any in Western Europe) this meant that the size of strips for each family tended to get smaller. This was another factor that fuelled the land hunger of the peasants and their hatred of the *pomeschiki* who made up 1.5% of the population but owned 25% of the land (land which the peasantry universally considered to be theirs).

The peasants had additional reasons for discontent. Not least was the fact that they were heavily taxed to pay for the first wave of Russian industrialisation in the last two decades of the nineteenth century. The result was a fall in peasant living standards in the 1890s. Sergei Witte, the Minister of Finance, pursued industrialisation tenaciously.

By keeping the rouble on the gold standard he encouraged foreign investment whilst his high tariffs were intended to promote import substitution. His key driving force was the building of railways across the huge Empire. In 1890 Russia was in fifth place among all states in terms of railway mileage but by 1900 only the United States had more. Building railways gave an enormous boost to the iron and coal industries which almost tripled in output. The role of the state in this process cannot be underestimated.

The state participated directly in the nation's economy to an extent unequalled in any Western country. In 1899 the state bought almost two-thirds of all Russia's metallurgical production. By the early 20th century it controlled some 70 per cent of the railways and owned vast tracts of land, numerous mines and oil fields, and extensive forests. The national budgets from 1903 to 1913 indicated that the government received more than 25 per cent of its income from various holdings. Russia's economic progress in the eleven years of Witte's tenure as minister of finance was, by every standard, remarkable. Railway trackage virtually doubled, coal output in southern Russia jumped from 183 million poods in 1890 to 671 million in 1900.[8]

The distinguishing characteristic of this industrial revolution was the concentration of the workforce in huge production units. By 1902 more than half of all workers were in workplaces employing over 1,000. Nowhere else in the world had this concentration of workers. But such a concentration also meant overcrowding. This meant that Russia's belated industrial revolution was accompanied by the most appalling social conditions which made the condition of Manchester in the 1840s, as portrayed by Engels, look preferable. In rural areas, industrial units were accompanied by barrack block accommodation, but in cities these were less common (only 7% of Petersburg workers were in such accommodation in 1915). Working class areas had no sewage, lighting, heating, paving or rubbish collection. They were huge fetid slums where overcrowding was the norm (over 4 people to a room in Petersburg). The consequences were dire. Contagious diseases were endemic. The death rate in these areas was high by European standards and was 2 to 3 times higher than in the more affluent areas of Russia. In Petersburg in 1915 a quarter of all babies did not make their first birthday[9].

And exploitation in the factories here was brutally primitive.

Wages were low, hours long, factories dangerous, living conditions squalid, discipline brutal, employment insecure and insurance non-existent. The large number of potential recruits to industry, particularly from the overcrowded villages of the Black Earth zone, meant that employers could hire and fire at will ... the majority [of workers] were simply short-term factory fodder who would be sacked at the first sign of insubordination, lack of discipline or unfavourable economic circumstances.[10]

There was thus no lack of motive for class conflict. These horrors of early capitalist industrialisation took place in a state which was determinedly autocratic. After the assassination of Alexander II by the People's Will group in 1881, his successors concluded that the problem was not that the reforms had been inadequate, but that reform itself was dangerous. The result was that the pillars of autocracy were strengthened.

The Orthodox Church, of which the Tsar was head, reinforced the message of his divine right to rule and any resistance to him was an affront to God. 80% of the population were peasants with massive levels of illiteracy and belief in the semi divinity of the "Little Father", the Tsar, was achieved relatively easily amongst them. However in the towns, and amongst Russia's intelligentsia, more draconian methods were called for. Tasked with this was the Department for Protecting Public Security and Order or *Okhrana*. The Okhrana was never that well-funded but specialised in infiltrating revolutionary groups, often getting their own men into leading positions in them (at least two of whom carried their double agency status to the point of killing important Tsarist ministers!). Torture was also extensively used and the Russian legal system could be relied on to exile revolutionaries to Siberia to keep them out of the way. The police state nature of the autocracy was defined for the urban population by both the activities of the Okhrana and the clumsy methods of state censorship.

The rise of nationalism in the rest of Europe had its counterpart in the unofficially supported "slavophile" movement. This racist movement not only had Russia posing as the defender of all the Slavs in Eastern Europe (and thus led to its involvement in the First World War) but also attempted to suppress and oppress all the other national minorities within Russia. Attempts at "russification" in education and employment only exacerbated opposition to the regime amongst all the Russian Empire's national groupings. After the crushing of the 1863 Polish revolt there were national risings amongst almost every linguistic minority in the Empire from Latvia to Georgia. It is no accident that members of these minorities were to be found in large numbers in all the various opposition parties and groups. This is no surprise given that places like Kiev, Kharkov, Odessa, Donbass, Warsaw, Łódź, Riga and Baku, where the national question was played out, were at the same time some of the biggest industrial centres of the Russian Empire. Worst treated of all were the 5.5 million Jews who were not only "not Russian" but not Christian either. They were repeatedly the subject of *pogroms* led mainly by the so-called Union of the Russian People, more commonly known as the "Black Hundreds". Some 200 of these were carried out from 1881 to 1907 when the Black Hundreds began to decline (and resistance to them began to be organised under the leadership of the Jewish Social Democratic organisation, the Bund). The repression and brutality of the autocracy formed a vital element in preparing the conditions for the coming revolution particularly amongst urban workers.

On the eve of the First World War Tsarist Russia was a long way from being "feudal" either socially or politically. It was in fact the sixth industrial power in the world, and already the world's fourth-largest producer of steel and its second-largest source of petroleum. Its population grew from 126 million in 1897 to 170 million by 1914. Only 15% lived in towns and 10% worked in industry but that still meant that Russia had more proletarians than any country in Europe outside Germany. The late development of a proletariat (whose numbers increased further during the war) under an autocratic regime gave a totally different character to its struggle compared to workers in Western Europe and the United States.

When gauging the class war we have to first remember that this late capitalist development also had an effect on the capitalist class. About half of all Russian heavy industry was foreign-owned but the Russian capitalist class was beginning to emerge from the shadow of the state. However, this industrial and mercantile bourgeoisie, though it may have wielded economic power which carried political weight, was deeply divided. In Moscow the industrialists' organisations were more like the bourgeoisie of Western Europe in wanting to see the gradual diminution of absolutism (and the role of the state) if only on grounds of capitalist efficiency. They formed the Progressive Party after the 1905 Revolution and, under the pressure of a rising working class struggle after 1912, called for an extension of representative government. In St Petersburg, on the other hand, the leading industrialists were hand-in-glove with the autocracy as they relied more on government contracts, and often government investment, especially in iron and steel production. The majority of their investment was provided by the state banking system[11]. As Koenker and Rosenberg put it;

The leading figures of St Petersburg industry moved easily in and out of government service, serving officially at times as ministers and deputy ministers ... Disagreements were reserved for ministry meetings and boardrooms where power still resided.[12]

Unsurprisingly they saw no need to compromise with growing working class resistance and responded to workers' strikes with lockouts, and by bringing in the military. In Marxist theory of course (and on the basis of what happened in other states) the capitalist class, the bourgeoisie should have been the spearhead of a "democratic revolution" which would abolish autocracy and begin the further development of capitalism in Russia. However this was not the case. They had little or no connection with the liberal intelligentsia who headed the democratic opposition. All the opposition political parties had the "democratic revolution" as part of their programme. Even the Social Democrats (Bolsheviks and Mensheviks) held the view that Russia was ripe only for the overthrow of Tsarism and the establishment of a democratic republic headed by the capitalist class. All these assumptions were to be challenged and turned on their heads by the 1905 Revolution.

The 1905 Revolution

As capitalist development speeded up in the late nineteenth century, the working class had increased and so did the annual number of strikes. In the period 1870-84 the average number was only 20 a year but in the ten years before the 1905 revolution this had reached 176 [13] with most of these coming after 1900. Indeed it was the rising strike wave which provoked the reactionary Minister of the Interior, Viacheslav Plehve to opine in 1904 that what the regime really needed was "a short victorious war". War against Japan duly followed, and although it was short, it was far from victorious. The reason for its shortness was not just military failure, but the fact that the privations brought about by the war led, less than a year after it started, to the most significant workers' attempt at revolution since the Paris Commune.

The 1905 Revolution's contribution to the later success of the events of 1917 cannot be underestimated. Not only did the practical decision of the various factory organisations to unify their separate strikes in a workers' council (soviet) provide a template for how workers' government might operate in the future, but it also educated and gave experience to both a young working class, and to the political organisations which aspired to give their struggles a political goal. Trotsky announced afterwards that the revolution of 1905 "… destroyed the myth of the 'uniqueness' of Russia" but this "majestic prologue"[14] did underline, in some ways, certain distinct traits of the Russian working class which were not experienced elsewhere.

In the first place the working class movement had none of the organisational baggage that encumbered the workers of Western Europe. Trades unions were weak and illegal and, as Trotsky himself noted, the political parties claiming to be socialist had only just been formed. At first they had few adherents and these were mainly members of the intelligentsia. 1905 turned the Social Democratic Party (still nominally uniting both Bolsheviks and Mensheviks) into a real workers' party. Even after their formal separation in 1912,[15] neither Party came to own a great deal of property or produce large circulation papers as social democracy did in other parts of Europe (although as Lenin bitterly noted the Mensheviks started off with a lot more money). Under the autocracy there was certainly little sense that economic and political action were separate forms of struggle. Indicative of the situation was the fact that the only thriving "unions" were those created by secret police chief Zubatov, and headed by his agents like the Orthodox priest, Father Gapon. It was ironically Gapon's attempt to lead a strike movement onto the terrain of a peaceful demonstration that sparked off the whole year of revolution. His idea was for workers to beg the Tsar to alleviate the suffering of the working class which the Russo-Japanese War had exacerbated. The Tsar however departed for his country residence, and left it to the brutal General Trepov to order the shooting of perhaps as many as 1,000 people in cold blood. The massacre of the unarmed demonstrators on "Bloody Sunday" [January 22 (modern style) 1905] led to calls for a general strike which began in Poland[16] and soon spread via other subject nations, like Finland, to the workers of European Russia. Half of all workers in Russia went on strike but in Poland it was over 90%. This was largely because economic factors dominated in Russia itself, but in Poland there was the added political opposition to Russification.

Nearly 3 million workers throughout the Russian Empire in 122 towns and localities were involved in some 14,000 strikes in 1905. As Trotsky put it;

> *For almost two months, without any plan, in many cases without advancing any demands, stopping and starting, obedient only to the instinct of solidarity, the strike ruled the land.*[17]

Thanks to state repression these mass strikes died down a little after March but they never went away. 1905 was not just significant for the creation of the first Soviet. As S.A. Smith noted

It was the 1905 Revolution which signalled the immense possibilities of shopfloor organisation. As the general strike swept across the country, starosty and strike committees developed dramatically as organs of working class self-activity and self-expression. In the autumn "factory commissions" proliferated which foreshadowed the factory committees of twelve years later. These commissions began to take charge of all matters affecting the internal life of the factory.[18]

The reference to "starosty" committees is interesting since they were made of "starosta" or stewards which by a law of 1903 were already the only legal representatives of the workers. The government was here trying to prevent the formation of unions by reproducing the village elder (starost) in the factory. Workers usually hated them as being basically mouthpieces for the management but revolution can convert even a supposedly conservative body into something more responsive to the working class. In reality in 1905 all this activity of the shop floor took some time to mature. Soviets thus did not appear until May 15. The first real one was in Russia's "Red Manchester", Ivanovo-Voznesensk (Moscow district)[19]. After that they appeared in Kostromo, Saratov, Samara, Bialystok, Tver, Odessa, Kiev, Rostov, Baku, Novorossisk, Ekaterinoslav, Krasnoyarsk, Irkutsk, Vladivostok "and many smaller towns and special factory settlements".[20] It was not until October that the St Petersburg Soviet made its appearance onto the stage of history.

The nine months of struggle and the development of grass roots workers organisation in 1905 meant that the soviet did not just spring from nowhere. Their unlikely inspiration came from a government attempt to calm the class war. The Shidlovsky Commission, set up in January 1905 by the government in response to the strike wave after Bloody Sunday, gave a practical example of how to organise across factories. Although the Commission failed, the workers delegated to it through elections in each factory continued to act as representatives of the workforce, even though the movement had splintered into many local strikes. By the end of the summer it looked as though the strike wave was about finished but then the printers went on strike in Moscow and set up their own council. This was followed by sympathy strikes in St Petersburg, soon to be joined by a national rail workers strike which began over pensions but was soon calling for political reform.

The St Petersburg workers thus now posed the question of uniting the movement in a more centralised fashion. The Menshevik "group", taking the suggestion from the newly formed liberal bourgeois party, the Constitutional Democrats (also known as Kadets) in St Petersburg, proposed the setting up of a workers' committee. After some agitation in the factories *starosty* were elected on the ratio of one delegate to 500 workers (a ratio derived from the Shidlovsky Commission). Only 40 participated in the first meeting of what would later be known as the St Petersburg Soviet in October 26 in the city's Technological Institute[21] but 4 days later 226 delegates representing 96 factories constituted the Council of Workers Deputies (*Sovet rabochich deputatov*). Krustalev-Nosar was elected permanent chairman of the Soviet alongside an executive committee of 22 members. At its height this movement now represented 250,000 workers. 3 delegates each from the Socialist parties (Bolsheviks, Mensheviks and Socialist Revolutionaries) were also admitted, in an advisory capacity only, to the Executive. From being a simple coordination body of a strike the Soviet continued after the strike ended and began to take on wider political tasks. It became in effect a workers' parliament since workers lacked any form of representation under the autocracy (unlike the liberal intelligentsia who could find some minimal representation in the Tsarist zemstvos[22] after 1864). Just as significantly it became a model for all such bodies across Russia both in 1905 and again in 1917. It was in fact the historically discovered form of how to reconcile the maximum participation of a mass of people with the need to organise politically.

At the very hour when the St Petersburg Soviet was formally being constituted Nicholas II reluctantly signed the October Manifesto drawn up by Sergei Witte. It was his only hope of holding onto power in a country where transport had virtually ceased and economic and social calamity threatened. The promise of a parliament, constitutional reform and greater freedom was enough to win over the liberal middle class. This left the working class to fight on their own but it did not stop the spread of soviets to other towns (Moscow though did not form one until early December). By this time some workers were realising that they should have been preparing for an armed insurrection but by then it was too late. The last appeal of the St Petersburg Soviet for a general strike in late November was not so well supported as before. This gave the Government the confidence to arrest its leaders. The baton passed to Moscow where its Bolshevik-dominated Soviet called for a general strike. This became an armed insurrection. A number of other towns heeded Moscow's call and insurrections followed in Nizhny Novgorod, Rostov, Kharkov and a few other places. In Moscow the barricades lasted more than a week as 2,000 insurgents, whilst facing a garrison of 15,000, enjoyed the solidarity of the surrounding working class areas. However their lack of arms and the fact that the Army remained loyal to the Tsar made the outcome predictable. On 30 December, with the final surrender of the textile district of Presna, the 1905 Revolution was over.[23]

After 1905

The counter-revolution had never gone away. Throughout the year of upheaval that was 1905 the workers' resistance was met by pogroms[24] and massacres carried out by the Black Hundreds. With the restoration of order though, it could now began in earnest. Witte was sacked (despite his part in saving the regime), the Fundamental Law affirmed that the Tsar's autocratic rule would continue despite the new Duma, and revolutionaries were now rounded up. The appointment of the intelligent butcher, Peter Stolypin, as Prime Minister, brought about the execution of thousands. Although there was no legal death penalty Stolypin sidestepped the law by handing arrested workers over to military tribunals for sentencing. The hangman's noose became known as "Stolypin's necktie". Stolypin also did not like the results of the first two Duma elections so they were annulled and the electoral law changed to make it virtually impossible for workers' representatives to be elected. The toothless Duma was thus reduced to an empty talking shop.

Stolypin, however had already understood that the regime lacked a strong social base. The indigenous capitalist class were weak and the gentry in decline. He saw the communal production of the *mir* as a barrier to improved agricultural output so set about breaking it up. He changed the law so that peasants could leave the commune, ended the payment of redemption dues (which should have been paid until 1918) and via cheap credit from the Peasant Land Bank set up a class of individual farmers. Some were able to buy land from a distressed aristocracy mired in debt and terrorised by the rural revolts of 1905. Stolypin saw the new class of peasants as the future conservative social backbone of the regime. How successful his reforms were remains a subject of debate. About a quarter of peasants left the commune according to some estimates but the resentment felt by the rest of the commune members to these *otrubschiki* (those who had left the commune) or *khutoriane* (independent farmers) seems to have only increased class conflict in the countryside. Stolypin had asked for twenty years without war to allow his reforms to succeed but he himself was assassinated in Kiev in 1911 and his policies did not long survive him.

There is no doubt however that, in the short term, repression was successful. There had been almost 3 million participants in equal measure in both political and economic strikes throughout 1905, but by 1910 the numbers had fallen to 3,777 for political strikes and 42,846 in economic strikes. Not surprisingly this low level of class struggle was reflected in the renewed weakness of the working class political parties and tendencies. The main two tendencies, the Social Democratic Workers' Party (RSDLP) and Socialist Revolutionary (SR) Party, had only come into existence in the last few years before 1905 (although the SRs could point to their descent from the 19th century populist tradition of groups like the People's Will and Land and Liberty). Both parties were highly factionalised. The Social Democrat split between Bolshevik and Menshevik factions is well-known but the SRs were equally riven between those who supported individual terror and those who did not, between those who stood for the Duma and those who supported the official position to boycott it. The Revolution of 1905 caught all of them unprepared and with, as yet, little influence amongst either workers or peasants. 1905 was to provide a steep learning curve for all of them.

It also brought them closer to the working class and as a result they began to recruit workers in small but significant numbers. These parties were now no longer largely made up of the intelligentsia leading small bands of workers. More worker activists joined them and even became the face of the party in working class districts. The strong class movement also promoted cooperation. Bolsheviks and Mensheviks often worked together in the grassroots of the movement in 1905. In 1906, the party of Rosa Luxemburg, the SDKPiL (Social Democratic Party of the Kingdom of Poland and Lithuania) and the Lettish Social Democratic Labour Party responded to the revolution by joining the RSDLP as autonomous sections at its Fourth Congress. However at the same Congress, the Mensheviks' tendency to argue against the armed uprising of the workers on the grounds that the December rising had failed, was roundly condemned by Lenin in a prefiguration of some of the debates of 1917.[25]

Today, with the benefit of hindsight we can see how significant the creation of soviets in 1905 was. It was not quite so clear cut to all those at the time. In her famous booklet on *The Mass Strike* Rosa Luxemburg for example, only mentions them once as "the general council of workers delegates" but does not seem to see any significance in them other than "The general council of workers delegates decided to achieve the eight-hour day in a revolutionary manner."[26]

From his cell in the Petropavlovsk Fortress Trotsky however wrote that: *The Soviet really was the workers' government in embryo ... The Soviet was, from the start, the organisation of the proletariat, and its aim was the struggle for revolutionary power.*[27]

After his dramatic escape from Siberia the former Chair of the St Petersburg Soviet would later write:

> *The Soviet is the first democratic power in modern Russian history. The Soviet is the organized power of the masses themselves over their component parts. This is a true, unadulterated democracy, without a two-chamber system, without a professional bureaucracy, with the right of the voters to recall their deputy any moment and to substitute another for him. Through its members, through deputies elected by the workingmen, the Soviet directs all the social activities of the proletariat as a whole and of its various parts; it outlines the steps to be taken by the proletariat, it gives them a slogan and a banner ... the first new wave of the revolution will lead to the creation of Soviets all over the country.*[28]

During 1905 Lenin had to polemicise against his own party on the significance of the Soviet. The Bolshevik St Petersburg Committee was suspicious of an organisation which had Menshevik origins and might turn out to be "another Zubatov union". Writing a letter from Stockholm to the Party paper *Novaya Zhizn* in response to a member of the St Petersburg Committee in November 1905 he disagreed with the attitude which put the Soviet in opposition to the Party.

> *I think it is wrong to put the question in this way and that the decision must **certainly** be: **both** the Soviet of Workers' Deputies **and** the Party ... I think it would be inadvisable for the Soviet to adhere wholly to one party ... It seems to me that the Soviet of Workers' Deputies, as an organisation representing all occupations, should **strive** to include deputies from **all** industrial, professional and office workers, domestic servants, farm labourers etc., from **all** who want and are able to fight in common for a better life for the whole working people, from **all** who have at least a degree of political honesty, from all but the Black Hundreds. (emphasis in original)*

Lenin then went on to call for an aspect of the soviets that only came about in 1917:

To my mind the Soviet of Workers'Deputies as a revolutionary centre providing political leadership, is not too broad an organisation but, on the contrary a much too narrow one. The soviet must proclaim itself the provisional revolutionary government, or form such a government, and must by all means enlist to this end the participation of new deputies not only from the workers but, first of all, from the sailors and soldiers, who are everywhere seeking freedom; secondly from the revolutionary peasantry, and thirdly, from the revolutionary bourgeois intelligentsia.[29]

For Lenin the challenge for the Social Democrats was to fight in all broader working class bodies like unions and soviets for the political programme of the Party. Although the 1905 Revolution foreshadowed what was to come in 1917 to an extraordinary degree, the soviets in 1905 were never even the "embryo" of a workers' government that Trotsky boasted about and Lenin called for. Had the Executive of the St Petersburg Soviet claimed itself as the provisional revolutionary government, they would not only have thrown down a challenge to the old order but given the working class a much clearer idea of what soviet power meant going into 1917-18. History though is full of what ifs and for the moment the Russian working class had made an enormous leap in class consciousness which would come back to reinforce their commitment to fight in February 1917.

This was already reflected in the fact that the Social Democratic and Socialist Revolutionary parties now found for the first time that they had a mass following. The combined membership of the Bolsheviks and Mensheviks in 1906 reached 85,000.[30] Lenin had already recognised at the start of that year that the Social Democrats had become a "mass party"[31]. This transformed not only its class composition but, at least as far as the Bolsheviks were concerned also its internal organisational nature. The tight-knit disciplined organisation of the clandestine period before 1905 was abandoned. It is no accident that Lenin in 1907 made his last ever reference to *What is to be Done?* and this was only to say that it was no longer relevant.

The basic mistake made by people who polemicise with What is to be Done? at the present time is that they tear this production completely out of a specific historical context, out of a specific and by now long past period in the development of our party.[32]

He never referred to it again in his lifetime. It was only as Lenin exited the political scene that it would get resurrected … by Stalin for his own counter-revolutionary purposes. Nevertheless it remains the bedrock of capitalist and anarchist critics alike, in their argument that Bolshevism had no confidence in the working class, and all along intended to usurp its role. This is actually quite laughable as the subsequent history of the Russian Revolution demonstrated. In reality, Lenin had already seen that the changed character of both party and period demanded a change in organisational theory and practice. In an article "Let the Workers Decide" he condemned the high handed action of the Party Central Committee which tried to go against the resolutions of the

Party Congress.

> *Social Democrats know that the whole Party organisation is built on a* **democratic** *basis. This means that* **all** *the Party members take part in the election of officials, committee members and so forth, and that all the Party members discuss and* **decide** *questions concerning the political campaigns of the proletariat, and that* **all** *the Party members* **determine** *the line of tactics of the party organisations.[33]*

This involvement of the entire membership also extended to the production of literature. In calling for the party literature to be the collective work of the whole organisation he proclaimed "Down with literary supermen!"[34] He went on to not only defend freedom of expression in the Party but also to abolish the distinction between writer and passive reader in the organisation.

> *There is no question that literature is least of all subject to mechanical adjustment or levelling to the rule of the majority of over the minority. There is no question, either, that in this field great scope must undoubtedly be allowed for personal initiative, individual inclination, thought and fantasy, form and content ... The organised socialist proletariat must keep an eye on all this work, supervise it in its entirety, and, from beginning to end, without any exception, infuse into it the life stream of the living proletarian cause, thereby cutting the ground from under the old, semi-Oblomov, semi-shopkeeper Russian principle: the writer does the writing, the reader does the reading.[35]*

There are many more passages in the same vein at this time and all suggest that the clandestine party of "professional" revolutionaries was now a thing of the past. As the Bolsheviks "are now becoming a mass party all at once, changing abruptly to an open organisation" the party is now "a voluntary association".[36]

As it was, in the period 1907-11 the various revolutionary parties found the working class movement ebbing and thus their newly-won influence dwindled again. As in all such periods of retreat their internal differences mounted[37] and police repression once again decimated their ranks. Workers saw their wages cut as employers took advantage of this repression and the speed that they were expected to work intensified (piecework at low rates being one of the main drivers of this). Although trades unions (and political parties) were technically now legal, in practice employers refused to recognise them and made joining them difficult. The state winked at this and responded to any appeal by an employer to send troops in to deal with a recalcitrant workforce.

This was what happened in April 1912 when some 200 striking mine workers in the Lena goldfield in Siberia were shot dead. This turned out to be another turning point in the class war as it sparked a revival in working class militancy which did not abate until after the declaration of war in July 1914[38].

Chapter 2
Against Imperialist War

In July 1914 what would eventually come to be known as the First World War broke out. Although long expected by many, including revolutionaries, its final arrival signalled a new epoch in both capitalist and working class history. Until 1914 the workers of Europe had, for the most part, given their allegiance to the Social Democratic parties which made up the Second International. At the head of the Second International stood the mighty German Social Democratic Party which had a million members, 90 newspapers, over a 100 MPs and garnered a third of all votes in elections. Although excluded from real power by Germany's monarchical constitution, its vast organisation of trade unions, cooperatives, party schools and all kinds of social clubs, made it almost a separate society within the state. With its MPs and union leaders now enjoying the fruits of their prestige in a good bourgeois life this turned out to be its undoing.

However, in the International, the German delegates voted for the motion Luxemburg and Lenin, together with Martov, had successfully proposed at the 1907 Stuttgart Congress of the Second International. This demanded that, in the event of war, socialists would do all in their power to utilise the economic and political crises caused by the war to rouse the peoples and thereby to hasten "the abolition of capitalist class rule".

This resolution was re-affirmed on many subsequent occasions like the Basel Congress in 1912. Even as late as July 1914 the Executive of the German SDP was insisting that: *"No drop of blood of a German soldier may be sacrificed to ... the imperialist profit-interests."* This was enough for Jean Jaurès the reformist anti-war French socialist, shortly before he was murdered by a nationalist fanatic in Paris, to confidently assert that,

> *If the Kaiser were to begin a war four million German Socialists would rise as one man and put him to death.*[1]

Jaurès hyperbole apart, *Vorwärts*, the SPD paper was still campaigning strongly against the war only three days before Austria-Hungary invaded Serbia. Its headline on 25 July 1914 was "Down with the War!".

The only real power the German Reichstag (Parliament) had was to withhold the budget from the Kaiser's Government. It was a power that the SDP had resolved to use time and again. However on 4 August 1914, two days after the German Reich had declared war on Russia, the 110 SPD deputies in the Reichstag immediately and unanimously voted 5,000 million marks to the Kaiser as war credits in the fight against "Russian despotism", with the justification that: "... *we make good what we have always affirmed: we do not leave the Fatherland in the lurch in the hour of danger.*"[2]

Against Imperialist War

Although its revolutionary members recognised that it was riddled with opportunism, none of them anticipated the great betrayal of the Second International in August 1914. The word "shock" is repeated in the memoirs of many at the time[3], and even before the 4 August vote, Rosa Luxemburg was paralysed by the realisation that there was to be no resistance to the war. Attending the Bureau of the International in Brussels (29/30 July) she was given a rousing introduction by Jaurès but refused to speak. Although "*again and again beseeched by the crowd she sat there motionless and lost in thought, deep sorrow written on her face*"[4].

According to Frölich, in this account, she could not bring herself to tell the crowd that the International was about to be drowned in a wave of nationalism. Overnight what she thought had been a mass socialist movement had disappeared. It would only be in December when Liebknecht became the first German socialist deputy to vote against a further extension of war credits that the pair of them, assisted by a small group which included Clara Zetkin and Franz Mehring could begin to work seriously on reviving the class movement.

Lenin and "Revolutionary Defeatism"

Luxemburg (and to some extent Liebknecht too) still clung on to the hope that this would come through the revival of the Second International at some point. However the Bolsheviks were already clear that this was "a bourgeois, imperialist and dynastic war" and that

> *The betrayal of socialism by most leaders of the Second International (1889-1914) signifies the ideological and political bankruptcy of the International.*[5]

This "tragedy", as Bukharin described it, was not only revealing the counter-revolutionary nature of the Social Democratic and Labour movements of most of Europe but was also forcing the Russian working class into the vanguard of the anti-war struggle which now slowly gathered momentum throughout Europe.

As noted earlier the Russian Social Democratic Labour Party (Bolshevik) only took on separate organisational existence after its Prague Conference in 1912 when they definitively split from the Mensheviks. The struggle with the Mensheviks had begun over the apparently trivial definition of a party member in 1903 but after the 1905 Revolution the two organisations parted ways over the very nature of the coming Russian Revolution.

For the Mensheviks there was no question that the coming revolution would be bourgeois. It would lead to a period of capitalist development which would then, in turn, at some unspecified distant point in the future lead to the proletariat, via its Social Democratic Party, taking over and installing socialism. The Bolsheviks though were beginning to develop a more radical understanding based on the experience of 1905. The liberals and other bourgeois forces had demonstrated their utter weakness to bring down the autocracy. It was the working class which had led the resistance in 1905. The conclusion was that the working class would have to complete the "democratic revolution" by setting up a democratic but not initially socialist dictatorship. This theory of the working class self-limiting itself to democracy and not socialism was an unhappy solution to a tricky issue and, as we shall see, led to a major showdown in the Party in April 1917. The one thing that separated the Bolsheviks from the Mensheviks was their open recognition that it would be the working class that would make the revolution, whatever its immediate character.

It also implied a different kind of party from the model that had developed in the final quarter of the nineteenth century. Whilst Western European parties grew big and fat on the cosy assumption that they might one day be elected to power, the Bolsheviks were forced to operate largely illegally, and thus never established a niche in the state (as the French Socialist Party did) or acquired the property which German Social Democracy and its unions amassed — a property which hamstrung it in 1914 and made it incapable of even contemplating a return to an illegal existence. August 1914 proved categorically that reformism and gradualism could not be the way for the working class to overcome capitalism. The future belonged, not to mass electoral parties which claim to represent the class, but the class itself, which will have to give birth to parties of the revolutionary Bolshevik type.

What that "type" was will become clearer in the rest of this analysis, but in the immediate term Bolshevism made a still greater contribution, not only in its opposition to that war, but also in the way it opposed the war. Whilst there were many pacifists around at that time who called for a 'just' peace (like Ramsey Macdonald), the Bolsheviks remained true to the Stuttgart resolution and tried to turn the First World War from a war between nations into a war between classes. Lenin's position is well-known, but it is worth emphasising here the theoretical basis of "revolutionary defeatism".

Revolutionary defeatism was based on the idea that "The European War is the greatest historical crisis; it means the beginning of a new epoch"[6]. And, as he spelt out in *Imperialism — The Highest Stage of Capitalism*, this was the epoch of imperialism, "of the decay of capitalism" or "a period of the end of capitalism"[7].

And, to underline that this was no passing perspective but the basis for a new political stand, he went on:

> *Let us raise the banner of civil war! Imperialism has put the fate of European civilisation at stake: this war, if there does not follow a series of successful revolutions will soon be followed by other wars ... If not today, then certainly tomorrow; if not during the present war, then after it ... the proletarian banner of civil war will rally not only hundreds of thousands of enlightened workers but also millions of semi-proletarians ... Overwhelmed by opportunism the Second International has died. Down with opportunism, and long live the Third International![8]*

Against Imperialist War

Lenin's revolutionary defeatism was then no mere tactic of the moment but was part of a long-term internationalist perspective. As already indicated, *Imperialism — the Highest Stage of Capitalism,* written in 1916, clearly set out the thesis that capitalism had entered an entirely new epoch, the epoch of imperialist war. This aspect of his thought cannot be emphasised enough since this was the basis of his break with Social Democracy in the period 1914-18 (i.e. the period of revolutionary advance). It is also the aspect of Lenin's ideas which is omitted or de-emphasised by so-called Leninists of the Trotskyist and Stalinist schools who, basing themselves on the Third International's embrace of social democracy in the 1920's, all seek to reincarnate some form of the minimum programme of Social Democracy within the working class. Thus the idea that capitalism had changed it character (even if still driven by the same basic laws) is something they have never grasped.

Class Struggle and Imperialist War

Classical bourgeois historians on the other hand conclude that Lenin was a master tactician (by which they mean a political opportunist) in adopting revolutionary defeatism — the class basis behind his tactics being, naturally enough, either denied or not understood. Their approach, common to bourgeois individualism, reinforces the "great man theory of history". References to Lenin's "lonely stand" at the socialist conferences against the war held in Switzerland (at Zimmerwald in September 1915 and Kienthal in April 1915) are numerous. We are told that only 8 delegates at Zimmerwald and only 12 at Kienthal supported revolutionary defeatism (the majority instead going for a pacifist declaration which looked forward to re-forming the Second International when the war was over). What, of course, this image leaves out is the fact that Lenin was not the prophet in the wilderness but part of a living class movement which, though temporarily checked by the rising tide of nationalist hysteria which accompanied the start of the war, had not disappeared.

There is no doubt that Lenin made his greatest contribution to internationalist political clarity inside the working class at this critical juncture. He immediately grasped that things would never be the same again. Less than three weeks after the German Social Democratic Party voted for the Kaiser's war, Lenin was explaining its significance in "The Tasks of Revolutionary Social-Democracy in the European War". After establishing the "imperialist" character of the war (although at this point he was not precisely clear about what that meant) and having denounced the "ideological and political bankruptcy" of the Second International he made clear that it was not enough to merely condemn the war and work for peace.

> *The opportunists have long been preparing to wreck the Second International by denying the socialist revolution and substituting bourgeois reformism in its stead, by rejecting the class struggle with its inevitable conversion at certain moments into civil war, and by preaching class collaboration; by preaching bourgeois chauvinism under the guise of patriotism and the defence of the fatherland, and ignoring the fundamental truth of socialism, long ago set forth in the **Communist Manifesto**,*

that the workers have no country, by confining themselves, in the struggle against militarism to a sentimental philistine point of view, instead of recognising the need for a revolutionary war by the proletarians of all countries , against the bourgeoisie of all countries ...[9]

From this approach Lenin produced the slogan "Turn the imperialist war into civil war", by which he meant "class war". For all but the minority of anti-war socialists this was going too far. Lenin's mental health was questioned, and when it was not, he was ridiculed for his hubris since there was at this time of jingoistic propaganda no widespread proletarian resistance to the war. However undaunted, he doggedly carried on meeting other socialists to persuade them that the war had to be fought, not just with plaintiff appeals to the capitalists to end it as the pacifists did, but by recognising it as an actual product of capitalist contradictions. Resisting imperialist war was part of the ongoing class struggle for socialism, not some temporary diversion from it, as the reformists maintained. He missed no opportunity to highlight any anti-war activity that took place, from the Christmas truce of 1914 to threats by the German High Command to treat any fraternisation as treason. He highlighted all those socialists who took a stance against the war from Liebknecht and Rühle to Pannekoek, Gorter and the Lichtstrahlen group. He mercilessly laid into all those "giants" of Social Democracy like Plekhanov and Kautsky who had betrayed socialism, and he did not polemically spare lesser-known figures like Potresov in Russia.

The First World War broke out at a time of intensifying class struggle throughout Europe. The mass strikes of 1904-5 in Russia, Poland and Belgium subsequently had their echo in every European country. An example was Britain where from 1910 until the outbreak of war there developed the "the largest wave of working class struggle... since Chartism"[10]. There was not one ruling class in Europe which was not mindful of the benefits imperialist war would bring in terms of social peace. On 2 August 1914 the Russian Tsar issued a typical example in his Imperial Manifesto which demanded that "in this hour of threatening danger, domestic strife be forgotten". And there was certainly plenty of domestic strife for him to worry about.

In 1910 the number of workers participating in political strikes had fallen to 4,000, but in 1912 the Lena Goldfield strikes, in which hundreds of workers were shot dead by the police, was the signal for a new wave of struggle. Over half a million workers took place in strikes in 1912 and in the first 6 months of 1914 this rose to 1,059,000 (Jan-June). Even in the first 3 weeks of July 1914 there were 42 strikes involving 200,000 workers. But:
> ... the outbreak of war in August 1914 defused the insurrectionary mood ... a wave of patriotic support for the war combined with repression by the authorities led to the virtual disappearance of strikes until July 1915.[11]

July 1915 broke the mould with 29 strikes (as opposed to the average of 5 in the previous year), and over 200 more in the last quarter of the year. In other words, the war had only bought Russian capitalism breathing space and, as Lenin had foreseen, the economic dislocation produced by the war was creating the conditions for an even wider and more intense struggle.

The composition and size of the working class also changed. The war economy demanded industrial expansion so the number of wage labourers had grown to 15 million overall. As in every other belligerent country, state control of industry increased and, as resources were switched to war production, some sectors (metallurgy, chemicals) grew at the expense of others (e.g. wood, textiles, food). Trade with the outside world collapsed dramatically in the first year of the war. Total imports fell from 10.4 million tons to 3.8 million tons[12]. In every country the printing press was liberally used to print money to finance the war but in Russia it produced the highest inflation of any of the major powers. By 1916 prices had more than doubled. This had the effect of reducing real wages though skilled metalworkers had enough clout to be able to demand more. Even so they too fell behind in late 1916 [13].

Some historians argue that Russia had the resources to make a functioning war economy, but lacked the transport and organisation to get supplies to where they were most needed. Trains were overcrowded and dominated by troop movements so that food for example had a hard time getting to northern cities, especially in a Russian winter. The strain on the economy was made worse by Tsarist refusals to allow local initiative offered by liberals in the *zemstvos* to organise war production[14]. The autocracy feared the liberals would use this as a pretext to demand constitutional reform. There is no doubt that the narrow reactionary Tsarist regime was incapable of fighting a modern capitalist war. In its final days even some of those who supported it were demanding change and wondering whether the regime was run by incompetents or traitors.[15]

After two and half years of war nearly two million soldiers and one and half million civilians were dead (and at least the same number "missing"). On the home front the bread ration got smaller and real wages for the majority had fallen due to inflation. As workers could see that the rich bourgeois and landowners were still living in "elegant grandeur"[16], there was plenty of combustible material around. Add to that the well-documented incompetence of the Tsar and his ministers, the horrors inflicted on soldiers at the front by a regime that could neither arm or clothe them properly, and it seems like a miracle that the Tsarist war effort lasted until February 1917.

There were similar stresses and strains in most of the belligerent powers by this time. Total war, imperialist war, is as much fought by economies as it is by armies. The strain of war, as Lenin had predicted, would see mutinies in the French army and the German Navy, strikes and the introduction of rationing in Britain, mass desertions and food riots in Italy and food shortages in the Central Powers of German and Austria-Hungary, but none were in so desperate a condition as Tsarist Russia.

The Bolshevik Party in the War

How did the Bolsheviks in Russia fare in this developing situation? It is often argued that the Bolshevik Party inside Russia did not mirror Lenin's own intransigence on the war issue. The usual evidence that is cited for this is the feeble performance of the Bolshevik faction in the Duma (or Parliament) at their show trial in February 1915. They had not even voted against the Tsarist war budget but simply left the Duma instead of voting on the war credits motion. Their leader Kamenev, apparently fearing that their trial would be moved to a military court (and thus could lead to the death penalty), denied the Bolsheviks were formally against the war and repudiated "revolutionary defeatism" on the formal grounds that it had not been voted on by the Central Committee. They were all sent to Siberia and the opportunity to use the trial to make propaganda was lost.

However, such failures "to display sufficient firmness", as Lenin mildly put it, were few, and did not extend to the rank and file of the Party. Although many of the local committees were unsure of the full meaning of Lenin's position, and often were without information, they contained very few who were to become social patriots. Many local committees independently took up anti-war agitation before hearing from the central bodies. The Petersburg Committee, as early as July 1914 (even before the Duma vote on the war), issued their first internationalist and anti-war leaflet. This proclaimed that the slogans:

> *Down with the War! War on war! must roll powerfully across ... the width of Russia. Workers must remember that they do not have enemies over the frontier; everywhere the working class is oppressed by the rich and the power of the property owners... Long live world wide labour solidarity!*[17]

The war made all the Socialist parties but especially the Bolsheviks even more working class in composition. Shlyapnikov, who was the chief Bolshevik organiser in Petersburg for most of the war, complained that at this time many of the *intelligentsia* deserted the struggles of the working class (often for jobs in the war effort) and that this made the work of producing propaganda harder. In addition the Okhrana (the Tsarist secret police) continuously tried to decapitate the Bolshevik Party inside Russia. Not only were the Bolshevik Duma deputies arrested in November 1914, but the Petersburg Committee was arrested in July 1914 and in May 1916. On top of this came the arrest of hundreds of the most active workers, all amidst a great shortage of funds. However, the Party organisation was never smashed thanks to the increased capacity of the local committees run by worker activists. They not only learned to do without the intellectuals but in fact became the real backbone of Bolshevism.

> *Almost everywhere workers' organisations found themselves without intellectuals but this did not paralyse their activity as in the previous period of pre-war reaction. The workers' organisations had thrown up their own purely proletarian leaders.*[18]

Thus the Bolshevik Party was able to operate for most of the war without a Russian Bureau (the Central Committee's representatives inside Russia). This was achieved because the Petersburg Committee was able to take on its role of co-ordination and leadership. And when its members were arrested the task passed to the Committee of the

Against Imperialist War

Vyborg District of Petersburg.

And it was these local committees which also gave life to the positions defended by Lenin on the international stage. As Shlyapnikov once again tells us:

> ... the central point of the ideological work of the illegal cells of our party, scattered around all the industrial centres of Russia was the attitude to the war, the struggle against chauvinism and "patriotic" exploitation... Evidence of the active work of the workers' organisations in the war is provided by the exile of thousands of organised workers, arrests and the posting of strikers to front-line positions.[19]

Shlyapnikov's memoir is full of the texts of anti-war propaganda issued by the Bolsheviks on every conceivable occasion, amounting on average to one leaflet for every week of the war. In every strike they always tried to get the slogan "Down with the war" included amongst the economic demands as well as the passing of resolutions against the war in every factory.

Typical of this was a resolution of September 1916 "adopted at general works' meetings in many major enterprises" and proposed by the Petersburg Committee of the Bolshevik Party:

Down with the War!

> We, workers of the ... ... works, having discussed the question of the sharpening food crisis, recognise that:

> (1) the food crisis observable in all countries is an inevitable consequence of the current war which has latterly acquired the character of a war of attrition;

> (2) the continuance of the war will entail a deepening of the food crisis, famine, poverty and the degeneration of the mass of the people;

> (3) in Russia the food crisis is complicated by the continued rule of the tsarist monarchy which places the country's whole economy in a state of complete dislocation, surrendering it to the whim of rapacious capital and ruthlessly suppressing any initiative by the mass of the people;

> (4) all piecemeal means of fighting the food crisis (e.g. co-operatives, wage rises, canteens etc.) can only marginally mitigate the effects of the crisis and not eliminate the causes;

> (5) the only effective means of struggle against the crisis is a struggle against the causes producing it, i.e. a struggle against the war and the ruling classes which plotted it; in taking all this into account, we call upon the Russian working class and all democrats to take the road of a revolutionary struggle against the tsarist

monarchy and the ruling classes behind the slogan of "Down with the war!"

As the party with the widest all-Russian organisation the Bolsheviks were already better prepared for the events of February 1917. They were spread very thinly but they were politically armed and active inside the wider working class. Neil Harding summarises this thus:

The Bolshevik section of the Russian Social Democratic Party (R.S.D.L.P.) had, ever since 1905, been unique amongst the socialist parties of Europe in that it not only believed in the imminence of revolution and laid great emphasis on the enormous educative role of revolutionary activity in raising the consciousness and developing the organisation of the workers – its commitment to revolution was even more unique in that it was not simply theoretical but practical. The Russian Bolsheviks, alone of all the parties of the Second international, took the business of preparing their cadres and, as far as they were able, the masses they led, for the actual physical confrontations that lay ahead. The other parties of the International, whilst theoretically acknowledging the conditions in Europe were ripe for socialist revolution, made no attempt whatsoever in the per-war era actually to prepare their members or their followers for the physical combat that this would entail.[20]

The Bolshevik model of the party was thus far from all the slanders about being a top-down organisation or dominated by middle class intellectuals, and it was also characterised by a lot of questioning, division and debate – all in a revolutionary framework. This is often denied by those whose view of history is polluted by the hindsight that the Bolsheviks would later replace soviet power with the party-state and thus become the agents of the counter-revolution. A key pillar of these critics is the assertion that the Bolsheviks support for soviets in 1917 was purely opportunistic, and that they only supported them until they got into power in order to liquidate them. This does violence to the actual process as we shall see later but it also ignores the evidence from before 1917. Other parties might support the idea of soviets but none of them advocated soviets as the form of a workers' government like the Bolsheviks. Lenin was already visualising this in October 1915. In his document *Several Theses* he not only calls for serious work in the coming struggles but makes it quite clear that soviets are the form of "revolutionary rule".

(3)We consider that the consolidation and extension of Social-Democratic work among the proletariat and its extension to the rural proletariat, the rural poor and the army are the immediate and pressing tasks. It is revolutionary Social-Democracy's most pressing task to develop the incipient strike movement ...

(4)Soviets of Workers' Deputies and similar institutions must be regarded as organs of insurrection, of revolutionary rule. It is only in connection with the development of a mass political strike and with an insurrection, and in the measure of the latter's preparedness, development and success that such institutions can be of lasting value.[21]

Against Imperialist War

At this point the Bolsheviks are still thinking that the task of the proletariat was to complete the bourgeois democratic revolution but behind it all lies the idea that the revolution would not stop there. The ambiguity of the formulation only reflected the ambiguity of the situation and it would be actual events that would settle which direction the future revolution would take. The Bolsheviks though were theoretically and organisationally the best equipped in their practice to play a leading role in those events.

The Nature of the Russian Working Class at the Beginning of 1917

The Bolsheviks may have had the best Marxist understanding of the nature of the imperialist war and the new crisis that had developed, but it would have been of little use if there had not been a working class receptive to their message. Despite all the stereotypes of the Russian workers as "culturally backward" and "illiterate"[22] the real picture is much more complex.

Russia's late industrialisation meant that its young proletariat faced squalid social and economic conditions like those described in Manchester in 1843-4 by Engels but some studies have shown that Petersburg workers were certainly materially better off than workers in Milan[23]. However there is one sense above all others where the situation in the Russian working class was unique. This was in the relationship between Russian workers and the state.

Elsewhere in Europe the labour movement had given birth to social democratic or labour parties and trades unions linked to them. Over time the social democratic movement had been able to wrest a few reforms regarding legal recognition and in some areas improvements in workers' conditions. This relative success gradually drew the social democratic parties into the orbit of the capitalist state. In fact within social democracy many concluded with Eduard Bernstein that the advances made by both workers and their social democratic parties meant that the Marxist doctrine of class struggle and revolution was now obsolete. In his *Evolutionary Socialism* Bernstein argued that capitalism could be reformed and made to work for workers.

The classic case was Bernstein's own German Social Democratic Party which went, within a few years, from being illegal under Bismarck to becoming the largest electoral party in the world. However this came at a price. As we saw on page 25, the Social Democratic Party in Germany had come to own a great deal of property. When war came in 1914 those Social Democratic leaders who were not out and out racists and imperialists (and they dominated the union apparatus) thought only of the loss of all they had built over four decades. As a result they voted war credits for the Kaiser and supported army recruitment. This was repeated in many countries in 1914. Social peace was now proclaimed across Europe and the socialist and labour parties now demonstrated they were "inside the system". Russia though was different. Sukhanov tells us why "Down with the War" dominated all the meetings of the February days"

The development of this slogan was quite inevitable. Russian Socialism, and the thinking Russian proletariat, unlike the Socialists of the Western European warring countries (with the exception of Italy), were for the most part resolutely against supporting the imperialist war. In the course of the war years our proletariat has been educated, as far as conditions allowed, in the spirit of Zimmerwald and the war against war. The defensist groups who had made themselves a niche in both capitals and here and there in the provinces had no authority whatsoever amongst the masses. There was nothing surprising or unexpected in the fact that a revolution against Tsarism should, at least amongst the proletariat of the capital, coincide with a movement in favour of peace.[24]

As a Menshevik (though on its "Internationalist" wing), Sukhanov is too coy to mention that the main Zimmerwald party which had long called for "war on war" was the Bolsheviks. Indeed there were many Social Democrats in Russia (especially Mensheviks) who would have liked to emulate the models coming from Western Europe but the conditions for such a development did not exist. Whether they liked it or not, the illegal status that they held until 1905 meant that there was no question of winning reforms or building a huge apparatus in Russia. After 1905 the socialist movement was in an ambivalent situation. Trades unions and socialist organisations were technically legal under the constitution but just about anything they did resulted in arrests of offenders and deportation to Siberia.

Firstly, the Russian unions were created in conditions in which there were no democratic freedoms: even after the publication of the Provisional Regulations for trade unions on 4 March 1906, constant police surveillance condemned them to a semi-legal existence. The unions, weighed down by state repression, were unable to accumulate experience in practical, day-to-day activities, and right up until 1917 they did not exert any deep influence on the workers' movement.[25]

As we saw in Chapter One, the Okhrana (secret police) was not generously resourced, but it was incredibly effective at infiltrating revolutionary organisations. Their ability to constantly decapitate the leadership of the revolutionary organisations ensured, not only the relative weakness of the latter at the start of 1917, but equally ensured that there was no danger that these organisations would reach an accommodation with the state.

Russian industrialists were heavily dependent on government contracts and thus for the most part were loyal supporters of Tsarism right to the end of the regime.[26] As a result in every strike, or attempt to resist the management of any factory, the bosses' first instinct was to call the police, who then arrested workers' leaders and attacked their demonstrations.

It was ironic, in view of Lenin's famous quotation of 1902 (taken from Kautsky) that *"the working class, exclusively by its own effort, is able to develop only trade union consciousness"*, that in the struggles in Russia from 1912-17 a trade unionist mentality was largely absent. Shlyapnikov, the leading Bolshevik organiser in the metalworkers' union, lamented the lack of union organisation and "trade union consciousness" in his memoirs.

> *There was little experience of persistent day-to-day struggle, as the trade unions were too weak; they lived under the threat of being closed down, and could not nurture or discipline a trade union type of struggle among the mass of workers.*[27]

Shlyapnikov, himself a highly skilled metalworker, focused on wages. He could not understand how the bosses got away with dividing the workers over pay rates which:

> *were not even uniform among workers in the same shops. The employers cunningly divided workers according to earnings. Workers in the same shop and in the same trade, turning for example, would earn anything from two to six rubles a day on tools and jobs of almost equal complexity and precision.*[28]

His explanation was that "the absence of trade-union organisation was apparent". However this did not mean that the workers were not militant. On the contrary, the lack of union intermediaries seems to have made them more militant since there was no real form of "mediation" with the bosses. Shlyapnikov returned to work illegally in Russia in 1914 after a seven year absence. He now found that: *"enormous changes had taken place in the attitude of the workers ... the absence of timidity and submissiveness which even then was strong in the plants of Petersburg, hit you in the eye. You sensed that the workers had matured considerably as individuals."*[29]

What it meant was that they had other ways of contesting the "frontier of control" with the management. Russian factory management was a long way from the more "scientific" exploitative techniques of Taylorism then being introduced in the United States.

> *Draconian forms of discipline, however, were as much a reflection of the political culture of Russia as of capital's needs to socialise labour into the norms of factory life. The violent exercise of management power within the factory mirrored the violent exercise of power without.*[30]

Humiliation of workers by foreman in the workshops, beatings, fines for breaking factory rules or poor work were daily occurrences. Petersburg also had the highest recorded instances for industrial accidents of any region in Russia. With the management refusing to talk to the nascent unions, the class struggle on the shopfloor was at its most naked.

> *The foremen, supervisors, engineers all exercised their power in the same arbitrary way, untrammelled by any notion of workers' rights. It is thus not surprising that workers who lacked any broad conception of the social system should have identified their main enemy not as the factory owner, but as the low-level administrators who were the bane of their everyday working lives. Strikes to remove foremen and their assistants were endemic prior to 1917 and demands for*

polite treatment by administrative staff figured prominently in strike demands ... commenting on the importance of "dignity" issues the worker Timofeev said 'the workers value proper treatment ... and if they get it, are often ready to put up with many of the darker aspects of their conditions and discomforts of their work'.[31]

"Dignity issues" lay behind many instant walkouts ("wildcat strikes" they would be called today, but in Russia at this time there really were no other kind). It was clear that despite the victory of the Tsarist regime at the end of 1905 (a victory that gave the regime 7 years of relative peace) the memory of that year of struggle had given workers new confidence.

From the Lena Goldfield strikes in 1912 to January 1917 (except for the quiet "patriotic" interlude that lasted for almost the first year of the War) the number of strike days in Petersburg rose and fell, but was generally on an upward curve from 40,000 to 200,000. And by January 1917 the number of "political" strikes was outnumbering "economic" strikes by three to one. Even in so-called "economic strikes" (i.e. those pertaining to factory issues) the strike was often more about the management of the factory or the actions of individual foremen. Workers sometimes demanded the dismissal of a foreman or did not simply wait for the management to agree before they wheeled him out of the factory in a barrow (often accompanied by other indignities). In the early days of the February Revolution this was to be the fate of many foremen and managers. Steve Smith recounts the fate of a hated member of the pogromist, pro-Tsarist organisation, the Black Hundreds:

In the engine-assembly shop, Puzanov, quondam chief of the factory's Black Hundreds, was tossed in a wheelbarrow, red lead was poured over his head, and he was ignominiously carted out of the factory, and dumped in the street.[32]

He was luckier than some others who were actually killed by angry workers, as workers settled scores with the most hated managers and foremen. The success of the February Revolution emboldened workers to push back the "frontier of control". Class war in 1917 was about to take on a new dimension in the factories.

Chapter 3
The February Revolution

History as a whole and the history of revolutions in particular is always richer in content, more varied, more multiform in character, more lively and ingenious than is imagined by even the best parties...[1]

International Women's Day

On International Women's Day[2] (23 February old calendar/8 March by today's calendar), women workers of both home and factory took to the streets of Petersburg. Five days of strikes, demonstrations and hundreds of deaths[3] later, the Tsarist edifice had crumbled. In these events, hundreds of thousands of men also took part but: *It was the women who initiated the action in most cases, primarily working women from the textile mills.*[4]

The final straw for the women workers had come with the breakdown in the supply of bread which began at the start of February when only half the food ordered for Petersburg arrived.

Long lines stretched in front of shops and bakeries. A winter unprecedented in severity had set in, filling the streets with ice and piling snowdrifts on the roofs of homes, sidewalks and bridges of the city. Shivering from cold, poorly dressed young people, women and old men waited hours for bread and often went home empty-handed. Food shortages provoked an even greater ferment among the masses. In line they discussed why there was no bread and why prices were still rising; they wondered who was responsible for the people's misery and who needed the war. The Petrograd Okhrana observed that on days of severe crisis the queues had the same force as revolutionary meetings and tens of thousands of revolutionary leaflets. The street had become a political club.[5]

The war made these conditions particularly exacting for women. Many were left having to work long hours in war industries after their men were conscripted for the front, as well as look after children, and spend what little free time they had in long lines queuing for bread and kerosene. Bread became the issue which sparked off uncontrollable rage. In the days before International Women's Day bakeries had been sacked and bread shops stoned, but what now transformed these bread riots into something more was that women (plus some male) workers held "stormy" mass meetings and decided to celebrate the day by going on strike, and not just demonstrating. Having decided to down tools in one factory they then went round others, sometimes throwing snowballs at windows to attract other workers' attention. Men and women poured out of factories to take part in demonstrations. And where the workers were better paid and more conservative, such as the Arsenal, it was more than snowballs that got thrown. According to the SR I. Mil'chik (a worker in the Ericsson factory) workers bombarded the Arsenal with rocks and pieces of iron until its workers stopped work (although they did not join the demonstrations but simply went home). Other places like the Cartridge factory were forced to stop in similar fashion. The demonstrators then set up pickets at the factory gates to ensure there would be no resumption of work.[6] All told that day somewhere between 80,000 and 120,000 workers, the vast majority of them women, went out on strike demanding bread, peace and, more ominously for the regime, an end to Tsarism.[7]

> *Workers stopped rapidly moving streetcars, forced motormen to halt, took away their operating wrenches, made passengers get out, turned the streetcars over and with shouts of "Hurrah!" moved on... Workers marched through the city's streets in a militant and joyous mood, singing "La Marseillaise", "Varshavianka", "Comrades, Boldly in Step", and other revolutionary songs. As they moved the demonstrations became living speakers' tribunes. Calling for struggle against the war and the monarchy, speakers were carried on the demonstrators' shoulders. Red flags waved here and there above the moving crowds. The revolution had begun.[8]*

The propertied classes were soon to know it. On 23 February/8 March it was mainly factories on the Vyborg side to the north of the city that were involved in striking. However Vyborg was only just across the River Neva from the city's administrative heart, the "Petersburg side" where ten factories had also gone on strike[9]. Here the famous boulevard of the Nevsky Prospekt was home to the headquarters of the leading Tsarist government institutions. In the various demonstrations, emanating from different parts of the city, the cry went up that they should march, as on the previous day, to "Nevsky".

Workers' tradition played its part here, as it would in so many of the events of the next few days. It was half way down Nevsky Prospekt, in front of the Kazan Cathedral, that the Narodniks (populists) had sponsored a demonstration back in 1876. From then on it had become a focal point for meetings, and so, in 1917, workers once again headed for the square in front of the Cathedral. To keep those from across the river joining the march on "Nevsky", troops and police blocked the bridges, especially the strategic Liteinyi Bridge which led from Vyborg (a Bolshevik stronghold, known for its militancy). However, it being winter, the Neva was frozen thick, so workers who could not get past the police patrols on the bridges, simply walked four or five hundred metres across the ice. At this point the police were under orders not to shoot in case it inflamed the situation.[10] The strike movement though was gathering momentum and the bitterness of the women workers on lower wages (who called on the men to support them[11]) animated the intensity of the class war. The depth of this feeling explains the use of violence to get the reluctant and hostile amongst the workforce to join the movement.

In initiating this strike action women workers went against the broad advice of the political organisations who wanted to confine this socialist anniversary, as previously, to a formal demonstration against the war[12]. V.N. Kaiurov, a worker on the Vyborg District Committee of the Bolshevik Party, later justified the advice he gave to keep calm.

The February Revolution

We could feel the storm coming, but no-one could determine how it would be manifested. The highly charged mood of the masses forced the district committee to stop agitating, cease direct appeals for strikes and the like, and focus attention primarily on the maintenance of discipline and restraint during the upcoming demonstrations.[13]

This wasn't the view of all Bolsheviks. Although Alexander Shlyapnikov, the engineering worker and leading Bolshevik organiser in Petersburg, shared Kaiurov's position he had earlier informed Lenin (in his Swiss exile) that: *It is reported from Kharkov that... certain comrades take the position that we are living in the era of social revolution.[14]*

There was no lack of evidence for this in Russia since there had been wave after wave of strikes since August 1916. It was at this point that a political strike movement, driven by acute food shortages and rising prices as a result of the war, had begun in earnest. From now on, *"three quarters of the strikes between September 1916 and February 1917 voiced political opposition to the autocracy and the war"*[15]. As a foretaste of things to come soldiers of the 181st Infantry regiment who were quartered in Vyborg (and thus an easier target for Left Socialist Revolutionary and Bolshevik agitation) joined workers on a march to the Finland Station on 17 October. Similarly, when news came through of the possible execution of revolutionary sailors in Kronstadt, 77 factories went on strike and the government had to back down[16].

Workers' memories were stoked by strikes and demonstrations on every occasion that demanded commemoration. On 9/22 January 1917, 109 workplaces had gone on strike to remember the anniversary of Bloody Sunday 1905.[17] Commenting on this strike only two days before the International Women's Day demonstrations, the last French Ambassador to the Tsar sent the following message to his government:

Please tell the President of the Republic and the President of the Council that you have left me very anxious. A revolutionary crisis is at hand in Russia; it nearly broke out five weeks ago and is only postponed. Every day the Russian nation is getting more indifferent towards the war and the spirit of anarchy is spreading among all classes and even in the army. About the end of last October a very significant incident occurred in Petrograd; I reported it to Monsieur Briand. A strike broke out in the Vibori [Vyborg – ed], quarter and as the police were very roughly handled by the workmen, two regiments which were in barracks in the vicinity, were sent for. These two regiments fired on the police. A division of Cossacks had to be hastily called in to bring the mutineers to their senses. So in case of a rising the authorities cannot count on the army. My conclusion is that time is no longer working for us, at any rate in Russia ...[18]

From this point on even the rumour of a revolutionary leaflet was enough to spark off a strike. Seeing this radicalisation, even the Menshevik-dominated Workers' Group in the War Industries Committees (set up by the state in 1915 to improve war production) also felt compelled to respond to the workers' growing anger but their initial response (in tune with their ideology of seeking the support of the liberal bourgeoisie) was to urge workers simply to strike in favour of a new ministry. However that was enough to get 11 of the Workers' Group arrested and within a week, on 22 February/6 March, a large strike at the Putilov works provoked the capitalist owners to lock out their workers. This strike and lockout gave added impetus to the next day's International Women's Day demonstrations to create a movement which would sweep away centuries of Tsarism.

However the Bolsheviks' Russian Bureau (the leading organ of the Party inside Russia) in Petersburg did not, at first, make the connection even though the Bolsheviks were, by most accounts, the best organised amongst all the revolutionary parties and groups in the capital with 3,000 members there. They thought that the simmering anger of the workers would not mature into a full-scale assault for a few more months, and that the ideal date would be the next great workers' anniversary on May Day. In the meantime they felt that they should not be provocateurs of something that would go off at half-cock. They considered, quite reasonably, that the consequences of a defeat would only have set the revolutionary movement back. It was thus the small Inter-District (in Russian *Mezhraiontsy*) Group of Social Democrats, to which Trotsky (then in exile in the US) belonged, which initially took the lead inside the women workers' movement. Whilst the Bolsheviks, led by Shlyapnikov, hesitated (their press had been seized by the Okhrana but in other circumstances they found ways around this) the *Mezhraiontsy* produced a number of leaflets,[19] including an appeal for International Women's Day which read:

> *Dear women comrades, are we going to put up with this in silence much longer, now and then venting our smouldering rage on small shop owners? After all they are not to blame for the people's suffering. They are being ruined themselves. The government is to blame! It started the war and cannot end it. The government is ruining the country and causing us to go hungry. The capitalists are to blame! The war brings them profits. It is high time to cry out to them: "Enough!" Down with the criminal government and its whole gang of robbers and murderers. Long live peace!*

The elemental movement of a working class that had reached the end of its tether swept aside all that caution.[20]

Ironically Bolshevik caution may have assisted the movement on that first day. The fact that the state knew that revolutionary leaders were urging caution (as we noted earlier, all political organisations were deeply infiltrated by the Okhrana) meant that the forces of repression also underestimated the strength of the movement on International Women's Day. On previous traditional workers' anniversaries like 9 January the regime knew about the revolutionaries' plans from their spies. They even knew how long strikes were planned to last. This was not the case on 23 February/8 March. General Balk, the Petersburg City Governor later admitted that,

> *Early on February 23 a strike involved half the factories and plants. I had no*

idea this would happen. This movement took us by surprise. No police units were on the streets. I called the units always available, mounted police, gendarmes and cavalry detachments.[21]

These units brutally attacked the demonstrators with whips and truncheons. 23 were arrested, but no-one was shot. This was a conscious policy of the military commander of the Petersburg district, General Khabalov. It appears that some members of the Tsarist ruling class had also learned lessons from Bloody Sunday in 1905. Although taken aback by the events on International Women's Day, Khabalov had previously drawn up general contingency plans to deal with "unrest" which the regime had long been expecting. Khabalov was later criticised as "indecisive" by other monarchists (and some historians) for not shooting down demonstrators from day one, but his approach was part of a policy of graduated repression. The idea was that the police (with mounted units) alone would deal with "disturbances" on the first day and would not fire on demonstrators. Instead they used their batons and *nagaikas* (whips with lead weights at the end) to crack skulls and lacerate bodies to break up any group of workers that they came across. Workers would run away and then regroup elsewhere, but demonstrations and street meetings remained fairly scattered. At the end of International Women's Day Khabalov could congratulate himself that things had gone pretty well. A few policemen had been badly injured but as this was just a "spontaneous" outburst then calm would soon be restored. His pre-emptive strikes a few days earlier, which included the smashing of the Bolshevik printing press and the arrest of many revolutionaries, should have ensured that no-one would be able to capitalise on the day's anger.

Or so he thought. Whilst the ruling caste was breathing a sigh of relief the Bolsheviks, particularly on its Vyborg Committee, were re-evaluating their position. In meetings that night in the Vyborg district they decided to take a more active part in spreading the movement if it continued. Shlyapnikov, the leading member of the Bolshevik Russian Bureau in the capital, heard about this decision but still thought the Vyborg Committee members were getting ahead of themselves. His continuing caution had a point, in that more workers had gone on strike on the anniversary of Bloody Sunday in January, as well as a later strike on 14/27 February.[22] Shlyapnikov, in his memoir of the February days, alludes to his indecision but finishes by recognising that this strike might not follow the same old ritual of a one or even three day strike.

We did not regard the movement that started on February 23 as the beginning of a resolute assault on the tsarist throne. But we took objective conditions into account. The workers' economic position had sharply worsened, people were dissatisfied with the war, the bourgeoisie was displeased with the failure to win the war, and also the entire economic ruin was intensifying and the reaction was fierce, and thus we admitted a revolutionary hurricane might arise even from such an insignificant wind. Therefore we watched the movement of February 23 with extreme care and attentiveness, and all organisations were directed to develop the movement, not to limit it to a fixed period as was common in those times.[23]

In truth it was those workers in the Vyborg Committee, who were closer to the actual strikers, who recognised that what was different this time was the intensity of class anger. It was they who took the decision that the Bolsheviks should go to work the next day and wherever they could lead workers back onto the streets. Similar decisions seem to have been taken by some anarchists, the *Mezhraiontsy,* the more radical SRs and even some Mensheviks. However the real dynamism of the movement at this point came, not from the relatively small politically organised parts of the class, but from the enormous mass of workers themselves, many of whom were participating in a strike for the first time. The revolutionaries, particularly the Bolsheviks, were important in this movement but they did not direct it, except for the fact (and this was significant) that this was the very movement they had long agitated for inside the wider working class. It was in this sense that Trotsky was right in stating that the February Revolution was led by "conscious and tempered workers educated for the most part by the party of Lenin".[24]

From Protest to Insurrection

As it was, on Friday 24 February/9 March the strikes developed a momentum which turned them from a protest into an insurrection. Workers went to their workplaces, but only to hold mass political meetings which decided to continue the strike and demonstrate as before. However, many more workplaces across the whole of the city from the Vyborg side, from Vassilievsky Island, from the Petersburg District and even the distant Narva district, which was home to the famous Putilov plant, now joined the movement. 200,000 workers were now actively involved. Serious fighting with the police and mounted troops now covered the city's streets.

If the women workers had led the way on day one the star turn was performed by the younger element (male and female) on day two.

> *Before the revolution progressive young workers had engaged in underground work, occupied themselves in study circles, distributed leaflets and participated in strikes. Now ... They marched in the front ranks of the demonstrators, attended rallies and clashed with the police... They were the first to inform the workers that troops and police were approaching, tell them where demonstrators were to assemble, what rallies were scheduled and so forth. Young workers organized pickets to prevent resumption of work. The police reported on February 24 that crowds consisting chiefly of young workers were stopping streetcars, singing revolutionary songs and throwing chunks of ice, bolts and other objects at the police.[25]*

Magnificent heroism but ultimately doomed to failure if, as in 1905, the troops remained loyal to the regime. Workers had not forgotten that it was the Semyonovsky Regiment which had finished the revolution with their assault against the barricaded workers' districts of Moscow in December 1905. It was imperative from the workers' point of view that they won over at least a part of the garrison in Petersburg.

The softening-up process began on 24 February/9 March. Although most of the mounted Cossacks initially did what they were told, there were one or two places where some sort of fraternisation or, more accurately, "sororisation", took place. It was again mainly women who went up to groups of soldiers telling them about their lack of bread, explaining that their men too were soldiers but at the front etc. Their aim was to shame the soldiers about the role they were playing.

The Bolshevik worker, Kaiurov, recalled the first instance where the troops' support of the regime began to crumble. On Bolshoi Sampsonievsky Prospekt (in Vyborg)

> *The Cossacks drew themselves up about sixty or seventy feet in front of the demonstration ... The officer's command rang out, and the Cossacks, sabres bared, drove down on our totally defenceless unarmed column ... Forcing their way through with their horses, their eyes bloodshot, the officers were the first to break into the crowd, and the Cossacks galloped behind ... But such joy! The Cossacks rode single file into the aperture the officers had just opened. Some of them smiled, and one actually winked at the workers ... Yells of "Hurrah" for the Cossacks rose from thousands of chests.*[26]

In Znamenskaia Square, the other traditional rallying point on Nevsky Prospekt, later renamed and still known today as "Uprising Square", the police were greeted with a hail of stones and wood from one of the biggest gatherings. The Cossacks, on the other hand, were greeted with cries of "Hurrah" to which they responded by bowing low to the crowd. A mass political rally then ensued in which speaker after speaker called for the overthrow of Tsarism and an end to the war. However such incidents of troops not attacking the demonstrators were rare on day two. Elsewhere the Cossacks assisted the police in harassing and beating workers.

These efforts to quash the movement failed and on Saturday 25 February/10 March the number out on strike rose to 300,000. More and more were trying to get to the great meeting places on Nevsky Prospekt, whilst more police and troops were detailed to stop them. The workers' strategy remained as before. Attack the hated "pharoahs" (the police) but avoid as much as possible any clashes with the soldiers. This did not stop the Ninth Reserve Cavalry Regiment gunning down nine workers on the steps of the Petersburg City Duma on Nevsky Prospekt. Elsewhere though, the discipline of the Petersburg garrison was beginning to waver.

> *In many cases, however the soldiers and Cossacks were passive and left it to the police alone to move against the people who neutralized the tsarist army. Male and female workers seized rifles pointed at them and pleaded with the soldiers to support the people. The workers' actions confused the soldiers and Cossacks and disorganized their ranks. Guns aimed at the people stopped firing. In some instances, soldiers and Cossacks indirectly aided the worker demonstrators and individual soldiers actually joined them. It was hard to capture such soldiers for the crowd helped hide them.*[27]

This was an important step because, as the mass of workers became more confident that the Army would come over to them, it meant that their courage increased and they took on the police more and more. The latter found it harder to arrest demonstrators and get them to prison as the workers would often fight back and release their comrades. Strikes and demonstrations were moving towards all-out insurrection. The demand for bread was now secondary to the demand for an end of Tsarism. And to make matters worse for the regime, this demand was supported by students who also went on strike, and even shopkeepers now shut up shop and joined the workers' demonstrations.

The crunch came on the evening of 25 February/10 March when the Tsar sent his famous cloth-eared telegram to Khabalov: *I command the disorders in the capital end tomorrow. They are impermissible in time of war.*[28]

It left the military authorities no option but to take the step they had been trying to avoid – calling on the troops to gun down the demonstrators. In a pre-emptive strike to try to decapitate the leaders of any actions Khabalov had over 100 people considered "seditious" arrested that night (this included the members of the Petersburg Committee of the Bolshevik Party). Posters were also put up warning the workers that weapons would be used against them if they re-assembled. Khabalov also saw that unless they solved the bread situation the demonstrations could not be stopped. The bread question was a constant issue which plagued all governments until NEP had been going for a year. Bakers though complained that they had only 60% of the flour they needed so there was no option left to Khabalov but to follow orders[29].

26 February/11 March became the second "Bloody Sunday" of Nicholas II's reign. Sukhanov reported that in the morning:

> *The streets were hung with General Khabalov's new proclamations and others, torn down and crumpled, littered the ground. Publicly admitting in them his own helplessness and implying that his previous warnings had been of no avail, he was once again threatening decisive measures and a resort to arms against disorders and mobs ... The last desperate throw was being made.*[30]

It certainly was. According to Chamberlin:

> *There was firing on the crowds in four separate places in the central part of the city; and on Znamenskaya Square the training detachment of the Volinsky regiment used machine guns as well as rifles, with the result that about forty persons were killed and an equal number were wounded.*[31]

This was true but not the whole truth. Some members of the detachment first got into conversation with the crowds and were reluctant to follow orders. A Corporal Il'in was arrested by the unit's Captain, Lashkevitch, who ordered new patrols to fire to break up the demonstration. However there was little sign of fraternisation elsewhere and more machine guns were put not only in the hands of the troops but also the police.

There was another uncomfortable moment for the government towards the end of the day which gave a foretaste of things to come.

> *Towards evening there was an outburst of rebellion in one company of the Pavlovsk regiment; but it was put down with the aid of other troops, and the ringleaders were imprisoned in the fortress of Peter and Paul.*[32]

The Government of the hapless Prince Golitsyn now felt confident enough to get the Tsar to dissolve the Duma[33] where the parties of the propertied classes had been negotiating to try to produce a government which "enjoyed the confidence of the country". It was an irrelevant gesture since the masses of workers were not counting on the members of the Duma anyway. The next morning "the decisive hour of the Revolution struck."[34]

> *The firing on the crowds on Sunday ... was the snapping point in the frail cord of discipline that held the garrison of the capital. The mutiny that was to transform the prolonged street demonstrations into a genuine revolution started in the very unit which had inflicted the heaviest losses on the demonstrating crowds: the training detachment of the Volinsky regiment. During the night the soldiers discussed their impressions of the day's shooting and agreed they would no longer fire on the crowds.*[35]

On Monday, 27 February/12 March the Volinsky Regiment told their captain (the same Lashkevitch mentioned earlier) that they would no longer shoot. He responded by reading out the Tsar's order. This only sparked off a mutiny in which the Captain himself was killed. The regiment poured out of the barracks and brought out the nearby Preobrazhensky and Litovsky regiments with them. For the troops this was no simple matter. Many had hesitated between risking the firing squad for breaking their oath to the Tsar and joining the revolutionary working class movement. However the "molecular interpenetration of the army" (Trotsky)[36] finally took its toll. Only 600 troops (mainly as individuals) had joined the demonstrators by the night of 26 February/11 March but the following morning 10,200 came over to the workers. By the end of the day this had swelled to 66,700.[37] Moreover, those troops who did not actually take to the streets with the workers, could not be relied on to come to the aid of the regime.

From this point the wave of insurrection was unstoppable. Although Shlyapnikov had refused to distribute the few weapons the Bolsheviks had (on the grounds that a few handguns would not make any difference when the main aim of the workers should be to win over the troops) some revolvers (often taken from the police) had found their way into workers' hands. These were used sporadically to pick off "pharoahs", as the police were called, a fact which seems to have encouraged the crowds to march more directly towards the lines of police and soldiers. In the demonstrations up until then workers had run down side streets to avoid fire, and then regrouped back on the main street whenever they could. Now, although some of them would be killed, they marched frontally towards the armed defenders of the state. They seemed to recognise that they could not waste time and only this step could bring victory closer. Whilst the police did not waver, the conscript garrison of Petersburg was not prepared to carry out further shootings.

By now Khabalov was witnessing the unravelling of his forces. He had ordered armoured cars to attack the demonstrators but the squadron commander told him they would be ineffective when surrounded by a crowd. Although the cars were then disabled the workers repaired them quickly. They then used them to assault police stations and, more importantly, the Telephone Exchange, which was still defended by the police. Once inside workers and students ordered the telephonists to disconnect all the lines to the government, whilst some soldiers acted as sentries to make sure that the telephone system continued to work (albeit inefficiently) for the revolution.

Whole sections of the city and key buildings were now in workers' hands. A last attempt to disperse the crowd by General Kutepov's punitive detachment led to many deaths on Liteiny Prospekt but the sheer numbers of demonstrators eventually overwhelmed them. As darkness fell, Kutepov realised he had lost his troops. They had simply melted into the crowd. The regime decided to retreat to defensive positions with the few reliable troops they had left, but even this turned out to be impossible.

Workers and soldiers now were fraternising in more direct ways. Several regiments crossed the Liteiny Bridge into the working class district of Vyborg. As they approached the Finland Station they met a crowd of workers coming from the factories. Among them was Mikhail Kalinin (future head of the Soviet state). According to him, the soldiers yelled "Where are our leaders? Lead us." Kalinin claims he jumped on a platform and replied "If it's leaders you want, Kresty (The Crosses) Prison is right here but first you have to free your leaders". There were 7,600 prisoners (in a gaol designed for 4,000) including members of all the opposition parties like the Bolshevik Petersburg Committee and the Menshevik leaders of the Workers' Group in the War Industries Committee. Thousands of workers and soldiers surrounded the prison and eventually they simply stormed the main gate. Not only were all prisoners freed, but all records were burned. The same scene was repeated at all the other prisons across Petersburg over the next few days.

By the morning of 28 February/13 March the few remaining defenders of Tsarism in the capital were counting on troops arriving from the front as their last hope. They came alright, but not to save the Tsar. As they came into contact with revolutionary workers and soldiers most of them went over to the revolution. Some even fought with their own officers who had tried to machine gun them. Even those stationed to defend the Tsar's family at Tsarskoe Selo came over to the revolution.

Although almost the entire Petersburg garrison had now joined the revolution, the battle for the capital was not over. The hated "pharaohs", having seen their police stations ransacked, spread out across the city. Donning civilian clothes or soldiers' greatcoats, they sniped at demonstrators from rooftops at strategic points (church belfries being a favourite) and tried to pick off as many of the demonstrators as they could. In combating this;

> The masses themselves displayed initiative and independence which was especially important in achieving this task.[38]

On the evening of 27 February/12 March a Military Commission (nominally under the Provisional Government that would come into existence that day) had been set up to coordinate the despatch of troops to where they were most needed. This was either to defend key points of the city or answer workers' demands to wipe out some machine gun nest or other. In the chaos of the moment it did not always work out neatly. The Military Commission were often too slow to act, so workers and soldiers took to guarding important public buildings on their own initiative. This was necessary not only against the "pharaohs" but also against looters, and those determined to take advantage of the breakdown of the system for their personal advantage. Amongst the latter were not only the criminals freed alongside the political prisoners, but those who still supported the regime. The latter egged on rioters to create chaos in order to discredit the revolution. Although bourgeois historians point to these and other criminal acts in February (and after) it is testimony to the remarkable self-discipline of so many workers in the revolutionary camp that despite some looting and other understandable acts of revenge (mainly against the police) very few of these attempts succeeded[39].

The Question of Who Should Rule After the Collapse of Tsarism

Although the formal abdication of the Tsar did not come for another three days, the regime was effectively finished on 27 February/12 March. However, sweeping away a hated old order is only the first task of a revolution. It immediately poses the question of what is to replace it. February 1917 would pose that question but it would not find an answer for another eight months. The working class had done the bulk of the fighting and dying on the streets.[40] In a real sense the February Revolution was a proletarian revolution which the bourgeoisie did all it could to recuperate for its own programme. Liberal bourgeois histories usually lament that the democratic revolution of February 1917 was stolen by those wicked Bolsheviks in October but this is just class propaganda. In fact it was the other way around. The proletarian revolution that had taken place on the streets in February was about to be usurped by the bourgeoisie with the full complicity of the leading Mensheviks and Socialist Revolutionaries.

The liberals and constitutional monarchists of the Kadets and the Progressive Bloc in the Duma huddled in their salons, discussing the horrors that were taking place on the streets. When the Tsar had simply ordered the dismissal of the Duma they were even more paralysed as they still did not want to act "illegally"!

It was only on 27 February/12 March, when soldiers, fearful of the reprisals they might face if the revolution failed, converged on the Duma's seat in the Tauride Palace. They wanted the Duma to absolve them of the breach of their oath to the Tsar and they thought that the Duma was the only body that could now aid them. Its ex-members had hastily decided to form a "Provisional Committee" (which would soon metamorphose into the Provisional Government). Their aim was quite clear as expressed by the Kadet, Kogan, who announced that "a revolution has begun and we must do everything to prevent 'irresponsible elements' from leading it.". The constant fear that the politicians of the old Duma had was that "the licentious passions of the *stikhiia*"[41], the elemental drive of the lower classes would get out of their control. A monarchist deputy, Shulgin recorded in his memoirs the rage of his class at the turn of events:

> *Machine guns – that is what I wanted ... Only the language of machine guns was accessible to the crowds in the streets ... only it, the lead, could drive this dreadful beast back to its den.*[42]

At the time he pointed out that the workers were already forming soviets; ... *if we don't take power, others will take it, those who have already elected some sort of scoundrels in the factories.*[43]

As Shulgin feared, those "scoundrels", aka the revolutionary working class, were already finding another solution to the political vacuum that the workers themselves had created. The legacy of 1905 had not been forgotten. As early as 25 February/10 March, shouts had gone up at the mass meeting in Znamenskaia Square, "Let's elect a soviet of workers' deputies". A Bolshevik worker present there later recorded:

> *On a teetering box by a lamp post, holding onto the grey pillars with one hand, stood a tall, broad-shouldered man with an animated face who looked like both a worker and a student. Gesticulating with one hand he cried "Comrades, the long-awaited hour has finally come. The people have risen against their oppressors. Don't lose a minute, form neighbourhood workers' soviets and draw soldier representatives into them".*[44]

And in factories across the city elections of factory committees and delegates had begun even before a central soviet had been proclaimed. Both Bolsheviks and Mensheviks supported the move though with different perspectives. In September 1915, after a year of defeats, the Russian liberal bourgeoisie, headed by the industrialist and monarchist Guchkov, had dreamed up the War Industries Committee to help organise supplies for the war. They were only papering over the cracks that had already appeared in the Tsarist state. The pro-war "defensist" Mensheviks had supported this (it fitted their notion of a gradual democratic revolution to see the bourgeoisie now playing "their real role" in the state) and under Gvozdev and Bogdanov[45] they created a Workers' Group to support the War Industries Committee. The Bolsheviks refused to participate in this, and instead made their first call for a workers' soviet, but not just as some coordinating committee. Even this early, they saw it as a potential Provisional Revolutionary Government.

However in February 1917 when the first Executive Committee of the Soviet was formed the Bolsheviks were hardly present at all. Why was this so? Bourgeois histories often argue that this was because the Bolsheviks played little part in the events of February. This is demonstrably untrue as the many memoirs of Bolshevik workers to the events testify. Marc Ferro tells us that on 25 February/10 March "the Bolsheviks were the main organisers of the strikes and parades."[46] Marcel Liebman probably sums it up most accurately;

> *The Bolshevik militants were not inactive ... they closely followed the events and took part in them. But they were unable to take the lead in the movement or put forward a clear programme of action...*[47]

This was hardly surprising given that their principal leaders were in exile, their next most experienced leaders (the Bolshevik Duma faction) had been banished to Siberia and even the Petersburg Committee had been arrested. Thus when, on 27 February/12 March, a crowd of 25,000, mostly soldiers from the nearby Preobrazhensky and Volinsky barracks, marched on the Tauride Palace (where the Duma sat) once again demanding "leaders" there were few Bolsheviks present.

Furthermore street fighting was still going on and left wing socialists and anarchists were still largely involved in that. As we saw earlier, the Bolshevik Petersburg Committee had been released that day, but decided to concentrate on ensuring the victory of the workers in the streets, and mostly remained in Vyborg (in fact Bolshevik workers there refused to go to the Duma building as they did not see the Duma as representative of their struggle). This allowed the Mensheviks led by Gvozdev, the pro-war leader of the Workers' Group of the War Industries Committee, to proclaim that they had set up a "Provisional Executive Committee of the Soviet of Workers' Deputies" in the Tauride Palace and appealed to workers to elect delegates to it that very evening. Shlyapnikov did get to the Tauride Place by 7.00 p.m. – the proposed start time of the first Soviet sitting. He saw amidst the chaos that the workers, and particularly Bolshevik workers, were not well represented. Amongst the delegates there was a preponderance of intellectuals, school teachers and even taxi drivers![48] He thus tried to delay the convening of the Soviet but the meeting went ahead with about 250, of which only 50 according to Shlyapnikov, really were accredited workers' delegates.

With fighting still going (and many workers not yet aware that there was a soviet to elect) the representational arrangements at this stage were ad hoc and haphazard. Even in the days that followed the informality continued. As the Petersburg Soviet of Soldiers' and Workers' Delegates took shape there was supposed to be one delegate for every 1,000 factory workers, and one delegate for each regiment. However, smaller factories, in which the Mensheviks predominated, could also send one delegate whatever the size of their workforce. The regiments elected far more delegates than they should have. Some were even represented by officers (commissioned and non-commissioned) who had gone over to the revolution. As the soldier element made up more than two thirds of the Soviet, it can be seen that the working class as a whole was under-represented in the first days of the Petersburg Soviet. There were so many other unsettled issues at the beginning of March. Tellingly there was not a single female delegate despite the vital role women had played in opening the floodgates to the February Revolution.

Chapter 4
Dual Power or Class War?

Faced with the "popular uprising" (the words are those of the Tsar's State Council), Nicholas II abdicated on 1/14 March. He, his Ministers and others of the Romanov dynasty, were eventually arrested. The autocracy which had oppressed the Russian people for centuries was overthrown. The landowners and capitalists who wielded economic power had at first thought of stemming the tide of revolution with a constitutional monarchy headed by the Tsar's brother. When they realised that the revolutionary masses would not tolerate this "solution" they put their trust in a "Provisional Government". Its declared aim was to govern the country until a Constituent Assembly could be elected to determine the final form of a new government apparatus.

Many of those who would end up in the new government were former members of the Duma but the Constitutional Democrat leader Pavel Milyukov realised that the new government could not seriously claim its legitimacy from that fact. He knew that the mass of workers would not trust a Provisional Government drawn from the old Tsarist Duma. After all, the Duma had been elected on the basis of a quota system intended to deny any real representation to either peasants or workers (under the old Tsarist census all workers were classed as peasants). Milyukov, thus took upon himself the responsibility of choosing the ministers of the new government. When he read out the list of capitalists and landowners to the crowds at the Tauride Palace there was some laughter and incredulity as no-one had heard of most of them. The most telling question came from the crowd itself, which asked "Who elected you?".[1] Milyukov replied "the Revolution" which was the first public indication that the bourgeoisie intended to steal "the Revolution" from the workers who had actually carried it out by defining it in their own terms. Milyukov himself wanted to restore the monarchy, but make it "constitutional" like the British system and, as we shall see later, wanted to maintain the Entente with the Western Allies in order to achieve the aims of Russian imperialism, with or without a Tsar.

Whatever schemes the bourgeoisie had, the new Provisional Government faced a major stumbling block. The real power did lie elsewhere. It lay with the war-weary workers and soldiers who had made the February Revolution, and who, as we saw in the last chapter, were already calling for the revival of the organs of popular democracy — the soviets — which had sprung up in Russia in the 1905 revolutionary uprising. This was soon recognised by Guchkov, once Chairman of the Tsar's War Industries Committees, now Minister of the Army and Navy in the Provisional Government. In mid-March he complained to one of his generals:

> *The Provisional Government possesses no real power and its orders are executed only insofar as this is permitted by the Soviet of Workers' and Soldiers'*

Deputies, which holds in its hands the most important elements of actual power, such as troops, railways, postal and telegraph service. It is possible to say directly that the Provisional Government exists only while this is permitted by the Soviet.[2].

The key words here are "insofar as". Also translatable as "to the extent", *postol'ku-poskol'ku,* was the condition on which the Provisional Government's authority rested from the beginning of the revolution.

It had its origins in "Soviet Order Number 1 to the Garrison of the Petersburg Military District", which the Petersburg Soviet issued on the same day the Tsar abdicated. This order called for wider elections to the Soviet by the rank and file throughout the armed forces, and stated significantly:

(3) In all its political actions, the military branch is subordinated to the Soviet of Workers' and Soldiers' Deputies and to the Committees thereof.

*(4) The orders of the military commission of the State Duma are to be executed, **only in such [postol'ku-poskol'ku] cases as do not conflict with the orders** of the Soviet of Workers' and Soldiers' Deputies.* [3]

This order was more or less dictated to the Soviet Executive by the soldiers who flocked to the Tauride Palace to protest against the order that the Military Committee of the Provisional Government issued. This ordered soldiers back to their barracks, and to obey their former officers. The soldiers could see that this was the first step in taking away what they had already won. The brutal treatment of soldiers by officers had led (as we have already noted) to many officers being killed by their own men. The soldiers were quite happy to have officers from those who had supported the revolution, but not the rest. Which is why they demanded the right to choose their own officers. They also feared that if they handed back their rifles they would be disarmed in the face of any counter-revolution.

The effect of all this was to make the Soviet — not the Duma's Provisional Committee (soon to be called Government), the body which controlled armed power. And in fact soviet power extended much further than issuing decrees. Based on the principle (although it would not always be adhered to) of directly elected and recallable delegates, it was the heart of the revolutionary process, and had the confidence of the masses. Local soviets were soon formed in every district of the city as well as in many towns and cities across the old Russian Empire. In Petersburg, transport, food distribution and the whole of the municipal administration were organised by the Soviet. Revolutionary Guards were dispatched to occupy such key institutions as the State Bank, the Treasury, the Mint and the Printing Office.

The paper authority of the Provisional Government which was recognised as the "official" government of Russia was not challenged by the Soviet at this point. Dominated by reformist socialists, the Soviet voluntarily maintained the fiction that the Provisional

Dual Power or Class War?

Government ruled. For the Mensheviks, who enjoyed the support of the large majority of Soviet delegates in the early stages of the revolution, this was just as it should be. According to their mechanical "Marxism", the revolution which was underway could only be the classical bourgeois democratic revolution whose task was to destroy the remnants of feudalism in Russia, and leave the way open for the development of Russian capitalism, which would, in some far-off future, create the conditions for a proletarian, socialist revolution. Since the revolution was a capitalist one, the formula ran, it was up to the bourgeoisie to wield state power. For the supposedly socialist Mensheviks, the Provisional Government was the natural source of authority. For them, the soviets were only temporary bodies which were good for calming workers' demands in the immediate term but at most could only be a kind of supervisor of the bourgeoisie to see that it carried out its democratic tasks.

Though it did not want to see the role of the working masses reduced to that of a mere spectator, or overseer of the capitalists' revolution, the activity of the Bolshevik Party was also initially constrained by the theory of the democratic revolution. In the aftermath of 1905, which revealed the weakness and political spinelessness of the Russian bourgeoisie, Lenin had outlined the tactics for a socialist party in the forthcoming revolution in Russia. Far from abstaining from taking political power, Lenin argued that the Russian proletariat must ally with the peasantry to establish a "revolutionary democratic dictatorship" and complete the bourgeois revolution themselves. This in turn would be the prelude to proletarian, socialist revolution. Although this was an infinitely more dynamic perspective than the Mensheviks', because it took into account the fact that the class struggle between workers and capitalists already existed in Russia despite its predominantly rural population, it still placed the tasks of the bourgeois democratic revolution first on the agenda of revolution.

February 1917 Opened Up a New Stage in Class War

So, when the February Revolution broke out the Bolshevik Party's Programme was still based on the idea that the first task was to complete the democratic revolution, and the initial activities of the various Party organisations in Petersburg, no matter what their political complexion, reflected this fact. Thus the Bolshevik Manifesto drawn up in February by the Bureau of the Central Committee in Russia (Shlyapnikov, Molotov and Zalutsky), whilst continuing the policy of revolutionary opposition to the war, called on the working class and the revolutionary soldiers to form "a provisional revolutionary government" in order to establish a democratic republic which would introduce such reforms as the 8 hour day, confiscation of landed estates, the creation of a constituent assembly on the basis of universal suffrage and secret ballot. After the formation of the Provisional Government the first seven issues of *Pravda*, under the direction of the Bureau, denounced it as "a government of capitalists and landowners" and called for the Soviet to convene a constituent assembly to establish a "democratic republic".

The more radical Bolshevik Vyborg District Committee, which as we have already seen, had played a leading part in the revolutionary actions there, envisaged a more significant role for the soviets. At its first ever legal meeting on 1/14 March it had already called for the Soviet to be the Provisional Revolutionary government. Its document rejecting compromise with the Duma was described by the historian Hasegawa "as like a time bomb in a powder keg"[4]. On 18 March/1 April it proposed to the Bolshevik Petersburg Committee that:

> *The task of the moment is the founding of a provisional revolutionary government, growing out of the unification of local Soviets of Workers', Peasants' and Soldiers' Deputies in the whole of Russia". The proposal went on to argue for the strengthening of the soviets in preparation for a "full seizure of central power" and limited recognition of the Provisional Government "only until the formation of a revolutionary government from the Soviets of Workers', Peasants' and Soldiers' Deputies and only in so far as its actions are consistent with the interests of the proletariat and the broad democratic masses.[5]*

But the Petersburg Committee leaders, headed by Shlyapnikov, were less inclined to dissociate the proletariat from the Provisional Government. Even before Kamenev, Muranov and Stalin returned from Siberian exile to take over the editorial board of *Pravda*, this committee accepted the Provisional Government as the agent of the democratic revolution, and refused to adopt the Vyborg Committee's motion. Instead it resolved not to oppose the Provisional Government unless it did anything against the working class. However, when Kamenev went even further in the pages of *Pravda,* and undermined the entire Bolshevik policy on the war by unashamedly calling for national defencism on the basis that a free people can only "*answer bullet with bullet, shell with shell*", there was uproar amongst rank and file Party workers.

According to Shlyapnikov: *The indignation in the Party locals was enormous, and when the proletarians found out that Pravda had been seized by three former editors arriving from Siberia they demanded their expulsion from the Party.[6]*

Protests from local committees such as that from Vyborg (which was printed in *Pravda*) meant that the new editors published no more articles openly in favour of the Provisional Government and its policy of national defence. But this only led to paralysis since the rank and file militants also kept silent and confusion remained. In the end the Party line towards the Provisional Government, proposed by Stalin, and apparently adopted by the Party's Conference in March, for the First All-Russia Conference of Soviets at the end of that month, was hardly distinguishable from that of the Menshevik majority. The Party Conference didn't manage to produce a resolution on the war, but at the Soviet Conference itself the Bolsheviks voted for the official "Resolution of Support for the Provisional Government" which recognised the "*necessity of gradually gaining political control and influence over the Provisional Government and its local organs so as to persuade it to conduct the most energetic struggle against counter-revolutionary forces, to take the most resolute steps towards a complete democratisation of all walks of Russian life, and to make preparations for universal peace without annexations and indemnities based on the self-determination of nations.*"[7]

Dual Power or Class War?

Small wonder that many sections of the Party thought that the re-unification of the Russian Social Democratic Party was now a possibility, or that in the provinces Bolsheviks and Mensheviks saw themselves as being in the same organisation!

Given the debates inside the Bolshevik Party, it is a mistake to explain the soviets' ceding of power to the capitalists as simply due to a low level of class consciousness, as reflected by the Bolsheviks' poor standing in the soviets. The February Revolution was the first to occur in the imperialist epoch. No-one, and no party had, or could have had, a fully-worked out strategy for how the proletariat should conduct the struggle. The Russian workers and soldiers had to learn for themselves how to struggle for soviet power. The idea that this might be the potential start of a world socialist revolution had occurred to some Bolsheviks in the Petersburg Soviet at this point[8] but the Party leadership in Russia did not reflect it. However one thing was clear from the start – the establishment of the Provisional Government was itself an act of class war and an attempt to deny the fruits of revolutionary victory to the working class.

February therefore was only the start of the working class fight for a better society. Russia now experienced an intensification of that class war. As 1917 wore on the battle lines became clearer and sharper. On one side stood "census society", that is the old privileged classes, the bourgeoisie, the capitalists, all the old supporters of monarchy (including most generals), and the Black Hundreds. On the other stood the "democracy" who supported soviet power. This included the Bolshevik Party, some of Martov's Menshevik Internationalists, the *Mezhraiontsy* (or Inter-district committee) to which Trotsky and Lunacharsky belonged, and the various anarchist groupings. The former represented the old order (although divided about how they could save it). The latter were all active inside the working class and in favour of breaking with the Provisional Government. In between them, but aiding and abetting the old order, were the Mensheviks headed by Tsereteli, and the Socialist Revolutionaries headed by Chernov. As long as these organisations supported the mythical idea that the Provisional Government ran the country, they acted as a barrier to the advance towards a real victory of soviet power and the working class. In their longer term plan the aim of the Right SRs and Mensheviks was to dissolve the soviets in favour of some parliamentary system.

However, the Russian-based Bolshevik Party leadership's initial attempt to cling to its programme of democratic revolution gave these Mensheviks and SRs the breathing space to work towards establishing the rule of the Provisional Government. Whilst confusion reigned, the Party's position on both the war and the future of the Provisional Government was unclear. These debates and arguments within the Bolshevik Party undermine any notion of its supposedly iron discipline of later Stalinist mythology (a myth also happily seized on by all those eager to prove that authoritarianism was the hallmark of Bolshevism). Before the Party could once again give a clear lead to the Russian working class, the debate within it had to be deepened to abandon the old framework and adopt a new one.

This was the task Lenin had already begun in his *Letters from Afar*, only one of which had been published (with significant cuts) by *Pravda*. On 16 April, 1917 Lenin returned to Russia from political exile in Switzerland. With his arrival in Russia he was in a better position to make his views felt, and to link up with the Vyborg workers who were already on the same hymn sheet.

"We Must Know How to Supplement and Amend Old Formulas"[9]

The astonishment of those who, like Sukhanov, heard Lenin's first speech at the Finland Station is well-known. The contrast between this and the direction the Party leadership had taken throughout March was certainly dramatic. In response to Chkheidze's (Menshevik Chairman of the Petersburg Soviet) official welcoming speech which hoped that Lenin would avoid sectarianism and pursue the supposedly common goal of "closing of the democratic ranks" in order to "defend the revolution", Lenin announced:

> *Dear comrades, soldiers, sailors and workers! I am happy to greet in you the victorious Russian revolution, and greet you as the vanguard of the international proletarian army... The piratical imperialist war is the beginning of civil war throughout Europe... The hour is not far distant when at the call of our comrade Karl Liebknecht, the peoples will turn their weapons against their own capitalist exploiters... The international socialist revolution has already dawned... Germany is seething... Any day now the whole of European capitalism may crash. The Russian revolution accomplished by you has prepared the way and opened a new epoch. Long live the worldwide socialist revolution.[10]*

For the Mensheviks and even some Right Bolsheviks, trapped within the sterile confines of the democratic revolution, Lenin's portrayal of the Russian Revolution as the beginning of the international socialist revolution seemed like the "ravings of a madman", or someone who had been away too long from the political reality of Russia. I.P Goldenburg (an old social democrat but defencist in the war) concluded that Lenin was now occupying "the throne vacated by Bakunin", whilst Skobelev (the member of the Soviet Executive who had written out Soviet Order No. 1 on the instructions of the soldiers) concluded with satisfaction that he was now "lost".[11] On the other hand, to many of the thousands of workers and soldiers mobilised by the Petersburg Committee (many from the Vyborg district where the Finland Station and Bolshevik HQ were) the speech must have seemed like a breath of fresh air, although not all were impressed. Some soldiers opposed his anti-war message, and wanted to pull Lenin down from the armoured car he was speaking from. It has to be remembered that this was at a time when nearly all the political forces agreed that the war should carry on and many, especially in the Petersburg garrison, were ready to invade any factory where workers were on strike, arguing that they weakened the war effort. Lenin was now giving voice to a real alternative.

His views on the war and world revolution were not extemporised on the spot. They were based on the theoretical contributions he, and Bukharin, had made to the Marxist analysis of imperialism. As we stated in Chapter Two, they argued that the First World War had opened up a new epoch in capitalist history. The epoch of imperialism was also the sign of the beginning of the "parasitism and decay" of the whole system. Capitalism was now ripe for overthrow and the Russian Revolution would only be the first step in the world revolution. This was the basis of the revolutionary defeatist policy Lenin had shaped for the Party, and the one the Zimmerwald Left had proposed on the war in 1915. What he now had to do was convince the Party that the framework for determining Party policy was no longer simply Russian economy and society, but had to be the situation of international capital, whose imperialist war had brought unprecedented devastation, and was creating an international revolutionary situation. In short, he had to prove that reality itself had gone beyond the programme of the so-called "democratic revolution", and that: *The formula is obsolete. It is no good at all. It is dead. And it is no use trying to revive it.*[12]

For Marxists "theory is not a dogma but a guide to action" and Lenin's *April Theses on The Tasks of the Proletariat in the Present Revolution* were intended to show the practical way forward for a proletarian party that was in danger of losing the advanced sections of the working class because of attachment to an outmoded programme. In the beginning Lenin was almost totally isolated amongst the party leadership. On April 4th he presented his *Theses* to two meetings: one of Bolshevik delegates to the Party Conference and the other comprising Bolshevik and Menshevik delegates to the Soviet Conference which had just finished. Only Alexandra Kollontai, a recent convert to Bolshevism, spoke in support. The *Theses* were published in *Pravda* as Lenin's personal view with a disclaimer by the editors who stated:

> *As for the general scheme of Comrade Lenin, it seems to us unacceptable in that it starts from the assumption that the bourgeois-democratic revolution is ended, and counts upon the immediate transformation of this revolution into a socialist revolution.*[13]

But this apparent isolation did not deter him. He was prepared to resign from the Central Committee, and argue his case as a rank and file member, rather than change his perspectives. As it was he spent the rest of April repeating the arguments of the *Theses* and developing the essential points for presentation at the forthcoming Party Conference. We can sum these up as follows:

• No matter the existence of a new government in Russia, the war is still an imperialist war fought for the interests of capitalism. Given that broad sections of the masses are being deceived by the bourgeoisie into believing that the war can now be fought as a war of revolutionary defence the task is to explain patiently "the inseparable connection existing between capital and the imperialist war, and to prove that without overthrowing capital it is impossible to end the war by a truly democratic peace". The Party must expose the contradictions between the Provisional Government's words about "peace without annexations" and its actions. This campaign should also be carried on at the Front alongside appeals for fraternisation. The latter should aim "to raise fraternisation from the level of an instinctive revulsion against war to a clear political understanding of how to get out of it".

• The Russian Revolution is now passing from its first to the second stage. The former, owing to "the insufficient class consciousness and organisation of the proletariat", placed power in the hands of the bourgeoisie. The next stage "must place power in the hands of the proletariat and the poorest sections of the state".

• No support for the Provisional Government. No breeding illusions that a government of capitalists can cease to be an imperialist government.

• So long as the Bolsheviks are a minority in the soviets, the Party's task is to explain the errors of the other parties who hold sway over the masses (Mensheviks, Social Revolutionaries) at the same time as preaching the "necessity of transferring the entire state power to the Soviets of Workers' Deputies".

• It follows from this that Russia should not become a parliamentary republic.

• The weight of emphasis in the Agrarian Programme is to shift to the soviets of Agricultural Labourers' Deputies and to separate soviets for poor peasants. All landed estates should be confiscated and put at the disposal of the Agricultural Workers' Soviets "for the public account".

• The need to convoke a Party Congress to change the Party's Programme on the issues of imperialism and war; the nature of the proletarian state; the out-of-date minimum programme; and to change the Party's name to the Communist Party.

• The need to take the initiative in creating a new revolutionary international.

The *Theses*, starting from the reality of the imperialist war and the existence of the soviets, provided a strategy and tactics for a party that was aiming to lead the working masses towards a socialist revolution in which the Soviets would be the state power.

"Let Us Create a Proletarian Communist Party; Its Elements Have Already Been Created by the Best Adherents of Bolshevism"[14]

Within a month the Party's attitude towards the *Theses* changed from ridicule and hostility to their broad acceptance as the basis for the resolutions at the April Conference. It is too easy, and simply untrue, to explain this by Lenin's charismatic leadership. Despite his undoubted standing in the Party, his views on return from exile had been dismissed as unrealistic by the Central Committee. It was reality itself which was to force on the leadership as a whole the validity of Lenin's perspective.

In fact, as we have seen, the *Theses* already reflected the feeling of rank and file members, in districts like Vyborg and Kronstadt, where there was no need to persuade the revolutionary workers and sailors of the need to oppose the Provisional Government, and establish soviet power. In other words, Lenin was much more in touch with the mood of the revolutionary working class than many of the other Bolshevik leaders.

But the longer the dual power situation lasted the more the folly of trying to pressurise the Provisional Government into acting in the interests of the masses became evident. While the ministers hummed and hawed about the fate of the landed estates, the peasants were already seizing the land. The food problem had not been solved; famine loomed and the price of bread was still rising. In fact the cost of living was increasing dramatically in 1917 to reach 14.3 times the level of 1914. Market prices rose 34 times in the course of the year.

In the factories the class war only intensified after February. Unions were formed and demands for the eight hour day increased. Organisationally though, the unions were not the most significant new bodies. The most striking feature was the increase in the number and self-confidence of the factory committees. Many of these were based on an older tradition of stewards (starosty) committees and were mostly elected by the whole workforce with responsibility for "control" (which, except for the state's war industry factories, meant supervision and inspection – at this point they did not aim to manage the factory). S.A. Smith compares them to the shop stewards committees on Red Clydeside and Sheffield, the *obleute* (revolutionary shop stewards) in Germany and the "internal commissions" in Italy.[15]

However, in one important respect the workers in the state enterprises devoted to war production went further, since they actually took over the running of the factories. This was because they had been subject to military discipline during the war and a greater degree of repression. The collapse of Tsarist authority meant that many of the military officers who managed the factories simply ran away. The workers thus had to take over in order to keep production going for the war effort (the Bolsheviks had less influence in these factories at this time). Not every factory committee was happy with this responsibility. On 15 April a meeting of factory representatives passed a resolution which stated

> Until such time as full socialisation of the national economy, both state and private, shall occur workers shall not take responsibility for the technical and administrative-economic organisation of production and shall refuse to take part in the organisation of production.[16]

This resolution demonstrates a high degree of sophistication, since it showed an understanding of the reality that workers managing capitalism is still capitalism. Workers can only start managing an economy when its social basis has shifted. At that time "control" or oversight (including veto over chosen managers and in some cases the hiring and firing of workers) was enough for the grassroots movement.

Meanwhile, the number involved in strikes escalated as the year went on. From

35,000 in April they rose to 175,000 in June and reached 1.1 million in September.

> *The geographical area covered by strikes broadened out from the Petrograd and Central Industrial Region in spring, to the whole of European Russia by autumn. All the time, strikes became more organised more large-scale and more militant. Strikes were a politicising experience for those who took part in them: they saw with their own eyes how the employers were going on investment strike, engaging in lockouts, refusing to accept new contracts or to repair plant; how the government was colluding with the employers, curbing the factory committees and sending troops to quell disorders.* [17]

Above all, the war dragged on. Peace seemed as far away as ever. The Provisional Government's policy of dragging the masses, via the soviets, into sharing responsibility for the war, under the guise of defending the revolution, floundered when Milyukov (Minister of Foreign Affairs) telegraphed a note to the Allies reassuring them that declarations about peace without annexations did not involve:

> *... any slackening on the part of Russia in the common struggle of the Allies. Quite the contrary, the aspiration of the entire nation to carry the world war to a decisive victory has grown stronger...* [18]

Immediately there were widespread demonstrations against Milyukov and the war throughout Russia. On 4/17 May 100,000 workers and soldiers in Petersburg demonstrated for peace. The Petersburg Soviet received resolutions protesting against Milyukov's note from soviets all over Russia. During this crisis, three days before the Bolshevik Party Conference, some local Party Committees (Kronstadt, Petersburg, Helsingfors) interpreted the slogan "Long live the Soviets" as a call for the immediate overthrow of the Provisional Government. The Kronstadt Committee led armed soldiers and sailors to the peace demonstrations carrying the slogan "Down with the Provisional Government". Even before the Party had formally adopted Lenin's resolutions and accepted "All Power to the Soviets" as the guiding slogan of the hour, the Bolshevik Party was presented with a problem which would reappear in the months to follow: that of militant sections overestimating the political maturity of the situation and falling into the trap of rushing into a premature attempt at insurrection. But this was a problem of a Party intent on creating the best possible conditions for a successful proletarian assault on power. In the aftermath of the April debates and the Party Conference the question the Bolshevik Party was asking itself was not whether the soviets should take state power but "How?" and "When?".

"For Actual Experience Will from Day to Day Shatter the Petty-Bourgeois Illusions." [19]

The bourgeoisie solved its political crisis by denying Milyukov's note meant what it said, but accepted the resignation of its author all the same. In this hour of need for the Provisional Government the Executive Committee of the Soviet came to the rescue once again by agreeing to enter a new coalition Government. Six so-called socialist Ministers were proposed by the Committee (SRs and Mensheviks). On 18/31 May a Bolshevik motion to the Petersburg Soviet opposing the idea of "socialist Ministers" received only 100 votes. Despite the massive anger of the workers, and thus the growing influence of the Bolshevik Party, it was still a long way from determining Soviet policy as a whole. At the beginning of May the Russian capitalists and their Allies still hoped to revive the crumbling war fronts, and win back popular support for a new military offensive by involving the Soviet in its Government. Kerensky, the self-appointed spokesman for the Soviets as Minister of Justice in the previous Provisional Government, now became Minister of War and the Navy in this new attempt to dupe the masses with arguments about strengthening Soviet control over the Government.

As Trotsky put it, the feeling was that if one Kerensky in the Government was all right then six Kerenskys would be even better. But while Kerensky himself was informing Buchanan, Ambassador for British imperialism, that "the soviets will die a natural death", the real socialists and revolutionaries, the Bolsheviks, were answering the petty bourgeoisie's empty rhetoric about revolutionary democracy with the now clearly-defined policy of patiently explaining the "need for the entire state power to pass to the proletariat and semi-proletariat". The Party as a whole now accepted that its task was "to increase the number of Soviets, to reinforce them and to consolidate the unity of our Party"[20] in preparation for a victory over the capitalists which could not be achieved "in a few days by a simple outburst of popular wrath" or by premature adventurist acts, but which required organisation and, above all, class consciousness – that is, the emancipation of even greater numbers of the proletariat from the influence of the Mensheviks and SRs.

Chapter 5
The July Days
"The Party Must Remain with the Masses"

In winning the battle to ditch the old Bolshevik programme, Lenin and his supporters in the grassroots had successfully "re-armed" the Bolshevik Party[1]. It now had a perspective which corresponded to the changed reality created by the February Revolution. How great a step forward this was for the Bolsheviks can be seen by the fact that Party membership rose dramatically. From less than 10,000 in February "at the end of July there were probably 200,000 Bolshevik members"[2] and support for the Party in all proletarian organisations in Petersburg has generally been estimated at about 30% by May 1917. This was particularly the case with the factory committees which had been established in most of the large factories by the later spring. At the end of May the first conference of Petersburg factory committees overwhelmingly passed a Bolshevik resolution on control of the economy.[3]

Becoming the most significant organised force calling for a completion of the revolution, and opposing any cooperation with the bourgeois ministers of the Provisional Government, may have put the Bolsheviks more in tune with the masses, but it also created a problem for them. Many young workers who were impatient for action entered the Party's ranks, particularly its Military Organisation and its soldiers' club, Club Pravda. These new elements understood that the Bolsheviks stood for *"All Power to the Soviets"* and *"Down with the Provisional Government"*. What they did not fully appreciate was that these were slogans of orientation. As Lenin stated in April:

> *The government must be overthrown, but not everyone understands this correctly. So long as the Provisional Government has the backing of the Soviet of Workers' Deputies, you cannot 'simply' overthrow it. The only way it can and must be overthrown is by winning over the majority of the Soviets.[4]*

This piece of advice came after spontaneous demonstrations against the Milyukov Note referred to in the previous chapter. Many Bolsheviks, led by the Petersburg Committee (and supported by the Kronstadt sailors) had wished to turn these anti-government demonstrations into an armed insurrection. They argued that the masses had already taken up Lenin's slogans against the Provisional Government. Many Bolsheviks actually joined in the demonstrations. A few days later at the Seventh All-Russia Party Conference Lenin underlined the message that it was too early to act:

> *The Government would like to see us make the first imprudent move towards revolutionary action... We cannot say that the majority is with us; what we need in the present situation is caution. To base proletarian tactics on subjective desires means to condemn them to failure.[5]*

The July Days

Lenin then went on to criticise those Bolsheviks who had supported the workers' use of the *"Down with the Provisional Government"* slogan against the Central Committee's insistence that only *"Long Live the Soviet of Workers' and Soldiers' Deputies"* was justifiable at the time. Lenin condemned this as *"disorganisation"*, *"a serious crime"*, concluding that *"Our organisational apparatus is very weak — our decisions are not being carried out by everyone"*.

This (and the debate over the change in the Party's programme) demonstrates that the Bolshevik Party was nothing like the disciplined monolith of later Stalinist mythology. It was a party of lively debate and wide differences which were well-known to all, as their debates were carried out publicly (which gave the Menshevik press plenty to gloat about). As Professor Smith states:

> In 1917 the Bolshevik Party was a very different animal from the tightly-knit conspiratorial party conceived by Lenin in 1903 ... Though considerably more united than the SRs, Mensheviks or anarchists, the Bolsheviks still embraced a wide range of opinion ... The city committees were the most important agency coordinating Bolshevik activity at the grass roots, and, to an extent they were left to their own devices.[6]

As we saw in Chapter 3 and as we shall see later, the capacity of local rank and file members to act on their own initiative to carry out the agreed policies of the Party was one of its strengths. However in May, June and July 1917 Bolsheviks were experiencing the growing pains of a proletarian party in an entirely new situation of rising class anger, and the rank and file of the party also reflected the unevenness of consciousness within the proletariat itself. By the end of May the Bolsheviks had a clear majority on the Central Bureau of the Factory Committees[7], a fact which only encouraged their young militants to think that the time to get rid of the Provisional Government was approaching.

The economic crisis, brought on by the war, and which had led to the overthrow of Tsarism, could not be solved by the Provisional Government. In February real wages had fallen to a third of pre-war levels and, despite large nominal increases for some workers, the position was no better in July due to massive inflation.

Food prices were doubling approximately every other month during 1917, and the fact that the Provisional Government was even worse at solving the transport question than Tsarism, meant that bread rations were cut from 1lb a day to three quarters of a pound by April. Worse was to come, since only 230 rail wagons containing food reached Petersburg each day in April 1917, compared with a daily total of 351 a year earlier. Only one third of coal needs were reaching the capital by May, and works like Putilov were closed down for weeks on end in August and September. In addition to these temporary closures, 568 factories went bankrupt, leading to increased unemployment. Not surprisingly this led to a massive increase in strikes, as we saw in the previous chapter. These radicalised the workers still further. As the leading academic analyst of these strikes concluded:

The strikes which swept Russia in the summer of 1917 had more than an economic significance. They were a sign of political disillusionment – a reflection of the fact that workers felt cheated of the gains they had made as a result of the February Revolution.[8]

In addition the Provisional Government could not solve the two other desperate problems of Russia in 1917, that of land distribution and that of the war. Even the arrival in the government of the supposed peasant party, the SRs, did little to shake the landowners in the Provisional Government. This was because the SRs were sternly patriotic and tried to get the peasants to abandon their land seizures until *"after the war"*. The peasants turned a deaf ear. They carried out their own spontaneous reforms by seizing the land and, where they met resistance, attacking the landlords. This further undermined the notion that the Provisional Government represented any but the propertied classes. And yet the Mensheviks and SRs who dominated the Soviet Executive still clung to the charade that this was the real government of Russia.

This *"voluntary surrender of state power to the bourgeoisie and its Provisional Government"* (Lenin)[9] only demonstrated the political bankruptcy of these organisations. This was further underlined by the events of June 1917. At the First All-Russia Congress of Soviets, when the dominant Menshevik minister, Tsereteli announced that: *"At the present moment there is no political party which would say "Give the power into our hands, go away, we will take your place." There is no such party in Russia"* ... Lenin replied rhetorically, without standing up, that there was.[10]

The rest of the Congress was a tussle between the Bolsheviks and other left groupings (like the Mezhraiontsy and the Left SRs) to get the other parties to vote for soviet power and the overthrow of the Provisional Government. Having failed in the Congress to get the other parties to agree to this declaration of war on the government, the Bolsheviks decided to put it to the masses by calling a demonstration for 10/23 June. The Soviet Executive denounced this plan and forced the Bolsheviks to call it off (for which Lenin was severely attacked within the Party for vacillation). However, the Mensheviks then overreached themselves. They thought that by calling a massive demonstration in support of the Soviets (i.e. **their** leadership of the Soviet) for the following week this would isolate the Bolsheviks and underline their weakness. This turned out to be a serious misunderstanding of the mood of the Petersburg workers. Sukhanov, who would join Martov's Menshevik Internationalists during 1917, could not believe how blind the Soviet Executive was to what was happening.

The capital was seething. The temper of the masses and the desire for decisive action was growing daily. In the capital there was no longer any need to agitate against the Coalition.[11]

When the demonstration took place on 18 June/1 July only a handful of banners expressed confidence in the Provisional Government (and, by implication, in Soviet support for it), whilst, according to Sukhanov, the slogans on the remainder were overwhelmingly Bolshevik.

> *The situation was absolutely unambiguous. Here and there the chain of Bolshevik flags and columns was interrupted by specifically SR and official Soviet slogans. But they were submerged in the mass; they seemed to be exceptions, intentionally confirming the rule. Again and again, like the unchanging summons of the very depths of the revolutionary capital, like fate itself, like the fatal Birnam Wood - they advanced towards us "All Power to the Soviets!" "Down with the Ten Capitalist Ministers!"* [12]

This success was however to bring the Bolshevik Party its severest test of 1917.

The July Days

Many bourgeois histories of the Russian Revolution argue that the July Days were a Bolshevik attempt to seize power which went wrong (unlike October which, they argue, was a successful coup of the same type). Typical of these is Richard Pipes who called the July Days "Lenin's greatest blunder". However, the evidence of various historians (particularly by A. Rabinowitch in his detailed study *Prelude to Revolution*) demonstrates that this was not the case. The origins of the July Days lay in the spontaneous revolt of the First Machine Gun Regiment in Petersburg against an order sending them to the front to participate in the Provisional Government's failing June Offensive. For some this was a provocation, but instead of trying to prevent a premature outbreak by this single regiment, it seems that the Bolshevik Military Organisation, against all party discipline, actually got carried along with the movement. Their paper, *Soldatskaia Gazeta*, called for the overthrow of the Provisional Government. They also helped to disseminate the news of the First Machine Gunners' revolt to the working class Vyborg district, and to the naval base at Kronstadt.

Here the Bolshevik representatives, Raskolnikov and Roshal, had already been warned by a telephone call from Kamenev to try to dampen down the movement. They were however unsuccessful, and were only able to delay the sailors participating in an armed demonstration for a few hours. And when thousands of demonstrating workers arrived at the Bolsheviks' headquarters in Petersburg on the night of 3/16 July both the Bolshevik Military Organisation and the Petersburg Committee agreed to support the demonstration and lead it on the streets.

The next day the Kronstadt sailors arrived, fully armed, at the Bolshevik headquarters in the mansion of the Tsar's former mistress, the ballerina Kseshinskaya. They, and the thousands of workers and soldiers with them, demanded that Lenin speak to them. Lenin, who was ill, had been absent from the capital for a few days' rest when he had heard of the new movement. If the Bolsheviks had really been planning the overthrow of the Provisional Government at this time they would hardly done so whilst their most known figure was recuperating. He had only returned to the Kseshinskaya mansion a short time before. At first he was reluctant to speak to the demonstration, but finally agreed to do so, murmuring to Podvoisky and the other leaders of the Military Organisation, as he went onto the balcony *"you ought to be thrashed for this".[13]*

His speech was a disappointment to the assembled mass since he only called for a peaceful demonstration and implied that victory would be theirs *"one day"*. To armed workers and soldiers, ready to finish off the class enemy there and then, this was incomprehensible.

Lenin was criticised, then and later, for *"an absence of leadership"* by more impatient elements of the Bolshevik Party. However, to understand his position we must look at the reality of the situation in 1917. There can be little doubt that had the Bolsheviks led the demonstration to attack the Provisional Government on July 4, it would have collapsed then. However, even if the Bolsheviks and their allies had overthrown the Provisional Government, what would have happened next? They could not give the power to the Soviets since these was still dominated by the Menshevik/SR policy of support for the bourgeoisie (one Kronstadt sailor gave vent to the frustration of the workers with this policy when in the course of the roughing up of the SR leader Chernov he shouted *"Take power you stupid bastard when it is being handed to you on a plate")*. And the Bolsheviks could not yet hold power themselves since they did not command enough support, even in the cities, to be able to carry out their programme. As Lenin himself summed it up in 1919,

> *Mistakes are inevitable when the masses are fighting but the communists* **remain with the masses,** *see these mistakes, explain them to the masses, try to get them rectified and strive perseveringly for the victory of class consciousness over spontaneity.[14]*

The July Days showed that, even against a bourgeoisie which was as weak, fragmented and politically bankrupt as that in Russia in 1917, the working class cannot overthrow it without uniting the bulk of its forces in a class wide organisation that commands the confidence of the wider class. The problem for the revolutionary movement in July was that there was an upsurge in support for the revolutionary cause (as represented by Bolsheviks, anarchists and other groupings to the left of the SRs) but this had not yet been translated into a majority in the Soviet. That still was nominally held by the Mensheviks and SRs and the Soviet remained key to the situation. This was further emphasised in the repression that followed.

It was not the Provisional Government which was able to call up the troops which carried out the repression against the workers who took part in the July Days. It was the Menshevik/SR Executive of the Petersburg Soviet that did it for them. Despite being an enormous setback in the short-term for the Bolsheviks, the July Days and their aftermath also emphasised the proletarian nature of Bolshevism against the majority parties in the Soviet. As Lenin repeated:

The July Days

> *... in order to gain power seriously (not by Blanquist methods), the proletarian party must fight for influence inside the Soviet, patiently, unswervingly, explaining to the masses from day to day the error of their petty-bourgeois illusions... Events should not be anticipated. Time is on our side.*[15]

This was what many in the Bolshevik Party overlooked. Burning with desire to rid themselves of the class enemy they did not see that subjective will was not a sufficient condition for the victory of the working class. However, if Lenin was critical of the putschists and Blanquists within the Party, he also recognised on 4/17 July that the class party had to remain with the class. This was also expressed by Raskolnikov in his memoirs of what had happened at Kronstadt. Despite Bolshevik arguments against the uprising:

> *...for our party to have broken with the spontaneous movement of the Kronstadt masses would have struck an irreparable blow to its authority. On the other hand, an armed uprising would have been doomed to certain defeat. We might have seized power with comparative ease but would not have been in position to retain it.*[16]

The Bourgeoisie Fail to Crush Bolshevism

This was further underlined in the days which followed July. By circulating the lie that Lenin was a German spy, and that the Bolsheviks were paid by the Germans to disrupt the Russian army, the Provisional Government persuaded many units in Petersburg to return to barracks. At the same time the Provisional Government were not slow to use the support of the Executive Committee of the Soviet in bringing back from the front troops loyal to the war effort. By the time *Pravda* announced the end to the demonstrations on 5/18 July the repression had already began. The *Pravda* offices were seized and its printing presses smashed (Lenin having left shortly before the detachment from the Government arrived), the arrest of Lenin, Kollontai, Kamenev and Zinoviev was ordered, hundreds of Bolsheviks were rounded up, many more were beaten up and threatened with lynching but amazingly only one, a young paper seller Voinov, was actually killed[17]. All kinds of reactionaries now crawled out of the woodwork to participate in the Bolshevik-baiting.

In this they were egged on by the Menshevik leaders in the Provisional Government, Tsereteli and Dan, who even ordered the closing down of Gorky's independent social democratic newspaper (*Novaya Zhizn*) after it printed Lenin's rebuttal of the accusations that he was a German spy! This only added to the attacks on workers and in fact led to the further polarisation of the class divide.

Once again, however, the Mensheviks and SRs found that their anti-revolutionary stance backfired. Soon they too found themselves under attack from the capitalist class, which did not shrink from supporting the anti-semitic and proto-fascist Black Hundreds, who had been one of the instruments of terror used against workers under the Tsars. The suppression of the Bolsheviks gave an enormous boost to the propertied classes who now turned from liberal sentiments to supporting blatant reaction. This naked assertion of their class interests only served to underline the fact that the great divide was between those who stood for working class power and the *burzhui* (bourgeoisie). To many workers the Mensheviks and SRs were increasingly revealed to be class collaborators. Although the Bolsheviks went through a temporary crisis of confidence in which some of their supporters in the factories dissociated themselves for a time from the Central Committee, and even put themselves under the control of the Executive Committee of the Soviet, within a fortnight the worst was over. Once the bourgeoisie's murderous intentions became clear, workers stuck with the Bolsheviks and it was this solid support amongst the masses, built over years, which explains how they were able to survive.

The Bolsheviks had championed working class interests for too long, particularly in the anti-war struggle, for the masses to abandon them now. Whilst the government blamed the July Days entirely on the Bolsheviks, their suppression by a reactionary government for aligning themselves with the masses ultimately confirmed their support amongst the working class, and especially within the working class heartlands of Petersburg. Thus most of the 32,000 Bolsheviks in Petersburg were able to take refuge in Vyborg and other working class districts where the Government forces dared not go. Although many factories (like Sestrorestsk) were raided for weapons, few were found, and Kerensky (who became Prime Minister on 7/20 July) knew that it would risk full-scale civil war to try to go further. In addition, the Menshevik and SR leaders in the Soviet Executive were cautioning a halt to the repression since its reactionary nature would backfire on the Provisional Government. It would only help the working class see even more clearly that the Bolsheviks were the genuine defenders of the working class.

Further evidence of this came from the decision taken by Trotsky and other members of the Mezhraiontsy who chose this particular moment to announce their fusion with the Bolshevik Party. Arrest warrants have been put out for Lenin, Kamenev and Zinoviev and Trotsky with his usual theatricality said that he should be equated with them. Lenin and Zinoviev, after some hesitation[18], went into hiding, but Trotsky along with his comrade, Lunacharsky, was immediately arrested. In the Kresty Prison they were joined by Kamenev, Kollontai and the Kronstadt Bolshevik leaders Razkolnikov, Roshal and Remnev.

The ineffectiveness of the repression against the Bolsheviks can be gauged by the fact that as early as 7/20 July the Petersburg Committee were able to issue leaflets again, and membership not only did not fall but was once again rising, as soon as the skeleton of the Party apparatus was reorganised.

On 26 July/8 August *"in a spacious private assembly hall in the heart of the Vyborg District",* the Bolshevik Party's Sixth Congress opened and continued, unmolested, to debate the new course for the Party for five days. The Party had already learned the need for greater cohesion within its own ranks. The Military Organisation was put under closer supervision by the Party. Its paper was taken over by the Central Committee to replace *Pravda* and its leaders criticised for their adventurism during the July Days.

The July Days

All Power to the Workers

The main topic on the agenda of the Sixth Congress was, however, the next step for the working class. Supporters of Lenin were circulating a text called *"On Slogans"*. The main thrust of this was to say that the July Days had shown that a peaceful development of the revolution was no longer possible. It was no good hoping for the Soviets to simply replace the Provisional Government since the SR/Menshevik leaders of the Soviets were hopelessly committed to the bourgeoisie. This point was fully shown by their support for Kerensky's repression against the working class instead of taking the power which the July demonstrators knew was there for the taking. From this Lenin concluded it was no point calling for *"All Power to the Soviets"* **at this time** since it was clear that the current Soviet was actually the biggest obstacle to this.

To all kinds of liberals, reactionaries and formalists, Lenin's wish to drop the slogan is enough to confirm them in their belief that the Bolsheviks did not really believe in the soviets as forms of proletarian democracy. However, this conclusion can only be reached by ignoring, both the long standing commitment the Bolsheviks had to the soviets since 1905, and the context of Lenin's argument, as well as the nature of the debate on the subject in the weeks that followed. Lenin first of all made it clear that he would have preferred the Soviets to assume power whoever held the majority:

> *Peaceful development would then have been possible, even in the sense that the struggle of classes and parties within the Soviets could have assumed a most peaceful and painless form, provided full state power had passed to the Soviets in good time.*[19]

But the key question which any revolutionary party must first consider is how to smash the last vestiges of bourgeois state power before the conditions for proletarian democracy can emerge. With the Soviet leadership entrenched in its support for the Provisional Government, and with the Bolsheviks more widely supported in the factories than in the Soviet (some Mensheviks were already admitting that the Bolshevik support was not properly represented in the Soviet), Lenin concluded that the Soviet, at least for the time being was no use to the revolutionary proletariat. But he was not against the soviet principle:

> *Soviets may appear in this new revolution, and indeed are bound to, but not the present Soviets, not organs collaborating with the bourgeoisie, but organs of revolutionary struggle against the bourgeoisie. It is true that even then we shall be in favour of building the whole state on the model of the Soviets. It is not the question of Soviets in general, but of combatting the present counter-revolution and the treachery of the present Soviets.*[20]

Lenin's opponents in the Bolshevik Party, such as Volodarsky, made it quite clear that they accepted Lenin's analysis of the current Soviet's political nature, but they did not accept that this would always remain the case. Being in Petersburg (and not in hiding in Finland), they could see that, by the end of July, Bolshevik support in the district Soviet was rising rapidly. Furthermore, more and more Mensheviks were deserting their class collaborationist party for the Bolsheviks. However, it was agreed that a committee be set up to look at the question of the Party's slogans. Although this meant that the Bolsheviks did not call for *"All Power to the Soviets"* for a month, it did not affect the work of building up support in those Soviets.

In this debate on slogans Lenin had argued that class antagonisms were sharpening and that given the abdication of responsibility by the Soviet majority: *"... power is in the hands of a military clique of Cavaignacs (Kerensky, certain generals, officers etc.) who are supported by the bourgeois class headed by the Kadet Party."* [21] Cavaignac was the general who had butchered the Parisian workers in June 1848 to save that revolution for the bourgeoisie. A month later the Russian bourgeoisie thought they had found their Cavaignac in the person of General Lavr Kornilov. He was to provide the Russian working class and its revolutionary organisations with their third major test of 1917.

Chapter 6
The Kornilov Affair Mobilises the Masses

As we saw when looking at the July Days, the Bolsheviks were able to survive the post-July repression because there was already a widespread class movement, and they had firm roots within it. The strength of the Petersburg workers in their own concentrations, especially in the Vyborg, Liteiny and Petrogradsky districts, enabled them to turn these areas into proletarian fortresses which could not easily be entered by the State.

Added to this was the chronic weakness of the Russian bourgeoisie which had failed at every turn to overthrow Tsarism. After the February Revolution its political project depended entirely on the acquiescence of the working class for its continued existence. They were only able to pretend to hold power so long as the workers did not realise that the aim of the Provisional Government was to dissolve the soviets at the earliest possible opportunity. However, as long as the Mensheviks and SRs still could claim a majority in the Petersburg Soviet (albeit an increasingly fragile one) they could still disguise what was going on. For the bourgeoisie the fall of the Tsar had only meant the removal of the greatest obstacle to winning the war against the German bourgeoisie. With the Mensheviks and SRs both supporting the idea that Russia was still undergoing a bourgeois revolution, "revolutionary defencism" (i.e, carrying on the war in defence of a supposed democratic revolution) was the order of the day. As a result they became increasingly disconnected from the working class and its aspirations.

Class war thus continued unabated throughout 1917. The proletariat faced continued privations throughout the year and increasingly turned to those organisations which had opposed the war since its beginning. By early August when the vote for the City Dumas showed an increase in Bolshevik strength of 14% on the May figure, it was clear that the July Days had resulted only in a brief check in the Bolsheviks' support. And as the Russian proletariat increasingly united itself in, and around, the revolutionary minorities, especially the Bolshevik Party, the bourgeoisie was beginning to turn further to the right and abandon any pretence of supporting a parliamentary system.

The "Kornilovschina"

The apparent defeat of the Bolsheviks in July had at first given new confidence to the bourgeoisie. Stiffer measures were introduced in the army, including the return of the death penalty, in an attempt to restore discipline. Prince Lvov yielded to the Socialist Revolutionary Kerensky as Prime Minister, since it was felt that he alone had the support of the majority of the Soviet and the will to destroy the Bolsheviks. However, when it quickly became clear that Kerensky was only prepared to pursue Bolsheviks, and was not yet ready to tackle the ascendancy which the Soviets had gained since February, the properted class immediately began to cast around for a real Napoleon figure. Egged on by the British and French ambassadors who constantly promoted the cause of General Kornilov, the party of the Russian liberal bourgeoisie, the Constitutional Democrats, now threw its weight behind a military dictatorship. Capitalists formed a "Society for the Economic Recovery of Russia" aimed at financing the Kadet's plans and, as if to underline the change in the tactics of the bourgeoisie, the Kadets opened their ranks to the proto-fascist ex-members of the Tsarist Black Hundreds, who were famous for their *pogroms* of Jews and workers under Nicholas II.

At the same time, the disaster of the June Offensive had forced General Brusilov to resign, and Kerensky, under pressure from the Union of Officers and the Allied Ambassadors, was forced to appoint General Kornilov as Commander-in-Chief of the Army. The latter had brought himself to the attention of the British because he was the first to call for an end to the offensive so that measures could be taken to restore the officers to full control in the army. He had already carried out this policy in his section of the front by dissolving units that refused to fight, disarming over 7,000 soldiers, shooting deserters and dispersing soldiers' meetings by force. Kerensky had himself favoured these policies and concluded that Kornilov could help save the war effort and freeze the revolution at the point it had already reached. He thus announced that *"Kornilov, whose views are similar to those of the Provisional Government, is the man to save the situation".*

Once Kornilov was appointed, the active scheme against the revolution gathered pace, as he became the darling of the bourgeoisie. Riga was yielded to the Germans on 21 August after troops of the Provisional Government's elite "battalions of death" fought the 2nd Latvian Rifle regiment and the militia instead of the Germans.[1] This convinced many workers that the cessation of Riga had been deliberate. Now Petersburg was within the front line zone, and therefore under military rule – a fact which signalled the start of the crisis. As Trotsky tells us, all that was now needed was a some act of provocation to implement the planned coup.

> *The strategic plan was simple. The three divisions coming from the south were to be transported by railroad to Tzarskoe Selo, Gatchina, and Krasnoe Selo, in order from those points "upon receiving information of disorders beginning in Petrograd, and not later than the morning of September 1" to advance on foot for the occupation of the southern part of the capital on the left bank of the Neva. The division quartered in Finland was at the same time to occupy the northern part of the capital.[2]*

We leave to bourgeois historians the task of analysing the degree of Kerensky's complicity in the early moves in the Kornilov affair. Kornilov had made it clear in repeated statements that he intended not just to smash "Bolshevik Petersburg" but also the Petersburg Soviet. Kerensky seems only to have broken with him when it became clear that he too would be removed by the budding military dictator. From the point of view of the working class the key thing to note here is that a divided governing class is a necessary, but insufficient condition for its overthrow. The consciousness and organisation of the proletariat itself is far more significant in the revolutionary process, and our task is to examine how these elements developed as a result of Kornilov's actions. To illustrate the impact of the new crisis let us quote at length from one of the first Western historians to have had real access to Russian archives.

> *In previous crises, in April, June and July, the spontaneous initiatives of Bolshevik and anarchist soldiers had caused street demonstrations. The leading elements in the Bolshevik Party had been forced, in the end, to assume responsibility for a movement launched by the young men of the military organisation. As the cinema films show, there were considerably fewer workers than soldiers or sailors.*

> *In the Kornilov affair, when the action was defensive, the reverse happened. The proletarian districts were the first to mobilise, recruiting 40,000 men and arming 25,000 from the factories through their committees or from weapons left by the Kronstadt sailors during the July Days ... A further difference was that since the disappearance of the anarchists as a motive force, the militant grassroots and the higher echelons of the Bolshevik party came closer together. They remembered the effects of the lack of discipline in July, and were prudent with action which might provoke hostile action; the authority of the party leadership which had been perspicacious in July, was greater. As the party requested, no demonstrations took place on 27 August. However the grassroots militants were ready for action; they responded instantly to the organisation's appeal against the Putsch because, unlike Lenin, who was preoccupied with questions of overall strategy, they were not "taken aback" at what happened, because they analysed things differently. Thus it was possible for the Petrogradsky district committee to organise defence by 23 August, four days before the appeals issued by Kerensky, Chernov, the soviet and the Bolshevik party. Under the leadership of the Bolshevik Skorokhodov, this committee co-ordinated its actions with the other committees of the capital, planning for cars to go round to maintain communication, guarding factories, arranging information briefings at set times and the like ... The people were mentally prepared, and the means for defence were made available, such that when the organisations appealed, every citizen, tree, house and stone was set to oppose the advance of Kornilov, whose telegrams failed to arrive and whose locomotives got no water. The ground crumbled under his feet.[3]*

These events revealed a new step forward in the consciousness and organisation of the working class. No longer was the running made by squads of impetuous sailors, but by the carefully considered actions of greater masses of workers, who recognised that the onward march of the counter-revolution had to be fought.

> *Spurred by news of Kornilov's attack, all political organizations to the left of the Kadets, every labor organization of any import, and soldier and sailor committees at all levels immediately rose to fight against Kornilov. It would be difficult to find, in recent history, a more powerful, effective display of largely spontaneous and*

unified mass political action.[4]

Resistance to Kornilov also saw the arming of workers on a wide scale for the first time. It was now that the Red Guards linked up with the soldiers of the Petersburg garrison, and it was also at this time that suspicion towards the antics of Kerensky, plus the Mensheviks and SRs in the Soviet, came to be replaced by outright hostility.

Moreover it once again showed the Bolsheviks caught unawares by another sudden shift in the situation. However, as on earlier occasions, the Bolsheviks in Petersburg responded quickly and decisively by making it clear in their declarations in the press that they were opposing Kornilov, without offering support for Kerensky. This was significant since it meant that the Bolsheviks were once again *de facto* legalised and more importantly could take up 3 of the 8 seats on the new "Committee for the Struggle against Counter-Revolution" set up by the Soviet. The fact was, the Soviet needed the Bolsheviks more than the other way round, as the Menshevik-Internationalist Sukhanov testifies:

> *The committee, making defence preparations, had to mobilise the worker-soldier masses. But the masses in so far as they were organised, were organised by the Bolsheviks and followed them. At that time theirs was the only organisation that was large, welded together by an elementary discipline and linked with the democratic lowest levels of the capital. Without it the committee was impotent.[5]*

Bolshevik Tactics

Lenin, who was still in hiding in Finland, was taken more by surprise than the other Bolshevik leaders. This was because he recognised that the failure of July had given the bourgeoisie the opportunity to roll back the revolution towards a military dictatorship. However, he had assumed that the bourgeoisie had found their dictator in Kerensky and, though he was only a caricature of a Bonaparte, that he had behind him "the counter-revolutionary Kadets and the military clique".[6] Lenin was wrong here but he was clear that the resort to dictatorship would step up the class struggle because "not a single important task of the revolution has been accomplished here".

Foremost amongst these tasks was the settling of the land and war questions. Even though Viktor Chernov, the leader of the Socialist Revolutionaries, the supposed peasant party, was Minister of Agriculture, the land seizures of the peasants were resisted by force. The peasants were told that they had to wait for a Constituent Assembly decided on the issue. But the calling of the Constituent Assembly was always postponed for one reason or another, but essentially because the Provisional Government feared the outcome of any election. And this prevarication by the Provisional Government and its allies in the Soviet was because they had no wish to break with the bourgeoisie and landowners. These propertied classes were now demonstrating their gratitude for this by looking for a general to sweep aside, not just the Soviet, but Kerensky and the Provisional Government along with it. This is why they committed political suicide by opting for the Kornilov adventure. It was this that caught Lenin by surprise. Once he saw what had happened he had no hesitation in supporting the actions of the Bolsheviks in Petersburg.

This episode rather undermines the picture given by both bourgeois and Stalinist historians (as well as a few Trotskyist writers, like Tony Cliff) that without Lenin the Bolshevik Party was incapable of acting. In this case Lenin's contribution was to analyse and frame the proletarian response to a dilemma which an event like the Kornilov Affair poses for the proletariat. In a letter *"To the Central Committee of the RSDLP"* (i.e, the Bolsheviks), he wrote:

> *The Kornilov revolt is a ... downright unbelievably sharp turn in events. Like every sharp turn, it calls for a revision and a change of tactics. And, as with every revision, we must be extra cautious not to become unprincipled. It is my conviction that those who become unprincipled are people who (like Volodarsky –) slide into defencism or (like other Bolsheviks) into a bloc with the SR's into supporting the Provisional Government. Their attitude is absolutely wrong and unprincipled. Even now we must not support Kerensky's government. This is unprincipled. We will be asked: aren't we going to fight against Kornilov? Of course we must! But this is not the same thing; there is a dividing line here, which is being stepped over by some Bolsheviks who fall into compromise and allow themselves to be carried away by the course of events. We shall fight, we are fighting against Kornilov, just as Kerensky's troops do, but we do not support Kerensky. On the contrary, we expose his weakness. There is the difference. It is a rather subtle difference, but it is highly essential and must not be forgotten ... we must campaign not so much directly against Kerensky as indirectly against him, namely by demanding a more and more active, truly revolutionary war against Kornilov ... by drawing the masses in, by arousing them, by inflaming them (Kerensky is afraid of the masses, afraid of the people) ...*[7]

Writing from his hiding place in Finland Lenin was ill-informed about what was actually being done by the Bolsheviks and the working class in Petersburg. To make amends for this he quickly added a footnote withdrawing his unfair criticism of Volodarsky, and congratulating the Bolsheviks in Petersburg on having already carried out the policy he was advocating. However, this stance by the Bolsheviks needs some discussion if we are to explain its real significance, particularly since the tactic adopted has been cited as an example on numerous occasions since by those who claim to be proletarian to justify opportunist and counter-revolutionary positions.

Bolshevik tactics during the Kornilov Affair have often been cited as the precursor for the united front of 1921 or the anti-fascist popular fronts of the 1930's. However, as Lenin (and even more so, Marx) often pointed out, the key to any understanding of political action is to locate it within its specific historical context. If we do this we can see the last two are expressions of retreat and defeat for the working class, whilst the former was correct because it was put together in an entirely different situation. In August and September the Petersburg masses were already moving forward in a confident fashion, as the quotation from Ferro above shows. In this context it was possible for the Bolsheviks to fight alongside the Mensheviks and SRs, but without compromising their political independence. Not to have acted thus would have been to turn their backs on an opportunity to demonstrate their capacity and resolution in practice. In 1921-2, the united front was an opportunist tactic dreamed up by the Communist International to try to attempt to build a mass class base in a situation of revolutionary retreat. The Stalinist Popular Front policy of the 1930's was not even that. It was simply part of the USSR's attempts to form an anti-fascist alliance for the imminent imperialist war. Both had reactionary consequences. The net result of these policies was to legitimise the forces of social democracy as proletarian and to associate the defence of the workers' interests with the defence of capitalist democracy. In the Kornilov Affair the defence of Petersburg took place under the aegis of the workers' own organs, the Soviets, so there was no danger that the defenders of capitalist democracy would gain from it. Whereas Kornilov's actions were dragging these forces further towards a revolution they wanted to avoid. Indeed the logic of the Kornilov Affair was for the Soviets to take over from the Provisional Government immediately to prevent any further plotting by Kerensky and the Right.

"All Power to the Working Class!"

This was not a step that the Menshevik or Right SR leaderships could take. After six months of support for a coalition with the bourgeoisie they were not prepared to abandon that policy now, however treacherous their erstwhile allies were. However, factory after factory was now coming round to the view that only the soviets could be relied upon to defend the revolution. The day after Kornilov was defeated, workers in the machine shop of the Petersburg Pipe factory declared that "*all power must be transferred to the soviet of workers', soldiers', and peasants' deputies*", whilst the 8,000 workers of the Metallist factory approved a motion of no confidence in the socialists who cooperated with the Provisional Government. These declarations were followed in all the larger Petersburg factories, and were soon echoed in the garrisons, even of those regiments that had suppressed the July Days. Three days after the defeat of Kornilov the Petersburg Soviet endorsed a resolution, proposed by Kamenev, that the Government should be replaced by one composed truly of workers' representatives. It was the first time a Bolshevik resolution achieved a majority in that body. What was clear was that the Kornilov Affair had led to an enormous leap forward in class consciousness;

> *The soviets, now distinctly radical in outlook, emerged from the crisis with their popularity amongst the masses immensely enhanced. Revolutionary Russia was more widely saturated than ever before with competing grassroots political organisations and revolutionary committees. Workers had become more militant and better organized, and significant numbers of them had obtained weapons. At the same time, democratic committees in the army, by virtue of their leading role in organizing soldiers against the Kornilov movement, were rejuvenated. Within the Petrograd garrison, control of many regimental committees passed from more moderate elements into the hands of the Bolsheviks.* [8]

The Kornilov Affair Mobilises the Masses

Far from taking advantage of this to assert the Bolsheviks right to power, Lenin raised the possibility that there could still be a peaceful development of the revolution if the Mensheviks and SRs would lead the soviets in the process of taking power. This was a complete reversal of his depression after the July Days. Unable to attend the Sixth Party Congress at the end of July, he had sent a short document, *On Slogans,* as his contribution. We already discussed this in Chapter 5 but here we want to look at it for a different purpose – what it said about the possibility of the peaceful development of the revolution. In *On Slogans* Lenin had argued for the abandonment of the slogan "*All Power to the Soviets*" because this was the slogan of the "*peaceful development of the revolution*".

> *Peaceful development would then have been possible, even in the sense that the struggle of classes and parties within the Soviets could have assumed a most peaceful and painless form, provided full state power had passed to the Soviets in good time.*[9]

However the repression that the Bolsheviks (and some workers attached to other organisations) had suffered since the July Days showed that no such peaceful development was possible. Lenin was not arguing against soviet power in *On Slogans,* as many anarchists assert, but against the sell-out of "these soviets" by the Mensheviks and SRs to the bourgeoisie. He was confident that new soviets were "bound to" appear "rejuvenated in the fire of struggle"[10] but to call for transfer of power to "the present soviet" in July was to deceive the people. Lenin's call was however rejected by the Congress (yet another instance which proves the Bolshevik Party was not simply his tool but a reflection of a wider class movement) and by such local party organisations like those in Saratov and Tsaritsyn[11] because the delegates knew that, despite the repression, the fact was that Bolshevik influence in the soviets was rising across the country.

And so, after the Kornilov Affair, the possibility of a peaceful development of the revolution was once again on the table. On 1 September Lenin called for compromise.

> *The Russian revolution is experiencing so abrupt and original a turn that we, as a party, may offer a voluntary compromise – true, not to our direct and main class enemy the bourgeoisie, but to our nearest adversaries, the "ruling petty-bourgeois-democratic parties, the Socialist-Revolutionaries and Mensheviks".*

> *We may offer a compromise to these parties only by way of exception, and only by virtue of the particular situation, which obviously will last only a very short time. And I think we should do so. The compromise on our part is our return to the pre-July demand of all power to the Soviets and a government of SRs and Mensheviks responsible to the Soviets.*

> *Now, and only now, perhaps during only a few days or a week or two, such a government could be set up and consolidated in a perfectly peaceful way. In all probability it could secure the peaceful advance of the whole Russian revolution,*

and provide exceptionally good chances for great strides in the world movement towards peace and the victory of socialism.[12]

      This hardly gives a picture of the power-mad vanguard partyist that some bourgeois and anarchist histories paint. Lenin does not demand Bolshevik Party power but soviet power, even if the soviets are headed by the Mensheviks and SRs. And contrary to Robert V. Daniels assertion that this offer was "neither consistent nor enduring"[13] it was no isolated comment. He repeated the idea of a peaceful development of the revolution a fortnight later.

Power to the Soviets – this is the only way to make further progress gradual, peaceful and smooth keeping perfect pace with the political awareness and resolve of the majority of the people and with their own experience. Power to the Soviets means the complete transfer of the country's administration and economic control into the hands of the workers and peasants, to whom nobody *dare offer resistance, and who, through practice, through their own experience,* would soon learn *how to distribute the land, products and grain properly.[14]*

      Whilst Lenin here accepts the existing framework of the Menshevik and SR soviets, where the government would only be "responsible to the soviets" and not elected directly by them, he also spelled out why soviet power would be fundamentally different to the other governments that had appeared in 1917:

The slogan "Power to the Soviets", however is very often, if not in most cases, taken quite incorrectly to mean a "Cabinet of the parties of the Soviet majority"... "Power to the Soviets" means radically reshaping the entire old state apparatus, that bureaucratic apparatus which hampers everything democratic. It means removing this apparatus and substituting for it a new, popular one, i.e., a truly democratic apparatus of Soviets, i.e., the organised and armed majority of the people—the workers, soldiers and peasants. It means allowing the majority of the people initiative and independence not only in the election of deputies, but also in state administration, in effecting reforms and various other changes.[15]

      The above passage not only gives the lie to those that keep quoting *What is to Be Done?* to demonstrate that Lenin only saw the masses as there to be manipulated but also, in clearly formulating what soviet power meant, puts the so-called democrats of the SRs and the Mensheviks on the spot. They could not bring themselves to abandon the Provisional Government since they, like Kerensky, feared the actions of the masses.

      They in fact regarded the appearance of the soviets as a temporary aberration, and had done all they could to undermine them (such as detaching the Soviet Executive from the body of the Petersburg Soviet which became largely a talking shop). Soviet Congresses were supposed to take place every 3 months and as the first had been in June the second should have been in September but fearing their loss of control the Menshevik/SR Executive Committee kept postponing it. The struggles of 1917 had already exhausted many worker-delegates and there was a real danger that the soviets might indeed wither away from the lack of progress in actually achieving what the working class had set out to achieve in February. Kerensky had already told the British Ambassador that the soviets' days were numbered.

In fact it was Kerensky's time that was up. On the one side, the bourgeoisie who had seen him as the demagogue who could tame the masses in March and July now hated him for his "betrayal" of Kornilov. If the parliamentary figleaf would not fool the masses the bourgeoisie, as ever, were ready to turn to dictatorship. Now that Kornilov's troops had melted away in the face of the fraternisation of the workers, his arrest was turned into a farce when Kerensky simply allowed him to reside at Bychkov monastery (from where he made an easy escape in November to lead the Whites in the civil war).

On the other side, Kerensky was now faced with a tide of popular agitation which he tried to put down by issuing decrees dissolving all *ad hoc* revolutionary committees (including the Committee for the Struggle against Counter-Revolution). Only the Mensheviks and Right SRs still stuck with him. This only isolated them too from the "real movement" and greatly boosted the worker base of Bolshevism. The fact that the Bolsheviks (joined as we saw in the previous chapter in July by Trotsky's Mezhraiontsy group) were the only party to coherently and consistently support soviet power now began to tell in their favour. By early September the Bolsheviks had won control of the Petersburg Soviet with 4 out of 7 seats on the Praesidium going to them. Trotsky once again became the leader of the Petersburg Soviet, a post he had last occupied in 1905. Six days later Moscow went Bolshevik followed by Kiev, Kazan, Baku and many other industrial centres. It was a similar story in the Army where, in units like the Moscow garrison, a June majority of 70% for the SRs and Mensheviks was turned into a 90% vote for the Bolsheviks in September. More stories could be told of Bolsheviks advances in local councils or city Dumas (in Moscow their representation rose from 11 to 475), in trade unions and even in sickness cooperative boards which, as Ferro argues, "*was the evidence of a very large-scale movement which came from the depths of society*". [16]

At the same time the refusal of the Mensheviks and the SRs to put their trust in the working class in the soviets brought about the break-up of their organisations. Whilst a split in the SRs resulted in the formation of the Left SRs who supported soviet power, the Mensheviks, already split into several factions, became a rump as many delegates flooded into the ranks of the Bolsheviks. However, soviet power could not come about just by making speeches or passing resolutions about it. First the old order would have to be overturned. The opportunity that presented itself now came in the lead up to the Second Congress of Soviets which the Soviet Executive at long last called for on 26 October/8 November.

Chapter 7
The Proletariat Takes Power

On the evening of October 24th [6 November new style] the Provisional Government had at its disposal little more than 25,000 men. On the evening of October 25th, when preparations were underway for the storming of the Winter Palace, the Bolsheviks assembled about 20,000 Red Guards, sailors and soldiers before that last refuge of the Provisional Government. But within the palace there were not more than 3,000 defenders, and many of those left their posts during the night. Thanks to the Bolsheviks' overwhelming superiority there were no serious battles in the capital from October 24th to October 26th, and the total number of those killed on both sides was no more than 15, with no more than 60 wounded.

During these critical hours, as all the main strategic points in the city passed under Bolshevik control (telephone and telegraph exchanges, bridges, railroad stations, the Winter Palace etc.), Petrograd continued on the whole to go about its normal business. Most of the soldiers remained in the barracks, the plants and the factories continued to operate, and in the schools none of the classes were interrupted. There were no strikes or mass demonstrations such had accompanied the February Revolution. The movie theatres (called cinematographias in those days) were filled, there were regular performances in all the theatres, and people strolled as usual on the Nevsky Prospect. The ordinary non-political person would not even have noticed the historic events taking place; even on the streetcar lines, the main form of public transportation in 1917, service remained normal. It was in one of those streetcars that Lenin, in disguise, and his bodyguard Eino Rahya travelled to Smolny late on the evening of the 24th.[1]

Thus the Soviet "dissident" historian, Roy Medvedev described the October Revolution. It's not quite the exciting image that John Reed's *Ten Days that Shook the World* or Eisenstein's *October* portray. Trotsky explained clearly enough why this was so.

Demonstrations, street fights, barricades — everything comprised in the usual idea of insurrection — were almost entirely absent. The revolution had no need of solving a problem already solved. The seizure of the governmental machine could be carried through according to plan with the help of comparatively small armed detachments guided from a single centre ... the very fact that the resistance of the government came down to a defence of the Winter Palace, clearly defines the place occupied by October 25th in the whole course of the struggle. The Winter Palace was the last redoubt of a regime politically shattered during its eight months existence and conclusively disarmed during the preceding two weeks.[2]

The Proletariat Takes Power

The Russian privileged classes had expected an orgy of looting and murder, political chaos and the collapse of all morality. Instead they were faced, at least in the capital, with an ordered transition which must have been even more terrifying for them. The proletarian masses had shown they had no need of rulers but could found their own forms of government. Of course, this ordered overthrow of the living corpse of the unelected Provisional Government was immediately turned into a caricature of the October Revolution by the historians of our class enemy who have portrayed the proletarian revolution only in terms of its final act. They could thus spread the legend that the insurrection was simply a putsch, a *coup d'etat* by a small, fanatical group whilst the masses passively sat on the sidelines. It is surprising that such a myth has not collapsed under the weight of its own absurdity.

Apart from the fact that the Bolshevik Party had 350,000 members, with deep roots in the factory committee movement, and had the active support of nearly every soldier in Petersburg (about 300,000 men) coups are carried out in secret. This was not the case here. The seizure of power was debated in the press of all political shades for over a fortnight before the final fall of the Provisional Government. As S.A. Smith pointed out, if it was a coup it was "a coup much advertised". The Bolshevik dissidents, Kamenev and Zinoviev had even publicly advertised it when they registered their disapproval of Bolshevik Central Committee's purely formal decision on 10/23 October to overthrow the Provisional Government by writing an article opposing it, in Gorky's independent newspaper, *Novaya Zhizn* (New Life). As Professor Smith concluded "*the Provisional Government had expired even before the Bolsheviks finished it off.*"[3]

The whole history of 1917 was one of intensifying class struggle in which the February Revolution was simply the opening act. The turmoil in the factories, in the villages and in the Army all attest to a growing radicalisation of the mass of the population. In some places like Latvia so-called "dual power" never took effect[4]. As we saw earlier in July the Bolshevoks had to act to try to dampen down the impatience of the revolutionary workers but they had also had to do this with the Kronstadt sailors in May after they refused to recognise the Provisional Government and again in June had disappointed the most militant by dropping plans for their earlier anti-Provisional Government demonstration. In many places throughout Russia (including the famous Ivanovno-Vosnesensk) soviets had actually replaced the local dumas well before October. This ferment created a process of selection which left the Bolsheviks, some anarchists and the Left SRs (who only emerged as a tendency in May 1917) as the only supporters of soviet power – the form of organisation historically-discovered by the Russian working class in the course of two revolutions. It was a form which reconciled the active participation of the mass of society with the need to organise to meet the needs of all of society.

And as we saw at the end of the previous chapter, the Bolsheviks already had a majority in the leading soviets around the country. After the Kornilov affair even more flooded into their ranks. This was expected to translate into a majority for them at the Second Congress of Soviets which other "socialist" parties were keen to postpone or abandon. Rosa Luxemburg perhaps summed up the process of how in defending revolutionary aims the Bolsheviks had broken with social democratic reformism and achieved their predominance inside the working class.

> ... *the Bolsheviks solved the famous problem of "winning a majority of the people," which problem has ever weighed on the German Social-Democracy like a nightmare. As bred-in-the-bone disciples of parliamentary cretinism, these German Social-Democrats have sought to apply to revolutions the home-made wisdom they say, applies to a revolution: first let's become a "majority." The true dialectic of revolutions ... stands this wisdom of parliamentary moles on its head: not through a majority, but through revolutionary tactics to a majority – that's the way the road runs.*[5]

This was how the revolutionary Russian proletariat made the Bolshevik Party their principal political and organisational instrument. We now need to look at how the tactics of the Bolsheviks were tested in the complex situation of September and October 1917.

Could an Insurrection Succeed?

Although not apparent to contemporaries, the fate of the bourgeois order in Russia was sealed from the moment that the armies of the Kaiser occupied Riga in August 1917. Instead of the Provisional Government's promised victories, the Germans were now poised to go all the way to Petersburg. Just as significantly, as we saw in the previous chapter, the Russian Army withdrawal from Riga now brought Petersburg within the military zone of the front line and thus theoretically meant that the soldiers in Petersburg were now subject to the command of leading generals. Kornilov even publicly seemed to welcome the fall of Riga. He asked: "*Must we pay with Riga the price of bringing the country to its sense of duty?*"[6]. Such sentiments were common amongst ex-tsarist generals and the propertied classes. They frequently voiced the idea that the German occupation of Petersburg would at least get rid of the Soviets and the Bolsheviks. These attitudes reflect the heightened class tensions in the capital which were narrowing down the options of all the main actors in this episode of the class war.

Lenin had been arguing for insurrection inside his party from the moment he realised that the other so-called socialist parties (the Mensheviks and the Right SRs), true to their theory of supporting a bourgeois system, did not intend to rule through soviet power despite being offered Bolshevik support if they did so.

But the Bolshevik Central Committee seemed to be ignoring his letters. What was worse for him was that, as he sat in hiding, the Bolshevik Central Committee seemed to be falling for Kerensky's attempts to bolster his tottering rule. In the aftermath of the defeat of Kornilov the Provisional Government called a "Democratic Conference" to try to rally the parties represented in the soviet around bourgeois rule. To Lenin's horror, the Bolshevik Central Committee fell for this ruse, and participated in this charade (Lenin singled out Trotsky for special praise for arguing for a boycott of this assembly). Furthermore, they also agreed to participate in the so-called "Pre-parliament" which Kerensky hoped to use to legitimise the position of his unelected government and sidetrack soviet power. Lenin responded in *From a Publicist's Diary*. After noting that that Mensheviks and Right SRs had refused the Bolsheviks' compromise offer, he maintained that the Democratic Conference and Pre-parliament were shams to divert the masses away from the soviets and the revolution. He ended by criticising the Bolshevik Central Committee:

> *There is not the slightest doubt that at the top of our Party there are noticeable vacillations that may become **ruinous** ... Not all is well with the "parliamentary" leaders of our Party; greater attention must be paid to them, there must be greater workers' supervision over them ... Our Party's mistake is obvious. The fighting party of the advanced class need not fear mistakes. What it should fear is persistence in a mistake ...*[7]

Not only did the Bolshevik leaders around Kamenev persist in their mistakes, but they made them worse by suppressing all Lenin's criticisms of their approach to the Democratic Conference and the future insurrection. Although Lenin wrote thousands of words to stimulate them into action they ensured that the key passages were edited out. In frustration Lenin finally submitted his resignation from the Central Committee on 29 September/12 October[8] but *"reserving for myself freedom to campaign amongst the rank and file"*. Although the Central Committee did not even discuss this resignation letter, it freed Lenin to take up private correspondence with individuals who were in other Party organisations besides the Central Committee. The best example of this was the Petersburg Committee. When it learned of the Central Committee's censorship of Lenin's writings they were outraged. The Petersburg Committee was dominated by "worker activists" who were closer to the class movement than the minority in the Central Committee of the Party who opposed the notion that the Russian Revolution would only be the first in a chain of workers' revolutions, the first step on the road to world revolution.

The international question was now obvious in the concerns of the Bolsheviks in Petersburg. In the debate over the need for insurrection, the most coherent opponent of Lenin's was Volodarsky (an ex-member of the Mezhraiontsy or Inter-district committee and a brilliant orator). He pointed to the backwardness of Russia and insisted that the Bolsheviks should mark time because the Russian Revolution could only succeed as part of a world revolution. Lenin's supporters agreed that the fate of the Russian Revolution was dependent on the spread of the world revolution, but they argued that the proletariat in backward Russia had been given a chance not yet offered to the working class anywhere else. They believed that the Russian working class must seize power immediately before the forces of reaction could undermine the soviet movement any further. After that they would have to hold on until the European revolution, which would sweep away all capitalist regimes, developed. This argument for not delaying any longer won the day. Lenin enshrined the internationalist position in his document *The Crisis has Matured*. This document, like many others written in this period, deserves to be read in full but we will content ourselves with just a few lines which indicate the internationalist essence of Bolshevism — the factor which, above all, made it so distinctively the party of the international revolutionary working class in the First World War.

> *The end of September undoubtedly marked a great turning point in the history of the Russian revolution and, to all appearances, of the world revolution as well ... This stage may be called the eve of revolution. Mass arrests of party leaders in free Italy, and particularly the beginning of mutinies in the German army are indisputable symptoms that a great turning point is at hand, that we are on the eve of world-wide revolution ... Doubt is out of the question. We are on the threshold of a world proletarian revolution. And since of all the proletarian internationalists in all countries only we Russian Bolsheviks enjoy a measure of freedom — we have a legal party and a score or so of papers, we have the Soviets ... of both capitals on our side and we have the support of a majority of the people in a time of revolution — to us the saying "To whom much has been given, of him much will be required", in all justice can and must be applied.*[9]

It was an argument which won over most of the leadership, and on October 10th, the Central Committee voted to accept **in principle** the idea of organising the insurrection. It was not simply a victory for one man, or even one party, but for the international working class. However, even then the insurrection did not come about according to any preconceived plan but was triggered by the class war for power itself.

The Soldiers Become Bolsheviks

As we showed in the previous chapter, the Bolsheviks won enormous support well before the Second All-Russia Congress of Soviets was called (which the outgoing Menshevik/SR Executive Committee managed to delay by a further five days until 25 October/7 November on the pretext of checking the credentials of delegates). In fact the Bolsheviks had emerged as the largest party in the Congress with over 300 of the roughly 650 delegates. With the support of about 80 Left SRs plus most of the 100 or so non-party delegates "soviet power" had a clear majority. However, this does not mean that the entire proletariat was imbued with a communist consciousness since this would have been an impossibility whilst capitalist conditions still prevailed. What they did have were concrete demands which accumulated as 1917 wore on. They wanted an end to the war and its associated miseries of food shortages and inflation. They had seen that coalition with the bourgeois Provisional Government only continued the war. Furthermore, the Germans continued to advance closer to Petersburg. This only seemed to confirm the hopes of the bourgeoisie that the revolution there could be crushed. Kerensky added to the fear by ordering the evacuation of the capital and then rescinded it after howls of protest from the working class organisations. All this simply increased support for the Bolsheviks since they had become the largest organised expression of what the working class really wanted. They opposed the war in unambiguous terms and had all along called for *"All Power to the Soviets"*.

By October 1917 ending the war and establishing soviet power had become tied together as barracks after barracks voted not to obey orders to go to the front, and to listen only to the Soviets. Typical of these resolutions was that of the Egersky Guards Regiment on 12 October:

> *The pulling out of the revolutionary garrison from Petrograd is needed only by the privileged bourgeoisie as a means of stifling the revolution ... We declare to all who listen that, while refusing to leave Petrograd, we will nonetheless heed the voice of the genuine leaders of the workers and poorer peasantry, that is the Soviet of Workers' and Soldiers' Deputies. We will believe in and follow it because everything else is pure treachery and open mockery of the world revolution.* [10]

This resolution was passed as part of the final critical struggle for control of the forces in Petersburg and also shows how deeply internationalist ideas had developed in the course of the imperialist war. On 9 October Trotsky had been able to get a resolution passed in the Petersburg Soviet which called for peace, the removal of the Kerensky government and, most significantly, proposed that the defence of Petersburg be undertaken by the Soviet itself. As a result of its acceptance this proposal created the famous Military Revolutionary Committee which was to coordinate the practical seizure of power on 7 November (25 October old style). Contrary to later Stalinist myths, the committee was not set up as a premeditated coordinator of the takeover. It only became so because the Mensheviks and Right SRs refused to take part in it. The Committee was thus composed solely of Bolsheviks and Left SRs who were united on the need to transfer power to the soviets. Furthermore, the resolution to set up the Military Revolutionary Committee came before the Bolshevik Central Committee finally accepted Lenin's arguments about an immediate seizure of power.

The final proof that the Military Revolutionary Committee was not foreseen as the organiser of the October insurrection was that Lenin, and most Bolsheviks (with the exceptions of Trotsky and Volodarsky), looked to the Bolsheviks' own Military Organisation to carry out the practical preparations. However, the latter, which had gone in for adventurism in July, had been so severely criticised within the Party that it now did not want to get its fingers burnt again. Their preparations were so deliberate and cautious that in the end they played a subsidiary, rather than a leading role.

Whilst all this was being debated inside the Bolshevik Party, the anti-Bolshevik campaign in the right wing and "moderate" socialist press was reaching new levels of hysteria in Petersburg. Thanks to Kamenev and Zinoviev they had plenty of advanced warning that the Bolsheviks were intent on *vystuplenie* (coming out) against the Provisional Government, and their papers poured out a stream of vitriol denouncing them. The right-wing though were hypocritical here, as they had thrown their weight behind a military dictatorship only a month earlier. The Mensheviks and the Right SRs were now left stranded as the last defenders of a Provisional Government which could not even claim to have been democratically elected. The civil war was already beginning. Cossacks led by Kaledin were beginning to dismantle soviets in the regions of Russia. It was clear that in this sense Lenin was right, and that the revolution had arrived at a critical point. It would though be Kerensky, not the Bolsheviks, who would make the fateful move.

Kerensky was desperate to get the Petersburg garrison out of the way be sending them to the front but, as the troops refused, he was effectively faced with a mutiny from the moment the soldiers put themselves under the leadership of the Soviet's Military Revolutionary Committee. By the time Kerensky, and his Petersburg commander, General Polkovnikov realised this, it was already too late. The Military Revolutionary Committee had already managed to get commissars loyal to the Soviet elected in most of the regiments. When Kerensky realised he had few reliable troops in the capital he telegraphed for troops from the front, but was told that the troops there were so *"infested with Bolshevism"* that they would refuse to move unless told the purpose of their transfer. In short the Provisional Government was already virtually paralysed. When Kerensky finally did act on 22 October/5 November it was to call for the arrest of all the Bolsheviks who were out on bail after the July Days (this included all the military leaders of the Party), and to close down the Bolshevik press for sedition. But in order to carry out these measures he could only rely on cadets from officer training schools, a women's shock battalion and a rifle regiment of war wounded.

Kerensky's forcible seizure of the *Trud* press, where *Rabochii Put*, a Bolshevik paper addressed to workers, was published, was the signal for the Military Revolutionary Committee to react on 24 October/6 November. The press was soon in workers' hands again and troops loyal to the Military Revolutionary Committee persuaded those thinking of responding to Kerensky's appeals for support to remain neutral. As with the Kornilov Affair, troops being moved towards the capital were also persuaded not to assist the counter-revolution. Militarily there were now no obstacle to a seizure of power but there remained the question of when and how. This debate, which had raged in the Bolshevik Party throughout September, had still not been finally resolved despite the famous vote of 10/23 October. Whilst some members of the Military Revolutionary Committee wanted the immediate overthrow of Kerensky, other Bolsheviks still saw such an uprising as either wrong or premature. Trotsky summarised the situation correctly:

> The government is powerless; we are not afraid of it because we have sufficient strength ... Some of our comrades, for example Kamenev and Riazanov, do not agree with our assessment of the situation. However we are leaning neither to the right or to the left. Our tactical line has been developed by developing circumstances. We grow stronger every day. Our task is to defend ourselves and gradually to expand our sphere of authority so as to build a solid foundation for tomorrow's Congress of Soviets. [11]

Lenin did not fully agree with Trotsky of course. After seven weeks of campaigning for an immediate uprising against a defeated enemy, he could not contain himself. For the second time in a month, he disobeyed the Central Committee's instructions to remain in hiding, and took his famous tram ride to the Bolshevik headquarters at the Smolny Institute. He had already sent an appeal to lower levels of the Party urging them to act before the Central Committee. It was a summary of all he had argued before:

> *History will not forgive revolutionaries for procrastinating when they could be victorious today (and they certainly will be victorious today), while they risk losing much tomorrow, in fact they risk losing everything. If we seize power today, we seize it not in opposition to the soviets but on their behalf. It would be a disaster, or a sheer formality, to await the wavering vote of 25 October. The people have the right and are in duty bound to decide such questions, not by a vote, but by force, in critical moments of the revolution ... The government is tottering. It must be given the deathblow at all costs. To delay action is fatal.*

In fact, both positions contain important elements of the truth. Trotsky recognised that there was little chance for a new Kornilov to appear. He saw that events were already quickly developing enough towards a final denouement (and Trotsky was amongst the most active in ensuring the process was speeded up). Trotsky also knew something Lenin didn't, namely, that the composition of the Second All-Russia Congress of Soviets would be overwhelmingly for the overthrow of the Provisional Government. Lenin feared that it would still contain enough Mensheviks and Right SRs to postpone any decision on soviet power until the Constituent Assembly met. He believed this *"... cannot possibly be favourable to us"* and wanted to present the other "socialist parties" with a *fait accompli*. If the Mensheviks rejected it then they would expose themselves as bourgeois in front of the working class. In fact this is almost how things turned out.

Proletarian October

The myth of the October Revolution, as seen in Eisenstein's film *October* and later Stalinist propaganda was that it was a dramatic but well-organised event. It is true that a militant proletariat, steeled in a class war that had lasted years and now with its own political instrument in the Bolshevik Party, took power in the most orderly of mass actions in history. However, this should not obscure certain facts which are characteristic of the relation between party and class. The Bolshevik Central Committee never, at any time, decided on the date for insurrection. It was forced to put the Central Committee's resolution into action by the march of events and it was the Bolshevik-controlled Military Revolutionary Committee of the Petersburg Soviet which directed the final attack. Even here though, the real initial action was to be found on the streets.

The October Revolution began when Kerensky sent officer cadets to close the bridges over the Neva (thus cutting Petersburg's centre from the working class districts on the Vyborg side) just as he had done in July. However:

> *...they were challenged by an irate crowd of citizens, many of them carrying weapons. Forced to give up their arms the cadets were escorted humiliatingly back to their academy; as nearly as can be determined, this action took place without any specific directives from the Military Revolutionary Committee. Similarly, as soon as the struggle for the bridges began, Ilyin-Zhenevsky, also acting on his own, saw to*

it that garrison soldiers took control of the smaller Grenadersky and Samsonevsky bridges ... [12]

In short, despite all the planning and all the debates, the revolution was not simply the work of a minority leading a passive majority. The Bolsheviks as a military directing centre were not as well-prepared as Stalinist histories, and indeed Trotsky, later made out. Their real success as a leadership of the working class was political in both reflecting and crystallising the clear goals of the mass movement in the months that preceded October. Thus the Liteiny Bridge was shut by workers acting on their own consciousness of the importance of the situation, whilst an individual Bolshevik (Ilyin-Zhenevsky) didn't wait for instructions from the "centre", but was able to act on his own initiative, in accordance with the demands of the situation, to rally troops to keep the bridges to the working class districts open. As we have shown throughout this work, the Bolsheviks' fitness for the revolutionary task was not the result of some assumed infallibility in strategy and tactics but in the fact that it was a party genuinely rooted in the class conscious vanguard of the working class – and a party capable of learning from its mistakes. It was not, as many bourgeois pundits of the Cold War used to proclaim, based on the tight conspiratorial party of *What is to be Done?* (a document which was long forgotten, even by its author). The October Revolution was a product of all that had happened to the working class under Tsarism and particularly in the First World War. It was the completion of what the working class had died for on the streets in February. The Bolsheviks had responded to the new reality the earlier revolt in February had created by updating its programme. It had related the war and its devastation to the way in which capitalism operated under imperialism. In this sense it was not just the guide and leader of the proletarian victory in the October Revolution in Russia. It was at that moment also the leader of the world-wide working class revolution. And, as for the canard that this was just a coup d'état, we can leave the final verdict to the Menshevik Sukhanov.

> *The Mensheviks and SRs, by the way, consoled themselves with this military conspiracy for several months thrusting it in the faces of the Bolsheviks. Incomprehensible! It would have been better if those sharp-witted people had looked and said: was the Petersburg proletariat in sympathy or not with the organisers of the October insurrection? Was it with the Bolsheviks, or were the Bolsheviks acting independently of it? Was it on the side of overturn, was it neutral or was it hostile?*
>
> *Here there can be no two replies. Yes the Bolsheviks acted with the full backing of the Petersburg workers and soldiers.* [13]

The final evidence that the Bolsheviks' programme chimed with the wishes of the masses came in the figures of the allegiance of the delegates to the Second All-Russian Congress of Soviets. They showed that the Bolsheviks had 300 delegates, the SRs 193 (of whom half were Left SRs who supported the overthrow of the Provisional Government), whilst there were 68 Mensheviks and 14 of Martov's Menshevik Internationalists. The remainder were mainly non-affiliated but, as the voting soon showed, largely followed the Bolsheviks. The Bolsheviks supported a motion by Martov to establish a coalition government of all the socialist parties, but this was sabotaged by the Mensheviks and SRs. They considered that soviet power would last only a few days, and made it clear that they were walking out of the Congress. They hoped to mobilise the proletariat against the Bolsheviks but all they achieved was to weaken their own position in front of the working class.

And it was also to have consequences for soviet power, as we shall see later. The Menshevik Internationalist, Sukhanov, realised this when his own faction led by Martov followed the main Menshevik group out of the Congress, He registered his anguish later when he wrote:

> *By quitting the Congress, we ourselves gave the Bolsheviks a monopoly of the Soviet, of the masses and of the revolution.*[14]

The same scene was apparently played out in towns across Russia where town councils (Dumas) representing the middle classes opposed the local soviets. In Saratov the soviet had called for the overthrow of Kerensky as early as 7/20 October. On the night of 26 October/8 November, the Mensheviks and Right SRs declared their support for the Duma and walked out of the Soviet. The response of the Bolshevik Antonov was greeted with applause and cheering:

> *I am answering on behalf of the Soviet. You are walking out. You are washing your hands like Pilate. So you're leaving. But remember that the workers and peasants will never forgive this. They will tell from generation to generation that in the greatest moment of our life, when we seized power and held off the furious attacks of the bourgeoisie, the Mensheviks and SRs abandoned us and went over to the enemy.*[15]

Back in Petersburg further attempts by Martov's Menshevik Internationalists to try to form a coalition of those parties which rejected soviet power came to nothing. Lenin himself was not interested, but the right-wing Bolsheviks, led by Kamenev and Riazanov sincerely tried to create a coalition. The Mensheviks and Right SRs however, were still not ready for any compromise and, in order to avoid agreement, made deliberately impossible conditions for a unity government (such as the exclusion of both Lenin and Trotsky from it). Chernov, the most significant Right SR leader, even decided to leave Petersburg before the Congress of Soviets was due to meet.

The Congress went on without them and overwhelmingly endorsed the insurrection. At about the same time the Winter Palace fell into the hands of the Military Revolutionary Committee and the members of the Provisional Government were arrested – the only arrests made by the working class side. Kerensky had earlier escaped to try to rally front line troops. This turned out to be another demonstration of the overwhelming victory of the Bolsheviks, since his efforts failed, and almost ended with his own arrest. After his few troops were easily repulsed at Gatchina, Kerensky's role was played out. He fled Russia in disguise to write his mendacious memoirs at Harvard Law School over the next half century. Meanwhile Lenin had emerged from hiding to greet the Congress of Soviets with the simple statement *"We shall now proceed to construct the socialist order"*. This was an aspiration. Transforming it into reality he knew could not be achieved in Russia alone. As everyone was well aware at the time the future of the Russian Revolution hung on the arrival of a world working class revolution.

Chapter 8
The "Honeymoon" of the Revolution

If further proof is needed that the October Revolution was an insurrection and not a coup, then its subsequent success in the rest of Russia's cities and towns gives us the evidence. Had the Provisional Government and its lieutenants inside the working class, the Mensheviks and Right SRs, had any meaningful support then this could have become the base for its revival. Though the revolution did not pass off so easily in many places as it did in Petersburg, the supporters of soviet power triumphed almost everywhere. What Donald J Raleigh points out was that soviet power on the Volga was more easily established in places where the Bolsheviks had separated themselves earlier from the Mensheviks, and/or where there were other radical groups who worked alongside them in promoting soviet power.

> *... Soviet power was recognized sooner in those Volga cities where the Bolsheviks had created party organisations early in 1917 (Saratov, Samara, Tsaritsyn) or where party organisations, united or otherwise, benefited from the strength of other radical groups (Kazan). Soviet power took longer to become established in those less industrialized centres where the Bolsheviks had formed separate organizations later in the year (Simbirsk, September; Penza, October; Astrakhan, August).* [1]

Most indicative of the class divide was the battle for Moscow where the supporters of the so-called "Committee of Public Safety", headed by the Mayor of Moscow, a right wing Social Revolutionary called Rudnev, fought against the Military Revolutionary Committee. This was headed by the Bolsheviks but was only set up **after** the October Revolution in Petersburg had been announced. This lack of preparation was to be costly. The Committee of Public Safety had on its side only about 10,000 officer cadets (junkers), officers and students whilst the Military Revolutionary Committee had the support of 50,000 soldiers, with about the same number benevolently neutral. However, the slow preparations of the insurgents and the superior training of the officers, gave the junkers the early initiative. They captured the Kremlin which had been in Military Revolutionary Committee hands (committing the first war crime of the civil war by shooting some of the defendants who had surrendered on the promise that their lives would be spared).

Every revolutionary knew that, as Rosa Luxemburg put it: "*In Russia the problem could only be posed. It could not be solved in Russia*". The Bolsheviks and a great number of Russian workers did not see their revolution as a "Russian" revolution *per se* but as the first step on the road to a world-wide workers' revolution. Peter Struve, an ex-socialist who became a supporter of the Tsar's war, and later of the Whites, could see this. Writing from hiding in 1918 he noted that the Russian Revolution: "*was the first case in world history of the triumph of internationalism and the class idea over nationalism and the national idea.*"[2]

Mensheviks then, and their descendants now, have never accepted this reality and hence could not, and cannot, understand the revolution, except in terms of a Russian-only revolution. The Russian Revolution was not a reckless gamble on the part of the Bolsheviks, but stemmed from the reality of the imperialist war, and in this sense was both part of, and an inspiration for, an international revolutionary wave which capitalist states around the world only survived with great difficulty. In 1917-18 however, whilst waiting for the anticipated world, or at least German, revolution the Russian working class could not just sit administering the old system and wait. They also had to start shaping society in a collectivist direction. This was no easy task given the inherited economic crisis and war.

There was no blueprint for how to proceed, and it was clear that the Russian working class would have to work it out for themselves. Lenin, in following Marx, also did not believe in drawing up blueprints. When asked in 1918 by Bukharin what the socialism of the future would be like he replied:

> *what socialism will be like when it reaches its final form we do not know; we cannot predict it.*[3]

Nevertheless he came the nearest to indicating what the new power should do. It was pretty skeletal. Although Soviet historians were forced to write, after Stalinisation, that the Bolsheviks intended to nationalise the economy from the start, the economic programme of the Bolsheviks before October had only three clear policies – land redistribution, nationalisation of the banks and workers' control of production. The Sixth Party Congress in August 1917 had called for "a number of syndicates in the oil, coal, sugar, metallurgy and transport sectors"[4] to be formed but beyond that Lenin seemed to think that the system would be some hybrid which he called "state capitalism". Although this was contested by Left Communists in the Party as "nonsense" (since the elimination of the power of capital was a precondition for socialism), for the most part the Bolsheviks seemed to accept that the social and economic backwardness of Russia meant that they would be administering some form of capitalist regime until the world revolution arrived. However, there was never a settled Bolshevik idea of what that would entail and, as we shall see, circumstance as much as ideology played a role in defining how the revolution advanced, and then retreated.

In the meantime, the new workers' government had to live up to their claim that:

> *The cause for which the people have fought, namely the immediate offer of a democratic peace, the abolition of landed proprietorship, workers' control over production and the establishment of soviet power – this cause has been secured.*[5]

A flurry of decrees, all endorsed by the Soviet Executive Committee (VTsIK), followed. The speed of this action was partially dictated by the fact that the Bolsheviks did not know how long, or even if, soviet power would survive. The *Decree of Peace* (October 26/November 8) was a carefully calibrated document which did not directly call for world revolution but did appeal to the workers of Britain, France and Germany to end the war and "at the same time emancipate the labouring and exploited masses"[6]. When, after almost two months, this evoked no response from any of the imperialist belligerent powers, a more explicit Appeal "to the toiling masses of all countries" was issued. This now stated that peace would only come when "the peoples of all countries dictate its terms by their revolutionary struggle".[7]

The *Declaration of the Rights of the Peoples of Russia* (2/15 November) gave "the right of the peoples of Russia to free self-determination, up to secession and the formation of a separate state" and brought into law the "abolition of all and any national and national-religious privileges and restrictions"[8]. The same document also condemned Tsarism's policies of "massacres and pogroms". Jews are not specifically mentioned, but they were the main beneficiaries as they were no longer restricted to the Pale of Settlement,[9] or discriminated against in law.

"National self determination" remained one of the most hotly disputed issues inside the left of the social democratic movement. Rosa Luxemburg, whose Social Democratic Party of the Kingdom of Poland and Lithuania often worked alongside the Bolsheviks in Tsarist Russia, had continuously campaigned for the Bolsheviks to remove the offer of national independence from it programme. Born into the supposedly oppressed nation of Poland, she belonged to a long line of Polish revolutionaries who had opposed national independence for Poland. Her argument was that Marx had never supported all national struggles. but only those which would have led to a further development of capitalism. and hence prepared the groundwork for the proletarian revolution since it would have entailed the expansion of the working class. By 1909 she argued the slogan had become obsolete as no new bourgeois revolutions could take place. Any national bourgeoisie that did emerge would be weak, and at the beck and call of the already established capitalist powers. This included the Polish bourgeoisie who were so "tied by chains of gold" to Russia that no real national independence could be achieved[10].

She was supported inside the Bolshevik Party by such figures as Yevgenia Bosch, Georgy Piatakov and Nikolai Bukharin. Indeed these three so strongly opposed Lenin in the first issue of *Kommunist* in 1915 that the second issue never appeared[11]. Lenin's position was that the Tsarist Empire was a "prison-house of nations" and thus offering the right of national self-determination was the only position for an internationalist. Anything else would smack of "Great Russian chauvinism". His hope was, of course that the new nations would then all voluntarily re-unite in some federated soviet body of the future.

No surprise then that in 1918 Luxemburg criticised this declaration as an abandonment of places like Finland and Ukraine to the capitalists. In reality however, there was little the Bolsheviks could do to assist the workers in either state at this time, even though the workers in Helsinki (Helsingfors as it was then) had already set up their own soviets.

These would soon be bloodily crushed by Baron Mannerheim, with the full support of German imperialism. Russian forces were not even minimally in a position to stop them. And indeed that was how the national question was settled everywhere in the period after 1917. Force determined the day everywhere. The Bolsheviks could not win back Poland, or the Baltic states thanks first to German, then Entente imperialism but in Ukraine, the Caucasus and Central Asia where they emerged victorious from the civil war soviet republics were set up which joined the Russian Socialist Federated Soviet Republic (the name "Union of Soviet Socialist Republics" was not adopted until 1923). Just how much this was a shotgun wedding can be seen in the treatment of Georgia by Stalin and Ordzhonikidze which was forcibly invaded in February 1921 and its Menshevik government, led by Jordania, overthrown. This was contrary to Lenin's wishes (he had even called for a coalition government in Georgia with the Mensheviks). For him the key thing was that every soviet republic should have the right of secession. Stalin's actions in Georgia made a mockery of this and Great Russian chauvinism was already on the march before Lenin died[12].

The same elemental class war that produced the October Revolution did not stop because of it. Many of the decrees simply sanctioned a process which was going on already. Peasants had continued to seize land throughout 1917 so the *Decree on Land* simply codified this. It abolished "landed proprietorship" except for "ordinary peasants". Contrary to the assertions of many bourgeois historians, and the anarchist Volin[13], this decree neither nationalised the land, nor did it just give "land to the tiller" (i.e. individual peasants), as is often stated but, in keeping with what the peasants were actually doing, vested redistribution in village (volost) committees, who would decide how to redistribute land for themselves. This shows that the Bolsheviks understood more about the traditional needs of the peasants, at least as far as the land question was concerned, than most histories give them credit for. Where they failed with the peasants was over trade, especially as this would have an impact on the food supply or bread question, an issue which would almost bring about the end of the soviet power, as we shall see. In 1918 however the theory was that the cities would meet the peasants' needs for goods of all types and these would be exchanged for grain. There were several problems though. In the first place retooling factories from war production was no simple matter (and in any case when the civil war restarted in earnest in June 1918 producing for the Red Army became a priority). Second the peasants did not want payment in kind but in money (which was at that time on the road to becoming worthless due to the increased issuance of roubles). Third, as Silvana Malle pointed out, self-subsisting peasants had little interest in most of what industry could offer[14].

Sending grain detachments into the countryside had been a feature of factory life even under the Provisional Government, but now it became a settled policy of the soviet power. In their increasing resort to grain requisitioning (*Prodrazverstka*)[15] from the start of 1918 onwards, the Bolsheviks thought that a class divide between rich and poor peasants existed which they could play on. It was a false analysis, which led to a desperate war between town and country, undermined the popularity the Bolsheviks had enjoyed until then, and helped pave the way for a civil war within the civil war as peasants attacked "the commissars" sent to seize the grain. It was also a major cause of the Kronstadt Uprising in 1921, not to mention the famine which followed that year.

In the towns and cities the very formation of soviet power was enough for the factory owners to start sabotaging the economy in 1917-18. They either deliberately reduced production, abandoned the factories, or refused to pay their workers. The workers responded in most cases by taking over production themselves.

There is no more vexed subject than the issue of workers' control in the Russian Revolution. Despite a recurring anarchist (and bourgeois) myth that the Bolsheviks intended only to establish "party power", Lenin was, at least initially, an enthusiastic supporter of the self-activity of workers. On 14/27 November the *Instructions of the All-Russian Central Executive Committee and the Council of People's Commissars on Workers' Control* was issued. The original had been drafted by the All-Russian Council of Factory Committees but their version was only about setting up a central apparatus to regulate the economy. Lenin redrafted it to include the right of workers in all enterprises to control all aspects of production and "decisions of workers control bodies" were "binding on the owners of enterprises".

This awkward fact makes nonsense of the claim in Western historiography that, once power was in his grasp, Lenin, the stop-at-nothing centraliser, proceeded to crush the "syndicalist" factory committees. In fact the reverse is true. [16]

In defending the Instructions in the All-Russian Central Soviet Executive (VTsIK) the Bolshevik (and Left Communist) Milyutin explained:

... we have been overtaken by events ... we have to coordinate the work of control organs set up in the localities ... We proceeded on the basis of control from below. [17]

At the time Lenin was equally adamant:

Creative activity at the grassroots is the basic factor of the new public life. Let the workers set up workers' control at their factories. Let them supply the villages with manufactures in exchange for grain... Socialism cannot be decreed from above. Its spirit rejects the mechanical bureaucratic approach: living creative socialism is the product of the masses themselves. [18]

It is often argued by libertarians (of which the most famous is Maurice Brinton in his *The Bolsheviks and Workers' Control*[19]) that the setting up of the Supreme Economic Council (Vesenkha) in December 1917 was the unmasking of the deep-rooted authoritarian tendencies of the Bolsheviks, but this does not fit the facts. In the first place, the Vesenkha was set up "apparently at the behest of the factory committee leadership"[20] to coordinate the socialisation of the economy that was already underway from the bottom up by the various factory committees that had emerged in the course of 1917. At this point too, Brinton's attempt to make a distinction between the Bolsheviks and the factory committees is a false one. The Bolsheviks had been the most vociferous defenders of the factory committees since the February Revolution, thus it was no surprise that the majority of factory committees were run by workers, who also just happened to be Bolsheviks.

Additonally, at the head of the Vesenkha were those Left Communists, as they were soon to be called, who most favoured the idea that socialism could only come about via the self-activity of the masses. Its Chair was Valerian Obolensky, who is more famous under his revolutionary name of Nikolai Ossinsky (or Osinsky)[21]. Also on this Council were Bukharin, Lomov and Vladimir Smirnov. All of them were future participants in the *Kommunist* project of March-June 1918. This not only opposed the signing of the Treaty of Brest-Litovsk but also the introduction of "scientific management" and the use of specialists that belonged to capitalism, all of which undermined the process of education which the mass of the class was undergoing as it wrestled with the need to maintain production. According to Brinton's prejudiced and ahistorical account these Left Communists were put in charge of a policy they strongly defended simply as a figleaf to hide the real aims of the Bolsheviks.

Until the Spring of 1918 Lenin enthusiastically endorsed the Left Communists' support for the self-activity of the working class, but he thought it should be worked out as they went along, as "the masses" operated by trial and error. The day before Vesenkha was set up Lenin wrote: "*There was not and could not be a definite plan for the organisation of economic life. Nobody could provide one. But it could be done from below, by the masses, through their experience. Instructions would, of course, be given and ways indicated but it was necessary to begin simultaneously from above and from below.*"[22]

Indeed it was the workers organised in their factory committees who were leading the drive for "nationalisation" (in short demanding that the soviet regime take responsibility for the socialisation, i.e. the workers' takeover of the factories). Many saw it as the sole alternative to the closure of the factory. Some took over the factory when the owners fled, others deliberately seized the factories from the owners when they realised that production was being run down[23] and still others just did it to get rid of the boss. Undoubtedly the *Instructions on Workers Control* gave them the legal green light to do this. In so doing however they were transforming workers control (of what the capitalists were doing) into direct workers' self-management of production. Some Bolsheviks (those closest to the Mensheviks, who argued along the same lines) even criticised what they saw as an attempt to build socialism where the material conditions for it did not exist. Others deplored the chaotic way it was being carried out from below. One member of Vesenkha, Gurevich grumbled:

Everyone who wished to "nationalise" did so; local "sovnarkozes" [councils of national economy], "ispolkoms" [executive committees], "voenrevkoms" [military revolutionary committees] and even the Chekas ... such action was prompted by some kind of motive in each individual case and was not due to any kind of plan.[24]

The "Honeymoon" of the Revolution

In fact many orders were issued by Vesenkha forbidding "nationalisation" by individual factory committees, but they largely fell on deaf ears. Almost 95% of the 850 or more factory takeovers[25] between November 1917 and March 1918 came as a result of the workers' own battles with the bosses. Eventually, the Bolsheviks bowed to the grassroots movement and announced the nationalisation of most enterprises in June 1918. Thus the nationalisations were primarily neither a product of utopian zeal nor of Marxist ideology, but born out of a class movement which demanded support for its actions as well as the growing economic chaos (which, until March 1918, Lenin accepted as the price of workers' initiative). The *Decree on the Nationalisation of Enterprises* actually highlights this dual aspect. Its first line states that the Decree's purpose was "*to overcome economic dislocation and to consolidate the dictatorship of the working class and the village poor*"[26]. For the Left Communists, and most factory workers at that time, nationalisation was seen as a partial step towards socialism. The Left Communists were its keenest supporters and inveighed against Lenin and the Bolshevik Right for wanting to do deals with capitalists. Ironically they accused Lenin of defending one form of state capitalism (which was more like post World War Two Keynesianism in the West) whilst unwittingly peddling their own form of it, in which the state would become the universal capitalist[27]. But we only can understand this now with the benefit of hindsight, based on this experience of the Russian working class. This was not the last discussion on the nature of the state and capitalism within Communist ranks. As we shall see in Chapter 15 the issue of state capitalism was still live after the introduction of the New Economic Policy in 1921 so we will discuss it further there.

The social achievements of the Revolution, both in the first one hundred days and thereafter, were in many ways its most admirable aspect. One statement of intent that this was a society in transition was that officials were paid only the average wage of a skilled industrial worker. Additionally Church and State were separated and freedom of religion was established (thus ending the legal oppression of Jews)[28]. Other social achievements were the introduction of free education (alongside a mass literacy campaign), as well as the removal of the Church from control of education.[29]

Perhaps the most radical steps were taken in relation to gender and sexual relations. Readers may recall that at the end of the February Revolution, despite the fact that women had started the uprising, there was not a single female delegate in the initial Petersburg Soviet. This state of affairs had not altered much by November 1917. However as the first political party in Russia to try to organise working women, the Bolsheviks already had an agenda for changing women's lives and encouraging them to change their own. New laws also brought in free maternity homes and nurseries, and equal pay for women. Divorce could take place at the request of either partner, and children "born out of wedlock" were granted equal legal status. In 1920 Russia became the first country in the world to legalise abortion. Kollontai tells us that

> ... *measures to protect and provide for motherhood were carried through in the first months of Soviet government by two People's Commissariats: the People's Commissariat for Social Welfare and the People's Commissariat for Labour. The*

latter drew up a series of statutes in the field of social legislation. The People's Commissariat for Social Welfare carried through the measures designed to mothers.

She went on;

... that the initiative on the issue of protection and provision for mother and child came from the working women themselves. At that time, very few working women actively participated in the Soviets. But from the very first days of soviet power, working women were able to contribute constructively to the work of the Soviets as regards lightening the burden of motherhood for women[30].

In the autumn of 1918 Lenin called for more women to be involved in the soviets[31] (a call he would repeat in 1921). Although they had been a little nervous of organising women separately (on the very real premise that it smacked of bourgeois feminism) the Bolsheviks eventually did set up a Women's Department in 1919 headed by Alexandra Kollontai and Inessa Armand. Kollontai was at pains to stress that:

Woman in Russia has achieved political equality. However she owes this achievement not to co-operation with bourgeois suffragettes, but to a joint, united struggle with her comrade workers in the ranks of her own working class.[32]

The comrade male workers did not always see the struggle for women to be treated as equals as something they should get involved in. In a civil war, where few women were under arms, macho attitudes persisted. Some of it was almost a caricature. Wearing a leather jacket, for example, became a badge of those males who wanted to look authoritative. Women were thus still often seen by men in their traditional roles, and on at least one occasion their presence in the Soviets was questioned by patriarchal Russian males who considered that if women were in the soviet then so should children![33] Such social transformations have to be fought for and can take time. The soviet power had at least set down a pointer for what gender relations should be, and it had no equal anywhere else at the time. However, as with the vast bulk of the changes of this early Bolshevik honeymoon period, they were rolled back or abandoned by a Stalinism which in the 1930s saw women simply as the bearers of the next generation of soldiers for the future imperialist war.

Soviet Russia was only the second country in the history of the world (after Revolutionary France) to decriminalise homosexuality. Many anti-Bolshevik sources say this came about simply by default. The idea that the Bolsheviks simply "forgot" to criminalise it is not born out by the evidence. In the first decree on marriage[34] gender is not mentioned. The Bolsheviks were

indirectly influenced by Magnus Hirschfeld, a German scientist who founded the Institute of Sexology in Berlin. Hirschfeld often spoke in public of his conviction that homosexuality was not a disease, but a natural manifestation of human sexuality. [35]

This is why the 1922 penal code reinforced the decriminalisation of gays. It was explained and defended by Dr Batkis of the Social Hygiene Institute at the University of Moscow, in a pamphlet called *The Sexual Revolution in Russia*. In it he wrote:

> *Whilst European legislation defines all this as a breach of public morality, Soviet legislation makes no difference between homosexuality and so-called "natural" intercourse. All forms of intercourse are treated as a personal matter. Criminal prosecution is only implemented in cases of violence, abuse or a violation of the interests of others.*[36]

Of course it did not always reflect reality on the ground in a country that was culturally as undeveloped as Russia, and assaults on gays still took place. Some Soviet doctors also still argued that homosexuality was a disease. They proposed removing the testicles of the "sufferer" and replacing them with those of a heterosexual! However these views were ignored and at least one provocative attempt to prosecute gays (in 1925) was thrown out by the courts citing the 1922 legal code.[37] In terms of the time it was an enormous step forward.[38] Even more so if we consider that in the UK until 1967 anyone who was found to be gay was offered a choice of prison (where they would be routinely beaten up) or chemical castration "for their illness". Stalin, of course, explicitly recriminalised homosexuality in 1933 in a new penal code.[39]

The Left Socialist Revolutionary Isaak Steinberg, who became Commissar for Justice in the new government, thought the October Revolution had come as a relief after eight months of class tension. For him it opened up a whole new series of revolutionary possibilities.

> *All aspects of existence – social, economic, political, spiritual, moral, familial – were opened to purposeful fashioning by human hands. Ideas for social betterment and progress that had been gathering for generations in Russia and elsewhere seemed to wait on the threshold of the revolution ready to pour forth and permeate the life of the Russian people. The issues were not only social and economic reforms and thoroughgoing political changes: with equal zeal the awakened people turned to the fields of justice and education, to art and literature. Everywhere the driving passion was to create something new, to effect a total difference with the "old world" and its civilization. It was one of those uncommon moments of self-perception and self-assertion. The storm passed nobody by; neither those who hailed it as a blessing nor those who spurned it as a curse.* [40]

The October Revolution was thus not simply the Bolshevik "power grab" of bourgeois histories but about something much deeper and widespread than the mere shifting of power from one group to another. It was the living proof of what Marx had written in *The German Ideology* about what it takes to alter the consciousness of masses of human beings. This: "*can only take place in a practical movement, a revolution; this revolution is necessary, therefore, not only because the ruling class cannot be overthrown in any other way but also because the class overthrowing it can only in a revolution succeed in ridding itself of all the muck of ages and become fitted to found society anew."* [41]

As you would expect in a real revolution this self-activity of the masses took many forms.

Soviet Russia was the first nation in history to witness the birth across its land of thousands of communal organizations spontaneously engaging in collective life.[42]

Indeed Stites tells us that the word *kommuna* (commune) became "a regular part of the Soviet lexicon"[43] right after October. Communal experiments in living were set up across the country. First amongst these social experiments was the Kronstadt Commune which the anarchist historian Paul Avrich called "a lost revolutionary utopia". For over three years it supported the Bolsheviks but during that time it was virtually an independent republic. About half of the 50,000 inhabitants of the island were sailors. Here they formed communes of 40-60 people where everyone worked on urban garden plots and "were rewarded according to labour or special needs".[44] Housing and building plots were dished out according to family size and rations were shared. Decisions of vital issues were settled in noisy meetings held in Anchor Square. Some have seen in this a continuation of the peasant mir or commune but here there was no domination by rich peasants or village elders. The Kronstadt Commune remained a supporter of the power of the working class as expressed in the soviets until its brutal end in March 1921.

Russia also seemed to have gone committee mad. Committees to govern every aspect of life were spontaneously created from housing committees, which had the right to requisition and reallocate housing, to people's courts and tribunals, which sprang up everywhere (see Chapter 12). Even hostile observers tell of railway passengers forming travel committees which regulated the (always overcrowded) train until it reached its terminus! Clearly none of this was a result of any Bolshevik master plan and the socialisations went far beyond what the Bolsheviks had thought possible at that time. The soviet power tried to keep pace with these initiatives by regularising them (e.g. in November 1917 all courts had judges elected by local Soviets[45]).

This flowering of proletarian activity at all levels was not without its problems. Local factory committees often saw newly socialised factories as their collective private property and there were some instances of factory committees selling off the factory machinery. The railway workers at the Alexandrovsky Station in Moscow turned railway carriages into their own homes. This localism also affected local soviets so that some positively medieval situations arose such as the taxation of oil travelling from Baku to Moscow by every soviet on the route.

At first, none of this discouraged the Bolsheviks from supporting the experiments. Lenin called these problems "the disease of growth" and pointed out that the proletariat would only learn from these experiences.[46] There are few if any signs at this point that the Bolsheviks were intent on a one-party state. Indeed it seemed as if the Bolshevik Party was dissolving itself into the masses rather than the other way around. Not only were about 1 in 6 of the Russian working class actual card-carrying party members but the Party organisation itself had no plans for expansion. It had only two politically responsible secretaries with a total office staff of 4. That it functioned so well was due the extraordinary memory and energy of Jakob Sverdlov. Sverdlov was not only "organiser in chief" of the Bolshevik Party (he had no official party title) but was also President of the All-Russian Soviet Executive Committee (VTsIK) as well as the first President of the Soviet Republic. His death from "Spanish flu" in 1919 was a harsh blow to the Communist Party, and definitely altered things. It was followed by the creation of a growing party apparatus which did not work well until Stalin was given the role of General Secretary in 1922. No-one at the time saw the significance of allowing this "grey blur" (as Sukhanov described him in 1917) to get his hands on party appointments. However this is to anticipate events.

In July 1918 when the Constitution of the Soviet state was drawn up the Party was not mentioned as having any role to play. As Neil Harding put it:

> *The role of the Party apparatus ... was simply to enthuse the mass of the people to undertake this momentous transformation.*[47]

On the Left of the Party, Preobrazhensky even suggested that the achievement of proletarian power had now rendered the party's special position in relation to the class as a whole redundant, and that it should therefore dissolve itself into the soviet structure. In practice this was at first what actually started to happen. Indeed just as the October revolution seems to have given creative impulse to the working class as a whole, it also seems to have fired the imaginations of the members of the Party:

> *...the victory of the revolution appeared at first to relax the bounds of party discipline and led to an outburst of unfettered dissension and controversy unprecedented in the annals of the Bolshevik Party or perhaps rare in those of any other... a winter of free speech and hard hitting argument in the central committee culminated in the famous debates in February and March 1918 on the Brest-Litovsk negotiations; ... in these Lomov openly said "we must take power without Vladimir Ilyich".*[48]

This is hardly the behaviour of a party with dictatorship already in its DNA.

As we shall see, not everything was perfect in early 1918, but most of the social and cultural advances outlined above survived throughout the 1920s and only disappeared, or were watered down, under Stalin with Jews, gays and women being the main victims.

As it was the first few months of workers' power was a time of political hope and social experiment. The Left Bolshevik economist Lev Kritsman described it in the title of his book as *The Heroic Period of the Great October Revolution,* which was a defence of the entire period of "war communism", but which would have been better restricted to the first 8 months of soviet power. Up to this point Lenin was still repeating his faith in the capacity of the working class to take control of its own destiny. This culminated at the Seventh Party Congress in March 1918 where, he repeated his mantra of the winter of 1917-18:

> *It is important for us to draw literally all working people into the government of the state. It is a task of tremendous difficulty. But socialism cannot be implemented by a minority, by the Party. It can only be implemented by tens of millions when they have learned to do it for themselves.* [49]

This was not the last time that Lenin would express such confidence in the mass of the working class but the echoes of it became ever fainter as the economic consequences of what they had inherited from the previous regime began to hit home. We will turn to the consequences of this economic situation in Chapters 10 and 13 but first we have to deal with the signing of the Treaty of Brest-Litovsk in March 1918 which many wrongly identify as the first step towards counter-revolution.

Chapter 9
The Treaty of Brest-Litovsk

It was one thing to decree peace as the Second Congress of Soviets did on the second day of the revolution. It was another thing, in the midst of a brutal imperialist war, to achieve it. The Bolsheviks though owed a great deal of their dramatic rise in popularity in the working class to precisely this aim. The governments of the Tsar and Kerensky (backed by the SRs and Mensheviks) had all been rejected because they wanted to continue the imperialist war "to victory".

The fraught question was what kind of peace would the Bolsheviks be able to obtain? The real intention of their appeals for peace were not aimed at just Germany but at all the belligerent powers in the hope of bringing about a general peace. This did not happen. Instead, finally signing the Treaty of Brest-Litovsk with Germany in March 1918 the Bolsheviks, and particularly Lenin, were both denounced by nationalists for selling out the Russian motherland and assailed from the Left by those who accused them of undermining the prospects of world revolution. This even included some of their own leading members who as we shall see became known as the Left Communists.

Revolutionary defeatism and the need for peace

As we saw in Chapter Two, the Bolshevik Party distinguished itself in 1914 as being in the vanguard of the international working class when it came to "revolutionary defeatism". Lenin, in particular, had worked body and soul for this against the ridicule of the ruling classes of Europe, accompanied by most of the leaders of the collapsed Second International, and even the doubts of some Bolsheviks like Kamenev. At the beginning of 1918 the proletariat had only succeeded in winning the class war to put an end to the imperialist war in one country – Russia. This success posed its own problems so long as the workers in the rest of Europe did not follow the Russian lead.

Since 1915 the Bolsheviks had been committed to offering immediate peace to all nations. Now at the summit of soviet power they began cautiously. Lenin spelled out the conditions under which peace would be offered, and with what perspective, as early as September 1917.

> *The Soviet Government must IMMEDIATELY formulate proposals to all belligerent countries (that is simultaneously to their Governments and to the masses of workers and peasants) to negotiate a general peace on the spot on democratic terms, and to conclude an armistice at once, if even for only three months such a peace will evoke such an explosion in the whole world for the workers revolt against the war grows with undiminished vigour.*[1]

The promise was fulfilled in the first international act of the "provisional workers' and peasants' government" on 8th November 1917. The *Decree on Peace* which Lenin had spent the first night of workers' power drafting was, as we saw in the previous chapter, really an appeal to governments and peoples to end the war. It was deliberately not couched in revolutionary terms. There was nothing in it about imperialism as the cause of war, or that only a proletarian seizure of power could prevent more wars in the future. The aim was to give the capitalists no excuse for continuing the war, thus exposing them in front of their own people.

In this sense it was successful since the US President Wilson was forced to issue his famous 14 Points for "a just and democratic peace" only two months later. But whilst the racist windbag in the White House was mouthing sentiments about "open covenants, openly arrived at" the Bolsheviks were publishing the secret treaties that the Russian bourgeoisie had signed with their friends in Britain and France to carve up the world. Henceforth Trotsky told the Soviet Executive:

> There exists for us only one unwritten but sacred treaty of the international solidarity of the proletariat.

In fact "international solidarity" had been the main plank in the argument for the Bolsheviks to take the lead in overthrowing the Provisional Government in October. Lenin had argued that *"the international situation gives us a series of objective grounds for believing that if we come out now, we shall have all proletarian Europe on our side"*.

Seven weeks passed but there were no responses from any belligerent to the appeal sent out by the Soviet Congress and equally there was, as yet, little evidence that the working class anywhere was stirred by the revolution in Russia. By the end of December 1917 the difficult question of coming to terms with German imperialism could not now be avoided.

What the Bolsheviks initially hoped to do by entering into negotiations with the Germans at their Army Headquarters at Brest-Litovsk was to buy time. With no army worthy of the name to resist further German advances they could only rely on the fact that the Germans were preparing to hold the Eastern Front whilst the "knock out blow" would be delivered in France. In this respect the October Revolution did not change German policy. Indeed the German desire to achieve a peace in the East which would need less troops to police it was one of the reasons why first Joffe, then Trotsky, were able to spin out the negotiations for close to four months.

If the Bolsheviks were united behind the idea of trying to keep the negotiations going to await the world revolution, they were divided on the perspective to be adopted if this failed.

From the start Lenin was quite sanguine about the fact that a peace would have to be signed, and on German terms. His position was no less internationalist than his opponents in the Party. As he wrote in an open letter to American workers (published in English at the end of 1918):

> *He is no socialist who does not understand that the victory over the bourgeoisie may require losses of territory and defeats. He is no Socialist who will not sacrifice his fatherland for the triumph of the social revolution.*[2]

Trotsky's perspective was no less internationalist than Lenin's. He too staked the survival of the Russian proletarian revolution on the activities of the Western European workers.

> *If the peoples of Europe do not arise and crush imperialism we shall be crushed – that is beyond doubt. Either the Russian proletarian revolution will raise the whirlwind of struggle in the West, or the capitalists of all countries will stifle our struggle.*[3]

On the other hand, Trotsky, with his usual over-confidence, thought that he could play off the imperialist powers against each other. He told the Entente powers exactly what Soviet Russia was doing and invited them to join in the peace talks. When the draconian nature of the German terms became clear he tried to get the Allies to come to military terms, and asked them what material aid could they offer for a resumption of the war. But his requests, not surprisingly, fell on deaf ears. Thus

> *We began peace negotiations in the hope of arousing the workmen's parties [sic] of Germany and Austria-Hungary as well as those of the Entente countries. For this reason we were obliged to delay the negotiations as long as possible to give the European workmen time to understand the main fact of the Soviet revolution and particularly its peace policy.*[4]

However, the French and British bourgeoisie feared the Russian workers' experiment with Soviet rule more than they did German imperialism. After all, Trotsky had already revealed the rapacious imperialist contents of their secret treaties. Thus when Kamenev was sent to Britain his diplomatic luggage and his money was seized and after a short imprisonment, and a brief talk to the Foreign Office, he was deported back to Russia.

Even in the signing of the armistice with the Germans at Brest-Litovsk, the Bolsheviks tried to balance the shame of negotiating with imperialism with the need to spread revolutionary propaganda. Not only did they get the Germans to agree to halt the transfer of troops to the Western Front during the period of the armistice (the German General Staff had been gradually doing so since the collapse of the Provisional Government's June Offensive) but also to agree to fraternisation between the two armies and to allow revolutionary literature into German-held territory. Radek had already begun organising German and Austrian prisoners of war and even produced a newspaper for them (*Die Fackel — The Torch*) which was also provocatively distributed to German troops at the Brest-Litovsk station by the Bolshevik delegation!

"Peredyschka"

Trotsky was able to hold up the Germans for three weeks but on 18th January 1918 the German ultimatum was finally presented. An outbreak of mass political strikes in Austria on 14th January, which lasted for almost a week, had compelled the Habsburg Emperor Karl to send a message to Count Czernin, Austro-Hungarian representative at Brest-Litovsk on 17th January. The sense of panic lies in his words.

> *I must once more earnestly impress upon you that the whole fate of the Monarchy and the dynasty depends on peace being concluded at Brest-Litovsk as soon as possible ... If peace be not made at Brest there will be a revolution here, be there ever so much to eat.[5]*

It meant that Czernin who until then had been trying to ensure that the Russians did not walk out of the peace talks now had no options left. Ironically this also brought Trotksy's filibustering to an end. Czernin had to just go along with anything the Germans proposed. The German Generals now could make their military demands which made no pretence of respecting principles like "national self-determination". Their demands were brutal. All Polish, Lithuanian, and half of Latvian lands were to be German whilst Ukraine was to be given its "independence". These were the offerings Trotsky took back to Petersburg. It was at this point that all the different perspectives latent within the Bolshevik Party made themselves felt. Lenin was in no doubt that there was no option but to accept. He immediately drew up his views in his "Theses on the Question of the Immediate Conclusion of a Separate and Annexationist Peace". He still maintained that

> *There is no doubt that the socialist revolution in Europe is bound to happen and will happen. All our hopes of the FINAL victory of socialism are founded on this conviction and on this scientific prediction. Our propaganda activity in general and the organisation of fraternisation in particular must be strengthened and developed.*

But

> *it would be a mistake to build the tactics of the socialist government on attempts to determine whether the European, and in particular, the German socialist revolution will happen in the next half year (or some such short time) or will not happen.[6]*

To Lenin making peace at all costs would be the best advert for world revolution since the war-weary workers would have no better contrast than the rapaciousness of imperialism and the peace of the socialist republic. This reasoning did not find much support from the other two tendencies in the Party. Trotsky had all along said he would never sign a shameful peace with Germany so he could not bring himself to sign the proposed terms. On the other hand he recognised, like Lenin, that there was no possibility of serious resistance at that time as the Russian Army had further disintegrated once the soldiers were told by Kirilenko in December that the armistice had been signed. This is why he came up with his formula of neither signing the peace nor fighting the war.

The majority at this time were for rejection. Lenin dubbed this group the "Muscovites" since its core was the Moscow leadership around Bukharin, Lomov and Ossinsky and the journal *Kommunist* which actually came into existence over the opposition to signing Brest-Litovsk. For these "proletarian communists" as they styled themselves, but Left Communists as they were called by Lenin, the issue was one of principle. To sign the peace was to abandon the Western European revolution, which they believed imminent, to German militarism. They rightly claimed that they were holding to Lenin's old position. However they added the idea of fighting a revolutionary war against Germany and even talked of retreating to Siberia whilst conducting a guerrilla war against the Germans wherever they could. Although the biggest faction, the Left Communists did not command an overwhelming majority and Lenin threw his support behind Trotsky's formula rather than accept the Moscow position, on condition that if Trotsky's gamble that the Germans would not advance further, even if there was no peace treaty, failed then Trotsky would support Lenin's call for acceptance.

Trotsky was allowed to return to Brest-Litovsk to make his unilateral declaration of "No war, no peace". This aroused high hopes amongst Bolsheviks. Ilyin-Zhenevsky recorded the tension, the drama and his own personal tragedy at this time.

> *Several days passed in agonised waiting. Each day that went by peacefully instilled fresh hope. Why were the Germans not advancing? Perhaps the revolutionary infection really had penetrated so deeply in to the German Army that the soldiers were refusing to take up arms against the red banners of the revolution? In that case Trotsky had calculated correctly when he made his beau geste. Then suddenly, as though out of a clear sky, came the thunderclap. The Germans started to advance and pressed with incredible speed towards Petrograd.*

> *I shall never forget the heavy oppressive mood that then came over our people in the Party and the Soviets ... It seemed that all was now lost and that we were going to be crushed by the armed might of German imperialism ... The first person who fell victim to this mood was my wife (Lydia Borisova née Witmer – JD). After suffering torment for a whole day through her anxiety over the fate of the revolution and the Soviet Republic, in the evening of February 20 she shot herself.*[7]

In this crisis Lenin proposed an immediate offer of renewed negotiations but lost by one vote in the Central Committee. The vote was Trotsky's. He argued for waiting to see what would happen in Germany and Austria. But within twenty-four hours, when news of the German capture of Dvinsk, and most of Ukraine, reached Petersburg, he had abandoned his position. Now the Central Committee voted to accept the original terms offered by the Germans.

However, the Germans now upped the price of peace. In addition to the earlier terms, the Russian Army had to abandon the Baltic Provinces and the whole of Ukraine and

Finland. The new even more draconian terms revived the divisions in the Bolshevik Party. Lenin repeated his earlier arguments that;

> *Germany is only pregnant with revolution. The second month must not be mistaken for the ninth. But here in Russia we have a healthy, lusty child. We may kill it if we start a war.*

The Left Communists though renewed their call for a revolutionary war. The first issue of their journal *Kommunist* contained an article by Bukharin and Radek which stated that *"No conscious revolutionary would agree to such dishonour"* as the treaty and that *"we should die in a fine pose, sword in hand, crying 'Peace is dishonour, war is honour!'"*

This kind of language sounds more like that of Don Quixote than serious revolutionaries but there was a genuine concern behind this call. The Left Communists were seriously worried that the Bolsheviks were abandoning the internationalist principles which had marked them out from virtually every other socialist party in Europe. In the light of the further degeneration of the revolution into Stalin's "socialism in one country" it has to be seriously asked if Brest-Litovsk was the first step on the road to the abandonment of the world revolution in favour of defending Russian state capitalism. As Lenin was himself proposing "state capitalism" as the economic programme of the revolution pending the extension of workers' power to other areas, it would seem that there is a degree of coherence in this. However, Lenin's aphorism "facts are stubborn things" marked out his method in this debate rather than any change of principles.

To him signing Brest-Litovsk was a **tactic**. The stubborn fact was that the Bolsheviks had no alternative unless they wanted German bayonets to wipe out what was left of "Red Petersburg". In addition, he still expected that a German Revolution in a few months would wipe out all treaties (and in November 1918 he was to be proved right). His speech at the Seventh Party Congress on 6th March was probably the most hard-hitting of his career. He severely castigated the "fools" who talked of "dishonour" and argued that:

> *all that I foresaw has come to pass in place of the treaty offered at Brest-Litovsk we have one that is far more crushing. The blame lies with those who refused it. By this refusal we are helping German imperialism by handing over millions of tons of our resources - guns, ammunition and food. We had to do it nevertheless to gain a breathing space .. but the Kommunist makes light of the peredyschka (breathing space)."[8]*

Because there was now no other outcome to the debate the Congress voted by 30 votes to 12 to accept "the humiliating peace treaty". In the meantime Lenin's response when presented with the treaty document was

> *I don't mean to read it and I don't mean to fulfil it, except in so far as I am forced*

to.[9]

In response the *Kommunist* group argued that

> *the conclusion of the peace has a negative effect on the spiritual and psychological development of the international revolution.*[10]

They pointed to the fact that the German and Austrian ruling classes would now have the grain lands of Ukraine to offer bread to their workers to support imperialism. Further the work of fraternisation and propaganda with the armies of the Central Powers would have to be abandoned.

These "facts" however turned out to be wrong. In the first place the German General Staff needed 1 million men in Ukraine to enforce their robber peace. Hoffman, the German commander in the East was soon complaining to his superiors that these troops were unreliable since they had become infected with the "Bolshevist virus".

And the Ukrainian peasants failed to cough up the grain which the Germans and Austrians had hoped to entrain for Berlin and Vienna. It was after all nearly the end of the winter. As a result Brest-Litovsk did not prevent that increase in starvation of the German and Austrian masses. A quarter of a million died in Germany alone at this time due to the wave of influenza amongst a weakened population. This carried on throughout 1918. By August in Berlin,

> *Food was scarce and expensive – being largely of the Ersatz variety – and the whole appearance of the city and its inhabitants were shabby and desolate. House windows once broken remained unmended, pavements had fallen in, and rubbish and refuse remained uncollected in the streets. People and horses collapsed through lack of nourishment; the very street cars constantly broke down and the passengers dejectedly alighted to the muttered command of the conductor "Alle aussteigen; der Wagen ist krank".*[11]

This economic privation contributed to the revolutions of October and November 1918 in both Austria and Germany and it was this which brought about an end to the war. The Treaty of Brest-Litovsk was therefore only in force for about eight months. This hardly bears out the fears of Bukharin and others that the peace had held up the world revolution. But by then both Bukharin and Radek had recanted in their opposition to the peace.

As for the ending of revolutionary propaganda, it was one of the terms of the Treaty that there should be an exchange of ambassadors. Joffe was sent to Berlin where he was extremely successful in directing literature about the situation in Russia, and the hope for world revolution, to the most advanced sectors of the German working class. His problem was that the Spartakists, the largest revolutionary group, were still only a fraction inside the centrist USPD (Independent Social Democratic Party) and its main leaders Luxemburg and Liebknecht were in prison. It cannot therefore be said that Brest-Litovsk held back the promotion of world revolution. On the contrary it was the failure of the working class in Germany and Western Europe to defeat the more entrenched bourgeoisies of the West that left the world revolution isolated in its Russian outpost.

In September 1918, Rosa Luxemburg was worried that the Bolsheviks' "mistake" in signing the peace would put them under the heel of German militarism. She had some rationale for her view since the Germans had continued to put pressure on the Soviet government since March and on 27th August Joffe had signed a further treaty which gave up Estonia and Livonia, recognised the independence of Georgia, made oil concessions (Russia was to sell Germany 25% of Baku's oil production as a quid pro quo for the return of Baku) and agreed to pay an indemnity of 6 billion marks to Germany. In return Germany was to evacuate White Russia, the area around the Black Sea and give Russia access to the sea in the Baltic Provinces. Russia agreed to resist the British invasion from Murmansk and Germany would come to Russia's aid if it could not do so alone. Although these terms were no better or worse than Brest-Litovsk, it underlined the continuing weakness of soviet power. Luxemburg's concern that the revolution would be lost by default was understandable.

> *If this were to be happen, all the sacrifices until now, including the great sacrifice of Brest-Litovsk, would have been totally in vain, for the price of the sacrifice would ultimately be moral bankruptcy. Any political destruction of the Bolsheviks in a honest struggle against the overwhelming forces and hostile pressures of the historical situation would be preferable to the moral destruction.*

With the benefit of hindsight we can see that these were prescient words. However, the "moral destruction" of the revolution did not come about in the way that Luxemburg posed it. She, in her prison cell, did not know that her immediate fears were groundless as "German militarism" was at the time on the point of collapse. Ludendorff had secretly told the Kaiser over a month earlier that the gamble of outright offensive had failed and that he should seek a way of making peace. The Bolsheviks not only were now in a position to ignore the new treaty (only an instalment of the indemnity was paid) but the Germans also soon retreated from Russian territories. For the rest of her analysis she perhaps gave the fairest assessment of the situation of the revolution in 1918 which is worth quoting at length.

> *The Bolsheviks have certainly made a number of mistakes in their policies and are perhaps still making them – but where is the revolution in which no mistakes have been made! The notion of a revolutionary policy without mistakes, and moreover, in a totally unprecedented situation, is so absurd that it is worthy only of a German schoolmaster. If the so-called leaders of German socialism lose their so-called heads in such an unusual situation as a vote in the Reichstag, and if their hearts sink into their boots and they forget all the socialism they ever learned in situation in which the simple abc of socialism clearly pointed the way – could one expect a party caught up in a truly thorny situation, in which it would show the*

world new wonders, not to make mistakes?

> *The awkward position that the Bolsheviks are in today, however, is, together with most of their mistakes, a consequence of basic insolubility of the problem posed to them by the international, above all the German, proletariat. To carry out the dictatorship of the proletariat and a socialist revolution in a single country surrounded by reactionary imperialist rule and in the fury of the bloodiest world war in human history – that is squaring the circle. Any socialist party would have to fail in this task and perish – whether or not it made self-renunciation the guiding star of its policies.*[12]

If Brest-Litovsk did not appreciably hold back the world revolution it also did not bring about the "peredyschka" or a breathing space that Lenin claimed was needed for the survival of soviet power. Within three months the imperialist war had become a civil war across Russia's vast territory but not the one the Bolsheviks envisaged in 1914. The White armies led by counter-revolutionary generals were soon assisted by 14 Allied armies from Britain, France, the United States and Japan as well as a host of lesser powers. The isolation of the revolution was complete. When the Left SRs split from the Soviet government and began a campaign of assassinations against leading Bolsheviks and German diplomats, the Bolsheviks were left as the only party completely committed to the soviets. As Luxemburg suggested, the Bolsheviks had made many errors before Brest-Litovsk but after March 1918 a new phase in the Russian Revolution opened up. Isolated as it remained, workers' power in Russia was faced with some unpalatable choices which in the end would undermine its proletarian character. It is to this that we will turn in our next chapter.

Chapter 10
Soviet Power and the Bolshevik Party

When in hiding from Kerensky's arrest warrant after the July Days, Lenin wrote to Kamenev that if the capitalists "should do me in" there was a notebook on "Marxism and the State" which he had left in Sweden and which he would have liked published in the event of his death. This notebook (later published separately) was the basis for *The State and Revolution* which Lenin actually completed in hiding that summer (but which was not published until months after the October Revolution). These biographical details undermine the arguments of legions of bourgeois and anarchist historians, starting with the anarchist Volin, who, in their anxiety to condemn Bolshevism as *a priori* anti-working class, maintain that the Bolsheviks only paid lip-service to the idea of workers running society themselves. The fact that Lenin wanted his political testament to be *The State and Revolution* and the fact that he did not actually publish it before October dent the premises of this argument.

The State and Revolution has been called Lenin's flirtation with anarchism but in fact it was an attempt by him to draw together what Marx (and other Marxists from Engels to Pannekoek) had written about the nature of a the state, and to relate this to the extraordinary political consciousness which he had seen awakened in Russia following the February Revolution. It is by no means perfect and leaves many problems of the transition to socialism untouched, but this was not its purpose. This was to re-affirm what the Marxist position on the state was against all those Social Democrats who had leapt to the defence of the imperialist nation-state at the beginning of World War One.

For Lenin the premise was that a Marxist is someone "who extends the recognition of the class struggle to the recognition of the *dictatorship of the proletariat*". This term dictatorship has been repeatedly seized on by the defenders of capitalism to insist that "dictatorship" is what Marxists aim at all the time (and, of course there was Stalin wasn't there?). But the term dictatorship when used by Marx stems from the material fact that this is really what the state is in **any class society**, whatever democratic institutions it clothes itself in. Thus the bourgeoisie today exercises a dictatorship over society by virtue of the parliamentary regime which gives an appearance of openness, but which in fact is easily dominated by those who control the means of production (and hence the means of production of ideas).

In this sense the dictatorship of the proletariat would be no different. It would also be an instrument of class rule but against the bourgeoisie and their allies. The main difference would be that this new dictatorship means a vast extension of democracy *"which, for the first time, becomes democracy for the poor, democracy for the people, and not democracy for the money-bags."[1]*

But since this dictatorship was one of majority over minority the minority would be absorbed or socially wither away so that the State which emerges from the proletarian revolution "begins to wither away immediately". The final establishment of communism, and the disappearance of what Lenin dubbed "the semi-state", were thus synonymous.

Once the October Revolution had taken place the mood of optimism about the speed of advance to "socialism" did not abate, nor did events immediately force Lenin to revise his ideas. All kinds of liberal bourgeois historians and not a few anarchists have sought to portray Lenin's use of the slogan "All Power to the Soviets" as a piece of opportunism to disguise his real aim of a party dictatorship but, as we have demonstrated earlier, there is not a shred of evidence for this assertion in the events from October until just after the signing of the Treaty of Brest-Litovsk in March 1918.

What these critics usually rely on is reference to Lenin's earlier works like *What is to be Done?* where he repeats the Social Democratic mantra of Kautsky that "the working class left to itself can only achieve trade union consciousness". However using this single passage as evidence of Lenin's lack of faith in the working class comes up against several objections. First, after the 1905 revolution Lenin wrote (in 1907) that *What is to be Done?* had been overtaken by events and in the new situation had been superseded.

> *The basic mistake made by those who now criticise What Is to Be Done? is to treat the pamphlet apart from its connection with the concrete historical situation of a definite, and now long past, period in the development of our Party.*

Later in the same document he explains that *What Is To Be Done?* "*is a controversial correction of Economist distortions and it would be wrong to regard the pamphlet in any other light.*"[2]

No further reference to it was made by Lenin. As we shall see, it was only resurrected by Stalin, and his supporters, for entirely different purposes, when Lenin was already ill. Anyone who has actually read the whole pamphlet will also see that in several places Lenin also demonstrates his greater confidence in the working class than he had in those social democrats who claimed to defend it.[3] This did not stop it being identified by a whole raft of Western historians during the Cold War[4] as the key to Bolshevik elitist thinking on working class organisation thus being a handy explanation for their future creation of an authoritarian society.

Furthermore, when Lenin wrote *What is to be Done?* Kautsky was still seen as the "Pope of Marxism". This undeserved reputation was maintained because he (alongside real revolutionaries like Rosa Luxemburg) had led the fight against the "revisionism" of Eduard Bernstein in the last years of the old century. However as we saw in Chapter 2, Kautsky's failure (along with most of German Social Democracy) in August 1914 to condemn German imperialism had turned Lenin's idea of what constituted social democracy on its head. Kautsky now became a "renegade" from revolutionary Marxism and his writings now came under new scrutiny.

The key issue was imperialism. Whilst Kautsky, alongside many other social democrats now opted for pacifism and tried to argue that imperialism was somehow an aberration so that the struggle for socialism would have to wait until after the war, Lenin was having none of it. He began a withering attack on all those who had failed to support the resolutions of the Second International against war at successive Congresses. More than that though, after the betrayal of the Second International, he had to rethink what socialism was, and where the working class now stood in relation to the capitalist system as a whole at that point in time. As Neil Harding[5] has convincingly demonstrated Lenin's whole framework for revolution changed on this issue.

Lenin, the orthodox Social Democrat had thought that the "democratic revolution" was on the agenda in Russia, but the war changed all that. The war revealed that capitalism had changed and so to had the tasks of the working class. He first recognised that something was new under capitalism in *Under a False Flag*.

The first epoch from the Great French Revolution to the Franco-Prussian war is one of the rise of the bourgeoisie, of its triumph, of the bourgeoisie on the upgrade, an epoch of bourgeois-democratic movements in general and of bourgeois-national movements in particular, an epoch of the rapid breakdown of the obsolete feudal-absolutist institutions. The second epoch is that of the full domination and decline of the bourgeoisie, one of transition from its progressive character towards reactionary and even ultra-reactionary finance capital. This is an epoch in which a new class—present-day democracy—is preparing and slowly mustering its forces. The third epoch, which has just set in, places the bourgeoisie in the same "position" as that in which the feudal lords found themselves during the first epoch. This is the epoch of imperialism and imperialist upheavals, as well as of upheavals stemming from the nature of imperialism..[6]

And it was the nature of imperialism that he turned to next. Borrowing factual material from the liberal Hobson, and the Kautskyite Hilferding, he developed a "popular outline" of imperialism which took its Marxist inspiration from *Imperialism and World Economy* written in 1915 by Lenin's younger Bolshevik colleague, Bukharin.

This is not the place to give a resumé of Lenin's *Imperialism – the Highest Stage of Capitalism*. Its significance is that it defined his whole political outlook up to and after the October Revolution. He now concluded that the imperialist war was not an aberration, as Kautsky maintained, but central to the process of capitalist accumulation. From this he concluded that capitalism had entered a new stage. We were now living in the era of "the parasitism and decay of capitalism"[7].

Revolution should not proceed country by country as each one arrived at a full capitalist condition as in the social democratic schema. Now the question was posed internationally because capitalism as a whole, whatever form it took in any single state was now a global system and moreover one in decay, "rotten ripe" for a world proletarian revolution. It was on this premise that the Bolsheviks committed themselves to leading the overthrow of the Provisional Government.

But in doing this they did not see themselves as a new ruling class. From the start there is powerful evidence to show that Lenin and his party had come to believe that the wider Russian working class itself was capable of administering its own affairs. We outlined some of this in Chapter 8 but there was much more. After the revolution Lenin continued to insist that "Living socialism is the work of the popular masses themselves"[8] and, as we saw earlier this is what broadly happened. Over 400 new soviets were set up throughout Russia in the months following the October revolution. Partly this was a consequence of spontaneous activity following the success of the Soviet takeover but there was also a great deal of activity in this direction by local Bolsheviks. They were encouraged everywhere by circulars like that of the People's Commissariat of Internal Affairs of January 5th, 1918 which decreed that "The entire country must be covered with a network of local soviets" which would take over all the administrative functions of the old bureaucracy. Proletarian democracy was beefed up in December when the *Decree on the Right of Recall* was issued which established the proletarian principle that:

> No elective institution or representative assembly can be regarded as truly democratic...unless the electors' right to recall those elected is accepted and exercised. [9]

In other words, Bolshevism at first tried to give the green light for the spread of a working class democracy which was vastly superior to the parliamentary representative model. On 5th November 1917 Lenin appealed to workers to show the same energy now that they were the ruling class as they had done in eliminating the old regime.

> Comrades, workers! Remember that from now on **you yourselves** are administering the State. Nobody is going to help you if you yourselves do not unite and take over **all** State affairs. Rally round your Soviets: make them strong. Get to work there, at the base, without waiting for orders.[10]

This is not an isolated reference. Throughout the whole period before the Seventh Party Congress (held in March 1918), and before the signing of the Treaty of Brest-Litovsk with Germany, Lenin reiterated time and again the message of *The State and Revolution*. To the Congress of the Fleet on Nov. 22, 1917 he said;

> The oppressed masses are confronted with the most difficult task in the whole world; they have to build a state unaided ... The labouring classes have nothing to rely on except themselves. We must have confidence in our own forces ... [11]

Whilst to the Third Congress of Soviets in January 1918 (a few days after the dissolution of the Constituent Assembly) he stated:

> Anarchist ideas now assume living forms in this epoch of the radical demolition of bourgeois society. However it is still necessary, first of all, in order to overthrow

bourgeois society, to establish the strong revolutionary power of the toiling classes, the power of the revolutionary state ... The new tendencies of anarchism are definitely on the side of the Soviets.[12]

This is strikingly similar to passages in *The State and Revolution* where he concludes that the anarchists never understood the real Marxist position on the "withering away of the State" because this had been downplayed by the revisionists of Social Democracy. The latter had abandoned the whole idea that revolution was necessary. Lenin and the Bolsheviks though differed from the anarchists in that the working class would first have to establish at least a "semi-state" until the bourgeoisie was finally defeated. The assumption was that this would be based on the armed soviets who once they had overcome, integrated and rooted out the bourgeoisie on a world scale, would then convert themselves into the means by which the workers would administer society for themselves in building a new way of doing things. Thus the "state" or "semi-state" would wither away.

The "Workers' State"

So much for the theory. What about the actual practice? It should be clear from what we have already demonstrated that the Bolsheviks initially played a positive role in the extension of Soviet rule and until the early summer of 1918 there is little doubt that the same mass activity which had made the Bolsheviks the dominant force in the Soviets continued after October. However, as most Bolsheviks had recognised during the debate over the need to overthrow the Provisional Government in October, the real class struggle would intensify with the establishment of a workers' system of government. We have already seen how this affected the class war on the factory floor in Chapter 8.

There are still two factors which the critics of the October Revolution always point to as evidence that a single party dictatorship was the real aim of Bolshevism. These are the undeniable fact that by the summer of 1918 the Bolsheviks wielded power alone in most soviet bodies, and the dissolution of the Constituent Assembly in January 1918.

Let us take these separately though there is a degree of connection between them. The October Revolution was a decisive watershed in the history of the Russian (and international) working class. Nowhere was this clearer than in the attitudes and policies of the so-called socialist parties like the Socialist Revolutionaries and Mensheviks. Until October they had been able to face two ways. As parties in the Soviet they could claim to represent a working class not yet ready to take power whilst as members of the coalition Provisional Government they were also propping up the bourgeois regime.

The overthrow of the latter forced them to make a choice. Either accept soviet power and take up their opposition within the soviet, or demand the return of the Provisional Government, and the preparation of a parliamentary regime, via the Constituent Assembly. At the Second All-Russian Congress of the Soviets both the Right SRs and the Menshevik majority refused to accept soviet rule despite Bolshevik readiness to accept a Menshevik Internationalist motion calling for a coalition of all the socialist parties represented in the Soviet Congress. The SRs' response (later endorsed by the majority Menshevik faction) was to demand that troops supporting Kerensky be allowed into the capital unhindered and that any government should not include either Trotsky or Lenin! In short a reversal of the October Revolution that had just begun. They then announced they were walking out. This *coup de théâtre* was somewhat undermined by the fact that about a third of their own delegates did not follow them. It was still further undermined when Boris Kamkov got up to announce that the Left SRs supported soviet power and would remain.[13]

With the Right SRs and Mensheviks officially gone, Martov, the leader of the Menshevik Internationalists, had no grounds for keeping on with his compromise proposal. Although he recognised that, "almost the entire proletariat supports the Bolsheviks", he too led his Menshevik-Internationalists out into "the dustbin of history" as Trotsky memorably shouted after them. This did not please about half of the Menshevik Internationalist delegation. One of them, Sukhanov, summed up what they had achieved.

> By quitting the Congress and leaving the Bolsheviks with only the Left SR youngsters and the feeble little Novaya Zhizn group we gave the Bolsheviks with our own hands a monopoly of the soviet, of the masses, and of the revolution[14]

This abandoning of the Soviets to the Bolsheviks only underlined the class divide between these supposedly "socialist" forces. The SRs and Mensheviks both split into several factions. Within days the Right SRs under Gotz and Avksentiev had joined forces with Purishkevich's monarchist supporters in the army in an attempt to carry out a real coup. This insurrection came two days after the Second Soviet Congress opened but:

> found itself surrounded by a mass of poorly organized but determined workers against whom there was little point in struggling in view of the obvious lack of success in other parts of the city. Polkovnikov in the name of the Committee to Save the Fatherland gave the order to surrender, and by late afternoon nothing remained for the Bolsheviks to do except mop up a few pockets of resistance. When Lieutenant Colonel Krakovetski emerged from staff quarters, the impression he received was one of a small island surrounded by a raging sea; and while a professional soldier could only disdain the armed rabble, he no longer could harbor any illusions as to where the sympathy of the populace lay.[15]

It was this mass support that made the Bolsheviks' position so undeniably strong. In theory the SRs should have had millions of peasant supporters but, as the historian of their movement, Radkey makes clear, they were in fact mainly a group of intellectuals in the tradition of the old Populists of the 1870s. They may have been able to count on peasant votes but in the actual struggle these were largely passive supporters, whereas the Bolsheviks' support amongst workers was always a more active one. And where peasants were often active was in the Army where they were much more likely to support the anti-war policies of the Bolsheviks and the Left SRs.

Throughout the civil war after June 1918, the SRs actually at times threw in their support for the Whites with some of their leaders even going over to monarchism. They eventually set up their own anti-soviet government in Siberia (the so-called KOMUCH - which was overthrown by the White Admiral Kolchak) and, in a return to their populist past, carried out terrorist campaigns which claimed the lives of popular Bolsheviks, like Volodarsky and Uritsky (and led to the woundings of Lenin, Bukharin and others).

As for the Mensheviks, their membership declined from around 150,000 in November 1917 to 40,000 by late 1918, and their equivocations and splits only weakened them further. Some entered anti-Bolshevik governments in Samara, Omsk, Ekaterinburg and Baku.[16] Others set up an anti-soviet government in Georgia under Zhordania, and gave support to the Czech Legion which was in arms against the soviet power. But they never actually came out in favour of the Whites in order to retain what minimal working class support they still had. Bukharin catalogued the anti-working class actions of both Mensheviks and SRs, denouncing the hypocrisy of these "heroes of social treason" in an article of the same name in *Kommunist* in April 1918.[17]

Though the Mensheviks were harassed throughout the civil war and their press was closed from time to time by the Cheka, they were not prevented from holding Congresses (to which they invited anti-soviet SR leaders like Chernov). They even returned to the soviets in 1919 and were present at the Eighth Congress of Soviets in 1920 alongside anarchists and some SRs. Unlike bourgeois parties (like the Kadets) Mensheviks and SRs were not declared to be illegal at this time (this would only occur after Kronstadt) but were expelled from the VTsIK. The VTsIK urged other soviet executives to do the same but this did not always happen.

The Left SRs went through a different evolution. Led by younger revolutionaries like the iconic Maria Spiridonova and Boris Kamkov, they had chafed at the support the Right and Centre SRs had given to the Provisional Government. With the October Revolution

> *the vigorous left wing of the (SR) party ... now at last emancipated itself from the fetters of sentiment and ideology and broke away from the parent body, carrying with it much of the party's youth and zeal and-even more seriously – a substantial portion of its peasant following.*[18]

They announced that they accepted soviet rule and voted for all the early Bolshevik decrees in the VTsIK, but at first did not take up the seats offered to them in the Council of People's Commissars (Sovnarkom). They had still hoped that the anti-soviet parties would join a broad "socialist coalition" but the intransigence of their own former comrades made this impossible. However as the Bolshevik *Decree on Land* was close to the policy they had campaigned on for years, and as peasant soviets were put on a nominally equal footing with those of the workers, they took up seven seats in the Sovnarkom in December 1918. They then played an important part in setting up both the Red Army and the Committee for Combatting Counter-Revolution and Sabotage or Cheka, as it was known, with a leading Left SR, Peter Alexandrovich becoming Dzerzhinsky's deputy. We'll deal with the Cheka and what became the "Red Terror" in Chapter 11.

However with the signing of the peace of Brest-Litovsk the Left SRs quit the Sovnarkom over the concessions to German imperialism. They even held talks with the Left Communists inside the Bolshevik Party (who had all resigned their posts too) over a joint campaign to reverse the Treaty. These came to nothing and for a time they continued to hold their places in the Soviet Executive (the VTsIK). However, as full-scale civil war throughout Russia was getting under way, the Left SRs decided to try more direct methods to reverse course. The plan was for Left SR members of the Cheka to assassinate the German Ambassador, Mirbach, in July 1918. This was supposed to reignite the war against Germany. At the same time the Left SRs took up arms against the government in the middle of the Fifth All-Russian Congress of Soviets. Although the assassination was a success, it did not provoke a German response and the confused insurrection was easily suppressed.

The Bolsheviks still did not proscribe the Left SRs. They merely held the actual plotters (who escaped) individually responsible. However by the summer of 1918 the Bolsheviks were the only organised political force left in the soviets. But, as many historians from S.A. Smith to E.H. Carr have pointed out, this was hardly planned, rather it stemmed from the fact that by mid-1918 "no opposition party was prepared to remain within legal limits" of a soviet democracy.[19]

Prior to the October Revolution, the precise role of the Bolshevik Party (or "Russian Communist Party [Bolshevik]" which it became in March 1918) after the overthrow of the old order had hardly, if ever, been discussed. True, in reply to the statement by Tsereteli, the Menshevik leader, in June 1917 that no party in Russia was ready to take power, Lenin had rhetorically retorted from his seat "there is" but he then followed it up by calling in his own speech for "All Power to the Soviet" in which the Bolsheviks were still at the time a tiny minority.[20] In *The State and Revolution* reference to the party is noticeable by its absence, but the increasing isolation of the Bolsheviks in the soviets in 1918 threw the party-soviet question into sharp relief. As we have already seen the Bolsheviks initially did not see the building of socialism as the task of the party, but as one for the class as a whole. Indeed the evidence is that many (like Preobrazhensky, see Chapter 8) now thought the party had no further role to play. In Petersburg, Mary McAuley quotes one Bolshevik memoirist, Shelavin

> ... the best party people were throwing themselves into the surge of construction ... when the Vasilievsky island district soviet moved from the 16th line to a new building on Middle Prospect, the party committee got shoved up to the fifth floor on the grounds that it did not have any particular work to do.[21]

Ilyin-Zhenevsky claimed that "*Many Party members even formed the view that Party work was somehow second-class work*".[22]

But there were also many party members (especially amongst those who supported the Left Communists) who still thought that their tasks of propaganda, agitation and education were not over. They deplored the fact that so many Party members put their work for the soviets first so that a bureaucracy was developing. It was not even an efficient one as there was administrative chaos in attempts to deal with the declining food supply, the collapse of industry, and the growth of corruption. As the economic situation worsened McAuley records *"The party organization was fading, as an organization..."*.

As evidence she points to the Northern Region Conference in early April 1918 where

> *Zinoviev agreed that all the party forces had gone to work in the new state institutions (the state had swallowed up the old party, as he put it) but he refused to accept that the destruction of the old party had been as complete, and the degeneration of the soviet apparatus had been as serious as the Left Communists claimed.*[23]

In fact the real problem was that, as workers abandoned the cities in search of food, the Bolsheviks lacked enough people to maintain a separation between party and soviet work. Though the debate went on inside the party as to the relative importance of each institution right through the civil war, in the final analysis the two were increasingly forced to merge. As McAuley concludes

> *... faced with fewer and fewer people, a strategy of merging the party and soviet leadership was a rational one. It was though simultaneously one that kept the Soviet, not the party, in command.*[24]

Since it was the same personnel some might think the distinction is perhaps academic. However the historical record shows that the one party system came about first through the development of the material circumstances of the civil war period. It was not planned, but by the end of 1920, with the civil war won, the party was now officially promoted as the body which carried out what the working class as a whole wasn't capable of doing. This was a return to the social democratic idea (also held by Rosa Luxemburg and most German Social Democrats) that the political minority, the party, wasn't just a minority of the most class conscious but was a mass party which did not just represent the class but **was** the class.

However this is to anticipate. In 1917-18 the Russian proletariat and the Bolshevik Party were breaking new ground. There was no model to follow as to how to organise a new society. As the isolation of the revolution to Russia continued immediate problems had to be faced and practical solutions found. No-one knew what would happen to a party, built on the dedicated commitment of its predominantly working class membership, when that party (in the soviets) increasingly became the main organiser of just about everything. The first was that careerists entered its ranks looking for a marginally easier life in the midst of an appalling economic crisis. The second is that the old tolerance of factions, arguments and debates that characterised the life of a rising revolutionary party now came under strain.

This was seen in the treatment of the Left Communists in their opposition, first to the signing of the Treaty of Brest-Litovsk, and second in what they considered to be the anti-working class drift of administrative policy such as the introduction of one-man management as a "cure" for industrial chaos.

The Left Communists of 1918 have often been criticised both for their short existence and the feebleness of their fight. Their journal, *Kommunist* started off as a party-sponsored paper in March (eleven issues) but ended as a private initiative which produced only four issues. Their protest at the course the revolution was taking, despite attracting the support of many workers, largely failed because the Bolsheviks had gone from being a revolutionary party in opposition, to being responsible for day to day policy on the eve of a civil war, in which everything was sharply reduced to a question of choosing sides. Debate was no longer just about some aspect of revolutionary theory of a party in opposition, but about life and death decisions pertaining to the survival of the revolution until the world revolution should come and transform the situation. It was a factor which would undermine, first the democratic basis of the soviets, and then the class character of the party, as the civil war unfolded.

The Left Communists, who may even had represented a majority view in the party for a brief time in March 1918, were thus subjected to the most relentless political pressure by the other Party bodies and members. Most of their supporters ended their opposition before the summer of 1918 was out. Indeed, some like Bukharin and Radek would soon abandon their left communist stance in defence of proletarian self-activity and, under the pressure of the events of the second half of 1918, move to the right of the party. Some like the Democratic Centralists (or Dekists) would continue their fight to try to restore the proletarian heart of the revolution well beyond the end of the civil war but had little hearing in the Party, and even less in the class. The fact was that though, from the point of preserving the proletarian essence of the revolution, they were often right, the objective circumstances of isolation, civil war and economic collapse reduced their critique to irrelevance. Only revolution outside Russia could have revived their campaign. However this was also the view of nearly all the leading Bolsheviks. Everyone knew that without world revolution the Russian experience was doomed but, whilst waiting, they were faced with the question of how best the revolution could survive in Russia in the meantime.

The Constituent Assembly

The other great confrontation between proletarian and bourgeois democracy took place over the Constituent Assembly which was elected in December 1917 (only 3 weeks or so after soviet power was established) and scheduled to meet in January 1918. Throughout 1917 the bourgeoisie had continually postponed the calling of the Assembly to decide on Russia's future constitution. Successive ministries were hoping for a more favourable moment to call the election (such as a victory at the front) but for them matters simply got worse. Kerensky finally fixed the election for the end of November and the Bolsheviks, who had continually campaigned for the Constituent Assembly, did not hesitate to honour this once they were in power. The elections took place on the basis of electoral lists drawn up the previous June. They did not reflect the growth of the Bolsheviks' popularity since then, and certainly did not give any time for putting the new situation to the voters. In many places in that vast territory many who went to the polls had not even heard of the October Revolution.

To some revolutionaries today it has remained a mystery as to why, with soviet power achieved, the Bolsheviks went through with an exercise which seemed loaded against them. Why did they not postpone the vote for just a few weeks when it would have been a verdict on soviet power? If they had postponed it yet again it would also have given their allies, the Left Socialist Revolutionaries, time to clarify their split with the Right SRs to the peasantry which might have then given their combined forces a majority in the Russian people, and would have silenced all the Western propaganda since then about the lack of legitimacy of a regime based only on soviets. It would also have allowed the question of soviet power to be properly debated first.

Answering this puzzle in 1920 Lenin justified going through with the elections because, he said, it would demonstrate to the working class that the SRs and the Mensheviks were against soviet power. This is not very convincing. As the account we have given so far shows the working class already knew where they stood. It was the vast majority of peasants who still needed time to grasp what was happening. More likely the election went ahead because the Bolshevik right, led by Kamenev and Riazanov, who still sought a coalition with "other socialists", demanded that the Bolsheviks stick to their promise to hold the election. It was really the Bolshevik Right rather than the working class that needed to see exactly what the Mensheviks and SRs stood for.

The results were predictable. Whilst the Bolsheviks won 175 to the Mensheviks' 16 seats in the towns, in the countryside the peasant vote went to the SRs who obtained 410 (only about a tenth being allocated to the Left SRs by the Rightist leadership despite being supported by about half the peasantry) of the 707 seats. If the Constituent Assembly had been allowed to determine the future of Russia it is clear that it would have done so on behalf of the bourgeoisie and petit bourgeoisie against the working class.

Now the Bolsheviks worked to delay its opening whilst the Right SRs endeavoured to arm workers, win over some of the best regiments left from the old army and tried to bring soldiers back from the front to counter the overwhelming support the Bolsheviks had within the Petersburg garrison. When all these efforts came to nothing, they plotted to kidnap the entire Sovnarkom, and did actually make an attempt on Lenin's life. Lenin was saved by the Swiss socialist, Fritz Platten who, riding in the car with him, pulled him down, the bullet striking his hand.[25]

In the event the Right SR majority in the Constituent Assembly, in their total disregard for the depth of support for soviet power in the working class, cut its own throat by refusing to accept the Bolshevik and Left SR motion which concluded;

> *Supporting the soviet power and the decrees of the Council of People's Commissars, the Constituent Assembly recognises that its tasks are confined to the general working out of the fundamental principles of the socialist reconstruction of society*

The Bolsheviks and Left SRs left the Assembly in the early hours of the morning, but the SR majority, with the small rump of Mensheviks tried to then carry on as if soviet power did not exist. After twelve hours of unreal discussion, which included an endless speech by Chernov on a land reform the SRs has refused to sanction when in the Provisional Government (and which had already been carried out by the Bolsheviks since), the Constituent Assembly was finally closed down at 4.00 a.m., when the anarchist sailor Zheleznyakov told Chernov that they had to stop now because "the guard was tired". The Constituent Assembly was not allowed to resume its meanderings the next day. Although there was a demonstration in support of the Assembly it was easily dispersed by troops. Its dissolution caused hardly a ripple of protest, and a few days later the VTsIK (the Soviet Executive) prorogued it for good. For this, as one Right SR stated at the time "The Constituent Assembly was blamed more than the Bolsheviks who dispersed it." As Carr commented

> *It was one more demonstration of the lack of any solid basis, or any broad popular support, in Russia for the institutions and principles of bourgeois democracy.[26]*

Six days later the Third All-Russian Congress of Soviets accepted that

> *Russia is hereby proclaimed a Republic of Soviets of Workers', Soldiers' and Peasant Deputies. All power, centrally and locally, is vested in these Soviets.[27]*

Soviet power, which had been waiting to be recognised as the real government of Russia since February, was now formally established.

Of course not all was perfect with this workers' democracy – it would have been astonishing if it had been the case. For example, the creation of Sovnarkom, the Council of People's Commissars, owed rather too much to the bourgeois idea of parliamentary government in which the executive power is separated from the legislative. In fact it was yet another "provisional" government (Russia's fourth in 8 months) which was supposed to dissolve once the Constituent Assembly met. Given the refusal of the latter to endorse soviets, Sovnarkom just carried on. It would have been more in the spirit of soviet power if the VTsIK (the Soviet Executive) had acted directly as the executive of the state but in the conditions of late 1917, and early 1918, Sovnarkom acted more as a response to the masses (e.g. in its nationalisation decrees) than as a government in the bourgeois sense. Indeed, given the fact that it had, at this time, no bureaucracy (the Commissar for Agriculture did not even have a desk when he took office!), the Sovnarkom really only acted as a beacon for the revolution. Its decrees could not be carried out unless the masses organised in soviets all over Russia enacted them. The problems though of an executive from a single party (after June 1918), and not directly responsible to the mass organs of the working class would come back to haunt the revolution as it continued to be isolated.

The honeymoon period of a revolution founded on mass action came to an end in the late spring of 1918. At the Third Soviet Congress in January, VTsIK was instructed to prepare a new soviet constitution for the next Congress which was fixed for March 1918. However by that time the debate over the signing of the Brest-Litovsk treaty with Germany overshadowed everything. This, as we have seen, led to the break-up of the alliance of the Bolsheviks with the Left SRs and to the military intervention of the British, French, Japanese, US and ten other states in Russia. They gave support to various ex-tsarist generals some of whom the Bolsheviks had released in October 1917 on the promise that they would not fight soviet power. From April 1918 to the end of 1920 this imperialist intervention helped to sustain a devastating civil war which, alongside the economic crisis, was to have the deepest consequences for the future of soviet power.

Everything now took second place to the fight against the Whites and their allies, both amongst the other "socialist" parties, and international imperialism. There was little time for the luxury of social experiment, though surprisingly many of these continued despite the economic and military pressures. Instead the revolution began to build the very institutions of state power that it had intended to dismantle. In some ways this was unavoidable in a war. Even long-established bourgeois states suspend freedom of the press, elections and persecute any opposition to the war effort. Even the anti-statist Makhno in his corner of Ukraine, despite enjoying tremendous support amongst the peasantry, was forced to adopt a degree of revolutionary terror to defend the basis of his power.[28] What chance did a young proletarian power have in a relatively backward economy of working out what were the best institutional forms for working class emancipation in these circumstances?

So, instead of a workers' militia the Red Army was formed and the Cheka rose to become a semi-independent power in its own right as it pursued a Red Terror not only against the White Terror but even in the end within the working class itself. At the same time soviet power gradually began to decline. There were fewer new elections, and some of those were annulled or ignored. And in order to feed the starving workers forcible requisitioning was employed against the peasantry leading to what amounted to a class war in the countryside. A new state bureaucracy (aided partly by the members of the old bureaucracy) began to replace local soviet initiative just as one management became the dominant feature of the new economic life. These developments did not immediately kill the revolution, but the chapters which follow are devoted to an examination of how each of these phenomena taken together ultimately ripped the proletarian heart out of the revolution.

Chapter 11
Red Army and Civil War in the International Context

The Railway War or "First Civil War"

When Kerensky fled Petersburg on 7 November, he sought out General Krasnov who agreed to march a force of between 700 and 1,000 Cossacks on the city. At the same time a "Junker mutiny" of officer cadets, linked to the Right SRs, was planned, but the Military Revolutionary Committee knew of it, and it was crushed on 11 November (see Chapter 10). The next day a "ragtag of workers, soldiers and sailors"[1] came up against Krasnov's Cossacks who they outnumbered 10 to 1, at Pulkovo Heights. Although shots were fired, victory, as would happen so often in this first stage of the civil war, was won politically. Propaganda teams quickly persuaded the Cossacks that it was pointless to lose their lives to keep their officers in control. They handed Krasnov over to the soviet troops. By this time Kerensky had escaped, disguised as a sailor. Krasnov was soon released on signing a pledge not to attack soviet power, a promise he immediately broke (see Chapter 10).

The immediate internal military threat was not over, although it now came from further away. Cossacks (*Ka zak* is Turkic for "free man") in Ukraine, Don, Kuban and elsewhere had long had their own semi-independent institutions but generally policed the borders of the Russian Empire against Ottoman and Polish forces. Although occasional Cossack revolts (e.g. like that of Pugachev) had led to the disbandment of their "hosts" or communities they were usually later amnestied and remained an arm of the Tsarist state. In the Russian imperial expansion of the eighteenth and nineteenth centuries they fought in the Russian army. By the end of the nineteenth century they were mainly used as an internal police force putting down peasant risings and intimidating strikers. They should have been the backbone of resistance to soviet power.

In 1917 the thirteen various Cossack "hosts" stretching across the south of Russia from Ukraine to beyond the Urals numbered 4.5 million people, of which 300,000 men (*frontoviki*) had fought in the First World War[2]. This huge semi-autonomous region became a magnet for many reactionaries and liberals, appalled by the workers' take over of the towns and cities. There were initially two main threats. The first was from Ataman Dutov, elected leader of the Orenburg Host, who overthrew the soviet in Orenburg and began to widen the area under his control. The second and greater threat came from Kaledin, Ataman of the Don Cossacks. His call for the suppression of the soviets in August 1917 had made him the darling of the reactionaries. In November he was joined by Kornilov who "escaped" from the monastery at Bykhov, where Kerensky had so comfortably lodged him after his capture in August.

Both were dealt with in the same way, with the soviet power sending *eshelons* (trains) of revolutionary soldiers a thousand or more miles to take on their opponents. Dutov soon found that most of the younger Cossacks, the *frontoviki* were sick of war, and opted to stay neutral whilst many non-cossacks (*inogorodnie* or "outsiders") who had to rent land from the Cossacks, actually welcomed the October Revolution. Orenburg was retaken by Bolshevik forces on 31 January/13 February and the Host was driven into the Kirghiz steppes.

A bigger Red force under Antonov-Ovseyenko, the then Commissar for War, was sent south to deal with Kaledin in the Don. Kaledin faced similar problems to Dutov in that many of the *frontoviki* did not want to fight, and some even supported the revolution. He could only muster relatively small numbers of troops to take on much larger forces coming by *eshelon*. These trains emanating from the north gave the soviet troops a great advantage throughout the civil war since the railway network was based around the major cities they controlled. However they had other problems, as Evan Mawdsley explains

> *The Red Army did not formally exist ... and as the fighting went back and forth between key junctions there were frequent pauses for negotiations. Key decisions were made at mass meetings – continuing the 1917 tradition of **mitingovanie**. Some mutinous detachments had to be disbanded. Others were diverted to cope with a "war" in Ukraine.*[3]

Despite this supposed military inefficiency of having *mitingovanie*[4] (open mass meetings) to decide on military policy, the Reds still won. The critical factor in victory was, at it had been against Kornilov in August and against Krasnov in November, political. The appeals of the soviets led to the defection of *frontoviki* Cossacks who refused to support Kaledin, and set up a Don Military-Revolutionary Committee under a Left SR, Podtelkov. Kaledin, appalled at what he considered this betrayal of the Cossack tradition, resigned as Ataman and shot himself. A fortnight later, Rostov and the Cossack capital, Novocherkassk, were both taken by Antonov's troops and a Don Soviet republic was set up in March, to be quickly followed by another in the Kuban.

With Kaledin dead, the leadership of the counter-revolution in the Don region passed to the former Tsarist Generals Alexeev, Kornilov and Denikin. Kornilov had joined the other two in the Don where they had formed what was later known as the Volunteer Army. This was only 4,000 strong when the soviet troops arrived at Rostov so Kornilov marched his troops out into the steppe to undertake an epic "Ice March" which lasted seven weeks. Eventually they arrived in the Kuban and attacked its capital Ekaterinodar on 10 April, but were surprised by the strength of Soviet resistance. After three days of siege, Kornilov was killed when Soviet artillery hit the farmhouse where he had his headquarters. Denikin now took over the military command but he and Alexeev (who soon died of cancer) were forced to retreat back into the steppe.

At this point most Bolsheviks, from Lenin to the Left Communists, thought the civil war was all but over. Lenin admitted that there would still be skirmishes but "on the internal front reaction has been smashed"[5]. In the first edition of *Kommunist*, organ of the Left Communists, Ossinsky also stated that the civil war was over:

> *The intense period in which the military forces of the bourgeoisie (White Guards, Kaledin's forces, etc.) have been crushed is over; as is the sabotage by the bourgeoisie, and by the intelligentsia.*[6]

This was one of the Left Communist rationales for criticising the direction the revolution was now taking. For them there was no need for the soviet power to bring in bourgeois specialists or to make a priority of raising production. Instead it could concentrate on allowing the mass of the class the space to learn to develop the socialist character of society, whatever setbacks or disorganisation that entailed. As a clear conception of what socialism was all about it was unassailable and, as we saw in Chapter 8, Lenin himself had supported the Left Communist position until March 1918.

However, in his reply to the Left Communists, Lenin makes it clear that the dire economic situation, and the need to defend the soviet republic from all kinds of enemies whilst awaiting for an international revolution, had altered his perceptions. In the columns of *Pravda* he derided the *Kommunist* writers as "naïve" "*szlachcic*" (i.e. like romantic Polish noblemen – we would call them "quixotic") and "petty bourgeois", not just for their opposition to the signing of the Treaty of Brest-Litovsk, but also for their critique that Russia was headed for state capitalism not socialism.

Although the definition of state capitalism at this time was different from its later use, the key statement by Lenin was that, "state capitalism would be a step forward" for the Soviet Republic. There was no previous working class experience at this point to contradict him but, as it turned out, the concept opened the way to state building rather than anything else. Certainly no-one at the time considered that state capitalism would actually to turn out to become a barrier to genuine working class revolution however, and wherever, it developed around the world in the epoch of imperialism. At the same time all the earlier references to the fact that socialism could only be built by the mass of the class "learning to do it for itself" disappeared from his speeches and instead "iron discipline" and "control" were repeatedly cited as the main need of the hour.

Furthermore

> *This control must be established not only over "the insignificant capitalist minority, over the gentry who wish to preserve their capitalist habits" but also over the workers "who have been thoroughly corrupted by capitalism".*[7]

The quotation marks are Lenin quoting himself from *The State and Revolution* which had been praised by Bukharin in *Kommunist No. 1* for its revolutionary understanding of the need to smash the state. Bukharin's positive review was no innocent commentary. He was reminding Lenin of his previous "libertarian" views which he was now abandoning. It obviously stung Lenin, but precisely why, Lenin (for once) did not make clear to the casual reader. Instead he quoted various passages from *The State and Revolution* in an attempt to show that he had not changed his mind since the summer of 1917. But he quotes himself out of context here. In *The State and Revolution* his remarks about "corrupted" workers were clearly aimed at only a minority of the class. Lenin was now expressing the general idea that, on its own, the Russian working class was, as a whole, not sufficiently culturally developed to create the basis for socialism.

This had been, and still was, one of the key Menshevik arguments against soviet power. Mensheviks intellectuals often expressed fear of the working class and the Russian masses in general. They often accused the Bolsheviks of playing a dangerous game by putting their trust in the *stikhiia* of these "dark forces" (i.e. the revolutionary working class) or in inciting them to revolt.

Lenin, of course, would not have conceded this for a moment. His constant consolation was that, despite all the setbacks and retreats, the working class were still in control via the soviets and that was the key to anything else that happens. However, as we shall see in the next chapter, from this point (the late spring of 1918) on, the soviets were gradually ceasing to be real representative organs of the class. What emerged in the civil war against the Whites and the forces of imperialism was instead a militarised state, dominated by a single party. The formation of the Red Army was, alongside the creation of the Cheka, one of the primary instruments in that transformation.

The Origins of the Red Army

The apparent victory over the Whites in early 1918 was short-lived and a new, greater military threat appeared in the form of the Czech Legion. These were former Austro-Hungarian prisoners of war who had been formed into an army of 38,000 well-armed troops by Tsarism. They were intended for use against the Austro-Hungarian Empire from whom the Czechs were demanding independence. By the summer of 1918 they were supported by the Entente powers, and had already had several run-ins with Red Guard units along the Trans-Siberian Railway. They wanted to use the line to exit Russia via Vladivostok so that they could return via the West to carve out a Czechoslovak state from the collapsing Habsburg Empire.

Trotsky, who replaced Antonov-Ovseyenko as Commissar for War after Brest-Litovsk, gave the erroneous and impossible order on 14 May for the Czechs to be disarmed (he clearly had no idea what kind of military force they wielded) and the result was that the Czechs revolted and seized various trains spread over more than a thousand miles of the Trans-Siberian Railway. So instead of the Czechs exiting Russia quietly they now occupied a large stretch of the Urals, cutting off the route to Siberia and straddled the Volga, Russia's most important river artery. They received political support from the Mensheviks and Right SRs who had set up a government covering the Volga and Urals. The Czechs now gave the SRs the military force their *Komuch* (Committee for the Members of the Constituent Assembly) government had hitherto lacked.

Red Army and Civil War in the International Context

August also saw the main invasion by imperialist forces as well as a renewed White offensive in the south. By 2 August British troops had also reached Archangel, and were giving material support to General Miller's regime in the north. On 4th August British troops landed at Baku. 12,000 Japanese troops had landed at Vladivostok, soon to be followed by 50,000 more. A US force under General Graves also landed there. The Germans were dislodging soviet rule in Ukraine and the Don and Kuban Hosts under Denikin now took advantage to retake these Cossack lands. In all, some fourteen different states would invade the territory of the old Russian Empire in the next 3 years and the British and French would send in addition large military supplies (although it often arrived too late to assist the White forces it was intended for). By 1919 there were close to a quarter of a million foreign troops in Russia, the majority in Siberia.

These new threats posed the issue of whether the soviets could fight armies which had the material backing of international imperialism with no army of their own. It was a fact that the Bolshevik victory in October precipitated

> *one of the most rapid and least controlled military demobilisations in history.*[8]

The order for demobilising the old Tsarist army was eventually given on 2 March 1918, but this was only a formal recognition of what had already happened. The army had been dwindling for months. In a sense this was part of the victory of the workers, for the army had traditionally been one of the main sources of repression of the Tsarist state. But now that the soviet power, despite all its propaganda for peace, faced invasion from so many directions how was it supposed to organise a response?

In the *State and Revolution* Lenin contrasts the state of the exploiters with that of the exploited which will "no longer [be] a state in the proper sense of the word". Instead of "special bodies of armed men" or a "special machine",

> *... the people can suppress the exploiters with a very simple "machine", almost without a "machine", without a special apparatus by the simple organisation of the armed people (such as the Soviets of Workers and Soldiers Deputies) ...*[9]

In short, a proletarian army should be made up of proletarian militias subject to the control and recall of the soviets. Local militias of workers and peasants did exist in the period after October and played an important political role in mobilising support for the overthrow of the Provisional Government. They embodied the same spirit of popular participation which characterised the rest of Russian working class society at this time. They still had soldiers' committees which frequently debated whether this or that course of action should be followed (with the officers waiting for a decision) no matter what the military situation (see the comment on *mitingovanie* at the beginning of this chapter). All commentators agree that they were too ill-disciplined to pose a serious alternative to the increasingly well-armed White armies backed by Allied imperialism. Most of these commentators are, of course, military historians not sympathetic to the revolution, or the new proletarian way of doing things, so we might dismiss them as being irrelevant to the discussion. However there were also contemporary criticisms from inside the revolution. Former anarchist, Victor Serge, describes how the professional soldiers of the Czech Legion who supported the Whites:

found themselves faced in battle only by improvised, undisciplined and anarchical units, good at most for a guerrilla war against an adversary exposed to the hatred of the masses. One corps of 1,105 bayonets, for instance, which held the front near ... Chelyabinsk, was made up of thirteen local detachments, the smallest of which contained nine men and the largest, from Perm, 570... Each detachment had its own leaders and tried to act as it liked. The basis of their organisation was the local factory. These bands sometimes fought very well, and sometimes very badly; they knew almost nothing of the art of reconnaissance, of the main forms of defence, of the most elementary precautions to be taken in a march across country. They might abandon a position to carry on a leisurely debate... These partisans were beaten with ease by the Czechoslovaks.[10]

Even the supposedly more class conscious and better trained Red Guards were not much to shout about. An American, William Brown wrote:

Many of them were mere boys. The idea that these men were to wield power in Russia for a long time to come had not even occurred to us.[11]

Some of this seems like caricature, and does not preclude the possibility that these volunteer Red Guards would not have learned in rapid order, but in the emergency situation of 1918, the solution was to build up the Red Army. The Red Army had already been decreed as existing in January 1918 although did not really take shape for another year. In this decree it was clearly recognised that a proletarian army could not be the same as a bourgeois army. The Decree of Sovnarkom (the Council of People's Commissars) stated:

The old army was an instrument of class oppression of the working people by the bourgeoisie. With the transition of power to the working and exploited classes there has arisen a need for a new army as the mainstay of the soviet power at present and the basis for replacing the regular army by the arming of the whole people in the near future, and as a support for the coming socialist revolution in Europe. The Workers' and Peasants' Red Army is built up from the most conscious and organised elements of the working people.[12]

All very good we might think. The aim appears to be a class conscious population voluntarily under arms – a basic prerequisite of a state which will ultimately wither away is that it has no monopoly of arms because the entire population is under arms. However in the material situation of Russia in 1918, where the working class made up less than ten percent of the population, this posed many difficulties. The idea that a volunteer army of class conscious workers would be sufficient to defeat what were believed to be well-equipped bourgeois armies foundered on the simple lack of volunteers. As for the class conscious element the numerical weakness of the Russian working class (as against the peasantry) hindered this too. In fact the needs of war forced Trotsky, as head of the People's Commissariat for War, to go back to traditional bourgeois conceptions (like conscription) and even to the organisational machinery and personnel of Tsarism.

The Organisation of the Red Army

The People's Commissariat for War was actually just the old Tsarist Ministry of War with the most reactionary elements purged from it. Trotsky himself spoke of

> ...unifying and organising the huge military apparatus inherited from the past, which though disorganised and disordered, is mighty owing to the quantities of values it includes, and adapting this to the army we now wish to form.[13]

The problem with this was that it meant also introducing the kind of formal discipline and organisation that had characterised the Tsar's army before February 1917 (minus the brutality and degradation used then). Saluting officers, special forms of address for superiors, separate living and eating facilities for officers, the death penalty for desertion or disobedience under fire, and the use of specialists, including ex-tsarist generals all dictated that the Red Army was hardly the epitome of proletarian principles. No wonder some Bolsheviks like Uritsky (assassinated on 17 August, 1918 – see next chapter) grumbled that:

> Confirmed counter-revolutionaries are running things in the army again, not elected persons.[14]

But what alternative did the isolated Russian soviet republic have? Some have argued that it would have been possible to build an army on the basis of the 'partisan' units which flourished behind German and White lines. However, as the earlier quotation from Victor Serge showed, their actions were not always co-ordinated and were geographically restricted. Trotsky did not discount their contribution which was sometimes crucial (e.g. against Kolchak in Siberia and the Germans in Ukraine) but 'partisanism' became a synonym for 'disorganised and chaotic'. Trotsky concluded that whilst the partisans were valuable:

> Nevertheless, we must formulate the incontrovertible rule: the revolutionary power works to incorporate the best partisan detachments and their most reliable elements into the system of regular military organisation. Otherwise these partisan detachments could undoubtedly become factors of disorder, capable of degenerating into armed bands in the service of petty bourgeois anarchistic elements for use against the proletarian state.[15]

The "petty bourgeois anarchistic elements" Trotsky obviously had particularly in mind were those in Makhno's relatively successful peasant army in Ukraine but we will come to them later. Faced with armies on a series of widely scattered fronts the conclusion was that the Soviet area needed a more centralised force if it was not to be overrun by the imperialists and the Whites. Given what Trotsky repeatedly referred to as "the lack of culture among the broad masses" it is not surprising that the centralised Red Army staffed by "experts" under the control of political commissars was seen as the only possible solution.

However today we must be clear that the formation of the Red Army, whilst an incredible organisational achievement, was the product of necessity and not choice. It was not a glorious step on the road to building socialism. The original idea, that only those who proved their class awareness of the socialist programme could join it, quickly collapsed. By the spring of 1918 volunteers of any kind were being called for and this was quickly followed by the April decree which brought in compulsory military training and conscription for all males between 18 and 40. This meant that the Red Army did not really take effective shape until 1919. Until then it was a mixture of partisans, *ad hoc* measures and local forces. In this form the Red Army survived on through the autumn of 1918, when the soviet area was under renewed pressure.

Trotsky faced a great deal of opposition to his use of former Tsarist officers (even if under the supervision of political commissars), and conventional discipline in the organisation of the Red Army, from inside the Bolshevik Party. These came to a head at the Eighth Party Congress in March 1919 in the shape of the Military Opposition headed by Vladimir Smirnov, a leading member of the newly-formed Democratic Centralist group (of which more later). Smirnov conceded the need for employing military specialists (other Bolsheviks were against this) but criticised the privileges for officers and the aping of the military regulations of a capitalist army. What he complained most about was the loss of workers' initiative through such conventional military practices.

> *Regulations are necessary but need to be made in correspondence with the experience which has been acquired, rejecting everything that has been evoked by the specific conditions of the pre-revolutionary period.[16]*

Despite such opposition Trotsky's policies were endorsed by 174 votes to 95 though the arguments of the opposition were conceded in the final resolution of the Congress.

> *The militia ideal of an army without barracks was affirmed for the future, and even the principle of electing officers was accepted as a desideratum when the maturity and stability of the army should permit it.[17]*

The idea of returning to a "socialist" militia system was again revived in the winter of 1919-20[18], but the need to finish off Denikin's offensive in the south followed by the Polish War of 1920, then Wrangel's last battles in the Crimea, again consigned these aspirations to the back burner. They were never to be revived. The one constant was the continual growth of the Red Army along the lines of a traditional army set down by Trotsky from the start. By the end of 1920 it had grown to an enormous 5.3 million soldiers, few of whom were proletarian and even fewer were communists.

Red Army and Civil War in the International Context

The Significance of Building the Red Army

Few historians doubt that in the end this numerical preponderance of the Red Army was critical to winning the civil war against the Whites (whose combined forces may have approached 2 million by spring 1920)[19]. The Reds had other advantages. Not least was geography. They were defending a unified territory whilst the Whites were spread along four different fronts from Siberia to Ukraine and the Arctic Circle. Additionally they had a unified command structure. Despite the occasional squabble (Stalin v Trotsky at Tsaritsyn, for example), or the debates inside the Red command, the political cohesion and coordination of the Communists was vastly superior to that between the rival White commanders.

However it was not just military logistics that enabled "Sovdepia" (as the Whites derisively called the area of soviet power) to emerge victorious but also wider political considerations. On the White side the early hopes of those Mensheviks and SRs who supported parliamentary democracy against soviet power (as in the Komuch in Siberia) were crushed by autumn 1918, and some of the SRs from the latter then threw in their lot with the reactionary Admiral Kolchak, whilst those who opposed him were either killed or gaoled. The White leaders generally kept quiet about whether they wanted a monarchical resurrection or not, but they made no bones about wanting to restore the old Russian Empire under some form of authoritarian regime. To the national minorities who had regarded that Empire as a prison house, Lenin's offer of national self-determination was a significant factor in winning their support, or at least their neutrality[20].

Additionally, the peasants, whilst carrying out a civil war within the civil war over the food requisitioning detachments sent to find grain, had at least been guaranteed that the land was theirs by the *Soviet Land Decree* of November 1917. This made the Bolsheviks more acceptable than the Whites despite the peasantry's visceral hatred of requisitioning. Some even used the slogan "Long live the Bolsheviks, Down with the Communists" which more or less summed this up, since the Bolsheviks had issued the land decree, but had changed their name by the time that requisitioning was really underway. Even more hated though, were the Whites who not only reversed the land reform, but on frequent occasions also hanged anyone involved in the land seizures.

Both regimes, like all wartime regimes, became increasingly authoritarian and brutal. The Whites though were increasingly unpopular for their racist brutality which was directed at "zhids and communists" (who were the same for them and their propaganda played on the fact that Trotsky and other leading Bolsheviks had Jewish backgrounds). It was not just confined to propaganda. In Ukraine especially they were accomplices in pogroms of 115,000 Jews in a dire echo of the policies of Tsarism. In the end White brutality was to cost it the support of its most efficient fighting force. In November 1919 the atrocities of the Kolchak regime, in which they had been forced to participate, led the Czechs to send the following to their Entente mentors;

Under the protection of Czecho-Slovak bayonets local Russian military organs commit acts which horrify the whole civilised world. The burning of villages, the beating up of peaceful Russian citizens by whole military detachments, the shooting without trial of the representatives of democracy on the simple suspicion of political unreliability, are a daily phenomenon.[21]

However we don't judge Communists by the same yardstick as we judge the agents of capitalism and reaction. We expect that Communists, even though they cannot materially move to socialism to at least lay the groundwork by encouraging the self-activity of the working class. But in fact the opposite was happening in Russia. Organs like the Cheka and Red Army, although nominally emergency bodies, were the backbone of a new state, and not one that was capable of "withering away" either.

The Red Army may have saved the regime but at what price for a workers' revolution? Amongst the Communist leaders (and not just the leaders) everyone knew that "special bodies of armed men" were the salient characteristic of all states throughout history. For the working class to be prepared to be in a position to do away with the state there had to be no monopoly of armed power by any section of the population. Instead of standing ready to dissolve the state when the bourgeoisie was overcome, the Bolsheviks had arrived at a situation where a new state was being built in the absence of workers' initiatives.

Many leading Communists at the time would have denied that this was what was happening, or rather excused it as a temporary necessity until either the civil war was over, or until the world revolution arrived (and, for some, both). There was no shortage of criticism although it was mainly inside the party, and not in the now increasingly moribund soviet organisations (see Chapter 13).

Everyone, from Lenin on, was aware that all was not well inside the Red zone. However they only saw it as a problem of the growing role of bureaucracy in the soviet republic without really understanding its full significance. "Bureaucratism" arose from the tendency for problems to be solved not by workers on the ground, as at the start of the revolution, but simply by administrative orders from the centre which laid down what should be done. Even Trotsky himself actually recognised that:

The necessity of maintaining a permanent army is likewise another source of bureaucratism.[22]

"Bureaucratism" was seen, not as the fault of this or that person nor even this or that policy. The problem was put down to the concrete situation of a relatively backward area of production attempting to continue an isolated proletarian revolution in a hostile imperialist world. Once the civil war was over and the world revolution had arrived these temporary measures would be replaced. However the expedients adopted to "hang on" until the world revolution became more and more anti-working class. Perhaps the most shocking, but also most telling, was the shift in the views of the one-time Left Communist, Bukharin. In his May 1920 book *Economics of the Transition Period* he seems well aware of the contrast between the self-activity of the working class and the situation that soviet power had arrived at by that time. However what he was now arguing was that:

> ... *the revolutionary class is most organized when it has constituted itself as a state power. For this reason state power constitutes the "concentrated and organized force in society."*

He goes further to add

> ... *this concentrated force turns* **inward**, *by constituting a factor of* **the self organisation and the compulsory self-discipline of the working people**.

"Compulsory self-discipline" sounds like an oxymoron but we might overlook it if "self-discipline" actually emanated from the class itself, but by this time it was no longer the case. And just to make this clear Bukharin then adds:

> *But even relatively broad circles of the working class bear the stamp of capitalist commodity relations. From this results the necessity of* **compulsory discipline**, *the compulsory character of which is that much more tangible the less the internal voluntary discipline, i.e. the less revolutionary the given group or stratum of the proletariat is.[23]*

Bukharin clearly did not think this was communism. That would only come about when

> *External coercive measures will begin to die out: first the armies and the fleet will die out as tools of the greatest external necessity; then the system of punitive and repressive organs; further the compulsory character of labour.[24]*

But Communist policies were not just taking the revolution in exactly the opposite direction, they were making it almost impossible to reverse course. The greatest weapons of the working class are its consciousness and its capacity for collective organised action. Bukharin glosses over the contradiction that this consciousness must be lacking if the "proletarian party" has to build a state apparatus in which coercion is the only way in which backward elements can be made to hold the whole show together. Socialism as the Bolsheviks well knew (and Bukharin first among them) in late 1917/early 1918, can only be built by the mass activity of the class and this cannot be turned off, and then back on, like a tap. As Ossinsky argued in 1918, "... *the construction of socialism ... can only be realised by the workers themselves.*"[25]

It will also not have escaped the discerning reader that Bukharin has also altered the definition of the word "vanguard". It no longer means just the clearest elements of the working class regrouped into a party of those workers who already realise the need for communism and which then stimulates the fight of the mass of the class to create society anew. It has come to mean simply the governing party of a new state apparatus. Little wonder that Bukharin, as editor of *Pravda*, was soon writing in support of labour armies and the militarisation of labour. When it came to organising the economy, "the model is given to us by the army" (18 December 1919).[26]

The Militarisation of Labour Debate

The debate over the militarisation of labour showed just how far the revolution had retreated as a consequence of the civil war. Despite his strictures on bureaucracy, Trotsky who was amongst the most statist[27] of all the Communist leaders, became the most prominent to call for the further militarisation of society in order to increase production once the civil war had been won. Initially this started with the conversion of the Third Red Army into a labour unit after its victory in Siberia in early 1920. Trotsky maintained that this initiative came from the soldiers themselves (but there is no verifiable evidence for this):

> On the whole, in the Third Army there remained about 120,000 Red soldiers in administrative posts, institutions, military units, hospitals, etc. In this general mass, mainly peasant in its composition, there were reckoned about 16,000 Communists and members of the organization of sympathizers – to a considerable extent workers of the Ural. In this way, in its composition and structure, the Third Army represented a peasant mass bound together into a military organization under the leadership of the foremost workers. In the army there worked a considerable number of military specialists, who carried out important military functions while remaining under the general control of the Communists. If we consider the Third Army from this general point of view, we shall see that it represents in miniature the whole of Soviet Russia.[28]

This was his argument for extending the principle of militarisation to the entire society. He saw this as the ideal way not just to solve the problem of economic organisation but as "*the inevitable method of organising and disciplining labour power in the period of transition from capitalism to socialism*".[29]

He was not coy about stating what the real meaning of the militarisation of labour was either.

> The very principle of compulsory labor service is for the Communist quite unquestionable. "He who works not, neither shall he eat." And as all must eat, all are obliged to work. Compulsory labor service is sketched in our Constitution and in our Labor Code. But hitherto it has always remained a mere principle. Its application has always had an accidental, impartial, episodic character. Only now, when along the whole line we have reached the question of the economic re-birth of the country, have problems of compulsory labor service arisen before us in the most concrete way possible. The only solution of economic difficulties that is correct from the point of view both of principle and of practice is to treat the

population of the whole country as the reservoir of the necessary labor power – an almost inexhaustible reservoir – and to introduce strict order into the work of its registration, mobilization, and utilization.[30]

As we have already seen, Trotsky was not alone and Lenin also supported it, though he only saw it as a temporary emergency measure and, like everything else done in the civil war, simply a means to hold on until the world revolution. But by the end of 1920 there were only a few in the RCP (B) who were prepared to dispute Trotsky's assertion that working class control meant Communist Party control. Or as he put it,

... control over their work remains in the hands of the working class, in the person of its Communist Party.

Whilst

Our compulsion is applied by a workers' and peasants' government, in the name of the interests of the laboring masses.[31]

The Left of the party came out against this planned militarisation of the whole economy, led by Vladimir Smirnov of the "Military Opposition":

If it were carried out in all branches of industry, it would radically alter the whole physiognomy of our party, smashing that continuous interaction which now exists (although this to an insufficient degree) between the upper and lower ranks. In this case the party would resemble a man trying to lift himself by his hair.[32]

Smirnov went on to add that the outcome would

... destroy the democratic power of the rank and file to influence the leadership and the leadership would become responsible only to itself.[33]

It is interesting that he talks here only of party democracy. This in itself is a decline in the aspirations of the Left of the RCP(B). In 1918 they had been fighting for the democratic self-activity of all workers but now they fought only for party democracy. And they were still largely ignored. Twelve years later Gavriil Miasnikov would identify what went on at the Ninth Party Congress as a "petty bourgeois coup d'état".

The decision of the Ninth Congress of the Russian Communist Party (Bolshevik) dissolved the few Soviets of Workers' Deputies that still existed. The proletariat was demoted from its rank of dominant class; the Soviets of Deputies of Workers' and Peasants', the cornerstone of the November Revolution, "essential nucleus of the Workers' State" (Programme of the Russian Communist Party (Bolshevik)), were dissolved and replaced with bureaucracy.[34]

Its not exactly clear which measures Miasnikov was referring to, but from this point on the opposition of Miasnikov's Workers' Group would grow, so that by 1922 he, and many of his comrades, would be expelled from the party. These elements of opposition show that there was no lack of understanding at the time that the drift of revolution was not in the direction the RCP(B) still officially claimed. However throughout the civil war the great hope of all Communists was that the workers of the world would soon come to the aid of the Russian Revolution and thus re-open the real prospect of socialism. At times the desperation for that revolution would affect war policy as well.

Exporting the Revolution by Bayonets?

The key Bolshevik assumption that a proletariat in power in Russia would only be the first step in a world socialist revolution was then, and is, often derided today by their critics (whether social democratic or reactionary), but at the time it was more than just wishful thinking. Over three years of an imperialist war which was the first "total war" in history which dragged in whole populations, and not just armies, the First World War represented the greatest crisis the capitalist world order has ever faced. It was to the credit of the Bolsheviks that most of them recognised what was at stake.

The Bolsheviks, as we saw, earlier had hoped to buy time and a breathing space until the revolution broke out elsewhere. Signing Brest-Litovsk was designed to save the revolution at home until the war eventually brought such privation that revolution would break out elsewhere. In this they were not disappointed.

Little more than six months after the signing of the Treaty of Brest-Litovsk the First World War was ending. On 23 October 1918, Karl Liebknecht, the Spartacist leader and most prominent anti-war figure, in Germany was released from prison. To the astonishment of the Majority Social Democrats this sparked

> ... *huge demonstrations in Berlin, and other cities, with crowds far larger than anything the Spartacists or the Independent Socialists had been able to produce until now. Liebknecht, the man who once had no popular following, rode through the streets of Berlin in a flower-filled carriage pulled by workers.*

> ... *Only a few weeks before, the Majority Socialists had been absolutely confident of their authority within the working class. But now they were not so sure. Philip Schiedemann, who had advocated Liebknecht's release on the grounds that he was much less dangerous outside prison than inside, was frankly dumbfounded – 'Liebknecht has been carried shoulder high by soldiers who have been decorated with the Iron Cross. Who could have dreamt of such a thing happening three weeks ago'.*[35]

Schiedemann immediately found an excuse to expel Joffe, the Soviet ambassador and his staff (who had been spreading propaganda works throughout Germany until this time) but the significance of this news was not lost on the Russian Communists either. After all Lenin had even stated at the Finland Station in April 1917 that it would not be long before in Germany *"at the summons of our comrade Karl Liebknecht, the people will turn their weapons against their capitalist exploiters"*.[36]

The naval mutinies at Kiel and Wilhelmshaven came exactly a week later on 30 October 1918 thus sparking off a wave of revolution across Germany. On the same day a huge demonstration of workers and soldiers in Vienna led to the fall of the Habsburg Empire and a social democratic government was sworn in. On 2 November it was news of the latter that reached Moscow first. A leaflet was quickly circulated and on Sunday 3rd November thousands took to Moscow's streets. Radek tells us that

> *From every corner of the city demonstrations were marching towards the Moscow soviet ... I have never seen such a sight. Workers, both men and women, and Red Army soldiers filed past until late evening. The world revolution had arrived. The masses of the people were listening to its iron step. Our isolation had ended.*[37]

Lenin told the Sixth Soviet Congress a few days later, and a year after the October Revolution, that Russia was now marching in step with its international allies in Austria and Germany as

> *...this war is leading the whole world as well as Russia to a world proletarian revolution and the workers' triumph over capitalism.*[38]

Unlike the Bolsheviks, however, the Spartacists had not organisationally separated themselves more distinctly from the mainstream of social democracy, and revolutionary ideas were thus more a spontaneous product of the war weariness that finally engulfed the German working class. This meant that there was no challenge until November 1918 to the Majority Social Democrats leadership of the working class (which was deeply rooted after decades of organisation building). The German SPD was the largest electoral machine in the world at the time, with massive property and hundreds of newspapers. It had preserved itself relatively intact by siding with German imperialism in the war. This different balance of forces meant that the German Revolution would need more time to absorb the significance of the Russian Revolution as conditions matured in the post-war world. Rosa Luxemburg, the other outstanding Spartacist leader understood this, but Liebknecht fatefully allowed himself to be carried away into prematurely proclaiming a "socialist republic" in Berlin in January 1919, only a few days after the Spartacists had formed the German Communist Party. In the disaster that followed, the SPD did a deal with the Army and crypto-fascist Freikorps, who militarily defeated the armed workers in the streets of Berlin. 400 communists were killed in cold blood in the days and weeks that followed, including Liebknecht and Luxemburg. Lenin in his *After the Murder of Liebknecht and Luxemburg*[39] was not slow to contrast the Social Democrats' hypocrisy about extra-judicial killings they sanctioned and their call for an enquiry into what happened.

With the benefit of hindsight it can be averred that this was also another nail in the coffin of a revolution in a single country whose success was entirely dependent on an international revolution. It was not so clear to contemporaries who saw it as a mere setback. Lenin finished the article referred to above with the words *"the exploiters all over the world are not strong enough to prevent the victory of the world proletarian revolution"*. And in 1919 the revolutionary movement seemed to be still on the rise. Not only was the Communist or Third International founded in March but soviet republics were formed in Bavaria and Hungary. Although short-lived, they demonstrated that a revolutionary wave was rising, and the capitalist class had not yet managed to impose its new world order on the working class.

The Hungarian Revolution in April 1919, largely led by returning prisoners of war from Russia, posed a dilemma for the Soviet Government. If they could give military assistance to Budapest they might break the blockade and open a bridgehead to the West through which world revolution might develop. As it turned out the Hungarian Soviet Republic only lasted until August, defeated by the incompetence of its leadership and an invasion from Romania. Attempts to send it military aid (in the form of a diversionary attack on Romanian forces in Bessarabia) came to nothing when Grigoriev's partisan brigade who had been asked to carry out the task abruptly renounced support for the Bolsheviks. Grigoriev issued an anti-semitic manifesto and undertook a series of pogroms, the worst being at Elizavetgrad in May 1919 where at least 1,000 Jews were murdered. Grigoriev later joined with the anarchist Nestor Makhno, who eventually killed him over his support for the Whites. However the significant fact was that the Red Army was not strong enough at this point for such offensive operations.

The question was posed again but in much starker form in the Polish War[40]. The Piłsudski Government in Poland, egged on and materially supported by France and Britain, had invaded Western Russia in 1920 with the aim of incorporating much of Ukraine into the new Polish state. The Red Army not only defeated Piłsudski's forces but began to drive them towards Warsaw.

At this point there arose a debate in the Bolshevik Central Committee. Lenin and Zinoviev wanted to drive on to Warsaw, throw out the Piłsudski government and establish a soviet republic. Trotsky and Radek (who was himself from Polish Galicia) were more realistic. They saw that an invasion by the Red Army would only give the Polish ruling class the opportunity to play the nationalist card. As a result the workers of Warsaw would remain passive, or even support their "own" nation. In the event Radek and Trotsky were proved right, and the Red Army with its supply lines over-extended was outflanked, and then defeated in front of Warsaw.

This episode once again underlined the fact that socialism cannot be imposed from outside by bayonets alone. Throughout the civil war and now in the Polish War the political factor always remained significant in the fortunes of the Soviet regime. Where class consciousness was high and there was a willing embrace of the communist idea victory was often achieved with hardly a shot being fired. Where class consciousness and class participation was less forthcoming the outcome depended on the relative military strengths of the two sides. If for the bourgeoisie war is the extension of politics by other means (as Von Clausewitz put it), for the working class, politics (or rather, political consciousness) is the extension of war by other means. Class consciousness is the real weapon of the proletariat even in armed conflict. Self-activity of the mass of the working class cannot be replaced by mere military force, and its absence makes the construction of socialism impossible.

The Red Army after Victory

With the defeat of Wrangel in the Crimea in December 1920 and the withdrawal of the British and French (who had plenty of problems at home of their own) the Soviet Republic had won a major military victory. But, as we have seen, at a tremendous human and political cost.

The calculation of that cost varies wildly with some arguing that as many as 10 million died (perhaps by adding on the figures for the 1921 famine which followed the war, in which something like 5 million may have perished). At least 4 million died in the three years that cover 1918-20. Of these less than 350,000 seem to have been directly killed in battle on all sides. The rest died from hunger, literally freezing to death and disease, including close to 1 million soldiers in both Red and White armies. A population weakened by malnutrition was already prone to disease but in the civil war this was compounded by the acute lack of soap. As Lenin famously announced to the Seventh All-Russian Congress of Soviets in December 1919:

> Comrades, it is impossible to imagine the dreadful situation in the typhus regions, where the population is broken, weakened, without material resources, where all life, all public life ceases. **To this we say, Either the lice will defeat socialism, or socialism will defeat the lice!**[41]

As the result of the lice five million people contracted typhus during the civil war, of which, about a third died. A further 700,000 died from typhoid, cholera and dysentery.[42]

Not only had so many millions died (including many of the politically conscious workers who had been the drivers of the October Revolution); not only was the country wracked by famine and economic catastrophe; but the whole process of fighting the war had distorted the very nature of the soviet ideal.

The proletarian base of the October Revolution had been undermined in the early days of 1918 by the food shortage which saw up to half the working class quitting the cities in search of food. The constant mobilisations of the most conscious workers into the Red Army further undermined this working class base. To take Moscow as one example there were four major mobilisations of party workers in 1918, with a further five in 1919-20, so that by 1921 almost 70% of Moscow's Communists had served, at one time or another, at the front.[43] If we add to this all those party members mobilised to requisition grain, keep transport moving, work on the land etc. the conclusion must be that the civil war did much to undermine the Bolsheviks as a party of the working class.

Increasingly, whether they recognised it or not, they were the shock troops of a new state apparatus. A state apparatus increasingly divorced from the working class.

With the war winding down Lenin wanted to cut the Red Army by two thirds. Trotsky, having failed to turn the entire working class into a militarised labour force, was now trying to get the Red Army to become the shock battalions in the battle for the economic revival of the country. Neither were to achieve their aims and the Red Army (from which Trotsky was eased out soon after Lenin's death in January 1924) as "a special body of armed men" now became a pillar of conservation of the new state, alongside, as we shall see in the next chapter, the Cheka.

The lesson of the experience is that, whatever the immediate problems, of this or that situation, if a standing army has to be formed which operates outside the control of the organs of working class rule, this is not just undesirable but also a real obstacle to the process of building socialism. The Red Army may have won the civil war, but its victory turned out to be a Pyrrhic one which sounded the death-knell of the kind of society most Bolsheviks, and the majority of the working class, had envisaged in 1917.

Chapter 12
Proletarian Justice and Red Terror in the Civil War

In the *State and Revolution* Lenin outlined what constitutes the main bulwarks of state power.

> *A standing army and police are the chief instruments of state power. But how can it be otherwise?*[1]

Lenin then concluded that under the "dictatorship of the proletariat", the armed people "such as the Soviets of Workers' and Soldiers Deputies" would be enough to suppress the exploiters without the need for "a special machine" like the State.[2] The test of this theory would come almost immediately after the October Revolution. This took the form of the many acts of sabotage and violence carried out by the defenders of the old order. Both the Military Revolutionary Committee and the Red Guard militias seem to have struggled to deal with them.

Yet, ten days after the overthrow of the Provisional Government, Lenin was still insisting that:

> *We are reproached for using terror. But such terror as was used by the French revolutionaries who guillotined unarmed people we do not use and I hope shall not use ... When we have made arrests we have said "we will let you go if you will sign a paper promising not to commit acts of sabotage". And such signatures are given.*[3]

Carr points out that the signatures were given but that didn't mean the promises were kept. The Red Guards who stormed the Winter Palace released the officer cadets who had fought against them on a promise that they would not take up arms against the revolution. Most then did. Krasnov, who had been the last General to try to save Kerensky, signed one of these papers, then immediately went off to the South of Russia to organise the White Army in the civil war against the Soviet Republic.[4] Such early leniency by the Bolsheviks was only matched by the ruthless ferocity of the Whites. This was the case from the very start of "the dictatorship of the proletariat" in Russia. In October the Winter Palace had been stormed with hardly a casualty. As we saw in Chapter 8, it was not the same in Moscow. Here the Whites set the tone for the coming civil war by massacring, in the Arsenal and in the Kremlin, hundreds of workers who had surrendered to them on the promise that their lives would be spared. Even in the face of this, the Bolsheviks passed a resolution in the Soviet congress banning the death penalty in the army, which Kerensky had re-introduced shortly before his fall.

Communists know that the capitalist class will resort to any extreme to hold on to their power and wealth. Historically its acts of terror have far outweighed any acts of revenge by the working class. One has only to compare the massacre of the 40,000 Parisians by Cavaignac in the June Days of 1848 or the 20,000 Communards murdered in the "Semaine Sanglante" of 1871, with the 63 hostages the Communards shot in desperation, to see that workers have never been the initiators of mass terror. Even in the February Revolution it took the deaths of hundreds of mostly unarmed workers to win over the forces of repression to the side of the workers. In the July Days of 1917 it was the provocation and violence of the Menshevik and Right SR supporters of the Provisional Government that ensured the vast majority of the 700 deaths were sailors or supporters of the demonstration.

The Cheka

The first response of Sovnarkom to the threat posed by the counter-revolution was to set up Revolutionary Tribunals (the choice of name was a conscious nod towards the French Revolution). These were set up by a decree of 22 November/5 December 1917. They were the only bodies which had to the power to mete out the death penalty (despite the fact that at this time the death penalty was outlawed in the rest of the soviet legal system – it was not restored until June 1918, in response to the SR terror campaign which took the lives of Bolshevik leaders like Volodarsky). The Decree stated that:

> In order to fight the counter-revolutionary forces and to protect the revolution and its gains against them, and also for the purposes of trying cases of marauding and pillage and the sabotage and other misdeeds of merchants, industrialists, officials and other persons, worker-and-peasant revolutionary tribunals shall be instituted consisting of a chairman and six alternate assessors elected by the gubernia or city Soviets of Workers', Soldiers' and Peasant Deputies.[5]

In other words, at this point, the counter-revolution was to be dealt with by bodies which were directly responsible to the class-wide bodies, the soviets. They were later (May 1918) given further powers to prosecute cases of spying, "pogroms" (riots, as described below), bribery, forgery and "hooliganism".[6]

However their work was undermined almost from the beginning by the rise of a rival body, set up only two weeks later. The Cheka (the name is an acronym of the first two words of its full name, the Extraordinary (or Emergency[7]) Commission against Counter-Revolution and Sabotage) which was set up in December 1917. Critically, whilst the Revolutionary Tribunals were soviet bodies, the Cheka was set up as a body answering directly to Sovnarkom – the Council of People's Commissars, so the soviets had no direct control over it from the start. Initially the Cheka was only supposed to investigate cases of sabotage etc., and then hand them over for trial to the Revolutionary Tribunals. However in the febrile atmosphere created by the threat of a new German advance on Petersburg in February 1918, the Cheka was also given new powers of summary trial and sentencing, including the death penalty. This was itself supposed to be a short-term emergency measure linked to the Sovnarkom appeal "The Socialist Fatherland is in

Danger". Originally thought to have been drafted by Lenin (it is in is *Collected Works*[8]) it is now known to have been written by Trotsky (who later claimed authorship[9]) it underscored the dire situation the soviet power was in. It stated that:

> *The Socialist Republic of Soviets is in gravest danger. Until the proletariat of Germany rises and triumphs, it is the sacred duty of the workers and peasants of Russia devotedly to defend the Republic of Soviets against the hordes of bourgeois-imperialist Germany.*

The appeal concluded with an eight point series of measures, the last of which stated that:

> *Enemy agents, profiteers, marauders, hooligans, counter-revolutionary agitators and German spies are to be shot on the spot.*

This boosted the idea of summary justice which not only undermined the Revolutionary Tribunals but would also turn out to be a fateful step for the revolution. The first acts of summary justice though did not come from the Cheka. Even before it was formed the failure of Red Guards and local workers' militias to deal with criminal acts such as the so-called "wine pogroms" created a problem. Ever since the February Revolution there had been a rise in criminal activity. After the October Revolution criminal elements were joined by agents of the bourgeoisie intent on creating mayhem. This unholy alliance was thought to have been behind these "pogroms". "Pogroms" were usually carried out by lynch mobs against people (overwhelmingly against Jews under Tsarism) but the 1917 usage derived from the fact that crowds would suddenly turn up at places where they had been mysteriously informed that the bourgeoisie had stored huge quantities of alcohol, break in, and simply drink as much as they could. Even some militia sent to stop them would join in the bacchanalia. And behind it all some criminal gangs made small fortunes by grabbing their share.[10] Victor Serge tells us the solution that finally came to be adopted:

> *In the suburb of Vassili-Ostrov, the Finland regiment, which was led by anarcho-syndicalist elements, decided to shoot the looters on the spot and blow up the wine cellars.*[11]

The Cheka was set up a few days after this, and soon adopted the same policy. Serge tells us that a week later the wine pogroms had ceased. Summary justice, it seemed, worked. Initially the Cheka limited its actions to this type of work, hunting out food hoarders and speculators, or fighting economic sabotage by the bourgeoisie. The board of eight people, mostly ex-members of the Military Revolutionary Committee, had a staff of only 40 to start with. It was not exclusively a Bolshevik body, as the Left SRs had by this time joined Sovnarkom. Not only was the Commissar for Justice, Isaac Steinberg, a Left SR so too was the Deputy Head of the Cheka. Steinberg was in favour of revolutionary violence but not revolutionary terror. The distinction was that the first was spontaneous and included individual acts of terrorism (a concept shared by many

SRs) whilst the latter was a collectively chosen policy of the revolution. This seems an odd distinction for the chief legal officer of any regime to make but whilst he was in office (until March 1918) there was no official use of terror. As E.H. Carr points out "*no regular executions either by summary judgement or by normal judicial process appear to have taken place in the first three months of the regime.*"[12]

People's Courts

We should not forget too that the Cheka at this time was seen as a temporary necessity. It was not how the Bolsheviks conceived of the wider idea of justice under a proletarian social formation.

In the *State and Revolution* Lenin, paraphrasing Engels, also affirmed:

> *We set ourselves the aim of abolishing the state, i.e. all organised and systematic violence, all use of violence against people in general ... the need for violence against people in general, for the **subordination** of one man [sic] to another, and one section of the population to another, will vanish altogether since people will **become accustomed** to observing the elementary conditions of social life **without violence** and **without subordination**.*[13]

Obviously he was writing about the ultimate goal but in one respect soviet power did get close to prefiguring what a communist society might look like. As we showed in Chapter 8, in the early days of the revolution the development of many institutions might have been inspired by Sovnarkom decree, but were only really effective when they were carried out at local level by popular initiative. Amongst these were the People's Courts which were set up in the same *Decree on the Judicature* (22 November/5 December 1917) which had also set up the Revolutionary Tribunals. In these People's Courts judges "should henceforth be elected" alongside two alternating assessors (initially appointed by local soviets until the system got going). No special legal training was required, so any "upstanding citizen" of either sex could carry out the functions of prosecution, defence and investigation. There were no rules or procedures so that:

> *Court participants had little to guide them, which in effect empowered them greatly.*[14]

In fact because there was no codification of soviet law before 1922, the People's Courts prefigured an idea of justice that would be based on consensus, and real life experience, rather than a rigid system of law.

> *The People's Courts were not to be regarded as repressive or antagonistic institutions, but ones that would aid in the solution of the problems of everyday life. The removal of "counter-revolutionary" crimes from the jurisdiction of the People's Courts paved the way for an absence of government interference in local matters.*[15]

Proletarian Justice and Red Terror in the Civil War

This had its downside in some, mainly rural, areas where the lack of education led to some draconian and unjust sentences being passed,[16] but generally the People's Courts were, in many ways, a forerunner of how justice and disputes could be settled in a non-antagonistic way, as if in a fully classless society. The fact that the Courts did not deal with state issues or "counter-revolutionary" crimes means that they were pointers to the future rather than the representative of justice across the whole society at that time of upheaval.

Discussion of this early experience of the People's Courts has largely been buried under the weight of the Red Terror and the activities of its main instruments, the Cheka and the Revolutionary Tribunals. This has everything to do with the civil war against the counter-revolution which started in earnest in the early summer of 1918. From this time on far more cases were dealt with by the Cheka, and military and Revolutionary Tribunals. On 12 April 1919 Revolutionary Tribunals were given precedence over the People's Courts in all cases. On 21 October 1919 the Cheka then took precedence over the Revolutionary Tribunals when it established its own "Special Revolutionary Tribunal". By 1920, according to the Commissariat of Justice, only 22.3% of criminal cases were dealt with by the People's Courts. Even so the system itself appears to have had much to commend it. Of the 582,571 they found guilty only one third were given prison sentences and of these 40% were suspended.[17] It should also be added that juvenile crime was not dealt with by the courts at all but was seen as a welfare issue.

However, once the civil war started in earnest, the seemingly mundane everyday work of the People's Courts takes a back seat. The wave of terrorist attacks on leading Bolsheviks after June 1918 increased the Cheka's influence and power dramatically, and in time they were to become a law unto themselves, despite several attempts to rein them in.

The Cheka and the Anarchists

The Polish revolutionary Felix Dzerzhinsky,[18] who headed the Cheka and its successors, until his death in 1926, always defended "the Red Terror" as an alternative not only to White Terror but also to individualistic class terror or those seeking revenge. In the early days of the revolution it is undeniable that some arbitrary acts of class revenge were carried out by individuals and groups outside Soviet control. Most notorious of these were the murders of the two Cadet ex-ministers Shingarev and Kokoshkin in the Marinskaya Hospital in January 1918 by sailors from the Baltic Fleet with the connivance of the Red Guards supposedly guarding them. This was condemned at the time by the Bolsheviks (the Red Guard commander Basov, who justified himself on the grounds that it was "two less bourgeois mouths to feed", was gaoled, but the sailors were never traced) but the incident may have given an added boost to the extension of the powers of the "organised terror" (Dzerzhinsky) of the Cheka in February 1918.

The Cheka was supposed to be different from the secret police of the traditional capitalist state. Apart from its temporary status, Dzerzhinsky, himself no stranger to prisons in Tsarist times, considered the Cheka as something morally superior to the past. He warned one Chekist A.K. Artuzov to:

> *Beware of becoming a simple technician of the apparatus with all its bureaucratic insufficiencies. That would place us on the same despicable level as the political police of the capitalists.[19]*

And no doubt Dzerzhinsky was thinking of his own experience when he drew up instructions on how to make arrests and searches in 1918:

> *Let all those who are assigned to conduct searches, take people into custody and imprison them behave solicitously towards those being arrested or searched. Let them be more courteous even than to good friends. Let them remember that the incarcerated cannot defend themselves and that they are in our power. Each and every one must remember that they represent the soviet power, the workers' and peasants' government, and that any verbal use, rudeness, injustice or impropriety is a blot upon soviet power.[20]*

Unfortunately this was completely at odds with the experience of most (but not all) of the Cheka's later victims. And as the civil war rolled over the territory of the old Russian Empire soviet power was increasingly in a poor position to control this organisation which was supposed to "represent it". To begin with, as Carr suggests, *The development of the Cheka was a gradual and largely unpremeditated process.*[21] Many soviets (with the encouragement of the All-Russian Soviet Executive Committee) did originally set up their own Cheka organisations. There was soon a Cheka for just about every aspect of life, including in the Red Army. Some local Chekas acted with more restraint than others, as we shall see, but in the course of the civil war they were all gradually integrated into the central apparatus (the VCheka). During the civil war the increasing arbitrary nature of the Cheka would become an issue but there were signs that it was at odds with other soviet institutions even before that conflict began.

The first indication that the Cheka had taken on a life of its own was the attack on the anarchists in Moscow and other towns in April 1918. Less than three months earlier, Lenin had been telling the Third Congress of Soviets:

> *Anarchist ideas now assume living forms in this epoch of the radical demolition of bourgeois society ... The new tendencies of anarchism are definitely on the side of the Soviets.*[22]

However Paul Avrich tells us that:

> *During the spring of 1918, local anarchist groups began to form armed detachments of Black Guards which sometimes carried out "expropriations", that is, held up banks, shops and private homes. Most of their comrades – especially the 'Soviet Anarchists' – condemned such acts as parodies of the libertarian ideal,*

which wasted precious lives, demoralized the movement's true adherents and discredited anarchism in the eyes of the general public.

After the bitter opposition of the anarchists to the treaty of Brest-Litovsk, their formation of armed guards and occasional underworld excursions led the Bolsheviks to act against them. On the night of 11-12 April 1918, the Cheka raided twenty-six anarchist centres in Moscow, killing or wounding some forty anarchists and taking more than five hundred prisoners.[23]

The presence of criminal elements, who were just engaging in self-aggrandisement under the cover of being anarchist "expropriators", obviously played into the hands of the VCheka. The raids on anarchist premises could be justified as mere police actions but since the anarchists were also well armed (their arms included machine guns) over 50 died in the fighting (about 40 of them anarchists). Despite the bloodshed, many of the 500 arrested, who could demonstrate they really were "political" anarchists, were released, and only the criminal elements detained. Anarchist publications were still allowed to appear. Nestor Makhno himself came to Moscow in the summer of 1918 and met Lenin. According to his account, the Moscow anarchists were carrying out "a paper revolution" with their publications.[24] This is where we find the first denunciations of the April attack in the anarchist press that:

We have reached the limit! The Bolsheviks have lost their senses. They have betrayed the proletariat and attacked the anarchists. They have joined the Black Hundred generals and the counter-revolutionary bourgeoisie. They have declared war on revolutionary anarchism.[25]

This was followed by more violence on the anarchist side which unleashed a chain reaction of terror. Avrich again:

The campaign of terrorism continued for many months, reaching a climax in September 1919 when a group of "underground anarchists", in league with the Left SRs, bombed the Moscow headquarters of the Communist Party, killing or wounding sixty-seven people. This only led to greater repression ...[26]

Throughout this time, the Cheka stepped up harassment of anarchists, and not just those who were in open opposition to Sovnarkom. Even "soviet anarchists" (those who accepted soviet power and worked within the soviets to turn them towards anarchist ideas) like Iuda Roshchin, were sometimes arrested. The bitter irony here is that this cycle of violence was started against the clear wishes of the Communists in Moscow. The Moscow Communists had not only opposed the attack on the anarchists on 11-12 April 1918 but, through the soviet, had even been supplying them with weapons beforehand![27] The Moscow Soviet had formed its own Cheka a few days before the entire Sovnarkom governmental apparatus arrived from Petersburg on 10 March 1918. With it came the central All-Russian organisation of the VCheka. The Moscow body was thus united with the VCheka on 19 March. Technically however Cheka operations in Moscow should still have been under the control of the local Moscow Soviet but, in a foretaste of what the future would hold, they were not. The Deputy Head of the Cheka, Jakob Peters tells us that "*In Moscow in general at that time there was a peaceful mood ... The Muscovites basically did not welcome the Cheka*". Peters himself tells us that, when, weeks later, he spoke in the Moscow Soviet, he was greeted with shouts of "Okhrannik", meaning he was an agent of the Tsar's secret police. Writing about this episode, Martin Latsis, who became head of the Moscow Cheka summed up the Chekist mentality in his memoirs (written in 1926).

> *Nowadays this seems amazing but at the time there were not a few comrades ... for whom the principle of the inviolability of the individual was placed higher than the interests of the revolution.*[28]

Latsis poses a false alternative here. The question was not about the inviolability of the individual but the integrity of the workers' dictatorship. Any workers' power obviously cannot stand by and leave the counter-revolution a free hand, but in this case the Cheka even alienated some of the most committed supporters of soviet power. And to what purpose? In April 1918 in Moscow the Cheka action not only was out of all proportion to the damage done by a small proportion of those who called themselves anarchists, but also initiated the process of breaking up the tacit, but shaky, "pro-soviet" alliance between anarchists, minor pro-soviet socialist parties, Bolsheviks and Left Social Revolutionaries which had emerged in 1917 in opposition to the anti-soviet Right Social Revolutionaries and Mensheviks.

The Left SRs "Revolt"

Despite the actions of the Cheka in Moscow in April 1918 many anarchists bravely carried on fighting for the soviet system in the civil war. Indeed Lenin, in a letter to Sylvia Pankhurst in August 1919, singled out the "very many anarchist workers [who] are now becoming the most sincere supporters of soviet power".[29] Others gave it critical support until 1921, but as a result of this attack, many also abandoned the cities to join Makhno's peasant army in Ukraine. We will pick up that story later, but the next, and more significant, breakdown in the informal pro-soviet camp came when the Left SRs also took to armed opposition in July 1918.

Although they had resigned from their posts in Sovnarkom in March in protest at the signing of the Treaty of Brest-Litovsk, the Left SRs had remained inside soviet institutions. However, by July the differences between the Communists and the Left SRs had gone beyond that of the peace with Germany. Food requisitioning expeditions against the peasantry and the expulsion of the Right SRs and the Mensheviks from the Soviet Congress were added to the list of grievances. The Left SRs were still however in control of some Cheka units, and this was what gave them the chance to try to reactivate the war against Germany by assassinating the German ambassador Count Mirbach. Using forged credentials from Dzerzhinsky, two Left SR Chekists managed to gain access to him and, despite a bungled first attempt, carried out their plan to try to incite a revival of the war.

Proletarian Justice and Red Terror in the Civil War

The assassination not only triggered German demands that they be allowed to send troops to Moscow, but also led to a confused series of confrontations between units loyal to the Left SR party and those loyal to the Bolsheviks. There appears to have been no serious plan by the Left SRs to overthrow what had now become the Bolshevik government, but given that they took Bolshevik leaders (including Dzerzhinsky and Latsis) hostage in order to safeguard their own delegates who were then in the act of walking out of the Fifth Soviet Congress, it certainly gave the Bolsheviks the serious impression that this was part of a plan.

As the last major organisation supporting the soviets alongside the Bolsheviks, the defection of the Left SRs was a serious blow to soviet democracy. It was made all the more serious by the fact that this party of younger revolutionaries now suffered from "a bewildering number of splits [which] had appeared in their ranks".[30] It cost them two thirds of their membership (which had once stood at 100,000). It meant that the revolution also lost what could have been a valuable bridge to the peasantry. Instead it led to a more general intensification of SR terror of both Right and Left against the Bolsheviks, who retaliated in kind.

The Right SRs, using funds supplied by the French government, had already organised a failed attempt to seize power in Moscow. This was followed by a series of insurrections they tried to get going in the provinces, the most serious being that of Boris Savinkov in Yaroslavl in early July. Volodarsky, the most popular of the Bolshevik street speakers, had already been murdered in Petersburg on 20 June. He was to be followed by Uritsky in August, the same month in which Lenin (just) survived the SR Fanya Kaplan's attempt to kill him.

Sovnarkom's response was to bring back the death penalty. Dzerzhinsky now defended the Red Terror in Gorky's paper, *Novaya Zhizn*:

We stand for organized terror – this should be frankly admitted. Terror is an absolute necessity during times of revolution. Our aim is to fight against the enemies of the Soviet Government and of the new order of life. We judge quickly. In most cases only a day passes between the apprehension of the criminal and his sentence.[31]

Lenin, in a departure from his earlier high hopes about not shooting anyone, now fully backed Dzerzhinsky, and told the Fifth All-Russian Congress of Soviets that:

... a revolutionary who does not want to play the part of a hypocrite cannot renounce capital punishment. There has never been one revolution or civil war where there were not shootings.[32]

However, the dangerous situation in which the regime was in after the civil war was resumed by the Whites and led to a further aggrandisement of Cheka power. On 28 August 1918 the VCheka now instructed its local agencies to, "refuse to submit to any interference by the soviets: on the contrary, it was these local agencies that were to impose their will upon the soviet bodies."[33] The Soviet Executive Committee followed this up on 2 September 1918 by adopting a resolution which stated that:

> *To the White terror ... the workers and peasants will reply by a mass red terror against the bourgeoisie and all its agents.*

The Red Terror was now official. It was not aimed at the other "socialist" parties despite their bloody actions. The actual murderers of Mirbach escaped (one, Blumkin, later joined the Bolsheviks!) but the Left SR leader, Maria Spiridonova, who admitted that attacks like the murder of Mirbach had taken place on her orders, was arrested alongside hundreds of her party. She, and all those not directly involved in the Mirbach plot, were however released from prison before 1918 was over. Indeed there was a slackening of the Terror in general. According to Carr this was because:

> *The thirst for revenge had been slaked; fears of the counter-revolution at home were less acute; the German collapse had, momentarily at any rate relieved external pressures[34].*

The Red Terror was less lenient towards members of the old privileged classes.[36] Despite exceptions the clearest characteristic of the Terror (both Red and White) was its class nature. Whilst the White armies crucified workers, hanged miners as well as peasants who had seized land from landowners in their thousands, and carried out pogroms against hundreds of thousands of Jews, the Red Terror primarily sought out former Tsarist ministers and other members of the old ruling class who were involved in the campaign of sabotage of the Soviet resistance to the Whites. Some 512 were shot in the period immediately after the publication of the Soviet Executive's order but this paled in comparison with the numbers killed by the Whites. The Commander of the US troops in Siberia reported that:

> *I am well on the side of safety when I say that the anti-Bolsheviks killed one hundred people in Eastern Siberia to every one killed by the Bolsheviks.[37]*

Kornilov had already set the tone by instructing his Volunteer Army in the Kuban "*Take no prisoners. The greater the terror the greater will be our victory.*"[38]

Terror expanded dramatically in the civil war and it increasingly became arbitrary and was a law unto itself on both sides. In the context of a brutal struggle, where quarter was rarely given by either side, it is difficult to see how it could have been otherwise. However a proletarian movement ultimately aiming to usher in a new society which will be classless and stateless and hence eschew violence will always be judged by higher standards than its class enemies. When the Cheka added "profiteering" to the list of crimes for which it was responsible for combatting during the civil war, it meant not just dealing with racketeers but also with purely economic transgressions like those of starving workers who returned to their villages to get bread. This put them in danger of arbitrary arrest or worse. In this context it has to be said that the work of the Cheka attracted many who sought class revenge in the most brutal and ignorant way, and these became a source of shame for the Red side.[39] Victor Serge, returning to Russia in 1919 tells how as he worked for the International he was frequently telephoned by *"panic-stricken women who spoke of arrests, imminent executions and injustice and begged me to intervene at once".*[40]

On several occasions Serge and prominent Bolsheviks or socialists like Gorky, had to intervene (usually by a direct appeal to Lenin) to prevent prominent scientists or doctors being executed. Sometimes innocent victims were ordered to be released by Sovnarkom, only for it to find that the Cheka had already executed them.[41]

Serge's own conclusion sums it up reasonably well:

> *Since the first massacres of Red prisoners by the Whites, the murders of Volodarsky and Uritsky and the attempt against Lenin (in the summer of 1918), the custom of arresting and, often, executing hostages had become generalized and legal. Already the Cheka, which made mass arrests of suspects, was tending to settle their fate independently, under formal control of the Party, but in reality without anybody's knowledge. The Party endeavoured to head it with incorruptible men like the former convict Dzerzhinsky, a sincere idealist, ruthless but chivalrous, with the emaciated profile of an Inquisitor: tall forehead, bony nose, untidy goatee, and an expression of weariness and austerity. But the Party had few men of this stamp and many Chekas.*

> *I believe that the formation of the Chekas was one of the gravest and most impermissible errors that the Bolshevik leaders committed in 1918 when plots, blockades, and interventions made them lose their heads. All evidence indicates that revolutionary tribunals, functioning in the light of day and admitting the right of defence, would have attained the same efficiency with far less abuse and depravity. Was it necessary to revert to the procedures of the Inquisition? By the beginning of 1919, the Chekas had little or no resistance against this psychological perversion and corruption. I know for a fact that Dzerzhinsky judged them to be "half-rotten", and saw no solution to the evil except in shooting the worst Chekists and abolishing the death-penalty as quickly as possible.*[42]

What Dzerzhinsky actually said to Lenin was that you either had to be a "saint or a rogue" to do the work of the Cheka, but now he was "only left with the rogues". Serge's criticism of the Cheka actions in 1919 is hard to dispute but there are two caveats. The first is that no attempt was made to hide what the Cheka was doing. The whole point of the Red Terror was to make it clear to the White and other terrorists exactly what the consequences of their actions were. The Cheka, on Lenin's insistence published the names of victims where they could in the papers. Serge's overall verdict that the Cheka was out of the control of the party is bad enough, but more importantly it was outside the control of the class wide bodies of the working class, the soviets.

In 1918 though the VCheka was not yet so dominant and different ideas of how the soviet power should combat terrorism prevailed elsewhere. In Petersburg after the VCheka left for Moscow, a Petersburg Cheka (PCheka) was set up under the Left Communist, Uritsky. Despite being threatened with an imminent German invasion and with growing problems of cholera and hunger, his policy in Petersburg was markedly different from that of the VCheka. Rabinowitch tells us that:

> As soon as it was on its feet, the PCheka began to arrest suspected counter-revolutionaries, speculators and thieves. However many of these suspects, especially political detainees were released soon after being deposed (sic). The shooting of prisoners in Petrograd by authorized agencies other than the PCheka continued primarily for particularly heinous crimes (the VCheka had begun conducting such shootings in late February). Also theft and killings by criminals, many of them members of gangs, with an extraordinary high percentage posing as Chekists, skyrocketed. So did wild shootings, often by newly recruited Red Army soldiers, Red Guards and anarchists. Every night Petrograd's hospitals received piles of bodies picked up on the street ... Yet Uritskii as head of the PCheka, steadfastly refused to sanction shootings. His emphasis was less on the restoration of order through terror than by concrete measures at halting violence, economic crimes and abuses of power.[43]

Rabinowitch goes on to add that Uritsky was soon to get support from the new Commissar of Justice in the Petersburg Soviet, Nikolai Krestinsky. Also a "Left" communist, he was against extreme repression of political opponents after he took up his post on 4 April. Before the end of the month he issued public guidelines which stated that "no institutions in the city of Petersburg had the right to conduct shootings".[44] This held good throughout the summer and even after the assassination of Volodarsky on 20 June. However acts of terror like this against Communists meant that Uritsky and Krestinsky were increasingly fighting a rearguard action against those who wanted to make terror an instrument of policy. Inside the PCheka, all Uritsky could do was to get the Soviet to agree that any shootings should come only after a vote of the PCheka collegium. When the question of shooting some accused SRs arose in August 1918, he argued against them, and in the vote abstained. The shootings were then carried out. Uritsky was murdered a few days later (17 August) by a former officer cadet, Kannegiser, who was avenging a friend who had died in those shootings.[45] Kannegiser cannot have known what was discussed in the internal meetings of the PCheka so Uritsky's death was thus one of the great tragedies of the first year of the revolution. In Moscow, thirteen days later, Lenin was shot several times by the SR Fanya Kaplan, and for a few days his life was feared for.

Lenin had survived the first attempt on his life in January 1918 but this had not brought forward any demands for Red Terror. After March/April 1918 however, the economic crisis, the growing hunger and unemployment, which was soon accompanied by cholera and typhoid brought about a change in his attitude towards those actively trying to destroy the revolution. Additionally there was also increasing concern about how long the Bolsheviks and the soviets could "hold on" until world revolution arrived. The revival of the civil war in July 1918 also brought about a change in Lenin's view on terror. At moments of greatest danger for the Red side in the civil war he was issuing orders to all fronts. Where the danger was the greatest he called for the most brutal suppression. In August 1918 he was sending orders for the suppression of a White rebellion in Nizhni Novgorod. However, his orders go beyond the mere suppression of the Whites and the bourgeoisie. He told Bolsheviks there to "*organise immediately mass terror, shoot and deport the hundreds of prostitutes who are making drunkards of the officers.*"[46]

Many more such messages were issued calling for the same to be done to "kulaks", officials who failed in their duty, or troops who became undisciplined. The official announcement of the policy of Red Terror, which came on 5 September 1918, was not the end of the story. The terror was relaxed at the end of the year when the initial campaign against the Bolshevik government weakened, and the threat from the German imperialists declined after the outbreak of revolution in that country. Thus the Sixth All-Russian Congress of Soviets (the first one which was almost totally Bolshevik, and held in Moscow to celebrate the Revolution's first anniversary) ordered an amnesty and release of all those imprisoned by the Cheka.

This did not undermine the authority of the Cheka which carried on its grim work, including surveillance and harassment of other parties. Relations with other "socialist" parties fluctuated according to the attitude they held towards the soviet power throughout the civil war. Having denounced the October Revolution which gave power to the soviets, having refused to join the Soviet government and having, in some cases, taken up arms against it, Mensheviks and Socialist Revolutionaries, who continued to argue for the return of the Constituent Assembly (i.e. an end to soviet power) could hardly hope to escape the vigilance of the Cheka. At the Seventh All-Russian Congress of Soviets in December 1919, Lenin re-affirmed, against Martov's complaints, that "both Terror and the Cheka are absolutely indispensable". Despite this, the Mensheviks had still been able to hold their own 5 day conference in Moscow in October 1918 (and were still holding these meetings at the end of 1920 and beyond).

Lenin also saw the terror as limited. In February 1920, with the civil war in its final year, he told the All-Russian Central Executive Committee

We were forced to use terror in response to the terror employed by the Entente, when the mighty powers of the world flung their hordes against us, stopping at nothing. We would not have lasted two days had we not replied to these attempts of officers and white guards in a merciless fashion. This meant the use of terror, but this was forced on us by the terrorist methods of the Entente. But as soon as we had gained a decisive victory, even before the end of the war, immediately after the capture of Rostov, we renounced capital punishment, and we have therefore proved we intend to carry out our programme as we had promised. We say that the use of violence arises from the need to crush the exploiters, the landowners and capitalists. When this is accomplished we shall renounce all emergency measures.[47]

He then called for the Executive Committee to endorse the Sovnarkom decision to renounce the death penalty (although reserving the need to re-employ it should the Entente resume its war against the revolution).

It did not last. Wrangel's offensive and the Polish War later in the year once again heightened the emergency and thus the work of the Cheka, as did the outbreak of yet more peasant revolts in provinces like Antonov's *jacquerie* in Tambov. And of course the Cheka played a massive role in the execution of those Kronstadt rebels who fell in to their hands after March 1921.

However a liberal source tells us that

> *Once the civil war (1918–21) ended and the threat of domestic and foreign opposition had receded, the Cheka was disbanded. Its functions were transferred in 1922 to the State Political Directorate, or GPU, which was initially less powerful than its predecessor. Repression against the population lessened.*[48]

This was to be the case for much of the 1920s. Although many of the same personnel would follow Dzerzhinsky into the new body, the terror as practised in the years 1918-22 gradually ceased. The new body became an adjunct of the People's Commissariat of Internal Affairs (NKVD) and with the adoption of the new legal code in 1922 was supposed to deliver the enemies of the state over to the courts. The last act of the old class war terror of the civil war epoch was the arrest and expulsion of 160 prominent anti-soviet intellectuals (including the philosopher Berdyaev, and Kerensky's former secretary, the sociologist Pitirim Sorokin) between August and October 1922. It signalled the ending of the emergency situation where enemies of soviet power were shot or sent to labour camps. It was in fact one of a number of signals that the state was now consolidated but it was soviet in name only. In 1924, after the Russian Soviet Federative Socialist Republic (RSFSR) became the Union of Soviet Socialist Republics (USSR) on 30 December 1922, the GPU changed its name to the OGPU (Joint State Political Directorate), but it was still under the NKVD. At this point there were many calls by leading communists for the state security apparatus (which now had a personnel of 200,000) to be reduced and Dzerzhinsky spent the last two years of his life resisting them.[52]

In 1934 the work of the OGPU was transferred to the GUGB (Main Directorate for State Security). After this time the name of its governing body, the NKVD, becomes synonymous with a new cold and calculating terror which had nothing to do with the survival of soviet power but everything to do with preserving Stalin's grip on power. We will never know precisely how many perished under Stalin, as the files in the Lubyanka were emptied on his death, but the numbers are obviously so astronomical that they bear no comparison with the Red Terror of the civil war. However, the argument that Stalin was in continuity with the revolution rather than the sexton who buried its corpse, has long been the strategy of the defenders of capitalism in its Western form.

Proletarian Justice and Red Terror in the Civil War

More serious and sincere liberal historians do point to the continuities and no issue is better for their speculation than how the regime dealt with political opponents. Besides a secret police they also point to the civil war labour camps where the bourgeoisie and other enemies of soviet power were sent to do forced labour. But if that is the case Stalin's real model was the Tsarist system (which he, Lenin and thousands of others had all experienced). From 1754, on Siberia was the place of exile both for opposition intellectuals and anyone who committed crimes. Until the 1890s and the completion of the Trans-Siberian Railway convicts, chained together had to walk to the camps where they would be brutally treated as they worked in various industries. About one and half million were sent there under the Tsars.[53] The number actually in them grew from 85,000 in 1905 to 183,000 in 1912. However by the time the Red Terror was over this had fallen to 65,000. Although this would nearly double by 1927 it pales into insignificance compared with the one year for which a reliable figure under Stalin is known. In 1938 it was 16 million or one in ten of the then population of the Soviet Union.[54]

Aside from the numbers question, the difference is that, as noted earlier, Lenin was always upfront about the role of terror in the midst of a civil and imperialist war. Terror had a purpose and was an "emergency" measure. Stalin was under no threat (apart from the one he conjured in his own head) and operated secretly behind his minions, often pretending to his victims that he was interceding on their behalf. And of course Lenin justified the terror in terms of class war whereas Stalin's Great Terror was aimed equally at the revolutionaries in the old Bolshevik Party and kulaks and their like.[55]

Even Rosa Luxemburg saw the terror and the signing of Brest-Litovsk as unpleasant necessities forced on the Russian revolution.[56] For anyone concerned about the nature of a working class revolution the issue here is about control. The Red Terror had begun as a response to the given circumstances of the time (the White Terror) and the creation of the Cheka had originally been endorsed by the Soviets with many soviets creating their own more accountable bodies to combat the local counter-revolution. However, when the proletarian heart of the soviets, which were drained of much of their working class lifeblood in the early days of the civil war, ceased to beat, then the Cheka took on a life of its own. After June 1918 it simply became an instrument of a growing party-state which was bit by bit abandoning the ideals of the October Revolution.

Serge suggests how it could have been done differently when he argues that "*all the evidence suggests that Revolutionary tribunals, functioning in the light of day ... and admitting the right of defence would have attained the same efficiency with far less abuse and depravity*".[57] Given the fact that the tribunals already existed it would not have been too difficult to make them the instrument for the defence of the revolution and they could have been more easily controlled by the soviets as intended when they were set up.

In fact the opposite happened. Once the government moved to Moscow in March 1918, and Dzerzhinsky set up a more professional office in the Lubyanka, the Cheka personnel increased and it gradually became a state above the state. Despite attempts at various times (most notably in 1920) to limit its power, both at Communist Party and Soviet levels, the Cheka carried on with its grim work and carried on growing until it was dissolved after the civil war.

By this time, however, the October Revolution was a distant memory and the party-state which had replaced the soviet power of 1917 was in itself an expression of the victorious counter-revolution. It is to this process that we turn to next.

Chapter 13
The Road to Kronstadt

From the start the premise of this brief history has been that the October Revolution could only have succeeded as part of an international working class revolution. This is not just a judgment based on hindsight. Every leading revolutionary and, as we have seen in earlier chapters, the class conscious cream of the Russian working class at that time, knew that socialism could not be built in Russia alone, or in any other single country for that matter.

International revolution was the antithesis to imperialist war, but the Bolshevik party was the only major European party of the decrepit Second International to oppose the war with revolutionary demands. It was the Bolsheviks who led the split at the Zimmerwald and Kienthal Conferences with the centrist and pacifist socialist majority. And when the Bolsheviks came to power in Russia they shared exactly the sentiment of Rosa Luxemburg that:

> The question of socialism has been posed in Russia. It cannot be solved in Russia.[1]

At the Third Congress of Soviets in January 1918 Lenin stated, as he was to do repeatedly in the years that followed:

> The final victory of socialism in a single country is, of course, impossible. Our contingent of workers and peasants which is upholding soviet power is one of the contingents of the great world army.[2]

And in March, at the time of the acceptance of Brest-Litovsk he repeated this:

> It is the absolute truth that without a German revolution we are doomed.[3]

In his April Theses of 1917 Lenin had posed the need for a new International to replace the Second which had gone over to imperialism in August 1914. The war itself began to provide the material basis for this international as workers and former social democrats stepped up their resistance to their own governments. The First World War's end was hastened by the strikes in Vienna, in Hamburg and Bremen and all across Germany. In the previous chapter we already quoted Radek on the spontaneous workers' demonstration that occurred outside the Kremlin when this news arrived. He was not alone in believing that:

> The world revolution had arrived. The masses of the people were listening to its iron step. Our isolation had ended.[4]

This turned out to be a bit premature. Although many workers and ex-soldiers around Europe were increasingly supportive of the soviet idea, this had not taken the concrete form of new communist parties in most countries. Even in a place like Germany, as we discovered in Chapter 11, the revolutionaries had failed to distinguish themselves clearly and early enough from the social-chauvinist Socialists.

Although Luxemburg, Liebknecht, Zetkin and others, had formed the International Group in 1914, it was not until 1916 that they formed the Spartakus League. However this remained inside the German centrist USPD (which included Kautsky and Bernstein) as they feared isolation from the mass of the class. This only confused workers, and kept the Spartakists apart from the smaller, but politically clearer, groups such as the Bremen Left and the International Socialists (IKD). Given too that the Social Democrats did not openly oppose soviets, but worked behind the scenes to destroy them, it meant that the Spartakists were not seen as the only supporters of workers' councils (as had been the case with the Bolsheviks in Russia). The greater sophistication of the Western European bourgeoisie, which incorporated so-called socialists into their defence, was a major factor in defeating the spread of revolution to Germany and beyond.

As it was, the news that the Second International was re-forming in January 1919 forced the Communists[5] to send out feelers for a new International, which they intended to be held in Berlin. Before it could meet, the Spartakist uprising had been crushed by the Social Democrats, in alliance with the proto-fascist Freikorps. Liebknecht and Luxemburg were brutally murdered. The planned first meeting of the new International now had to be moved to Moscow. The move was meant to be temporary until revolution broke out in the West. However this was the first step in the process of intertwining what went on in Russia with the fate of the International. Because it was the Russian party which physically, and, due to its prestige, ideologically dominated the International, it very quickly became an organ for defending soviet power in Russia, rather than focussing on promoting world revolution. In the event the First Congress of the Communist International did little more than declare its existence. The fifty delegates who assembled in Moscow did not all have formal mandates, a factor which already presaged the dominance of the Russian party over the new body. This wasn't quite how Lenin saw it when he announced in *Communist International* that:

The new third "International Workingmen's Association" has already begun to coincide in a certain measure with the Union of Soviet Socialist Republics.[6]

By this he meant that the process of unfolding of the world revolution would also be accompanied by the advance of socialism in Russia. Unfortunately for the proletariat the process was to go in the opposite direction. The growing counter-revolution in the USSR would eventually come to dominate, and then destroy, the revolutionary aims of the Third International.

However this could not be seen in 1919, when world revolution and capitalist counter-revolution were locked in deadly embrace, and the existence (however feeble) of the Third International was a banner around which workers everywhere could rally. Earlier in the year, revolution had broken out in Bavaria and Hungary, where Soviet Republics were proclaimed. The Allied powers (Britain, France and the USA) were faced with mutinies in their own armies in Russia. Lloyd George, the British Prime Minister announced that the British intervention was not only finished, but the revolts on the Clyde and in South Wales were alarming the British state at home. He told the Paris Peace Conference that:

> *[...] if a military enterprise were started against the Bolsheviki, that would make England Bolshevist and there would be a Soviet in London.*[7]

At this time, Lenin was talking about July 1919 as "our last difficult July" since, within a year, there would be the victory of "the international Soviet republic". However the heady atmosphere which seemed to pose such a threat to capitalism did not last. By the end of May the Bavarian Soviet Republic, isolated even in Germany, had collapsed. It was followed in August by the Hungarian Soviet Republic, which succumbed due to internal squabbles, and the invasion of a Romanian Army supplied by the Entente. By the autumn the Whites in Russia had made their most threatening moves yet. Yudenich was at the gates of Petersburg, Kolchak was moving from Siberia and Denikin from Ukraine. In October and November the continued existence of soviet power hung by a thread.[8]

To add to the misery, the young German Communist Party, which had lost its best leaders in the murders of January to March 1919, was split by Paul Levi at its Heidelberg Congress in October 1919. The Party had adopted the tactics of using existing parliamentary and trades unions means to increase its influence, but only by the narrowest of votes. Not content with this victory Levi (against the advice of the Russian Communist Party) proposed the expulsion of all those who had voted against the majority. The Left wing which constituted half the party, and controlled its North German sections (including Berlin), left to form the German Communist Workers' Party (KAPD). Similar difficulties occurred in different forms in other countries. This was a blow to Lenin who tried to win all those who rejected social democratic reformism to the Third International, including anarcho-syndicalists. At this time he also told the British groups negotiating to form a party that, while he himself was in favour of using trades unions and parliamentary tactics, he did not condemn those who called for different tactics. At this point the hope was that a real International would be formed which would break the isolation of the Russian workers who had now been holding on through a devastating civil war.

The Economic Crisis Deepens

As it was, the situation in Russia remained precarious. "Holding on" until the world revolution was posing its own problems for the soviet experiment. What did it mean? There was no manual of how to proceed. Were they to try to move in the direction of socialising the economy or were they simply to administer capitalism until the world revolution arrived? As we saw earlier, there was no agreement within the Bolshevik Party on this. The Communists' enormous popularity began to wane as early as the first quarter of 1918. There was no mystery behind this. As we stated in Chapter 10 they had inherited an economy in meltdown. The Left Communist economist, Lev Kritsman described the situation as one of an economic collapse "unparalleled in human history".[9] Edward Acton, a modern historian and no supporter of the Bolsheviks, agreed, and pointed to the wider consequences:

> *In the aftermath of October, the country suffered an economic collapse on the scale of a modern Black Death... The capital lost no less than a million inhabitants in the first six months after October as workers streamed from the capital in search of bread.*[10]

The US historian, Diane Koenker tells us that,

> *Economically the period was a nightmare. Real wages plummeted and nominal wages became meaningless as more and more compensation came in the form of uniform food rations.*[11]

And even those workers who had jobs still had to spend their time looking for food. Demoralisation was compounded by mass absenteeism. Once the civil war started the situation only got worse. By 1920 Petersburg's population which had been close to 2 million in 1910 was only one third of that. Moscow lost a third of its population. The rule was that the further south and the smaller the city the fewer workers would be lost because food sources were easier to find near them. In some places like Rostov, Tsaritsyn or Perm, the population actually went up.[12] Places in the North were not only far from the grain producing provinces but the transport system, which had been inefficient under the Tsars, was even more decrepit after a further three years of civil war.[13]

There were other consequences. In the factories themselves the problem of absenteeism was compounded by the fact that skilled workers frequently pilfered materials from factories to make objects, like cigarette lighters, which they could trade for food with the peasantry.[14] This probably started in the winter of 1917-18, when the armistice with Germany meant that war production declined, but became a tradition throughout the civil war.

Economic chaos had deepened since the summer of 1917 and the situation was not any better in the early months of 1918. 1917 had produced the poorest harvest of the century and most parts of Russia received only 12 or 13% of the normal grain supply in the winter of 1917-18. A British nurse of reactionary views described the famine in Moscow in January 1918 where a horse pulling a sleigh dropped dead in the streets. It was almost immediately cut up where it lay by starving people.[15] By April the grain ration was halved again. Jacques Sadoul, a French officer who later joined the Third International, wrote of the consequences in:

...epidemics of typhus, smallpox, children's diseases. Babies are dying en masse.[16]

Indeed disease was to become a greater killer than either hunger or the fighting.

... the sudden spread of disease furnishes the most important clue to the rising mortality curve. Unsanitary conditions within a population weakened by cold and hunger produced periodic devastating epidemics whose effects are cruelly apparent in the yearly mortality record of Petrograd. Until 1918 the figure remained close to the prewar level (22 per thousand); that year it doubled, and in 1919 almost doubled again rising to the astounding rate of 80 per thousand (owing principally to the typhus epidemic).[17]

Add to this, unemployment had been growing since the summer of 1917. This was mainly due to the shortage of supplies for factories, although employers claimed that excessive demands by workers (an 8 hour day mainly) were also causes. This did not improve with the October Revolution. In Petersburg:

The crisis in the war industries, which began to build up during the summer of 1917, came to a head in the winter of that year. As soon as the Bolsheviks sued for peace, the bottom fell out of the capital's economy.[18]

The loss of jobs was compounded by the continuing bread shortage. The ration was cut to 150 grams at the end of January 1918, and by the end of February had been further reduced to 50 grams. Under the twin threats of a possible German occupation and starvation, 40% of the working class had abandoned the city by April. Of those who remained 60% were unemployed. Any party based in the working class had to share the same fate. Of the 43,000 who were in the Bolshevik Party in Petersburg in October 1917 only 13,472 remained by June 1918.[19] The political and social consequences for the revolution were dire.

Under the impact of the "balkanisation" of the economy the Bolshevik constituency fell apart.[20]

Chamberlin sums up how serious an impact this had on the political situation:

If human misery were an infallible barometer of revolutionary action the Soviet regime could scarcely have escaped overthrow in 1918.[21]

And Mary McAuley adds that;

by July 1918 the Petrograd party leaders were seriously concerned about the haemorrhaging of party strength at the grass roots and this in turn was affecting the soviets.[22]

All this was the product of the economic meltdown. It also had an effect in the factories themselves. Attempts by Communists on the factory committees at this time, to increase labour discipline in the face of all the problems mentioned above, led to new delegates being elected who were more compliant with the workers' demands. Eventually though even these newly elected factory committees began to be more concerned with labour discipline and output. In the court of history the Communists could not win on this one. Historians determined to defend the virtues of capitalism condemn the "chaos" and "anarchy" of those early days of workers' initiative, whilst in the anarchist/libertarian demonology this was, of course because "the Bolsheviks" suppressed that same initiative in the factory committees.

There is little doubt that the mounting chaos and intractable economic crisis were the main reasons for a gradual shift in Lenin's thinking. As we showed in Chapter 10, until March 1918 he defended all that the workers had done, and dismissed those who criticised the economic problems with the argument that this was just part of the learning process of the class. Eventually however the mounting economic crisis could not be ignored. The first sign of a shift in his thinking can be seen in the pamphlet *The Immediate Tasks of the Soviet Government,* published as an article in *Pravda* on 28 April 1918. It signalled the beginning of a new emphasis. Lenin began by still insisting that;

> *... a revolution can be successfully carried out only if the majority of the population, and primarily the majority of the working people, engage in independent creative work as makers of history. Only if the proletariat and poor peasants display sufficient class consciousness, devotion to principle, self-sacrifice and perseverance will the victory of the socialist revolution be assured.*[23]

However, he went on, the "central task" was now that of "administration". With the Left SRs having resigned from the government, he now stressed for the first time that it was "We, the Bolshevik Party" that "convinced Russia" so that:

> *For the first time in human history a socialist party has managed to complete in the main the conquest of power and the suppression of the exploiters, and has managed to **approach directly** the task of **administration**.*[24]

This is the first time that the identification of soviet power with the Communist Party was made absolutely explicit. And what "administration" entailed soon became clear too. In order to raise the "productivity of labour", bourgeois specialists (*spetsy*) would have to be called in, and paid well for their services. He acknowledged that this was "a step backward" for "our socialist Soviet state power" and a "departure from the principles of the Paris Commune" but the soviet government had to be honest with the population. "Labour discipline" and using the "most modern techniques" of capitalist management plus the "strictest accounting" were equally necessary. The most modern techniques included the return of piece-work and "applying much of what is scientific and progressive in the Taylor system".[25] Finally it was necessary that:

> *... unquestioning subordination to a single will is absolutely necessary for the success of processes organised on the pattern of large-scale industry.*[26]

In short, one-man management should be the order of the day in the factory. Calls for "everyday labour discipline" littered this article[27] and every Lenin speech at this time. This reflected the depths of the situation in early 1918. As hunger increased so too did more examples of indiscipline. Absenteeism to find food, theft of materials to have something to exchange with the peasantry for food, and drunkenness, all increased.

Another shift apparent in Lenin's thinking in *The Immediate Tasks of the Soviet Government,* is on the question of "the state". Lenin now spells out that whilst the soviets are at the same time both a higher proletarian form of democracy, and the embodiment of the "dictatorship of the proletariat", they are also a state apparatus. Gone is the idea posed in *The State and Revolution* that the dictatorship of the proletariat is only "a semi-state". Now he emphasised that:

> *Dictatorship is iron rule, government that is revolutionary, bold, swift and ruthless in suppressing both exploiters and hooligans. But our government is excessively mild, very often it resembles jelly more than iron.*[28]

And just to underline the point the writer who had, two months earlier, praised "anarchist ideas", concludes this part of his argument by insisting that:

> *If we are not anarchists, we must admit that the state, **that is coercion** is necessary for the transition from capitalism to socialism.*[29]

Party and Soviets

All was not yet lost. The bedrock of the whole revolution remained soviet power, and Lenin still accurately mapped out its essential characteristics.

> *The socialist character of Soviet i.e. **proletarian** democracy ... lies first in the fact that the electors are the working and exploited people; the bourgeoisie is excluded. Secondly ... all bureaucratic formalities and restrictions of elections are abolished; the people themselves determine the order and time of elections, and are completely free to recall any elected person. Thirdly it lies in the creation of the best mass organisation of of the vanguard of the working people, i.e. the proletariat engaged in large-scale industry, which enables it to lead the vast mass of the exploited ...*[30]

As long as soviets involved the mass of the class then the proletarian character of the regime would be safe. At this point in 1918 Lenin's description of how the soviets were operating was roughly accurate. As we have seen earlier, Sovnarkom not only encouraged the extension of soviets across Russia, but also endowed them with such procedures as the right of immediate recall of delegates. The reality was of course a bit messier than this, since the soviets, at various levels, operated differently in different places. Even the first constitution which announced the birth of the Russian Soviet Federative Socialist Republic (RSFSR) in June 1918, does not state how soviets were to be elected, and confined itself to the vague statement that:

Elections are conducted according to custom on days fixed by the local soviets.[31]

In his study of the Petersburg First City District soviet, Alexander Rabinowitch confirms Lenin's picture for that time. His analysis found that the soviet went through three phases which we can see was roughly mirrored in all aspects of the Revolution. Before October 1917 the soviets were *"lively, relatively democratic forums for the articulation of popular concerns and interests but not much more"*. We showed earlier that is just what the Mensheviks and SRs wanted them to be confined to, and there is some evidence that the numbers attending the soviets was actually declining as 1917 wore on, due to their perceived lack of influence. In "the first eight months after October" though:

... the workers, soldiers and sailors who had supported the overthrow of the Provisional Government rushed to realize their aspirations – most fundamentally power to ordinary citizens exercised through revolutionary soviets – they became the new regime's primary institutions of urban local government.[32]

However;

... during the Russian Civil War (roughly speaking between June 1918 and January 1920), the power and independent authority of these institutions were gradually decisively undermined, with the result by the war's end, generally speaking, they were effectively eliminated as significant autonomous political entities.[33]

To begin with though in the months after October;

... there is little indication that the Bolshevik citywide Petersburg committee, or lower-level party committees, controlled or even attempted systematically to guide the district soviet's work.[34]

Indeed "confusion and disorganisation" were "prevalent" at this time, as Chamberlin makes clear:

No matter how many decrees might be issued by the central government, every province, every town, every factory was to a considerable extent a law unto itself.[35]

It was the chaos of this period, in one sense was so rich with social promise, that was behind an increasing tendency for calls for discipline, and the beginning of a siege mentality within Communist ranks, even before the civil war began in earnest in July. As Mary McAuley showed, the key was the inability to feed the workers in the cities which not only led to a series of riots across the country, and not only led to many of their supporters deserting the towns (and thus the factories) but also cost them actual support amongst some sectors of the class. All this was leading to a waning enthusiasm for participating in soviets.

> *In the spring of 1918 the district soviets were in trouble too. Novaia Zhizn wrote at length of 'the crisis in the soviets' and the Bolshevik press made no attempt to refute the claim. The problem was they were being abandoned by their constituents; no longer were the factory delegates coming eagerly to meetings, willing and anxious to participate in soviet decisions.[36]*

As early as April 1918, in the giant steel and locomotive plant at Sormovo,[37] near Nizhni Novgorod, discontent over the dramatic food shortages, as well as abuses by local commissars led to a new election to the soviet. The Communists won the most votes (5,336) but the combined votes of the SRs and Mensheviks (7,674) outnumbered them. Given the dire food situation, and the fact that even in October 1917 Sormovo had been a stronghold of the Socialist Revolutionary Party,[38] this could have been seen as a success of a sort. But it is clear that the Communists misread the implications of this vote. They thought that their loss of support meant support for a return to the Constituent Assembly (which was what the Mensheviks and SRs openly campaigned on), but in fact the workers were really protesting against the food crisis, unemployment, and the behaviour of some local commissars (often former workers themselves) who abused their new power. Instead of seeing the vote as a useful barometer of where the Sormovo workers stood, the "solution" was to circumvent the election by forming a new Sormovo bureau attached to the Nizhni Novgorod soviet.

That was not the only incidence of elections going against the Bolsheviks, according to Diane Koenker:

> *Although the Bolsheviks had not lost their mandate to rule there were ... a string of Menshevik successes in local soviet elections in the summer of 1918.[39]*

The most dramatic occurred in Izhvesk in May and June. Izhvesk was a centre of Tsarist military production run by officers in the Tsar's Army. Given the food situation, the Communists and their Socialist Revolutionary Maximalist allies there, lost the soviet election to Right Socialist Revolutionaries and Mensheviks, so they dissolved the council. This would have dire consequences in August when the Whites took Kazan, and most Communists went to take part in its recapture. This allowed the Socialist Revolutionaries to rise in revolt and, being munitions workers, they were well armed. Their revolt spread to the nearby town of Votkinsk. It was not until Kazan had been recaptured in November that the revolt was finally defeated, with most of the rebels ending up in exile in the USA.[40]

Actions like this were not only to undermine the soviets as credible organisations of workers' power (although it did not yet bring about their demise) but was a complete reversal of all that the Party as a whole had earlier stood for.

How did this reversal come about? The whole way of framing debate in the period between February and October in 1917 had been in terms of parties. As we have seen, the Bolsheviks were not alone in supporting soviet power, but they were the ones who were most visible and the best organised. When the smaller Mezhraiontsy group of Trotsky and Lunacharsky merged into the Bolshevik Party, only the anarchists stood alongside, but outside, them in the struggles of 1917. The Left SRs were not formed until after the October insurrection and thus came late to the alliance with the Bolsheviks. By April 1918 they had resigned from Sovnarkom, so that in organisational terms, in the polarised world of Russia in 1918, the Bolsheviks increasingly saw themselves as the one embodiment of the working class revolution. What made this even more complete was the waning of working class participation which only increased when the civil war demanded that more and more Party members and workers join the largely peasant Red Army.

The civil war only intensified the siege mentality inside the soviet regime. This should come as no surprise. In every modern war even the most developed, sophisticated and democratic of capitalist states locks up "aliens" (however innocent, like the Jews who fled Nazism sent to the Isle of Man by the British Government in World War Two), censors the press, and mobilises the entire population to meet the emergency. After July 1918 it was little different in Soviet Russia, although intensified by the fact that this was also a class war as well as one against international capitalism.

Unsurprisingly, the civil war was to have a further negative impact on all soviet institutions. Marcel Liebman tells us that:

> The 'de-Sovietisation' of political life developed quickly and made itself felt at the centre as well as at the local level.[41]

At local level the pattern was for an increasing centralisation after the civil war started. In the First City District of Petersburg, for example, the evolution of the system went from the proposal for the central city Soviet to be made up from delegates from each district soviet in the summer of 1918, to one where the central soviet took over the tasks of the district soviets in December. This was almost certainly a pragmatic decision based on the declining numbers in the city, but its consequences were disastrous for the vitality of soviet democracy.

> Almost immediately ... In the First City District soviet, attendance at general meetings in January and February dropped to new lows; continual appeals to absent deputies, alternating with threats of expulsion, failed to measurably improve the situation.[42]

The pattern now set in for the rest of the civil war of local soviet committees taking the place of the full soviet. These committees too increasingly became one party committees. The original idea of having proportional representation of all parties in the soviet was already being abandoned before the civil war got really started. In June 1918 in the Petersburg First District the Mensheviks and Right SRs got 27% of the delegates, but the Communists and Left SRs were able to get a motion passed giving the majority parties all the posts on the local executive.[43] This was in compliance with the VTsIK request which on 14 June had excluded *"Right SRs and Mensheviks from its ranks on the grounds of their association with counter-revolutionaries and recommended all local soviets to do likewise"*.[44] When the Left SRs revolted against the Soviet government in July 1918 two of their three members on the committee denounced the rising, and joined the Communists whilst the third went into hiding. The Left SRs shattered and many joined the Communists who were now the only party left in government. The party now began to assign its members to local soviets thus further undermining their autonomy. It got worse as the regime came under serious military threat in 1919:

> *Here again, a major contributing factor was horrendous personnel losses, which had already begun to sap the soviets' vitality soon after October ... However at the height of the May emergency, the district party organization was suddenly ordered to ready 20 per cent of its membership for the front.[45]*

These included most of the remaining Bolshevik veterans of 1917 so that there was not only a drop in the quality of those remaining, but even a total collapse of local institutions. What is more:

> *During these critical months, largely as a result of the severe personnel shortage, structural distinctions between party and soviet all but disappeared. Indeed in the early summer of 1919, the district soviet as such, and even its executive committee, virtually ceased to function.[46]*

In fact this was the beginning of the end for the district soviet and with it the withering of grassroots democracy in the civil war. In any state form, wars favour arbitrary action and the centralisation of power. In a situation where a young proletariat was grappling to work out what the best way forward was in an economic crisis of gargantuan dimensions it was a miracle that the system did not collapse altogether.

Problems at a higher level too were magnified by the militarisation of the state. We have already pointed to the error of 1917 in creating the Council of People's Commissars (Sovnarkom) as the government which stood outside the soviet structure. At the time many did not see the problem. Not only was Sovnarkom supposedly temporary until the Constituent Assembly met, but it was also nominally subject to constant scrutiny and control by the Central Executive Committee (VTsIK), elected by the All-Russian Congress of Soviets. The first VTsIK after October included 62 Bolsheviks, 29 Left SRs, plus 10 Right SRs and Mensheviks elected in proportion to the number of their delegates at the Second Soviet Congress. The second was similarly elected by the Third Congress with 160 Bolsheviks, 125 Left SRs, 2 Menshevik Internationalists, 3 Anarcho-Communists, 7 SR-Maximalists, 7 Right SRs and 2 Menshevik Defensists. Initially these Congresses were supposed to be held every three months, and a major task was to elect a new VTsIK (the old VTsIK would resign at the outset of the Congress). This is what happened for the first four Congresses (October 1917, January, March and July 1918) after the overthrow of the Provisional Government, but in the June 1918 Soviet Constitution the frequency of Congresses was reduced to two a year, unless either the VTsIK, or a petition from lower soviets, called for extra ones. In practice, from the end of 1918 they were held only annually and became a bit of a ritual rather than the central expression of working class power.

VTsIK itself went through a similar decline. Although initially conceived as a body in permanent sitting, its meetings became rarer. Not surprisingly, this "controlling organ" only ratified 68 out of 480 of the decrees of Sovnarkom in its first year.[47] One problem was that its membership, which started at 100, rose to 306 as early as January 1918. It thus became too large to be an executive. In 1919, in an attempt to keep its power, and its status, VTsIK gave special powers to the management committee of its principal officers as a Praesidium. It was given the power to ratify or veto the decisions of Sovnakom in between sittings of VTsIK. It could also issue regulations in the name of VTsIK. This move weakened the authority of VTsIK, in that it gave the Praesidium virtually unlimited powers. VTsIK did not meet at all between 14 July 1918 and 1 February 1920.[48] In 1921 its meetings were limited to only three sessions a year, but by that time the Communist Party Politburo had usurped the roles of both Sovnarkom and VTsIK.

Lenin himself acknowledged as early as the Eighth Party Congress, held in March 1919 that all was not what it should be with soviet power. It makes a sharp contrast with his optimism about the capacity of the working class in Russia a year earlier.

> ... so far we have not reached the stage at which the working class could participate in government. Apart from the law there is still the question of culture which you cannot subject to any law. The result of the low cultural level is that the Soviets, which by virtue of their programme are organs of government **by the working people** are in fact organs of government **for the working people** by the advanced section of the proletariat, but not by the working people as a whole.[49]

This blunt recognition of harsh reality implied that the working class were now becoming passive spectators in their own revolution, but Lenin had not yet given up hope of turning things round. In the same speech he was still arguing:

> We can fight bureaucracy to the bitter end to a complete victory only when the whole population participates in the work of government.[50]

The solution lay in "education" and "raising the cultural level" of workers so that the old bureaucracy could be rooted out. But this was easier to say, and to achieve would take time. Conditions of hunger and civil war were hardly a propitious background to even make a start on that project. In the meantime the solution for combatting "bureaucracy" (i.e. using administrative methods instead of relying on workers' self-activity) was... more bureaucracy. The Eighth Party Congress held in March 1919 had not only debated the military question but also tried to confront; a "... *a serious danger. Many members of the party assigned to ... state tasks are becoming cut off from the masses to a considerable extent and are becoming infected with bureaucratism.*"[51]

The sources of bureaucratism were denounced as "red tape, slipshod work, organizational diffuseness and narrow-minded local patriotism"[52] but the solution was for the party to assume "complete control" over all soviet organs which, as we have seen, were already withering. Lenin, like the majority of Communists in 1919, still had high hopes that the world revolution would come to the rescue of the Russian revolution, but in the meantime "hanging on" by any means possible meant that the predictions of Ossinsky et al. were already becoming fact, and the retreat towards party, rather than class, rule was already underway. As the *ABC of Communism* confessed in 1919:

> *What exists in Russia today is not simply the dictatorship of the proletariat; it is a militarist proletarian dictatorship. The republic is an armed camp.*[53]

By July 1919 Lenin was confirming that the Party was now dominant.

> *When we are reproached with having established a dictatorship of one party and, as you have heard, a united socialist front is proposed, we say, "Yes, it is a dictatorship of one party! This is what we stand for and we shall not shift from that position because it is the party that has won, in the course of decades, the position of vanguard of the entire factory and industrial proletariat. This party had won that position even before the revolution of 1905. It is the party that was at the head of the workers in 1905 and which since then — even at the time of the reaction after 1905 when the working-class movement was rehabilitated with such difficulty under the Stolypin Duma — merged with the working class and it alone could lead that class to a profound, fundamental change in the old society.*[54]

The picture was enhanced by Kamenev, then Chairman of the VTsIK, at the Seventh All-Russian Soviet Congress in December 1919.

> *We know that because of the war the best workers were withdrawn in large numbers from the cities, and therefore at times it becomes difficult in one or another provincial or district capital to form a soviet and make it function ... The soviet plenary sessions as political organizations waste away, the people busy themselves with purely mechanical chores ... General soviet sessions are seldom called, and when deputies meet, it is only to accept a report, listen to a speech and the like.*[55]

Despite this, as the civil war dragged on, bringing in its wake hunger and disease, and even despite the growing Communist Party authoritarianism in a system fighting for its existence, the majority of workers knew that a Red victory in the civil war was the one hope for a return of real soviet power. At the beginning of 1920 Martov conceded this:

> *So long as we criticised Bolshevism we were applauded; as soon as we said a changed regime was needed to fight Denikin successfully ... our audience turned*

cold or even hostile.[56]

This reveals something significant about the Russian revolution. The individual parties like the Mensheviks and SRs may have opposed soviet power, and the Communists may have distorted it beyond recognition by 1921, but the working class as a whole largely remained loyal to its principles. This was true when the Constituent Assembly failed to endorse soviet power in January 1918,[57] and it was still true the end of the civil war, however denatured those soviets had become.

Bread and the Peasantry

We have already noted in Chapter 11 that the Communists were fighting two civil wars between 1918 and 1920. The first was the military campaign against the Whites, the second the war for food with the peasantry. At the beginning of 1918 the Bolsheviks could at least say that they had kept most of their promises. They were promoting the soviets, sanctioned the transfer of land to the peasants, had made an armistice with Germany. The one intractable problem, which had finally brought down Tsarism, and dogged all the Provisional Governments of 1917, was the question of "bread". This was not only the greatest single failing of the Communists, it arguably also undermined all the other achievements of the revolution, and ultimately was the cause of the near-death experience of the regime after November 1920, which culminated in the Kronstadt Revolt of 1921.

The Bolshevik/Communist policy towards the peasantry takes some explaining. By legalising the seizure of land by the peasantry Lenin always freely recognised that Sovnarkom was carrying out part of the SR programme, and not the Bolshevik ideal of some form of collective farming. He declared this openly, as he saw that there was no alternative, as the peasantry made up 80% of the population of Russia. The "black repartition"[58] of the land had been their dream for generations, and as noted earlier, they credited "the Bolsheviks" with acquiescing in it. Given this piece of pragmatism, and given the fact that it had long been established that Russia could only reach socialism on the back of revolutions elsewhere, it is something of a surprise that the Communists started "a war on the rural bourgeoisie" as the Commissar for Food, Tsiurupa, called it,[59] within the civil war, against the peasantry.

The crisis of food supply began in the midst of the First World War and had contributed massively to the fall of both the Romanovs and the Provisional Government. The Tsarist regime had resorted to *razvyortska* which was compulsory purchase of grain from peasants, at fixed prices, for the Army. This was a response to the fact that the amount of grain being sold had dropped from a quarter to one sixth of all the grain produced. By 1916 peasants were refusing to sell grain at the official price, and shortages (compounded by another constant problem of the whole situation, the collapse of the transport system in the war) increased. The Provisional Government had tried to solve this by creating a state grain monopoly but *"attempts to force peasants to sell their grain at fixed prices provoked them to conceal stocks and turn it into alcohol.*"[60]

And 1917 produced only a poor harvest so massive food shortages in the first winter of the Soviet government were inevitable. By February 1918 a workers' daily ration in Moscow was 306 calories, not even a tenth of what was needed for a healthy diet.[61] The consequences for the working class we saw in Chapter 10. There was no agreed Bolshevik plan as to how to solve the bread problem, but given the apparent failure of the free market and, the assumption that state control was, somehow or other, a step towards socialism, the balance was tipped in favour of maintaining the state grain monopoly, and also adopting a new and more aggressive form of food requisitioning, the so-called *prodrazvertska*.

The Bolsheviks thought they could divide the peasantry and make an alliance with the poorest in the villages who were rural labourers and often with no land. This was an article of faith for Lenin who had identified this possible class component in the countryside as long ago as his *The Development of Capitalism in Russia* (1899). It was a disastrous error. The Committees of Poor Peasants (*Kombedy*) that were set up in June 1918 were simply seen by the vast majority of the peasants as outside interference by the state. They frequently consisted of party workers, members of requisitioning squads and military personnel. They also included many outsiders who had returned to the village in early 1918 as urban life became unbearable. A study of Tambov region showed that a third of the *Kombedy* members had never done any farming[62]. They were supposed to assist the requisitioning detachments (*prodotyads*) who seized grain from the peasants, but could also impose fines on recalcitrant "kulak" or richer peasants and arrest them if they resisted.

And resist the peasants did. Maxim Gorky tells us that the *prodtyads* would sometimes return with bread, and at other times just carrying the dead bodies of comrades.

> *Many of the villages are now well-armed, and seldom does a bread expedition end without victims ... At the first report of a requisitioning expedition the whole volost (rural district) is mobilised ... and comes to the defence of the neighbouring village.*[63]

7,309 members of food detachments were killed during 1918 and the Cheka counted over 100 peasant risings before the end of the year. This was bad enough but the political consequences for the revolution were even more dire. Within even a few months Lenin was grumbling that the *Kombedy* were attacking the middle peasants as much as the kulaks, and this in itself was critical for soviet power. The Left SRs had resigned from Sovnarkom over the Treaty of Brest-Litovsk but had remained within VTsIK. Relations might have been repaired if it had not been for the Communists' refusal to sanction a free market in grain. The class base of the Left SRs was in the middle peasantry and the *Kombedy* and requisitioning "destroyed all possibilities of agreement or compromise".[64] Thus the Left SRs prepared their insurrection in July 1918 which ended in their ejection from the VTsIK, although not from the soviets as a whole. Some Left SRs actually denounced their Party's attempted coup. Others even joined the Bolsheviks (who, as we saw earlier) tended to leave them out of any general repression. However, the factional disintegration of the Left SRs after July 1918 robbed the soviet system of a party which, given its dominance in peasant soviets, could have been a vital bridge to the mass of the peasantry, i.e the mass of the population.

In January 1919 some attempt to give the system more coherence was introduced. Quotas for each province were introduced but the seizures continued. It is calculated that peasants got paid (at government fixed prices) for about 50% of their grain in 1918 but this fell to 20% in 1919. The situation in the countryside thus only got worse with less and less land being sown (or sown with crops like buckwheat which were hardly urban staples) so that the food crisis only got worse. By 1920 only 10-20% of the 1913 figure was reaching the towns[65]. Many historians (most notably Roy Medvedev[66]) posit the idea that if the Bolsheviks had only accepted a free market in grain (as they were to do in March 1921) earlier, then not only would a lot of suffering have been alleviated, but even the drift to a one party dictatorship could have stopped. The economic policy destroyed the alliance with the Left SRs, and prevented renewed cooperation with Menshevik Internationalists and anarchists who championed the peasantry. Furthermore risings like that in Tambov in 1920, or the *Makhnovschina* from 1919-22, and even Kronstadt, might have been avoided.

As it was, free trade was equated with speculation. Speculation undoubtedly existed but the attempt to eradicate it by putting more and more items of food supply under the state monopoly did not stop it. "Bagmen" (*Meshochniki*) appeared on trains up and down the land selling grain and many other items. Some peasants would travel in armed groups into towns ready to meet any attempt to stop them. In Moscow the Sukharevka market operated quite openly. There was a similar market in every town. They were reluctantly tolerated by the Communist government. They had to be, as they accounted for more than half of people's food supply,[67] although at prices ten times what they got from their ration/wage. So this black market was essential but constantly harassed and facing obstacles like the road blocks designed to catch "speculators" who were often just desperate people trying to barter something for food. The policy began to collapse under the weight of its own absurdity. Avrich, quoting the anarchist Alexander Berkman, explains the situation as the civil war drew to a close in 1920,

Laborers were sapped of their physical energy and fell victim to every form of demoralization. By the end of 1920 average productivity had sunk to a third of the 1913 rate. Driven by cold and hunger, men abandoned their machines for days on end to gather wood and forage for food in the surrounding countryside. Traveling on foot or in overcrowded railway cars, they brought their personal possessions, and materials which they had filched from the factories, to exchange for whatever food they could get. The government did all it could to stop this illegal trade. Armed roadblock detachments (zagraditel'nye otriady) were deployed to guard the approaches to the cities and to confiscate the precious sacks of food which the "speculators" were carrying back to their families. The brutality of the roadblock detachments was a byword throughout the country, and complaints about their arbitrary methods flooded the commissariats in Moscow.[68]

One such came from the chair of the Novgorod provincial soviet on 7 March 1920:

The food detachments are completely unable to carry out their task. They stir up the villages where they go against soviet power. Rudeness, illegal demands for food for themselves, confiscation of cattle and their demonstrative slaughter in case of refusal ... Cases of straightforward theft (accordions, rings, kerchiefs etc.). The province is starving. A huge quantity of peasants is eating moss and other rubbish.[69]

By this time life expectancy for men had fallen to 19.5 years and 21.5 for women.[70] In this dire situation and with the civil war ending it might be assumed that there would have been a rethink in policy. But it did not occur, although all kinds of debates which had been building up under the shadow of the civil war, now broke out within the Communist Party. They would come to a head at the Ninth Party Congress.

The Ninth Party Congress

The Ninth Congress of the All-Russian Communist Party (Bolshevik) took place between 29 March and 5 April 1920, as the civil war was coming to an end, and most foreign armies were in the act of leaving Russian soil. Did this mean that there could be a return to the politics of the "honeymoon" period of the first months of the revolution? The Congress was opened by Lenin. He posed the situation optimistically:

And after these victories we may now proceed with calm and firm assurance to the immediate tasks of peaceful economic development, confident that the present Congress, having reviewed the experience of over two years of Soviet work, will be able to utilise the lesson gained in order to cope with the more difficult and complex task of economic development that now confronts us. From the international standpoint, our position has never been as favourable as it is now; and what fills us with particular joy and vigour is the news we are daily receiving from Germany, which shows that, however difficult and painful the birth of a socialist revolution may be, the proletarian soviet power in Germany is spreading irresistibly.[71]

Having affirmed that policy has been dominated since the Eighth Congress (March 1919) by the slogan "Everything for the war" Lenin admitted that *"it was necessary to deliberately and openly leave some of the most essential needs unsatisfied, and time and again to deny assistance to many."*[72]

It was only because of the Party's "iron discipline" that it had prevailed. And Soviet Russia was still under siege from imperialism, so it was necessary to maintain the militarised dictatorship.

Our army offers a real guarantee that the imperialist powers will not make the slightest attempt or encroachment on us; for although they might count on certain ephemeral successes at first, not one of them would escape defeat at the hands of Soviet Russia.[73]

However with the civil war close to being won, and the regime apparently safe, dissent, both inside and outside the Communist Party, re-appeared. Inside the Party during the civil war,

... this period of life-and-death struggle and of great sense of purpose, the Communist Party closed its ranks. All shades of opinion within the party realized the seriousness of the struggle with the counter-revolution, and submitted to extreme centralization of authority and to measures of discipline which amounted to the militarization of the party.[74]

But now that the crisis of survival seemed over the party was faced with more direct opposition, both from within and without. The Democratic Centralists (or Decists) rejected the way in which proletarian initiative had been lost and that "centralism" without the "democratic" had come to dominate both society and party. Their most prominent leaders, Ossinsky, Sapronov and Vladimir Smirnov had all been part of the 1918 Left Communist group that published *Kommunist*. Ossinsky wrote in *Kommunist* that given

... the fatigue and the general overwork of the current workers, it must be said that all these capitalist temptations [introduction of one man management, Taylorism and piecework – JD] will enormously increase the passivity of the class, the inaction of the Russian proletariat.[75]

This would be quite prophetic. The Decists were still at it in 1920, arguing that "the party should not impose its will on the soviets" and called for a return to a real "dictatorship of the proletariat". Although they garnered some interest, even on the right of the Communist Party, they received few votes at the Congress. However their criticism was, in part, echoed by Mensheviks like Dan and Martov.

At the Seventh All-Russian Congress of Soviets in December 1919 Martov had seemed like one of the Left Communists when he identified a weakness which was already becoming an increasing problem for soviet power. This was *"an apathy of the masses nourished by centuries of slavery under under Tsars and serf-owners, a readiness to throw all responsibility for ones fate on the shoulders of the government".*[76]

It would have been easy for most Communists to dismiss this (and Lenin did in reply) since Martov, who had refused to accept soviet power in 1917, talking of "the apathy of the masses" was just a stick with which to beat the Communists.

More tellingly, in a speech to the Eighth Congress of Soviets (22-29 December

1920), the Menshevik leader, Fyodor Dan:

> *went so far as to charge that, with the stifling of popular initiative, the whole system of soviets had ceased to function except as a mere facade for a one-party dictatorship. Free speech and assembly, said Dan, had been brutally suppressed, citizens imprisoned or banished without trial, and political executions carried out on a mass scale. Decrying these terrorist practices, he demanded the immediate restoration of political and civil liberties and called for new elections to the soviets in every locality.*[77]

There is also an element of hypocrisy in all this since Dan had been no supporter of soviet power in 1917 or 1918, but for those communists who knew that the self-activity of class conscious workers is the only way to socialism, such a criticism was significant. It also signalled a revival of Menshevik support in the working class in the wave of strikes which broke out in Petersburg in November 1920. These were to be the forerunner and inspiration of the Kronstadt Revolt which we turn to in the next chapter.

Chapter 14
Kronstadt and Beyond

As we saw in the last chapter, the economic situation as the civil war was coming to an end was desperate. In the winter of 1920-1 it got worse, as heavy snow, breakdowns of locomotives, and fuel shortages prevented more grain deliveries to the starving cities. In Petersburg, on 22 January 1921, the already meagre bread ration (which, given the inflation of prices on the black market, was now the mainstay of the "natural" wage) was cut by a third. At the same time attempts to get more fuel for the city had failed. People were even pulling up their floorboards and burning them to stay warm, and credible rumours that many were dying of cold at home circulated. Given the fuel shortage, the closure of 93 factories employing 27,000 was also proposed.[1] This was around a third of the 80,000 who remained of the once mighty proletariat of Petersburg in 1917.[2]

It was the last straw. With the civil war over but the country left in a state of ruin (production, even by the most optimistic estimate, was less than 25% of 1913 levels), living standards were simply getting worse rather than better, and so the floodgates of protest burst open. Sporadic and short-lived strikes broke out in early February in both Moscow and Petersburg. In the latter, even in factories which did not strike, workers passed resolutions *which contained demands for free trade, and end to the check-point patrols, free labour and equal rations*".[3]

By 24 February the movement was only getting stronger. In some factories (presumably where the Mensheviks or SRs were present) there was the odd demand for a recall of the Constituent Assembly. About 2,000 workers at the Laferm cigarette factory in Petersburg also struck but added, "Down with Communists and Jews" to their banners.[4] This identification of Jews and Communists was not new, but was now becoming an increasingly regular occurrence.

The position of the Mensheviks was, by this time, ambiguous. After October 1917, Menshevik support had declined, but a small nucleus of it always remained. At first they continued, in concert with the Right SRs, to call for the return of the Constituent Assembly (in which they had only received 2.3% of the votes). They simply assumed that the Bolsheviks and Soviet power would not last long. Although also originally boycotting the Soviets, the Menshevik Internationalists and other elements on the left of the party, eventually returned to take up their minority seats in the Soviet Executive (VTsIK). However they refused to break with the Menshevik right which maintained its alliance with the SRs. As the latter had taken up arms against the Soviets this gave the VtsIK grounds for banning the Mensheviks on 14 June 1918. The ban was repealed in November 1918, but throughout the civil war Mensheviks were harassed, in a cat and mouse game of arrest and release followed by periods of toleration, by the Cheka.

By 1919 the most anti-Soviet Menshevik leaders were increasingly sidelined by their own party. Fyodor Dan and Iulius Martov, as we saw in the previous chapter, now recognised soviet power *de facto,* even though they did not support it, in order to voice a critical opposition within it. Both spoke in Congresses of Soviets in 1919 and 1920 and, in a sign that the end of the civil war was leading to a more relaxed atmosphere, the Mensheviks even held their own conference in November 1920. Until then Mensheviks often operated as non-party delegates in the soviets, or in the trade unions (one of their real bases of support before October). This positioned them to articulate workers' grievances but, as Dan himself reported in his memoirs,[5] little more than that, since satisfying immediate demands was the only thing that mattered to suffering workers at the time. The suggestion that the Mensheviks were behind the Petersburg strikes of 1920-1, as Israel Getzler[6] has tried to maintain, is wishful thinking on his part. It was rather the other way round, as Avrich noted.[7] Workers now gave more attention to Menshevik leaflets which, given their continued sizeable support in the printers' union, were printed in their thousands. The Communist government of course falsely claimed that the Mensheviks were behind the strikes. There is nothing unusual in this. When faced with real workers' struggles, state authorities always look for political plots, but the truth is that the workers had more than enough material misery to provoke an elemental demand for real change. The Mensheviks just gave written expression to those demands. They were not strong enough to give a political focus for the strikers, and as we saw in the previous chapter, they knew that they certainly dare not call for an end to the soviets.

The Petersburg Committee of the RCP(B) seems to have understood that the movement of February 1921 was spontaneous, and decided to treat the workers' demands seriously, although it would take some time to meet them. To begin with *kursanty* (officer cadets) were ordered to police the demonstrations, but they were under orders to exercise maximum restraint though subject to "a barrage of abuse, snow and stones". One cadet was even wounded by a shot from the crowd.[8] Less tolerant was Zinoviev, who responded with surprising speed by setting up a Petersburg Defence Committee. This included Red Army commanders like Lashevich who were in favour of outright repression. He appears to have been behind the threats to fire workers, and then rehire them on an individual basis. The threat of starvation thus hung over them. The Committee also sent its best speakers to the factories on a propaganda drive, but workers were now tired of being told to wait for things to get better. The civil war was over, yet they were still cold and starving. The Cheka, of course, responded to the ongoing crisis by arresting known SR and Mensheviks (some 220 in all) and armed patrols were soon on the streets (they were already in the factories). However, without waiting for any kind of authorisation the Petersburg Committee abolished the "special ration" given to ex-bourgeois specialists and other key workers on 22 February. And with the approval of Zinoviev, the Petersburg Soviet passed resolutions on 26 February:

> ... *in favour of larger allotments, the release of the Labour Army recruits, the provision of trains for travelling out to get food, and the end of requisitioning of grain from the peasants.*[9]

When news arrived that the sailors of the *Petropavlovsk* had voted to support the strikers:

> ... *the authorities moved decisively, announcing ... the end of the check-point patrols, the workers' right to produce from the previous year's allotments, and the return home (with two weeks pay) for all those recently mobilized for industry.*[10]

In addition extra clothes and food were distributed. The combination of arrests, threats of lockouts and mass sackings, and belated concessions were enough to bring the exhausted and cold workers back to work. By 8 March most workers had returned, and the crisis in Petersburg was over by 16 March. But well before then, the focus of discontent had moved to Kronstadt.

On hearing of the outbreak of strikes, Kronstadt sailors sent a delegation to Petersburg to investigate. Kronstadt sailors had a long history of political radicalism. 3000 of them were imprisoned or sent to Siberian exile in 1905 and hundreds more in a mutiny in 1906 (after which 18 of their leaders were executed). The Russian Imperial Navy, with its enormous class gulf between privileged officers and men brutalised by savage punishments, was the ideal breeding ground for class war, as Eisenstein's film *The Battleship Potemkin* captures so graphically. It was no surprise that Kronstadt sailors killed their commander in February 1917, and took over Kotlin Island on which the naval base is located. It became an oasis of working class rule throughout 1917.

> *In May 1917 the maverick Kronstadt Soviet, led by Bolsheviks, anarchists, left-wing SR's and unaffiliated radicals of an anarcho-populist bent, refused to bow to the authority of the Provisional Government and proclaimed itself "the sole power in the city". Thereafter the Soviet exercised overall political authority, supported by the general meetings in Anchor Square, which were held nearly every day.*[11]

In Chapter 8 we saw how the Kronstadters had adopted their own collective forms right from the start of the October Revolution. In many ways it already was a commune, and a prefiguration of what socialist existence might look like once the last vestiges of capital had been removed. This continued after the October Revolution. The sailors were also the impatient ones who, together with the Machine Gun regiment, were in July 1917, in calling for the premature overthrow of the Provisional Government before the rest of the class was ready for it. Trotsky dubbed them then as the "pride and joy of the revolution", and Lenin, when ignored by his own more cautious party leadership, threatened more than once to resign and "go to the sailors" to get support for action.

Such facts convey the impression that Kronstadt had always been a Bolshevik stronghold. However, no tendency ever had predominance in Kronstadt. SR-Maximalists, anarchists, Bolsheviks and Left SRs were all well represented in 1917. This continued into 1918, until the revolt of the Left SRs in July led to their expulsion from the soviets. This changed the political equation in Kronstadt as well.

With the expulsion of the Left SRs in July 1918, complete Bolshevik domination of the Kronstadt Soviet was finally achieved. The Sixth Congress of Soviets in November 1918 saw Kronstadt represented for the first time by two Bolshevik delegates, Mikhail Martynov and Choderain, and by them alone. Elections to the Kronstadt Soviet in January 1919 returned seventy-three Communists, ninety-one Communist sympathizers, twenty-two nonpartisans, one Menshevik (in November 1918 the Mensheviks were readmitted to Soviet elections), and one described as 'in sympathy with the Maximalists'.[12]

As elsewhere, the civil war did the rest. Elections to the Kronstadt soviet were now controlled only by the Communist Party, and the grassroots vibrancy of the community withered away.

The liquidation of Kronstadt's multi-party Soviet democracy was completed with the gradual emasculation and subsequent destruction of its rich grass-roots democracy of base committees in workshops, factories, plants and army and naval units. These were replaced at the base by a growing network of Communist party collectives responsible only to the party committee.[13]

And the demands of the war effort called for the end of many of the practices that had developed between February 1917 and July 1918.

Naval democracy was finally destroyed on 18 January 1919 when Trotsky, chairman of the Military Council of the Republic, decreed the abolition of all ships' committees, the appointment of commissars to all ships, and the setting up of revolutionary tribunals to maintain discipline, a function previously vested in elected 'comradely courts'.[14]

1919 was indeed a time of great danger for soviet power. In June, as Yudenich's White Army approached Petersburg, the entire garrison of Krasnaya Gorka, one of Kronstadt's satellite forts on the mainland, went over to the Whites. Its commander called on Kronstadt, and the other forts on the Gulf of Finland, to arrest Communists and join the betrayal. Only one fort complied, but at the same time the Cheka discovered in Kronstadt itself:

a conspiratorial anti-Soviet organization of officers, including Captain Alexander Rybaltovsky, chief-of-staff of the Kronstadt naval base, and the senior artillery officers Iuvenalii Budkevich and Kuprianov, and some members of the intelligentsia...[15]

This did not prevent the sailors in Kronstadt from taking part in the recapture of Krasnaya Gorka, starting with "a devastating bombardment" from the *Petropavlovsk* when the insurgents fired on Kronstadt. It was known that the defection of Krasnaya Gorka had been organised by the Russian National Centre, in league with British Intelligence.[16] These precedents may have played some role in determining the

Communist government's rapid and violent response in the tragedy which was now about to take place.

The revolt began when the sailors' delegation that returned to Kronstadt convinced the majority to support the Petersburg workers so that, on the *Petropavlovsk,* on 28 February, a fifteen point resolution was passed. As it has been the subject of many distorted interpretations, particularly by Trotsky and his later supporters, it is set out here in full.

Having heard the report of the representatives sent by the general meeting of ships' crews to Petrograd to investigate the situation there, we resolve:

1. In view of the fact that the present soviets do not express the will of the workers and peasants, immediately to hold new elections by secret ballot, with freedom to carry on agitation beforehand for all workers and peasants;

2. To give freedom of speech and press to workers and peasants, to anarchists and left socialist parties;

3. To secure freedom of assembly for trade unions and peasant organizations;

4. To call a non-party conference of the workers, Red Army soldiers, and sailors of Petrograd, Kronstadt, and Petrograd province, no later than March 10 1921;

5. To liberate all political prisoners of socialist parties, as well as all workers, peasants, soldiers, and sailors imprisoned in connection with the labor and peasant movements;

6. To elect a commission to review the cases of those being held in prisons and concentration camps;

7. To abolish all political departments because no party should be given special privileges in the propagation of its ideas or receive the financial support of the state for such purposes. Instead, there should be established cultural and educational commissions, locally elected and financed by the state;

8. To remove immediately all roadblock detachments;

9. To equalize the rations of all working people, with the exception of those employed in trades detrimental to health;

10. To abolish the Communist fighting detachments in all branches of the army, as well as the Communist guards kept on duty in factories and mills. Should such guards or detachments be found necessary, they are to be appointed in the army from the ranks and in the factories and mills at the discretion of the workers;

11. To give the peasants full freedom of action in regard to the land, and also the right to keep cattle, on condition that the peasants manage with their own means, that is, without employing hired labor;

12. To request all branches of the army, as well as our comrades the military cadets (kursanty) , to endorse our resolution;

13. To demand that the press give all our resolutions wide publicity;

14. To appoint an itinerant bureau of control;

15. To permit free handicrafts production by one's own labor.

PETRICHENKO, Chairman of the Squadron Meeting

PEREPELKIN, Secretary[17]

This is a programme primarily aimed at the revival of soviet democracy. As Getzler rather sniffily pointed out, it called for an "exclusive"[18] soviet democracy for workers and peasants only. It does not even call for all who claim the title "socialist" to be legalised – only the "left socialists" and anarchists. It did not call for "soviets without Bolsheviks" as Trotskyist apologists like Binns, Harman and Cliff maintained.[19] It did call for "immediate new elections to the Soviets, freedom of speech for anarchists and Left Socialist Parties", but this did not exclude "Bolsheviks". At its core there is also a call for the abandonment of the policies adopted since the start of the civil war. The demand for equalisation of rations was a call to reject the extra rations that bourgeois specialists (and officials) were entitled to, but most of the economic demands centre around food requisitioning. This had been tolerated whilst the war with the Whites went on, but was now clearly seen as not only unnecessary, but increasingly counter-productive. Contemporaries would not have known the precise figure but the amount of land put to cultivation had fallen to 60% that of 1913. Kronstadt had not faced the same privations as most of the rest of the country for most of the civil war, but the start of 1921 saw it too suffering from reduced food and fuel.

It is true that, like so many Russian workers, the sailors still retained ties to the land via their families, and it appears that many of them saw the hardship they faced when they were home on leave. Relatives who had had their livestock, or last stock of grain, arbitrarily seized, complained bitterly to sailors (who were able to get leave for the first time in two years now the civil war was ending) about the injustice of a revolution that gave them nothing back in return. Thus the resolution proposed granting "freedom of action provided they do not employ hired labour" to the peasants, and, critically, an end to all barriers to trading food. It shows that Petrichenko and his comrades could see the dilemma where solving the food supply might open the floodgates to reverse the course the revolution had taken towards socialisation.

Trotsky did not concede this for a moment, and claimed that this demand made the Kronstadt programme just "the convulsions of the peasant petty bourgeoisie".[20] Yet, when prompted by Victor Serge, he had to admit that he had tentatively made similar proposals when he suggested "a transition to the NEP" in early 1920.[21] Lenin himself had also been drafting the NEP or New Economic Policy since November, but it would not be unveiled until the Russian Communist Party (Bolshevik) Tenth Party Congress which was then due to open in Petersburg. It too would offer concessions to the peasantry similar to those demanded by the Kronstadters. It was "a retreat" (Lenin) but given that the problem of socialism could not be solved in Russia without world revolution, a necessary one, in that it would at least have alleviated the immediate suffering of the population.

Trotsky also has some cheek in suggesting that the Kronstadters just demanded "special privileges for themselves". Another of the causes which provoked so much resentment in both the Petersburg strikes and in Kronstadt was the evident creation of a new privileged class. Someone did not have to have much to be considered privileged in civil war Russia. Access to a government canteen, boots instead of bark footwear and a leather or sheepskin coat were enough to mark out the "commiss-arocracy". Rumour suggested even more luxury for some. Though Lenin and Trotsky themselves lived frugally, there were many in the new regime who used their positions in arrogant and arbitrary fashion. New words were coined to describe this "Communist arrogance". Chamberlin quotes veteran Communist, Aaron Soltz (or Solts) who was known in his time as "the conscience of the revolution". In February 1921 he wrote a series of article in *Pravda*, one of which stated that,

> *The civil war made some Communists most devoted and heroic. But some being in power under a dictatorship, lost the feeling of comradeship and became indistinguishable from former rulers.*

Pointing to the way some lower ranking Communists tried to please their superiors by supplying them with luxuries like extra food, special trains, cars etc., he goes on to quote one Communist who resigned from the party because,

> *I do not believe in the realization of communism, in view of the privileges which are enjoyed by those Communists who occupy responsible posts.*[22]

Even inside the Communist Party, the hostility of the *nizi* (lower) to the superciliousness of some *verkhi* (upper) members was apparent. One sign of this disillusionment was that:

> *Between August 1920 and March 1921, the Kronstadt party organization lost half of its 4000 members.*[23]

In this context it should also be noted that not only the whole of the Baltic Fleet but also about half of the remaining Communist Party members in Kronstadt accepted the *Petropavlovsk* programme. This was because they saw it, as Victor Serge noted, as "a programme for the renewal of the revolution".[24]

It is also not true, as various Trotskyists try to maintain, that the class composition of the Kronstadters had altered much between 1917 and 1921. Most of the sailors had been of peasant origin in 1917, and perhaps a few more of them were so in 1921, but it was hardly a massive shift in class composition. You could also make the same generalisation about most of the Russian working class, given that most workers' parents had been peasants. What had changed, as Trotsky himself understood in 1938, was that the Kronstadt sailors so fiercely identified with the soviet cause that they were repeatedly called upon to send detachments all over Russia to support the often shaky raw Red Army recruits. This meant that the most politically committed Communists were continually being taken away from the base, exactly the same process that was going on in factories across the country, thus weakening the links between class and party. And in Kronstadt the remaining Communist Party members were of a newer vintage, who had joined the Party after the revolution, on the assumption that it was the one force that could defend the gains the workers had won in October.

Kronstadt and Beyond

After the Petropavlovsk Resolution was announced there were no real attempts at negotiation, despite the attempts of Emma Goldman, Alexander Berkman and Victor Serge, and their associates. Mikhail Kalinin, himself both of peasant and working class origin, and one of the more successful at talking to angry workers, was duly sent to calm things down. Victor Serge blamed him for making the situation worse but, as Avrich demonstrated,[25] this time he was hardly given a hearing. Instead Kuzmin and Vasiliev, the Communists nominally in charge in Kronstadt, simply harangued and threatened the mass meeting in Anchor Square. The US anarchist, Alexander Berkman (who was not present) later accurately described their contribution as "a firebrand thrown into gunpowder".[26] They were the first to be arrested by the Kronstadters but like the other 300 of the Party members locked up they were left unharmed, apart from having to give up boots and warm clothing to the sailors guarding the fort perimeter.

The arrest of the Communist officials turned the protest into an insurrection, and this was only compounded in Communist eyes when the Kronstadt soviet formed a Provisional Revolutionary Committee of five, headed by Stepan Petrichenko. From the government point of view it looked like a direct challenge to the rule of the Communist Party, and coming as the civil war was only just ending, looked yet like another crisis that could only be dealt with militarily. The White generals who had been backed by all the imperialist powers had only been defeated a few weeks before, after almost three years of a bloody and exhausting civil war. For the Communists in power, holding on to save the Russian bastion of the working class until the rest of the world's proletariat came to its aid, now demanded the rapid crushing of Kronstadt.

Lenin and Trotsky were only too ready to grasp the slightest evidence (said to have been furnished by Kalinin) that this was a "White plot". The irony is that Trotsky had built up the Red Army using ex-Tsarist officers like General Kozlovsky who was in charge of the artillery at Kronstadt. He should have taken over the command of its fortress once the Communist commander had fled. He refused, though the fact is the Kronstadters' class position probably meant they would not have accepted him anyway. He simply remained at his post to give "technical advice". However, his presence was all that the Party propaganda machine needed to be able to spread the rumour that Kronstadt was a White plot. Partially as a result, the exhausted workers in Petersburg, whose strikes had initially provoked the Kronstadt Revolt, made no move to support it. The use of the press like this came as a complete shock to Victor Serge, the ex-anarchist then working for the Communist International:

> ... the Press ... was positively berserk with lies. And this was our own Press, the Press of our revolution, the first Socialist Press, and hence the first incorruptible and unbiased Press in the world! ... The Kronstadt insurrection had shed not a single drop of blood, and merely arrested a few Communist officials, who were treated absolutely correctly ... all, the same the legend of narrowly averted executions was put around.[27]

The Petropavlovsk sailors had earlier sent a delegation of thirty sailors to Petersburg to try to tell the striking workers the truth about Kronstadt, but Avrich tells us it was never heard of again. Another group, sent to try to persuade the last ice-breaking vessel in the Russian Navy to leave Petersburg and make its way to Kronstadt, was arrested by the Cheka. Isolation from much of what was going on outside was to become one of the factors in both the continuation and defeat of the rising. Kronstadt did receive support from some units like the Air and Naval squadron at Oranienbaum, just five miles away on the mainland, but when the insurgents sent a detachment of 250 men towards it, they came under a heavy bombardment from troops loyal to the government and were forced to retreat. Ironically the supposed "White general" Kozlovsky's first piece of "technical advice" to the sailors was to make a serious attempt to take the fort at Oranienburg from where they might have been in a better position to contact workers throughout Russia. However the Provisional Revolutionary Committee seemed to think this was unnecessary as they thought the workers of Petersburg were already behind them. They also seemed to think that when the thaw came they would be able to use the *Petropavlovsk* and *Sebastopol,* to both defend the fortress, and further their cause. Kozlovsky apparently advised against this as well, and suggested using the battleships' guns pre-emptively to blast holes in the ice, so they could be manoeuvred into a better position, as well as create a "moat" in front of the fort. It is a telling piece of evidence to prove that there was no White "plot" at Kronstadt that the sailors did not wait a few weeks until the sea had thawed to improve their chances of success. Instead the Kronstadters busied themselves with reviving soviet democracy, improving social organisation and equalising rations on the island (with sick children getting increases). So, despite the fact that in February/March 1921 there were, at one time or another, strikes in 77% of all large and medium sized enterprises in Russia,[28] not to mention 118 peasant uprisings against requisitioning, Kronstadt was very much on its own.

The Suppression of the Revolt

As it was, Trotsky eventually arrived in Petersburg and, as head of the Military Revolutionary Council of the Republic, immediately sent an ultimatum to the sailors to surrender. This did not include the threat to "shoot them like partridges" as is sometimes asserted. That phrase was in a leaflet issued by Zinoviev's Petersburg Defence Committee. On 7 March the *Kronstadt Izvestia* (now edited by the SR-Maximalist Lamanov who had for a period been a candidate member of the Communist Party, but announced his resignation in the paper itself) rejected the ultimatum, labelling Trotsky "the dictator of Soviet Russia".

The first assault on the base across the ice of the Gulf of Finland began the next day. It was a failure. Five hundred were killed and many of the troops deserted to the Kronstadters. A new force was hurriedly assembled, made up of Cheka units, Red Army officer cadets (*kursanti*) and even 300 or more delegates from the Tenth Party Congress, then convening in Petersburg. The Military Revolutionary Committee were also in a hurry because the ice around the Gulf of Finland was expected to melt in the next few days. It was rumoured that the ice in the streets of Kronstadt had already started to thaw. This would not only have freed up the ice bound ships around the base, but also made it impossible to retake without a navy, and the only two battleships the Russian Navy still had were moored at Kronstadt. This in turn could have made it possible for capitalist governments and White exiles to supply the base, and then use it for a way to re-enter Russia. Despite the attentions of the various anti-Communist organisations who contacted them by radio, the Kronstadt sailors had no intention of accepting any of their anti-soviet offers, but the Military Revolutionary Committee which also heard those messages, could not have known this, and thought it was a race against time.

On 16 March Tukhachevsky launched the second attack. As was now Red Army practice, the Cheka remained at the rear to shoot anyone who dared to turn back. Fortuitously aided by a snow storm, which helped hide the attackers, the entire town was re-occupied by 18 March, after fierce hand to hand fighting. There are few reliable figures of casualties but the anarchist historian, Paul Avrich, estimated that 10,000 of the attacking force died under the Kronstadt guns (including 15 delegates to the Communist Party's Tenth Congress) whilst 1,500 of the defenders were killed and a further 2,500 were captured. Many of these were later shot by the Cheka. 8,000 did escape across the ice to Finland where they were interned. It was with no sense of irony that delegates to the Tenth Party Congress of the RCP(B) celebrated the fiftieth anniversary of the start of the Paris Commune on the very day that Kronstadt fell.

Despite his sympathy for the defenders of Kronstadt, and the fact that he saw in their programme a revival of the revolution's original ideals, Victor Serge ended by supporting the action against it.

> *After many hesitations, and with unutterable anguish, my Communist friends and I declared ourselves on the side of the Party. This is why. Kronstadt had right on its side. Kronstadt was the beginning of a fresh liberating revolution for popular democracy; "The Third Revolution!" it was called by certain anarchists whose heads were stuffed with infantile illusions. However the country was absolutely exhausted, and production practically at a standstill; there were no reserves of any kind, not even reserves of stamina in the hearts of the masses. The working class elite that had been moulded in the struggle against the old regime was literally decimated. The party, swollen by the influx of power seekers, inspired little confidence. Of the other parties only minute nuclei existed, whose character was highly questionable [...] If the Bolshevik dictatorship fell, it was only a short step to chaos, and through chaos to a peasant rising, the massacre of the Communists, the return of the émigrés, and in the end, through sheer force of events, another dictatorship, this time anti-proletarian.[29]*

This gives us an insight into the siege mentality brought about by civil war. We were still in a world where it was only "Reds" versus "Whites". Lenin himself encapsulated this when he admitted to the Tenth Party Congress a few days later that the Kronstadters were not really supporters of the Whites since,

> *... they do not want either the White Guards or our government – and there is*

no other.[30]

However this made them "more dangerous than Denikin, Yudenich and Kolchak put together", since they would have led, as Serge also suggests, to the revival of the counter-revolution. Lenin even lumped all the oppositions within the Communist Party alongside the Kronstadters (thus blackmailing them into showing their loyalty by volunteering to join the forces assembled for the second assault on the fortress). A week before that assault Lenin turned on Shlyapnikov, who had criticised the failures of the Commissar for Food Supply, Tsyurupa.

> *Are we seriously discussing discipline and unity in an organised Party or are we at a meeting of the Kronstadt type? For his is a Kronstadt, anarchist type of statement to which the response is a gun.[31]*

The tragedy of Kronstadt was amply summarised by Serge. Despite the illusions of Lamanov and others in the base, there was to be no "third revolution", and nor could there have been. This was a clash between two sections of the working class about what precise course the counter-revolution would take. Both sides knew that the policy of requisitioning had outlived any use it might once have had and the only alternative was to capitulate to the peasantry. The isolation of the Russian workers made this inevitable. The great merit of the Kronstadters was that they also wanted to restore the original revolutionary principles of soviet direct democracy, but they now faced a Party that had once understood the need, not just to smash the capitalist state, but to abolish the state in general. However in the course of a brutal civil war, it had not only ended up as the wielder of a new state power, but was now dominated by those who saw it as the only legitimate guardian of the revolution. The minorities in the Communist Party who might have once sided with the Kronstadters were reduced to the same position as Serge. They might have sympathised with the cause of Kronstadt but apart from the likes of Miasnikov, who would soon be expelled from the party, they found they had little support, and either remained silent, or ostentatiously expressed their loyalty by joining the assault force.

In the sense that "socialism" was now a prerogative of a Party-state, any hope that the working class character of the revolution could be recovered was lost at Kronstadt, even if it did not appear so to many, both at home and abroad, at the time. Other events in March 1921 brought further signs that the revolutionary retreat went beyond Kronstadt.

The Tenth Party Congress 1921

Within Russia, the Tenth Party Congress opened on the same day as the first assault on Kronstadt. If further evidence was needed that March 1921 provided a significant turning point in the Russian and world working class revolution, then this Congress provided it. There were three issues on the table. The first was the trades union issue which had remained unresolved since the Ninth Congress, and which we dealt with in earlier chapters, but which had continued to fester throughout 1920. The second was over the policy to be adopted towards the peasantry now that it was clear that requisitioning was no longer fit for purpose, and the third was the internal condition of the Communist Party itself.

There were three proposed "platforms" on the role of the trades union. Trotsky, ever the state-builder, as we saw in both Chapters 11 and 13, wanted to make the unions part of the state management apparatus as part of his militarisation of labour strategy. Most dramatically opposed to this was the platform of the Workers' Opposition. The Workers' Opposition was the latest in a series of oppositions within the Bolshevik Party which attempted to maintain (in various and diverse ways) the idea that a workers' revolution had to be the work of workers' themselves. As we saw in Chapter 8, this had also been the position of Lenin himself until he grasped the economic catastrophe facing the revolution by the spring of 1918. The debate in the Tenth Party Congress was really about where the revolution should go next.

The three factions of the Party had been agitating for their platforms in local parties and trades unions throughout 1920. It was clear that the Workers' Opposition headed by Shlyapnikov, Medvedev and Lutovinov were getting about the same support as Trotsky's but falling well behind Lenin's so-called Group of Ten. The fact of Lenin's prestige, plus the fact that he could mobilise central party resources in the campaign, made it hard work for the Workers' Opposition to gain ground. When the Tenth Party Congress (8-16 March 1921) opened only 45 of the 694 voting delegates supported the Workers' Opposition.[32]

In view of this Shlyapnikov asked Alexandra Kollontai because of "her passion and skill at swaying audiences",[33] to write something about the Workers' Opposition. The result was her famous booklet *The Workers' Opposition*. Printed only for the delegates it later found its way abroad, and was serialised by Sylvia Pankhurst in *Workers' Dreadnought* before the year was out. Kollontai had been the first to support Lenin's *April Theses* back in 1917 and was convinced she could persuade Lenin to change course. In fact she used language reminiscent of the Lenin of early 1918, except this time as a criticism of where the revolution was going. She said that something the party leaders have lost sight of is that,

> ... **it is impossible to decree Communism**. *It can be built only ... by the creative powers of the working class itself.*[34]

She went on:

> *We are afraid to let the masses do things themselves. We are afraid of allowing their creativity. We fear criticism. We no longer trust the masses. Therein ... lies origin of our bureaucracy. Initiative wanes, the desire to act dies out. 'If that's the way it is, let the officials take care of us.' In this way a very damaging division grows up: we – that is, the workers – and they – that is, the soviet officials, on whom everything depends. Here is the root of all evil.*[35]

It had the exact opposite effect to her intentions. Lenin read it on the platform of the Congress, shook his head and addressing her, but in earshot of many, accused her of writing the "platform of a new party" then added it contained the same slogans as the Kronstadters:

For this you should not only be excluded but shot as well![36]

Neither Shlyapnikov nor Medvedev supported Kollontai, so the pamphlet was effectively repudiated by the Workers' Opposition, but the damage was done, and in the ensuing vote only 18 voted for their platform. The Party also rejected Trotsky's proposal to turn the unions into organs of state discipline. Lenin's Platform of the Ten to make unions organs of workers' defence, and "transmission belts" between the working class and the Party, was claimed to be still necessary because "ours is not actually a workers' state" but "a workers' state with **a bureaucratic twist to it**".[37] Ironically the statement of the Platform of the Ten that the unions "are the one place ... where the selection of leaders should be done by the organised masses themselves" was in itself a confession that real soviet democracy was not going to be revived. Everything else was at the whim of the Party.

And not even all the Party. At the Eighth Party Congress in 1919 it was decided that the Central Committee had become too unwieldy to make decisions so it was decided to set up two smaller bodies – the Political Bureau (Politburo), and the Organisation Bureau (Orgburo). The former which consisted initially of five people (Lenin. Trotsky, Stalin, Kamenev and Krestinsky) now become the virtual government of the soviet republic whilst the latter organisation now became responsible for organising elections of officials and dealing with Party disciplinary matters. At the Ninth Party Congress in 1920 the Democratic Centralists (Decists), among others, objected to the extinguishing of democracy inside the party as local party committees were now no longer elected by local members but now replaced by centrally appointed "political departments". Daniels tells us that one of the most rigorous applications of this was in the coal mines of the Donets basin by Stalin. When he became Communist Party General Secretary in 1922 he would develop his "talent" for such work by appointing local party secretaries to organise the election of his own creatures as delegates to Party Congresses, but this is to anticipate. At the Ninth Congress Sapronov distinguished himself by first denouncing the appointments system:

You transform the members of the party into an obedient gramophone, with leaders who order: go and agitate: but they haven't the right to elect their own committee, their own organs.

He then presciently asked:

I then put it to comrade Lenin: who will appoint the Central Committee? You see, there can be an individual authority here as well. Here also a single commander can be appointed. It does not appear we have reached this state but if we do, the revolution will have been gambled away ... Comrade Lenin ... allow us ignorant ones to ask you a question. If you go according to this system, do you think that the result will be the salvation of the revolution?[38]

In some ways the struggle of all the Party "oppositions" must already have become imbued with a sense of failure since they had passed from struggling for workers' democracy in the soviets and factory committees, to struggling to preserve democracy in a Party where the organisational machine was already stacked against them.

The *coup de grace* was delivered by the ban on factions which was introduced at the Tenth Party Congress. As we saw in earlier chapters, the Bolshevik Party of the past had been characterised by vigorous debate which ran from local party committees like Vyborg in Petersburg, and Bauman in Moscow, to the Central Committee. The Party had not always followed Lenin, and certainly never unquestioningly. The various tendencies within the Communist Party had come to accept the demands for "unity" and greater centralisation and concentration of power as the price of fighting a war. However when the war was winding down all sections of the Communist Party now put forward different plans for the future. We have already seen the widely different visions that were presented on the trades union question at the Tenth Party Congress. This was the standard practice in the Party up until then. However, before the Congress could begin, Lenin produced a remarkable document, entitled *The Party Crisis*. It was remarkable in that it denounced every single opponent (including Trotsky and Bukharin) as not being really communist. As a result he complained:

The party is sick. The party is down with a fever.[39]

To be sure Lenin said, as he always did, that he valued these comrades, but he made it quite clear that the only legitimate criticism was that confined only to details like "bureaucratic excesses". He reserved his most trenchant criticisms for the Decists and Workers' Opposition, though not by name. Against the Decists, he gave his response to Sapronov's question of the previous year:

*We must combat the ideological discord and **unsound** elements of the opposition who talk themselves into repudiating all "militarisation of industry" and not only the "appointments method" which has been the prevailing one up to now, but all "appointments" that is, in the last analysis, repudiating the **Party's** leading role in relation to the non-Party masses.*

And on the Workers' Opposition

We must combat the syndicalist deviation, which will kill the Party unless it is entirely cured of it.[40]

And just as he did in relation to Kronstadt, the danger that he ends on, is that any break in Party unity could open the way for all the revolution's enemies, from foreign imperialists to now-departed ex-Tsarist generals, to take advantage. These seem to have been a constant and genuine fear which all the strikes and revolts of 1921 only nourished. The result was the resolution *On the Unity of the Party*. This banned:

> ... *all groups without exception which formed themselves on one platform or another, and orders all organizations to deal strictly with any factional manifestations by prohibiting them ... Failure to execute this decision of the congress will lead to immediate and unconditional expulsion from the party.*[40]

In the debate the mercurial, but sometimes prescient, Radek said he would vote for the resolution because "the best Central Committee may make a mistake, but this is less dangerous than the wavering we see now."
But before that he wondered if

> ... *a rule was being established which ... may even be turned against us.*[42]

Radek here was not just referring to the published resolution. A secret provision gave the Central Committee even more power to control the Party membership. It stated that "in order to realise strict discipline",

> ... *the congress gives the Central Committee full power to exercise, in case of violation of discipline or causing or allowing of factionalism, all measures of party up to expulsion from the party ...*[43]

One of the first members to suffer this fate would be Gavril Miasnikov, the best known member of the Workers' Group which had been formed in 1920 in opposition to the decisions of the Ninth Party Congress. He continued to agitate for a revival of the original working class framework of Bolshevism and was expelled in 1922.[44] The secret clause also allowed for the demotion and expulsion of Central Committee members – a power not used in Lenin's remaining two years but it would be central to Stalin's eventual control of the Communist Party. Radek's commentary was not the first time he would unknowingly prophesy the fate of the revolution. Back in 1918 in the pages of the Left Communist journal *Kommunist,* himself the future advocate of "National Bolshevism" in Germany, Radek predicted that a military victory alone would be no victory at all. It was a prescient warning:

> *If the Russian revolution were crushed by the bourgeois counter-revolution, it would be reborn from its ashes like the Phoenix; But if it loses its socialist character, and by this disappoints the working masses, this blow would have ten times more terrible consequences for the future of the Russian and international revolution.*[45]

In 1921, his 1918 nightmare that a counter-revolution which would claim to be a working class victory, was already taking shape before his eyes.

Further evidence of this came from the final momentous decision of the Tenth Party

Congress. This was the introduction of the "New Economic Policy" (NEP). The irony of the name lies in the fact that there never had been "an old economic policy". Many histories of the Russian revolution will describe the period of 1918-21 as that of "war communism" but it did not get that name until Lenin used it at the Tenth Party Congress. By avoiding the use of the convenient shorthand term "war communism" up to this point, we are not just avoiding anachronism, but also avoiding the suggestion that what had gone before was a coherent policy. Even Silvana Malle, who wrote the monumental and definitive study of the economics of "war communism", excused herself from giving a definition of the term. For the most part she found that the Bolsheviks-cum-Communists had responded to events in a largely "expedient" way, even though tinged with ideological preferences.[46]

Lenin actually coined the term "war communism" in his 1921 pamphlet "The Tax in Kind" specifically to dismiss it as a series of emergency measures forced on Soviet Russia by the civil war. As we saw in Chapter 8 he thought any vision of real socialism had to wait until the world revolution had made it possible. The more ideological defenders of the policies undertaken in the Civil War were to be found amongst the various Left Communists. Most striking of these was the economist, Lev Kritsman. The title of his book, which we have referred to before, *The Heroic Period of the Great October Revolution,* rather gives the game away as to his view of the 1918-21 period, but he too saw that:

> ... *war communism can be seen not as the transition to socialism but the organisation of the 'rear', not the organisation of socialism but the organisation of war, i.e. a simulated transition to socialism.*[47]

And initially, as we saw in Chapter 8, the impulse for the "Red Guard assault" (Lenin) on capitalism in 1917-18 had come from the workers, and not the party which was divided and hesitant. The whole party knew that the fate of the Russian Revolution would be decided by revolution in the more advanced countries, but in this early period some on the Left began to think that such things as the collapse in the value of money, and the takeover of factories by the workers, were already the germs of a socialist mode of organisation. Even the emergency grain requisitioning policy was seen as part of the process. Ossinsky was still demanding that they hold on to this in 1920 when both Lenin and Trotsky had hesitantly begun to realise it had outlived its usefulness. He did win support for his own scheme of compromise with the peasantry in December 1920. This involved setting up sowing committees as a response to the drastic drop in the sown area. According to Ossinky's scheme the committees would distribute seeds, advise on planting and as an incentive peasants would be allowed to keep a higher proportion of the crop.[48] With the introduction of the NEP the proposal, although still given verbal support by Lenin at the Tenth Party Congress, never really got off the ground. Requisitioning was not just ideologically supported by Left Communists during the civil war but had real support in the working class, especially in 1918. Even when food supply problems emerged in the summer of 1918 workers still thought it the best solution. Kevin Murphy recounts the discussion in a Moscow metalworking factory.

...one worker criticized the proposed food requisitioning plan and proposed alleviating the food crisis by implementing free trade with the countryside. Workers "listened attentively to the speaker, but when he called for the abolition of fixed prices and for free trade, rows of workers came alive with shouts of protest".[49]

However, by the end of 1920 famine was already stalking the Volga region, and peasant revolts were so widespread, that it was clear that concessions to the peasantry would now have to be made. The NEP not only restored the "free market" in grain but substituted requisitioning with what was originally a "tax in kind" on part of the peasant surplus. In time the tax in kind became a money tax. Many workers saw that Lenin was right. It was a "retreat" but many others still did not find it acceptable. Serge tells us that:

the confusion among the party rank-and-file was staggering. For what did we fight, spill so much blood, agree to so many sacrifices? asked the Civil War veterans bitterly. Usually these men lacked all the necessities: clothes, decent homes, money; and now everything was turning back into market value.[50]

The Party which at that time was trying to weed out those who had joined for careerist purposes, was now faced with a spate of resignations from its most committed supporters.

NEP allowed the peasants not only to market their grain but revived the role of money in the economy and recognised their right of private ownership. NEP did not come in time to prevent a devastating famine in the Volga and Southern Urals where the harvest was poor due to a rainless summer. It led to the deaths of 5 million people, from a combination of starvation and disease.[51] The death toll would have been higher but, unlike the famines inflicted by Stalinism, this was openly announced to the world and aid sought, which largely came from the USA. Yet peasants in the rest of Russia were soon doing well, and were selling food to starving workers at inflated prices by the autumn of 1921. Lenin had confessed when introducing NEP,

*that the **kulak** element under this system will grow far more than hitherto. It will grow in places it could not before.[52]*

And the rise of rich peasants was not the only example of spreading inequality. The industrial managers were also granted favours whilst small artisans and rural petty industry could both employ workers and trade on the same terms as the peasants. However, as far as workers were concerned the return of some industries to private management and control through a system of leasing industries to cooperatives or private owners was the worst aspect of NEP. Wages paid in rations were phased out and money wages which had become almost irrelevant in the civil war were, bit by bit, reintroduced. This had to be handled carefully, as Carr tells us:

The change from payments in kind to a monetary wage system was too unpopular to be introduced except by slow stages. The worker, unconcerned with theory,

was alive to the consequences of receiving, in the place of his guaranteed ration,
payment in a currency of uncertain and constantly declining purchasing power.[53]

The attack on workers did not end there. Not only did they lose their rations, but free rent and transport also came to an end. Perhaps worst of all was the rationalising of industry so that factories were consolidated with the consequent loss of jobs. The number of unemployed stood at 175,000 in January 1922 but had reached 1.24 million by January 1924. This was equivalent to an unemployment rate of 25% for which only one in five received any unemployment benefit.

The final evidence of how deep the concessions to the peasantry could go came in the winter of 1922-3. The "scissors crisis" arose because NEP had been a success in producing more grain. Its price fell as industrial prices rose sharply. To solve this grain was now exported to keep up prices (and build up currency reserves) whilst many workers were laid off to lower production costs in industry. Just how much workers' power had been turned into peasant power can be seen by the arch state capitalist Trotsky who (in the absence of the sick Lenin) now came up with the convoluted logic of "primary socialist accumulation" which entailed that,

The working class, being in power, has the possibility, when class interests
require it, of giving industry a credit at the expense of the worker's wage

which he clarified as meaning,

... there may be moments when the state does not pay a full wage or pays only a
half, and you, the worker, give a credit to your state at the expense of your wage.[54]

In Trotsky's head (and not just his) this could not be equated with capitalist exploitation because the state was "a workers' state". As it was, real wages had already declined before management started to delay them, a fact which made 1923 the first year that state industry turned a profit.[55] Little wonder that a wave of strikes broke out against the "workers' state" in August and September 1923. Miasnikov's Workers' Group and members of the group, Workers' Truth, both participated in the strikes. The GPU (successor to the Cheka) suppressed the strikes, arrested Miasnikov after he tried to organise workers' demonstrations and then other members of the Workers' Group, like Kuznetsov. The same fate befell the Workers' Truth group, but not before they had issued a ringing condemnation of the "New Exploitation Policy".

The working class ekes out a miserable existence whilst the new bourgeoisie
(responsible party workers, directors of factories, managers of trusts, presidents of
executive committees etc.) live in luxury and revives in our memory the picture of
the bourgeoisie of all ages. Their very material prosperity and the stability of their
positions depends on the degree of exploitation of the toiling masses. All this makes
inevitable a contradiction of interests, a rift between the Communist Party and the
masses.[56]

The Workers' Truth Group was still largely made up of Party members who were not only arrested, but were also expelled from the Party, as per the resolution of the Tenth Party Congress. Appeals for members of the former Workers' Opposition to join with them apparently went unheeded. Until 1928 the relationship between party and class would, not without much grumbling, become one where the workers' standard of living was gradually improved but everything was now under the party-state. It was also the time when the workers' initiative of 1917-18 was completely turned on its head in top-down mobilisations for this or that cause.[57] It was a model which all one party states would come to adopt in imitation of this new type of state capitalism. We will return to this in our concluding chapter.

The International Counter-Revolution

As we noted early, the Kronstadt crisis and the outcomes of the Tenth Party Congress, were not the only signs that the counter-revolution was in the ascendant. In the very same month, news came of the disastrous March Action in Germany.

In Germany, the Communists had split between the Communist Workers' Party (KAPD) and the official party (KPD) in 1919 and all attempts to re-unite them fell on deaf ears on both sides. For its part the KPD oscillated from its birth between putschism and passivity. After the deaths of Luxemburg and Liebknecht the leadership had fallen to Clara Zetkin and Paul Levi. Levi had been the one who had precipitated the expulsion of the KAPD against Lenin's advice and had blocked their entry, other than as sympathisers, to the Comintern in 1920. The KPD got an enormous boost when the left of the centrist USPD joined with it to form the United Communist Party (VKPD), thus raising its membership to something like half a million. It had become a mass party, but one with a critically divided leadership, between those who thought the time was now ripe for action, and those wedded to parliamentarism.

Its participation in the so-called March Action was a disaster which not only cost it two thirds of its membership (falling from 450,000 to 180,000 in three months) but really sapped the morale and revolutionary will of the working class. Partly the KPD responded to a provocation of the Army (which tried to disarm workers), partly to the encouragement of Radek and Béla Kun to help break the isolation of soviet Russia, and partly to be seen to act more decisively than it had done during the Kapp Putsch (1920) where it had let the SPD organise the strikes which overthrew that right wing attempt at a coup. At the end of the March Action tragedy turned to farce when the KPD leader, Eberlein tried to stimulate the workers to carry on fighting by staging "kidnappings" of leading communists, and blowing up KPD buildings – a stunt which backfired when it was exposed by the ruling class. The final fiasco came when workers in Hamburg, who wanted to carry on, ended up fighting workers who saw that the action was over.

Long before the defeat of the March Action in Germany, Soviet Russia was negotiating its survival in the post-war imperialist set up. This did not mean the automatic abandonment of the world revolution, simply a recognition of the weakness of the soviet economy and the need to re-establish foreign trade. On 16 March 1921, two days before the final suppression of Kronstadt, the British Government signed the Anglo-Soviet Trade agreement which involved *de facto* recognition of the Bolshevik government in return for the suspension of all propaganda against the British in Afghanistan and India. By October Chicherin, then Commissar for Foreign Affairs, was announcing that the Soviet Government "was willing to assume responsibility for Tsarist loans before 1914" in return for recognition of the Soviet Government and the end of all hostile acts against it.[58] The regime's isolation was ending but by re-integration into the capitalist world order rather than via a revolution against it. As we shall see, secret negotiations had, in fact, already started with the German Army and Government, so that even though the March Action was taking place a German trade mission under Rathenau came to Moscow. Krasin, the Soviet Commissar for Foreign Trade, even warned German workers at this critical point that striking would impede deliveries to the Soviet Union!

The final piece of evidence that the revolutionary wave was dying out came at the Third Congress of the Third (Communist) International in June-July of 1921. The debacle of the March Action, and the Kronstadt Revolt, lay heavy on the minds of the Bolshevik leaders who organised the main debates. Some delegates arrived in critical mood believing that it was the Russian Party which had pushed the Comintern to adventurism in Germany.[59] Lenin was at pains to disabuse them of this by singling out Béla Kun for blame and spoke in French to make sure he was more widely understood. Béla Kun had his own "theory of the offensive" but was likely to have been acting on the orders of Zinoviev. For the latter, action in Germany might relieve the crisis in Russia. According to Serge though, Lenin said Levi (now expelled from the KPD for a pamphlet condemning "the putsch") had been right and repeatedly talked of the "stupidities" (bêtises) of Béla Kun.[60] However behind this attack on Béla Kun was also an attack on all those communists, in whatever country, who were impatient for revolution. It did not matter that they all had different views, the important point to get over was that the time for revolutionary offensive was over. Trotsky, in agreement with Lenin, went even further. He told the delegates that in 1919 they had expected world revolution in a matter of months. Now they were talking about "a question of years".

No longer was the framework one of intransigent defence of revolutionary positions as in the 21 Conditions adopted by the Second Congress in 1920. At this point, the main concern was how to achieve a "mass" basis for Communist parties. "Going to the masses" was the slogan which emerged from the Third Congress. Given that the revolutionary wave was ebbing this meant seeking alliance with the very Social Democrats who had joined the imperialist camp in 1914 and had connived at the murder of hundreds of communists by the crypto-fascists. The Third Congress of the International was thus another watershed in the counter-revolutionary turn of 1921. It also indicated how the fate of the International would remain bound up with the course of the counter-revolution in Russia. This first became clear in the debate on what had previously been called "the national and colonial question". Previously the International had had an exaggerated policy of seeing national struggles against imperialism as linked to the struggle for communism. Now (only nine months after the Baku Conference) it did not even refer to "national and colonial struggles" but to the "eastern question". A Russian trade treaty with the British Empire plus treaties with Persia (Iran) and Turkey meant that these governments were not to be offended. Small wonder that the Indian Communist, M.N. Roy, delivered the only really heavyweight verdict on the debate by denouncing Comintern policy as "pure opportunism ... more suitable for a congress of the Second International."[61]

The same thing was also true of the shift in policy towards social democracy in general. The "united front" with the butchers of the working class would have been proclaimed at the Third Congress, if it had not already been associated with the disgraced German KPD leader, Paul Levi. Instead the exhortation of the Bolshevik leaders in the Third Congress was "to the masses". But the Communists had already been using this idea even when trying to split the social democratic parties. So what could the new slogan mean? Nothing other than a rapprochement with social democracy at all levels, as became clear in December, when the Russian Party adopted the slogan of the "united front" for the first time. It was clear that the idea was not about working with the rank and file but with the leaders – this was the first step in abandoning the revolutionary path on an international scale. It was not announced as such but *de facto* it was already that. If 1921 showed that the revolution inside Russia had now swung against the working class it was also the beginning of the process that led to abandoning the proletarian principles of internationalism – the one thing that had defined the Bolshevik Party back in 1914.

On May Day 1922 the slogan of "world revolution" was missed out for the first time from the slogans issued by the Russian Communist Party. To the revolutionaries of the time however the significance of this was not so obvious. Setbacks will always occur in any process, and revolutionaries have to maintain a rational optimism that such setbacks can be reversed. In the case of the "united front" though there was an important issue. When it was put forward at the Fourth Congress of the Communist International, most of the new Communist Parties had only broken from social democracy eighteen or so months previously. Now they were being told to go back and make alliances with the very same parties which had sided with the bourgeoisie (murderously so in the German case). Before the end of 1922 Bordiga was openly criticising "the danger of seeing the united front degenerate into a communist revisionism".[62] The Italian party tried to salvage something from the slogan by turning it into a "united front from below" (i.e. working with socialist workers in strikes etc. but not the organisations they adhered to). However, by 1924 it was clear that this was only leading to questions amongst workers who had chosen to be in the ranks of the communists. On top of this the social democrats were not interested in any united front with any revolutionary movement and the rebuff was a humiliation. Bordiga now demanded the abandonment of the "united front" and the "workers' government" slogans as total confusions.

By this time however further degeneration had set in with all the Communist Parties affiliated to the International subject to "bolshevisation" i.e. their leaders were chosen for their compliance to Moscow and to the interests of the Soviet state's foreign policy. Gramsci replaced Bordiga on Moscow's insistence and he used various organisational means to destroy the hold that the Italian Communist Left held over the Communist Party of Italy (even if it did take until the Lyons Congress of 1926). By this time, the Communist Left, which had founded the Communist Party of Italy at Livorno, had formed the Committee of Intesa (Alliance), whose Platform summed up their verdict on the whole fiasco of the Comintern's policy.[63]

> *It is mistaken to think that in every situation expedients and tactical manoeuvres can widen the Party base since relations between the party and the masses depend in large part on the objective situation.*[64]

What this signified was that, instead of the world revolution coming to save the proletarian heart of the Russian Revolution, the advancing counter-revolution in Russia was beginning to turn the Communist International into a foreign policy arm of a Russian state increasingly seeking to do deals with the same capitalist powers which had spent almost three years trying to to crush it militarily. Trade treaties were to follow with Britain and Sweden within months whilst the Treaty of Rapallo of 1922 wiped out all claims Russia and Germany might make against each other and offered "favoured nation" status to each other. That "favour" extended to a secret deal with the German Reichswehr which used Soviet territory to evade the limits set in its activities in the Treaty of Versailles. The Germans were also given concessions under NEP to take over failing Russian shipyards, aircraft and armament factories to the mutual benefit of both parties. The concessions largely failed economically but the German Army retained four bases from which to operate and to train Red Army officers, and cooperation on chemical warfare research appears to have been more successful. According to the German General behind all this, Hans Von Seeckt, Trotsky even agreed to Germany re-establishing its old Eastern border.[65] That is, he agreed to the re-partitioning of Poland – thus prefiguring the deal that would be struck by Stalin and Hitler in 1939. The contradiction of a secret deal with the Germany Army came home to roost in November 1923 when the Comintern pushed the German KPD into premature revolutionary action. In the fiasco that followed the USSR was arming both the KPD and their opponents![66]

The Communist International eventually followed the path of the Second International in coming to an accommodation with the capitalist world order. United fronts were only the beginning and the last meaningful act of the Comintern was to call for the formation of, not just "united fronts" with nominally working class organisations, but by 1935 was calling for "popular fronts" with any "anti-fascist" force it could find. All this was part of the preparation for the Second World War, in which, as mentioned above, the USSR first entered a pact with Nazi Germany, before forming the "anti-fascist" imperialist bloc against Hitler. If we take the "bolshevisation" project of the early 1920s as the end of the original revolutionary international of 1919-20, the unavoidable conclusion is that the working class was betrayed by two internationals within the space of a decade. An enormous historical defeat from which it has not yet politically recovered.

Chapter 15
Revolution is an Affair of the Masses

Inside Russia the suppression of Kronstadt might in hindsight have marked the end of the revolution, but it was not the end of the crisis for the Communist Party in 1921. Putting an end to requisitioning was designed to make peace with the peasantry but Lenin, when introducing the NEP, still referred to the revolution as "a besieged fortress". This was because the 118 revolts, mentioned in the previous chapter, continued, including the Makhnovschina in the Ukraine, a revolt in Armenia which led to the seizure of the capital Erevan on 13 February, and above all the revolt in Tambov which had begun in August 1920. Most of the Communist Party leadership believed that any of these could open the way for the Whites to revive the civil war.

The rebellion which was perceived to be the most dangerous was that headed by Alexander Antonov in the Tambov *uezd*. During the civil war both Reds and Whites pressed thousands of peasants into their armies, and many of these deserted at the first opportunity. Whilst some would return home, and others switch sides repeatedly, a number would also take to the forests with their arms to set up bands of "Greens" who rejected both sides. The Tambov rebellion had started over the attempted requisitioning of grain, which then led to brutal assaults on village elders who refused to say where the young men in the village had gone. The peasants had had enough, and several members of the requisitioning squad were killed. The rebellion soon spread from two villages until it covered the entire region. A thousand Communist Party members were killed in the next three months.

Vladimir Antonov-Ovseyenko was given charge of a special political commission to deal with the rising. Under him Tukhachevsky, fresh from the suppression of Kronstadt, was now sent to unleash a massive attack supported by planes, poison gas and 50,000 of the most committed troops, including Chekists and members of Komsomol, the Communist youth organisation.

The leader of the revolt, Alexander Antonov, had been an SR all his adult life, specialising in violent "expropriations" under the Tsars. For this he was sentenced to 20 years katorga (forced labour in Siberia) in 1909 as a common criminal. Freed by the 1917 revolution, he joined the militia in Tambov *uezd*, but after the revolt of the Left SRs, and the deaths of some of his friends in the Red Terror in 1918, he became the leader of his own "forest brotherhood" of about 150 peasants. The Tambov revolt transformed this into a fighting force of at least 20,000 which, given the ham-fisted Communist Party policies towards the peasantry, had plenty of local support.

The revolt had little success in attracting workers, and was almost entirely confined to the Russian-speaking peasantry of Tambov province,[1] but Tukhachevsky had to basically resort to scorched earth tactics to depopulate whole areas, thus undermining the local support for Antonov's guerrilla army. It seems too that, as the year wore on, the introduction of NEP and the end of *prodradverstka* (forced requisitioning) removed one of the main issues that had sparked off the rebellion. By July 1921 the last of the Antonov bands was defeated near Kozlov, though Antonov himself was not killed until the following year.

The Makhnovshchina

By this time the peasant threat throughout the old Russian Empire had ended, as Makhno's Revolutionary Insurgent Army of Ukraine had also been defeated by August 1921. Makhno's insurgency may have also been peasant-based, but its political significance was much wider. To begin with it had arisen as part of the revolution itself. In 1917 Makhno was released from the Tsarist prison where he had spent much of the last decade receiving further instruction on the works of Bakunin and Kropotkin by the Bolshevik-turned-anarchist, Peter Arshinov.[2] On returning to his home town of Guliaipole (Hulyai Pole)[3] he rejoined fellow anarchists, persuading them to build links with the local peasantry in "left bank" Ukraine.[4] In 1918 he persuaded his group that they had to prepare to resist the return of the counter-revolution. However, they could not prevent the fall of Guliaipole to the troops of Ukrainian nationalist Rada, of Simon Petlyura. Makhno then wandered round Southern Russia before eventually taking the train to Moscow in June 1918. There, according to his own account, he found the anarchists only engaged in a "paper revolution" but managed to stroll into the Kremlin to meet Sverdlov. After a brief discussion, the Chairman of the Soviet Executive Committee (VTsIK) suggested Lenin would be interested in discussing with him. During the encounter Lenin asked Makhno what he understood by the slogan "All power to the Soviets".

> The peasants, said Makhno, took the slogan "All power to the Soviets" to mean that power over their affairs must rest with the workers themselves at the local level. The other main bone of contention was the Bolsheviks' general lack of interest in the peasantry. Makhno claimed that Lenin told him that if there were other anarchists like him, the Bolsheviks might be willing to work with them to set up 'free producers' organisations'.[5]

Given Lenin's praise of anarchist ideas earlier in the year (see Chapters 8 and 10), and his later call for anarchist workers to join the Third International[6] he was probably quite sincere in this, although at the same time Lenin also justified to Makhno the Cheka attack on the Moscow anarchists (see Chapter 12), on the not unreasonable grounds that they were harbouring criminals, or "bandits" as he called them.[7] Even as Makhno was talking to Lenin, the civil war was starting in earnest, and the Cheka were arresting other anarchists back in the south. Makhno (and probably even Lenin) may not have known this, but he was well aware how the Germans, and their allies amongst the landowning class in Ukraine, were pillaging and looting the peasantry and was desperate to return to the fight. He was furnished with a false passport by Ukrainian members of the Russian

Communist Party (Bolshevik) in Moscow, and returned to Guliaipole on 29 June 1918.

Makhno was clear that, whilst he would not let known "Bolsheviks" operate in his territory, the main enemy were the Whites, the Germans and the Ukrainian nationalist movement of Simon Petlyura. Over the next couple of years, both Reds and Makhnovists engaged in wary cooperation sometimes punctuated by acts of mutual hostility. The first Communists to visit Makhno in Guliaipole, Antonov-Ovseyenko and Lev Kamenev in April and May 1919 respectively, had a high regard for what was happening there, both socially[8] and politically, and advocated military cooperation, which included supplying Makhno with weapons. Antonov-Ovseyenko gave a report on 2 May which:

> pointed out that the makhnovtsy were 'imbued' with revolutionary spirit, lived modestly, were open to other viewpoints and did not agitate against soviet power.[9]

This was never accepted by Trotsky and, in time, would not be the final position of Lenin either. Whilst Antonov-Ovseyenko was a "weighty voice in defence of the Makhnovist army as an ally in the fight against Denikin", on 2 June 1919 Trotsky was writing an article entitled "Makhnovshchina" accusing the Makhnovists of undermining soviet power. A few days later Makhno resigned the Red Army position he had been given by Antonov-Ovseyenko, whilst Trotsky banned the peasant congress he had called, and was soon arresting and shooting his supporters.[10]

For Trotsky, all partisan and local militia were militarily inefficient, and the aim from the beginning was to bring everything under the direct control of his new standing army. The Makhno movement though was not just a military one. The incredible feats of movement it performed were not just down to his cavalry, or the use of *tachanka*[11] but also determined by the fact that it was fighting a social war based on the peasantry. His forces could receive fresh horses to keep moving well ahead of their pursuers, or bury their weapons and melt back into the surrounding population. Anarchist individualism across the world has often enjoyed great success with peasant movements, the archetypal petty bourgeoisie, who want to defend their property against the encroachments of the state whatever its political colour. The Makhnovists thus had a rural base which gave them extremely solid support. They protected both the peasantry's newly acquired lands (thanks to the Bolshevik land decree, but some of them were only obtained with Makhno's direct assistance against local landowners) against White attempts to restore the old landlords (*pomeshchiki*), and their grain against the requisitioning squads of the Reds. *Prodradvertska* (forced requisitioning) was the main reason for both Antonov's Green Army and Makhno's Black Army support within the peasantry. It has been calculated that some 1,700 members of these requisitioning squads were killed in Makhno-run Ukraine,[12] a fact which would not have helped the cause of his defenders within the Communist Party.

The Makhnovists also proved that it was not only the Communists who found that the demands of war provoked actions which were not consonant with the aims of socialist or anarchist revolution. The fighting in Russia usually goes under the name of a civil war, but it was part imperialist war, part national or ethnic war, and part class war. And, as Kevin Murphy has accurately pointed out, there was nowhere in the world where class hatred was so bitter as in Russia.[13] Makhno took no prisoners (although you could avoid being shot if you joined his Army). Officers in both White and Red armies were shot out of hand (although Red Army officers whose men spoke up for them were spared). He had his own secret service, the Kontrrazvedka[14] run by Lev Zadov.[15] Justice could be just as arbitrary and summary as that meted out by the Cheka, or by the Whites. Iosif Gotman, of the South Russian anarchist *Nabat* journal, also told Alexander Berkman that:

> *there was no freedom of speech for Communists in Makhnovite-controlled areas, though there was for Maximalists and Left SRs.[16]*

In 1919-20 there were four agreements between Makhno and the Red Army to cooperate in the fight against the Whites. These agreements were marriages of convenience on both sides, but some military historians have credited Makhno's diversionary attacks with being critical to the defeat of Denikin in 1919. The last agreement signed at Starobelsk ensured that Makhnovist forces played a major role against Wrangel who, driven into the Crimea at the end of 1920, evacuated his White Army from Russia. With the Whites gone, the *makhnovtsy* faced the duplicitous accusation of disobeying orders in this final campaign, and were ordered to disband. This was a direct betrayal of the Starobelsk agreement, and was accompanied by the arrest of other anarchist groups, like the Kharkov-based *Nabat* federation, including Volin, who was sent to join other anarchists, like Maximoff and Iarchuk, in prison in Moscow.[17]

For the next few months, Makhno carried out what became an increasingly guerrilla war, as his army broke up into smaller groups. The Red Army, now with no other enemy to fight, swamped the area with massive numbers of troops who several times got close to capturing Makhno only for him to break out of the encircling troops. Once again, the use of ruthless scorched earth tactics on an already exhausted peasantry, plus the fact that another dry summer meant that the Volga famine had arrived in Ukraine, further undermined Makhno's base. Little by little his movement drained away. When grain requisitioning ended in March 1921 a major cause of peasant discontent also disappeared. In August, Makhno and his last remaining forces, reached the River Dneister. This formed the border with Romania where Makhno now intended to seek refuge.

> *He needed fresh horses and the men were exhausted; even the wheels of the tachanka lacked lubrication. Taking fresh horses provoked a hostile reaction from local villagers who attacked the insurgents while they were sleeping without having posted guards: in the mêlée Makhno was wounded in the legs ...[18]*

The fact that some peasants were no longer willing to assist him (perhaps because requisitioning had now ended?) indicates the corner Makhno was in. In the days that followed, Makhno was again wounded, this time in the face, in skirmishes with Red Army troops, rendering him unconscious as he was clandestinely taken into Romania on 28 August 1921. He would never return to Ukraine, and died of poverty and tuberculosis in Paris in July 1934.

Alongside the suppression of Kronstadt, the determined campaign to extinguish a movement which had encouraged the growth of communes, cooperatives and even soviets, a movement which could have brought some kind of collective social order to at least part of Ukraine, was not only an abandonment of the principles of October, it was also a lost opportunity, which confirmed that the counter-revolution was now in the ascendant. In their 1918 conversation Lenin held out the prospect of joining with Makhno "in working towards a free organisation of producers".[19] Like so much else that was promised in the revolution it vanished in the civil war. Some might argue against the idea of a workers' revolution making concessions to the peasants who supported Makhno, but in the situation of the revolution's continuing isolation in the old Russian Empire, what else was the NEP?

The Russian Communist Party (Bolshevik), of course, posed it the other way round. It remained for the former Left Communist, Bukharin, to justify the attack on Makhno at the First Congress of the Profintern (Red International of Trades Unions) in July 1921. Here, he created uproar amongst anarcho-syndicalist delegates, when he insisted that Makhno's forces were just "partisan gangs" who "play the part of the rich peasant vandals against the revolution".[20] A statement which is more an indictment of Bukharin, and the Communist Party, who now supported concessions to "those peasant vandals", rather than Makhno himself. By this time though the Communist Party was no longer the revolutionary force of 1917 based in the soviets. It had built a state around the Red Army, the Cheka and its increasing monopoly of power. By December 1920, even Kamenev was admitting that the soviets had already become, in Sakwa's summary of his speech, "moribund, bureaucratic and the plenums devoid of political debate".[21]

The Failure of the Communist Oppositions

Bukharin's political journey between 1918 and 1921 could serve as a template for the shift from Bolshevik dream to Communist nightmare. As the doyen of the Left Communists of 1918, he had initially argued for "the self-activity of the working class". His biographer tells us that in 1917-18:

> ... Bukharin took seriously the idea of a revolutionary "Commune state" — a state "without police, without a standing army, without an officialdom as Lenin (to Bukharin's enthusiastic applause) had sketched it in State and Revolution. The definitive feature of the "commune state" was to be its repudiation of bureaucratic political and economic authority. It would be a state without bureaucrats, "that is, privileged people alienated from the masses and standing over the masses".[22]

However, as we saw in Chapter 11 he had, by 1920, been reduced to identifying the dictatorship of the proletariat as the same as the dictatorship of "its vanguard".[23] A few months before his Profintern speech he had more accurately described the introduction of the NEP as, "the collapse of our illusions".[24] He could have been speaking for the entire project of the Russian Communist Party at this point. At the same time, in the Tenth Party Congress, whilst Lenin was dealing with the Workers' Opposition, Bukharin led the fight against his former comrades on the Left of the Party. The Democratic Centralist (Decist) proposals for greater democracy were an "unacceptable expression" of "SR labouring-people's-power politics". What was needed now was a "single party, with a single psychology and a single ideology". Even that was not enough for the real authoritarians in the Party. The head of the Red Army political department, Ivan Smilga, called for Bukharin's "liberal-pink policy" of making concessions to the Decists to end. What Smilga (who would later support Trotsky's Left Opposition) also wanted to end, was any criticism of any Communist in a position of responsibility, and this was effectively what the ban on factions in the Party instituted.[25]

At the Eleventh Party Congress (27 March-2 April, 1922), despite the nominal ban on factions of a year earlier, the sparring between Lenin and the leaders of the Workers' Opposition continued. In response to Lenin's assertion the previous day, that:

> the Russian proletariat had ceased to exist as a class in the Marxist sense, Shlyapnikov, with customary irony, congratulated congress delegates 'on being the vanguard of a non-existent class'.[26]

At the same Congress Lenin gave the political report of the Central Committee, and went further in confessing the reality of the situation. After reasserting the new orthodoxy, that with state power in the hands of the Communist Party the transition to communism was assured, he confessed to another problem.

> ... what is lacking is culture among the stratum of the Communists who perform administrative functions. If we take Moscow with its 4,700 Communists in responsible positions, and if we take that huge bureaucratic machine, that gigantic heap, we must ask; who is directing whom? I doubt very much whether it can be truthfully said that the Communists are directing that heap. To tell the truth they are not directing but being directed.[27]

There is some truth in this, but it glaringly contradicts the idea that putting state power in the hands of the Communist Party was a guarantee of a communist future. In 1918 the number of soviet officials was some 100,000 but by 1920 this had become 6 million.[28] If we consider that the Bolshevik Party had something like 300,000 members in October 1917 it is clear that two processes must have gone on during the civil war. Large numbers of the worker base of the Party would have had to have entered the state apparatus, either via the Red Army (which numbered around 5 million by then), or the administration of the Soviets. Whilst this was seen as early proof of the proletarian nature of Soviet power there was another consequence. Such a reduction in the number of Communist workers in factories etc. had the effect of weakening the link between the Communist Party and the wider working class. Indeed, the 1921 crisis made the Communist Party only too aware of this, but subsequent attempts to get Party members to return to the factories, unsurprisingly, met with modest success.

Furthermore, even if every pre-October party member went into the soviet administration, they could only have made up 4% of the chinovniks (bureaucrats), so where did the others come from? Lenin now confronted the fact that in Russia:

> *The idea of building communist society exclusively with the hands of Communists is childish, absolutely childish. We Communists are but a drop in the ocean, a drop in the ocean of the people.*[29]

In fact, because of their needed experience, millions of former Tsarist *chinovniks* managed to retain their positions as *sluzhashchie* (white collar employees) and with that experience of administration these alien class elements would have been easily able to guide the new worker-administrators.[30] However, if it was "childish" to think that the Communists could build communism on their own, why had the Communists not made a bigger effort to avoid the defections from the soviet system by potential allies in other organisations back in 1918? Obviously this could not include Mensheviks and Right SRs, but could encompass Left SRs, some Menshevik Internationalists, anarchists, and even the many "non-party" workers who remained staunch supporters of soviet power even after 1921.[31] It was also exactly what the *Petropavlovsk Resolution* of the Kronstadters had called for in 1921.

Lenin himself has to bear much of the responsibility for this. Whilst he knew how to make concessions and correct mistakes, these were only done when he himself recognised the problem his earlier policies had created. Those who had seen the errors of previous policy earlier were rarely acknowledged. His mocking speech, against Maria Spiridonova and the Left SRs at the Fifth Soviet Congress in June 1918, for example, was a clear indication that he would not treat any of the Left SRs' demands about the problems of forced requisitioning of food from the peasant majority (which they could claim to represent) seriously. It was one thing to demand that all delegates in the soviets should be loyal to that form of government. It was quite another to eventually equate this only with the policies of first, Sovnarkom and the Bolshevik Party, and then by 1920, just its Politburo. This dogmatic method, brilliantly honed in ideological arguments before the revolution, was actually an impediment to the development of a revolution which was going where no working class had gone before, and was thus feeling its way forward. In such a situation a degree of proletarian pluralism would have strengthened the identification of workers with some of the unpalatable decisions that were forced upon the soviets as a whole.

In fact it is central to any revolutionary change in the deepest sense. Working class bodies (like any other) will only flourish as long as there is a sense of purpose in participating in them. If there is no real discussion, if everything of significance is decided in advance elsewhere, the organ atrophies and the participants vote with their feet. That kind of apathy and passivity is what capitalist society relies upon. Demanding that we put a cross on a piece of paper, to indicate our trust in representatives who can do what they like for five years, is the sole political duty of the "citizen". Meanwhile the so-called democratic state represents only the interests of the propertied classes. Socialist society is different. It is not just about dispossessing the wealthy of their ownership of the means of production, even if abolishing both the law of value and exploitation are the bedrocks on which a new mode of production must arise. Socialism demands the active participation of all producers in the decisions that affect their lives. Its democracy is direct and based on the ability to recall delegates if they do not fulfil the mandate they were given by the collectivity. Although the system was never so firmly established in Russia it was moving towards this goal in the first months after October, but once the economic crisis deepened, the sovereignty of the soviets came under pressure.

The root of the problem went back to 1917 when the very future of the soviets was at issue. By dint of the fact that the Bolsheviks had been the most vocal supporters of "all power to the soviets", and were directly opposed by SRs and Mensheviks who were scheming to sideline them, the question of the future of the soviet system was largely decided along party lines. Defence of soviet rule was thus for a time associated almost exclusively with the Bolshevik Party, especially after the Bolsheviks led the October Revolution in the name of the soviets. But when the economic crisis and food shortages hit home around March-April 1918 some Bolsheviks began to see all opposition to their policies as opposition to soviet power itself. There was, as yet, no centralised concerted effort to rig elections but in some localities, as we have seen, elections were postponed or ignored. The Left Communists of 1918 tried to oppose any diminution of proletarian initiative in the factories and in the soviets. Ossinsky, like Bukharin quoted earlier, had warned several times that, if the self-activity of the mass of the class which emerged from the year of revolutionary ferment that produced the October Revolution was stifled, it would be impossible to achieve socialism:

> *Socialism will ... have a firm foundation and it will not be possible to eliminate it if the new economy is implemented by the proletariat, if it it subjects it as master, if mastering and organising it is taken on by the workers themselves.*[32]

Mass discussion on this question will involve the workers in the construction of socialism which can only be realised by the workers themselves.[33]

As we saw earlier Lenin had supported this until then but, with economic collapse staring soviet power in the face, he fell back on compromising with capitalist methods. The Left Communists at the time had widespread support in the Party including its working class base.[34] However, such was the authority of Lenin in late summer 1918, they did not put this to the test.[35] From then on, not only would one man management and the introduction of specialists increasingly replace worker initiative in the factory committees, but Soviet elections would, gradually but increasingly, soon be annulled or rigged. Even in the Party, appointment replaced election as the way to fill offices. By mid-1919, in the polarising situation of civil war, it became increasingly hard for dissidents who championed the self-activity of a class which was in process of being dispersed by the search for food and recruitment into the Red Army, to keep on insisting on it. The Left Communists were hampered by the assumption (not unreasonable from their perspective at the time) that counter-revolution was seen as something which could only come from without – not from within the Communist Party itself, whatever mistakes it made.[36] Increasingly the conflict between defending worker activism and the Party itself resolved itself in favour of the Party. It seriously weakened the ability of the Communist oppositions to pursue their causes as the civil war ground on. Some however kept fighting for it longer than others.

In March 1920 Timofei Sapronov, a principle leader of the Decists group which had been formed a year earlier, rhetorically asked the Ninth Party Congress:

Why talk about the proletarian dictatorship or workers' self-activity? There's no self-activity here![37]

At the time he was supported by all the Decists and others in the Communist Party. However a year later Ossinsky, like Bukharin earlier, also abandoned the fight for proletarian autonomy when, after Sapronov had come out in support of the Workers' Opposition, he joined in the attack on them in February 1921.

All talk of the self-activity of the masses under the circumstances, he argued, was nonsense. All that could be done was to involve them in 'active work' under the guidance of the party.[38]

This apostasy finished off the Decists as a coherent independent opposition. Some like Ossinsky, Sapronov and Vladimir Smirnov would participate in later intra-party fights, and sign such documents as "The Declaration of the Forty-Six" in company with what would later come to be known as the Left Opposition around Trotsky. This was, however, a different sort of struggle from the earlier one. It was a fight over the leadership of the state, not about wider democracy in the Party, and even less about the involvement of the wider working class in the revolution. In 1921-2 the task of defending workers' initiative would be carried on (with their differing emphases) by the Workers' Opposition, Miasnikov's Workers' Group and the Workers' Truth group. The days of all these oppositions were, however, numbered. As Ossinsky, Sapronov, Smirnov and their Left Communist comrades had predicted in 1918, bringing in bourgeois managers would not only just replicate capitalist relations, but would also kill off the self-activity which had brought the working class to power. They were very aware that revolutionary class consciousness could not be turned on and off at the flick of an ideological switch. Once lost then it could not be recovered without some new convulsive development (which all sections of the Party still continued to hope in 1921 would be the world revolution). Ossinsky[39] and Bukharin (and others) now put their faith increasingly in a Party which had by now assumed the mantle of the state.

This was a far cry from the early months of 1918 when the debate about how to proceed had still been open. Indeed, as we saw in Chapter 10, it was the Party which was in danger of becoming irrelevant, as members did more work in the soviets than for the Party.[40] In fact the relationship of party and class was never clearly defined. Even Bukharin and Preobrazhensky's *The ABC of Communism* (1919), which was almost an official programme of the period, hardly mentions the Party. There was, of course, a lot of discussion about the role of the Party, but the whole process, as in every other aspect of the October Revolution, was dictated more by circumstance than design. We saw in Chapter 11 that the civil war ensured that considerations of military survival predominated over everything. As the Kamenev quote above shows, this produced a tendency, at every level, for more and more decisions to be taken by fewer and fewer people. Once the Party in late 1918 decided that it "... *must become the controlling, leading and guiding force over the soviets to avoid a breach (razlozhenie) between party workers and the helplessness of the state apparatus*",[41] the pattern was set for the party fractions to meet in advance and increasingly become the real decision-makers in the soviets.

In criticising the "idea", that the Communist minority could make the revolution as "childish", was Lenin now accepting the ideas of the various Left Communists that the revolution could return to early 1918, when working class initiative played such an enormous role? Far from it. Lenin now exhorted the Communists to learn how to organise but once again his model was ... the bourgeoisie.[42] He specifically rejected the Workers' Opposition criticism that the Party was "under-rating the workers" or that they should be allowed "greater initiative". Instead, he equated the retreat the Party was then conducting via NEP, with the retreat of the entire working class despite the fact that it would in reality, as we saw in the last chapter, be its principal victim.[43]

This debate was broadly about two different understandings of what socialism or communism entailed. From the middle of 1918 the Communist Party majority under Lenin developed what we could call a productionist view of socialism. They became more and more obsessed with the "backwardness", both culturally and economically, of the territory that the working class inherited from Tsardom. The idea of becoming more "businesslike" (*delovoi*) becomes a constant refrain of Lenin's speeches and writings after April 1918. Ironically the roots of this productionist approach go back to the ideas of the Second International which Lenin had so decisively rejected in 1914. In the majority interpretation of Marxism in the Second International, every country taken singly had to have developed the productive forces to a certain level before socialism could be on the agenda. In this mechanistic Social Democratic vision, especially the version promoted by Kautsky, the notion of "productive forces" was associated with the development of industry and technology. Even Herman Gorter could write in his 1908 pamphlet on Historical Materialism, "*Technology, the productive forces, forms the basis of society.*" But then it did have an introduction by Kautsky who describes Gorter as "*my friend*".[44] However Marx had never restricted his conception just to the level of development of technology since for him "the productive forces" also included the working class. Lenin had shared the Kautskyist idea until 1914-16, when, devastated by Kautsky's lack of a revolutionary response to the war, he came to see that imperialism had now created "a world economy" (Bukharin) which would allow for a capitalist collapse at its weakest link, i.e. in a place like Russia. Then, with the help of a world working class revolution, that weak link could develop the material basis for socialist society. As Neil Harding[45] demonstrated so clearly, it was Lenin's understanding of imperialism and the internationalist vision he drew from it, that not only made the Russian party the leader of the anti-war struggle, but also brought him to espouse the overthrow of the bourgeois order in 1917.

The Mensheviks, of course, denounced him for "breaking with Marxism". For them Russia was not materially ready for socialism but, as we saw earlier, this perspective rendered them increasingly impotent and irrelevant in the revolutionary fervour of 1917. The Bolshevik Revolution was premised on internationalism, that is, the expectation that a world wide workers' movement would arise from the First World War. This was no leap in the dark. After all, capitalism could not have been in much more of a global crisis than an imperialist war, which eventually engulfed all the great powers of the epoch. There was no firmer basis for believing that the common struggle against war would lead to an international movement of the working class.

And in the end it was a close run thing for capitalism. The revolutions in Russia, Germany and even Austria-Hungary brought the world slaughter to an end. There were mass movements across the world from Seattle to Shanghai in support of the ideals of proletarian emancipation and against a capitalist system of exploitation and bloodshed. What saved capitalism was, not any particular strength of the system, but the Social Democrats (especially in Germany) and their trade unions, who had betrayed the Second International in 1914, supported or failed to oppose imperialism in the war, and in the post-war revolutionary wave rescued the system in its darkest hour by dividing the forces of the working class by peddling the myth that capitalism could be reformed in their favour. The Bolshevik perspective was that this was an illusion, and the war provided the opportunity for a generalised movement that would, in time, lead to the creation of a global socialist society. Most of the Party were united around this from June 1917 on, and in the first few months of the revolution there was no difference between Lenin and what would become the opposition view, that socialism could only be built through mass working class initiative. As we have shown previously the break between him and the "Left" came in the late spring/early summer of 1918.

A New Form of State Capitalism

We saw in Chapter 8 that the Left Communists of 1918 identified state capitalism as one of the greatest dangers facing the revolution. However, at this point we need to be clear about what was meant by "state capitalism". The kind of state capitalism they were worried about was one which we might call today "a mixed economy". They were objecting to the possibility that Sovnarkom would enter into deals with the old capitalists to carry on running industry. As it turned out their fears were not realised at that time, as the economic crisis and sabotage by factory owners had led to the spontaneous takeover of factories, etc., by workers. Eventually this forced Sovnarkom, applauded by the Left Communists, to decree the nationalisation of all major industrial plants in the summer of 1918.

However in 1921 NEP returned to the idea of allowing private ownership of some firms by leasing them to individual (often non-Russian) capitalists and this revived the criticisms of the opposition over the promotion of "state capitalism". Lenin remained unrepentant. In his 1921 document "The Tax in Kind" he repeated at length what he wrote against the 1918 Left Communists, in *Left Wing Childishness and the Petty Bourgeois Mentality*.

> *State capitalism would be a step forward as compared with the present state of affairs in our Soviet Republic. If in approximately six months' time state capitalism became established in our Republic, this would be a great success and a sure guarantee that within a year socialism will have gained a permanently firm hold and will have become invincible in this country.[46]*

A few pages later he repeated his 1918 insistence that:

> *socialism is merely the next step forward from state-capitalist monopoly.[47]*

And then makes explicit that the basis of socialism can only be through large-scale industry.

> *Socialism is inconceivable without large-scale capitalist engineering based on the latest discoveries of modern science. It is inconceivable without planned state organisation which keeps tens of millions of people to the strictest observance of a unified standard in production and distribution. We Marxists have always spoken of this, and it is not worth while wasting two seconds talking to people who do not understand even this (anarchists and a good half of the Left Socialist Revolutionaries).[48]*

He finally confirms that his vision of socialism is a technologically determined one when he argues that the one condition for the immediate transition to socialism is – electrification![49]

This productionist view went beyond Lenin. It was the basis of the Trotskyist Left Opposition in the early 1920s and it was, of course, the same mentality as that of Stalin who, in a throwback to the civil war, feared military defeat at the hands of the West. He thus openly declared his military purposes when he adopted the brutal industrialisation of the USSR in the years after 1928. All the Communists, including the Left Communists, shared the idea that nationalisation by a "workers' state" was the same as the socialisation of production. During the civil war Left Communists often saw the expedient measures of "war communism", where money lost its value, most of industry was put under state control and free trade was outlawed, as necessary steps towards socialism. This was an illusion, given the economic reality of living on a system of rationing which was almost unendurable in its harshness. The significant difference though was that the "Left" of the Party really thought that the "workers' state" should be run by the workers' themselves, and for at least six months Lenin was at one with them. Without the control of the soviets, and other bodies created by the class, like factory committees, any nationalisation was just a shift in ownership of the means of production from private to state capitalist. It did not do away with exploitation. The worst legacy bequeathed by the revolution was the myth that the new form of state capitalism which emerged in the USSR had something to do with "socialism".

Left Communists, key among them Bukharin, produced the most lucid analysis of how monopoly capitalism led to an increasing intertwining of capitalism with the state,[50] and how this was the root of imperialism:

> *Capitalism has attempted to overcome its own anarchy by pressing it into the iron ring of state organisation. But having eliminated competition within the state, it let loose all the devils of a world scuffle.*[51]

The great strength of Bukharin's analysis lies in his refusal to accept that state control can be identified with "socialism" in any form. In the First World War the fact that the whole of social and economic life was subject to the domination of the militarised state meant that amongst the capitalists there were many who claimed that this was "state socialism". Ironically Bukharin did not see that the same thing had happened in Soviet Russia as a result of the civil war. He could not see that the failure of the soviets to really represent the wider working class was the beginning of a new form of state capitalism. By 1920, like Lenin, Trotsky, Stalin and every other major Bolshevik figure, Bukharin had come to accept that the Party ruled instead of the class. Far from seeing this as a departure from what they had stood for in 1917, some Left Communists now came to accept that the Party itself was a guarantee of the proletarian character of the dictatorship.

In his 1920 book *Economics of the Transformation Period* Bukharin wrote at length on the need for the compulsion of labour in the Soviet state. He justifies it thus:

> *In the capitalist regime, compulsion was defended in the name of "the interests of the totality", while in reality it was in the interest of capitalist groups. Under proletarian dictatorship, compulsion is for the first time really the tool of the majority in the interests of the majority". [Lenin wrote in the margin "True!"]*[52]

Such doublethink made it possible to accept that the outcome of the revolution was more positive than it really was (and there was also the increasingly faint hope as the 1920s wore on that Russia's isolation would end). It prepared the way for a new form of state capitalism which replaced working class initiative with state-sponsored mobilisations for this or that goal from literacy campaigns to subbotniks (voluntary Communist work on Saturdays).[53] Some were achievements, in the sense of modernising some aspects of a previously backward society, but all redounded to the glory of the "workers' state" which in reality was the Party-State. It also played on the sense of pioneering of a whole new generation of young Communists, particularly in Komsomol, the Communist youth organisation. Many of them who had been teenagers in 1917 chafed at the "retreat" of NEP and formed communes and lived collectively whilst waiting for NEP to end. Many would be sympathetic to the "industrialisers" like Trotsky and Preobrazhensky in the

Revolution is an Affair of the Masses

Left Opposition who called for "primitive socialist accumulation". Stalin poured scorn on them in the early 1920s but he would become the greatest "super-industrialiser" of them all. Stalin's "left turn" of 1928 would convince these young Communists to throw themselves enthusiastically into the self-sacrifice of the Five Year Plans, in the belief they were returning to the ideas of 1917.[54] This was an illusion, but then they were the first young generation to experience a victorious workers' revolution. They had come to believe that the Party was the Party of the class, and thus did not see that the essential element for a socialist society was missing – soviets which were key instruments of a working class acting on its own initiative.

What thus emerged from the Russian Revolution was a new model of state capitalism which, in time, would become attractive to the bourgeoisie of "backward" countries and colonies of the Western colonial powers (like, Cuba, Vietnam, Mozambique, Angola, etc.). They could use the State to keep Western multinationals from bleeding the country dry, and try to "develop" independently through state mobilisation of the population. Devoid of real proletarian initiative, this was a flawed model, and even the Communist Party of the Chinese People's Republic abandoned Stalinism after the death of Mao by setting up Special Economic Zones to attract international capital and build a new Chinese capitalist class (so-called "socialism with Chinese characteristics"). What they have in fact returned to is the type of state capitalism that Lenin advocated in 1918, opposed by the Left Communists of that time. Across the world many workers in the Twentieth century thought Stalinism was the answer until the 1980s and today many in the former Eastern European bloc still think it was better than what they have now. But neither "state capitalism" nor "state socialism" are socialism as understood by Marx. Both depend on the exploitation of workers whose surplus value is the basis for capitalist profit and who have no actual political say in the system.

The Débacle of Party Power

Although the Bolsheviks had begun by promoting the extension of soviet democracy they put institutional obstacles in the way of the soviets acting as the direct rulers of the system from the start. Most notable was the setting up of the Council of Peoples' Commissars or Sovnarkom. Lenin had wanted to call it the Council of Ministers but Trotsky, as ever with an eye to public perception of what was "revolutionary", suggested the use of "commissars", a term already in use under the various Provisional Governments. It was not quite like a bourgeois cabinet in more substantial respects. To begin with it was nominally subject to control by the VTsIK or Soviet Executive elected by every Soviet Congress. These in turn met every three months in the early days of the revolution. However, as we saw in Chapter 8, Sovnarkom issued scores of decrees in the early months of the revolution without reference to VTsIK. These were intended both as practical policies and propaganda since there was no telling how long soviet power might last. And once there were no Soviet Congresses (and there were none for all of 1919) there was no renewal of the VTsIK mandate. In any case, the VTsIK, which was Bolshevik-only by November 1918 was also too large to act as a decisive check on Sovnarkom. Some on the "Left" of the Party could see the danger. As so often, it was in

Moscow, where the alarm was first sounded by the Democratic Centralists.

A specially convened city party conference on 18 January 1919 was the scene of a bitter debate over the relationship between central and local soviet institutions and between the party committees and fractions in the soviets. Ignatov (a Decist – JD) introduced a motion demanding changes to the soviet constitution, and in particular the elimination of Sovnarkom in order to enhance the authority of VTsIK and for the increased autonomy of soviet fractions.[55]

The debate summed up the difference between the Left and what would in time become the Party majority. Whilst Ignatov got support from several members of the Moscow Soviet Executive Committee for his view that the party should not take on the task of the soviets, Lenin, in reply, "argued that only centralism could overcome the two great evils of bureaucracy and speculation".[56]

The disease of "bureaucracy" was defined differently by different Communist leaders throughout the revolution and civil war. But from the beginning the "Left" of the Party had warned of consequences if the grass-roots movement of the class did not have control of its own destiny. The more every meaningful decision was put into the hands of administrators, from whatever social origin, the less initiative was required by the masses themselves, the greater the bureaucracy required to replace it. The creation of the Red Army in the civil war, as Trotsky admitted, was a significant source of it. Even when demobilisation came this only added to the problem:

The demobilization of the Red Army of five million played no small role in the formation of the bureaucracy. The victorious commanders assumed leading posts in the local Soviets, in economy, in education, and they persistently introduced everywhere that regime which had ensured success in the civil war. Thus on all sides the masses were pushed away gradually from actual participation in the leadership of the country.[57]

Trotsky was writing this in the 1930s so his understanding came too late, but Lenin never really grasped that increasing centralism was the driving force of bureaucracy. If the existing organisation did not function his solution was to add another layer as with the Workers' and Peasants' Inspectorate (*Rabkrin*) headed by Stalin. Supposedly an organisation to allow workers to make complaints and monitor the bureaucracy, it became:

an additional source of muddle, corruption, and bureaucratic intrigue. In the end it became an unofficial but meddlesome police in charge of the civil service.[58]

In his last public statements Lenin recognised that the People's Commissariat of the Workers' and Peasants' Inspection did not enjoy the slightest authority but qualified this with "at present"[59] and went on to to suggest it could be improved by reducing its membership from several thousand to a few hundred.

Revolution is an Affair of the Masses

The "Left" of the Communist Party in its various forms may have tried to resist the oxymoron of a "workers' state" at the beginning but as the civil war ground on it had its effect on their approach as well. As the civil war was ending, Richard Sakwa argues that:

> *The liveliness of the debates of 1920 undermines the argument that the civil war, like some terrible deus ex machina cut down the intellectual vigour of the party.*[60]

It is true that vigorous debates like those of 1918 did burst out again in 1920, but what cannot be ignored is their change of focus. Whereas the "Left" had been fighting for "revolution from below" in the soviets themselves in 1918-19, by the time the civil war was won they were now focussed on internal Party democracy rather than class-wide democracy. As we have seen Ossinsky no longer focussed on defending worker initiative, whilst Ignatov's concern for revolution from below had shifted from getting rid of Sovnarkom to defending internal party democracy. Ossinsky went from criticising the existence of Sovnarkom to defending its "collegiality" as something far better than the increasing control of the Politburo.[61] It all has the air of making the best of a bad job rather than about defending the basis of socialist society.

Power thus passed from institutions which took their legitimacy from the soviets, to those that were under the control of the Party. Trotsky's position brutally summed up how far the ideas of 1917 had become debased by 1921:

> *What is indispensable is the awareness ... of the revolutionary birthright of the party, which is obliged to maintain its dictatorship in spite of the temporary wavering in the spontaneous mood of the masses, in spite of the vacillation even in the working classes. This awareness is for us the indispensable unifying element.*[62]

This babbling about "the revolutionary birthright" of the Party which is "obliged" to maintain "its dictatorship" is an appalling confession of failure. In its dismissal of the working class it smacks of Brecht's *Die Lösung* (*The Solution*), the satirical poem he wrote after the East Berlin rising of 1953:

> *... the people*
> *Had forfeited the confidence of the government*
> *And could only win it back*
> *By increased work quotas. Would it not in that case be simpler*
> *for the government*
> *To dissolve the people*
> *And elect another?*[63]

Trotsky was not alone. In fact he was only expressing a commonplace for Party leaders like Zinoviev, Bukharin, Stalin and Lenin himself. For the dying Lenin the only thing that now really mattered was the internal health of the Communist Party leadership.

Re-writing of the Party's history had already begun. The most obvious expression of it had come in Lenin's own *Left-wing Communism – An Infantile Disorder*, written in April 1920. This is supposed to be his advice for newly-formed Communist Parties on how to develop and grow in order to spread the world revolution. However, Lenin does not take the example of how Bolshevism operated inside the class before October 1917 as his model. He starts with the two and half years in which the Communists were in power in Russia. In the second chapter, entitled "An Essential Condition of the Bolsheviks' Success" he tells us that the key to this was the *"strictest, truly iron discipline (that) had prevailed in our Party"*.[64] He does not mention that at every Party Congress there was an opposition to the centralising tendencies of the regime even during the civil war (although, given its fame, he could not hide the near split over Brest-Litovsk). And he noticeably avoids discussing the lively dissent of the period 1906-14 when the Bolsheviks and the Russian working class were suffering the hammer blows of reaction. The word "discipline" recurs frequently throughout the subsequent text because it was precisely the obsession of the Communist Party at this time. Almost as frequently comes the word "compromise", but Lenin plays fast and loose with this notion, highlighting only those compromises he wishes to draw attention to (and ignoring those he failed to make, with the Left SRs for example). Overall his demand is that the "left-wing communists" (all of whom had their own particular take on what revolutionary politics should be about in 1920) should all make compromises to line up with those "socialists" they had recently split from or, as in the case of the British communists, should apply for affiliation to the Labour Party. "Left-wing Communism" was really a preparation for the upcoming Third Comintern Congress where, as we saw in the previous chapter, the slogan "To the masses" was adopted as the forerunner for the adoption of the "united front" policy with Social Democracy at the Fourth Comintern Congress. The subsequent humiliation of the Communist movement over both policies in the years that followed only underlines the distance that Lenin had travelled from the intransigent revolutionary stance of 1914-17.

All those historians who think that Bolshevik substitutionist ideas on the party and class can be traced back to Lenin's *What is to be Done?* could do well to re-read *"Left-wing Communism"*. Lenin gives an extensive survey of the various periods in Bolshevik history but starts it in 1903 (the Congress where it emerged as a distinct tendency). *What is to be Done?* was written more than a year earlier but Lenin once again passes up the chance to refer to it.

Later in 1920 reference to *What is to be Done?* would be made – but not by Lenin. The first to make reference to it was … Stalin. Quoting both Lenin's early documents from the period of clandestinity, *What is to be Done?* and *One Step Forward, Two Steps Back*, Stalin claimed that it was really about the situation in 1920 and *"completely answered Russian reality and masterfully generalized the organizational experience of the best practical workers"*.[65] Stalin's lead would be followed by Aaron Soltz. We quoted him in the last chapter railing against the *komchvantsvo* (Communist arrogance) of some Communists who abused their authority. Soltz was chairman of the Central Control Commission, which came under Stalin's remit as Commissar for the Workers' and Peasants Inspectorate (Rabkrin). It was intended to enforce both the moral and political standards of the Party. Regarded as an upright and sincere revolutionary (sometimes referred to as "the conscience of the revolution"), at the end of 1920, he shared Stalin's view that there was too much debate going on in the Party and "*specifically cited Lenin's "What is to be Done?" to prove the need for discipline*".[66]

The myth that "iron discipline" was the key to the success of the Bolsheviks would now begin to replace the historic truth that they gave a lead to the workers in 1917 because of their deep implantation in the life of the Russian working class. Appointment had long since replaced election in soviet bodies and henceforth it would be the norm in the Party. Stalin's control over much of the organisation was gradually established (he was not only in the Politburo but also the Organisation Bureau and controlled the organs which dealt with discipline). In 1922 he thus became the logical choice for the new role of Party General Secretary. This completed his power base. He was now in a position to countermand elections in local party branches, and to appoint local party secretaries who conducted elections of delegates to Congresses and, more importantly, to the Central Committee. It took him until 1928 but gradually more and more of his men appeared in all the higher councils of the Party. Daniels describes the people who were attracted to Party organisational work as:

> *less concerned with the Bolshevik ideals of 1917 than those of 1902. Such were the individuals who made good apparatchiki — "apparatus men" — who carried out orders effectively and were resolute in combating opposition activity.*[67]

Lenin had created the conditions for the rise of Stalin, but like Dr Frankenstein the monster outgrew him. He suffered a cerebral haemorrhage on 24 May 1922 and from this time forward his involvement in political affairs was sporadic. Too late he realised, on 25 December 1922, that Stalin represented a real threat to the stability of the Party. He penned a postscript to his famous "Testament". This called for the removal of Stalin as General Secretary but significantly not from the Politburo. Despite Lenin's request, the "Testament" was only discussed in the Central Committee, and Stalin's offer to resign as General Secretary was rejected by Zinoviev and Kamenev. They had now formed a triumvirate with him, and during Lenin's illness Zinoviev had assumed nominal leadership of the Party. Fearing that any demotion of Stalin would lead to the elevation of Trotsky, Zinoviev and Kamenev not only supported him, but hushed up the letters of Lenin. According to Roy Medvedev, citing the unpublished parts of Yelizaveta Drabkina's memoirs[68] at the beginning of 1924:

> *Lenin sat alone for hours and sometimes even cried, apparently not only because of his helplessness but also from a sense of insult and frustration. According to Krupskaya, on January 19 and 20 1924 she read Lenin the just published resolutions of the Thirteenth Party Conference [sic – Congress], which drew a balance sheet on the debate with Trotsky and his supporters. Listening to the text of the resolutions, which were very sharply worded and often unjust, Lenin became agitated. In order to calm him, Krupskaya said the resolutions had been voted unanimously. That could hardly have re-assured Lenin; his worst fears were beginning to be realized.*

On the next day, in a state of severe emotional distress, Lenin died.[69]

Within days it was announced by the Central Committee that Lenin would not be buried next to his mother, as he had requested, but that his body would be embalmed and buried in the Kremlin Wall (and soon in a specially built mausoleum where he remains to this day). His widow, Nadezhda Krupsakaya, opposed this and further asked that nothing be named after him but:

If you wish to honour the name of Vladimir Ilich, build crèches, kindergartens, houses, schools, libraries, medical centres, hospitals, homes for the disabled, etc., and, most of all let us put his precepts into practice.[70]

She was ignored, just as she was ignored in her request that Lenin's "Testament" be read out to the Party Congress. Instead, Petersburg would now become Leningrad, the 21 January was to become a day of national mourning, and statues (which Lenin reputedly said were only good for "collecting bird shit") would soon appear everywhere.

Before the Central Committee had even discussed Lenin's "Testament", Stalin was already making a bid to shape the further course of the counter-revolution. This first took the form of lectures to new recruits to the Communist Party at the Sverdlov University. They were published in Pravda in April and May 1924, with a book, *The Foundations of Leninism* appearing shortly afterwards.[71] It was a clear attempt to define the legacy of the revolution. In its pedantic simplicity it was Stalin's master stroke. Talk of "Leninism" was not new to the Russian revolutionary lexicon but it had been generally used by the enemies of Bolshevism to deride it as a one man party. This distortion now suited Stalin's intentions perfectly as he did a cut and paste job on Lenin's work, both from his earlier and long forgotten *What is to be Done?*, and later period *Left-wing Communism: An Infantile Disorder*, to extract from them the necessary justification for his take on where the revolution now stood. To be sure he also quoted *The State and Revolution* in his section on the dictatorship of the proletariat. He claimed this was still to be found in the soviets. This was in blatant contradiction with the reality of the situation in the USSR, but then this would become one of the hallmarks of his regime. As we saw earlier the proletariat had ceased to hold power before Lenin's death, as the soviets had by now become bodies whose members were largely appointed by the Party. This would not have troubled Stalin since the whole message of this piece is not about soviet power because "*the Party is the highest form of class organisation of the proletariat*" and not the soviets. Since "*the Party is the General Staff of the proletariat*", all workers have to do is "*display their readiness to support the vanguard*".

And just to hammer home the message that the Party is always right he concludes:

The question then arises: who is to determine the line, the general direction, along which the work of all these organisations is to be conducted? Where is the central organisation which is not only able, because it has the necessary experience, to work out such a general line, but, in addition, is in a position, because it has sufficient prestige, to induce all these organisations to carry out this line, so as to attain unity of leadership and to make hitches impossible? That organisation is the Party of the proletariat.

Moreover this vanguard can brook no dissension because it is:

The Party as the embodiment of unity of will, unity incompatible with the existence of factions.

He did not waste the opportunity to take more swipes at oppositional factions. Stalin repeated Lenin's criticisms of the various international Communist Left organisations in *Left-wing Communism*, but twisted them to make them appear a criticism of the Russian oppositions who would have "cut the party off from the masses" and transformed the party into a group of "futile conspirators".

As he increased his grip over the Party machine anyone objecting to the course the USSR was taking was now, by definition, an anti-Party factionalist. All those who had supported the banning of factions in 1921 would regret it, as they were to find that they too were now trapped by that ban, as Radek had predicted. Stalin's writing just codified the counter-revolution that had been in progress since 1921.

Chapter 16
Aftermath: Party, Class and Soviets

In this enquiry our basic premise has been that the workers in Russia, for all their relatively recent proletarianisation in the years before the First World War, had attempted something unparalleled in history. In the end their revolution failed. But, since the world working class will never be in a position to talk of "victory" until it has finally rid itself of capitalist exploitation for good, that is not the issue. What we have focussed on here is the manner of that defeat, and what we take from it. The Paris Commune of 1871 was isolated to a single city, and lasted only 74 days, before being bloodily crushed by the capitalist state, yet it remains an inspiration down to this very day.[1] The events of 1918-21 have left us a more awkward legacy. A counter-revolution managed by the same Party that had led the original assault on a capitalist state in itself is hard to make sense of.

The process of trying to get to grips with it has not been made any easier by the ideological attempts at self-justification by competing capitalist systems. Thus we get the mutually reinforcing distortions of both the Stalinist heirs to the counter-revolution and Western historians intent on defending the superiority of free market capitalism. Whilst the former maintain that the USSR was "really existing socialism", the latter are only too glad to agree that the monstrous command economy and brutal dictatorship of Stalinism was the product of a "Marxist revolution". Between them they obscure the truth about what was really unique and revolutionary about the original revolution in Russia. As Orwell put it in *1984* both are acting on the conscious premise that "who controls the past controls the future" in the full knowledge that, as they control the means of reproduction of ideas in the present, they dominate the message about what the past itself is. A workers' history therefore is not simply an academic exercise but, in combatting these false interpretations, it makes an essential contribution to the class war itself.

Rescuing historical truth is no simple task, as reality is always more complex, and messy, than the glib slogans of ideologists. And few episodes have been richer and more complex than the revolutionary period in Russia between 1905 and 1918. The Russian workers did not start from a completely blank sheet. In the appalling conditions in which they lived and worked they had already begun to listen to the socialist minorities, albeit in small numbers, before 1905. These parties passed on to them the ideas and experiences of workers beyond Russia. Thus Russian workers could take inspiration from the revolutionary assault of the Paris Commune. In 1871 the Parisian workers had found that they could not "*lay hold of the ready-made state machinery*" of the capitalist class. It would have to be destroyed as an instrument of oppression and replaced with something "new"[2]. But as to what that "new" would be, the Commune did not survive long enough to leave anything more than the vaguest of outlines.

Aftermath: Party, Class and Soviets

The Russian working class for all (or perhaps because of) their relative inexperience would provide the next link in the chain. *"The finally discovered political form"* (Marx) of working class rule was a result of the Russian Revolution of 1905. The supposedly "backward" Russian working class' historical discovery of "councils" or "soviets" solved the riddle of how a mass society can operate, whilst still allowing the maximum of participation of all its members. Instead of electing a representative every five years who was free to ignore the electors for all that time, workers built on the Paris Commune experience in electing delegates who could be recalled (and if necessary replaced) at any time. Based on delegates elected from each factory, rather than a district, this embryo of working class direct democracy was also physically crushed by the end of 1905.

The idea, though, did not die. It was already part of the consciousness of the workers so that, in the first days of the February 1917 Revolution, the call for soviets soon arose on the streets. As we have argued here this prompted the frightened propertied classes (with the assistance of so-called socialist organisations) to create soviets to meet workers' demands. But the perspective of the Mensheviks and SRs, like the bourgeoisie, was always that these were unnecessary bodies that would have to be tolerated until the revolutionary mood abated. They were only conceded to recuperate the movement on the streets. Their plan was that they would be liquidated when the Constituent Assembly met[3] but as the revolutionary mood only became more radical, the election of a Constituent Assembly was continually postponed. Turning the *de facto* power of the soviets into the *de jure* government lay at the root of the class war of 1917. Workers' direct democracy, and the organs of class society, cannot remain in tandem for long. Either the Provisional Government or the soviets had to go. This was what made the October Revolution the last, and most important, act of the drama that had been begun in February. Had the capitalist political order not been overthrown in October 1917 then it is likely that the liquidation of the soviets would have followed, since Kerensky had already announced their day was past.

The October Revolution, led by a party which had massive support throughout the working class, made the Russian Revolution the seminal event of the last century for the world proletariat. It is the only time the working class has ever overthrown the capitalist state over an entire territory, and this is what makes it worthy of continuing enquiry. We will certainly not see the unique combination of circumstances that existed in 1917 in Russia again, but the experience demands the deepest study and understanding. Unlike the Trotskyists (ever seeking to provide the "right leadership" for workers) we will not be looking for a precise re-run or promoting any single "formula" for success. However, we cannot ignore the fact that the working class also made the Bolshevik Party its own during 1917. If the soviets were the weapons of the "dictatorship of the proletariat", the tool it forged to actually lead the final act in the overthrow of the Provisional Government was its political party. The Bolsheviks were not the only revolutionary tendency operating in the working class who supported soviet power. There were also anarchists, other left socialists like Trotsky's "Inter-district" (or Mezhraiontsy) group, and eventually Left SRs and SR Maximalists. Amongst these, what made the Bolsheviks the party that would grow to over 300,000 by September 1917?

The first factor was that they already, in 1914, had a skeletal network of an organisation across most of the Russian Empire that few other political organisations could match. This however would have meant nothing if they had not politically held the views that most closely coincided with a working class that was being radicalised. The most significant reason for the Bolsheviks striking such a chord with the wider working class was their response to the First World War. They stuck to the internationalist principles of socialism, as voted at congress after congress in the Second International, by opposing the war on class terms. This was no airy theory. The worker-activists of the Bolshevik Party translated Lenin's call to "turn the imperialist war into a civil war" into a campaign of "down with the war". This principled position did not win much support at first, but once the reality of the war began to hit home in 1915-16, the working class did not forget who had led the opposition to the war.

Bolshevik internationalism did not end there. As we showed earlier, they not only called for a new international to replace the defunct Second International (at Zimmerwald and Kienthal) but also undertook analyses during the war to show that this was not going to be capitalism's last. Capitalism had now moved into the era of imperialism, or of the stage of the "decay and parasitism of capitalism", to use the subtitle of Lenin's *Imperialism*. The working class internationally had been confronting the capitalist system more directly in the years before the First World War and now, in the midst of a great international crisis, it had the basis for an even greater assault on the system. The Russian Revolution could even be a socialist one, as long as it was linked to a world-wide revolution. The Menshevik argument that this perspective was a break with Marxism was based on the mechanical interpretation of Marxism we analysed in the last chapter. They thought only in Russian terms, but the horizons of the Bolsheviks were much wider. Despite the fact that many of the Petersburg factories were owned by foreign multinationals, the Mensheviks failed to recognise that capitalism had become a "world economy" (Bukharin). This internationalist perspective was the alpha and omega of the Russian Revolution. Everyone from Rosa Luxemburg, to that great number of Russian workers who celebrated every international victory of the working class, knew that the question of socialism could not be answered in Russia alone. However, with the collapse of the Second International, and the political betrayal of the working class by so many of its leading parties, the paradox of Bolshevism was that it would have to lead the way, in the rational expectation that workers elsewhere would take up the fight against war and exploitation. It was the **isolation** of the revolution to Russia which remains the fundamental underlying reason why it had arrived at a cul-de-sac by 1921.

However, if that was the end of the story, this book would have been even shorter. To be sure, isolation to any one country would have doomed any proletarian revolution. It was the specific Russian conditions which shaped the decisions made by the Russian Communist Party (Bolshevik) after 1918. Even if they had taken better decisions it would not have saved the revolution for the working class, but they could have provided us with a more positive legacy. This is not just the verdict of hindsight. Contemporaries were aware of what was at stake. We have already quoted Radek from the 1918 journal *Kommunist* in Chapter 14. He was not alone. In its final issue in June of that year, another of the Left Communists, Sorin wrote:

> *... we believe that in the interests of the international proletarian movement, it is preferable to lose at the hand of outside forces as a true proletarian power, than to survive by adapting to the circumstances, by eschewing communist principles and allowing the soviet power to degenerate until nothing of it remains but its external shell; the soviets might still be "labelled" proletarian, but their content has become thoroughly non-proletarian. This second path leads to decomposition, to the corruption of soviet power and to the dejection of the working masses in Russia as well as the West.[4]*

Another prescient comment on both the course of the future counter-revolution in Russia, and its consequences for the world working class ever since. The central focus of this study has been to understand how the same organisation, which had fought for a workers' revolution in the teeth of all kinds of adversity also eventually became the agents of new kind of state power, not of the workers, but over the workers. The lessons may largely be of the "what is not to be done" kind, but this makes them no less important in the formation of a class perspective for the future.

This investigation has shown that many of the widespread interpretations about the Russian Revolution have either no basis in fact or, at best, are ideologically motivated exaggerations. We could find no evidence for example that there was anything in the DNA of Bolshevism that would lead it to consciously and deliberately undermine proletarian power from the start. On the contrary they did all they could to encourage it for the first 6 months. Such accusations of course are made by those who already know the story ended badly, but to leave out the positive achievements of those early months is a distortion which denies the achievements of the working class in Russia.

After three and a quarter years of war the Tsarist regime and the Provisional Government had left the revolution with an appalling economic crisis. This was only made worse by the Revolution's attempt to bring about peace (since factories engaged in war production closed). The loss of Ukraine further added to this woe. This, and the continuing shortage of food, not only led to many workers leaving the cities, but also to strikes and demonstrations against the Communists demanding food. The response was to start rigging or delaying elections, at least in the most hostile areas. And if this was not enough, the summer of 1918 got worse. The Left SRs abandonment of Sovnarkom, the beginning of the civil war proper and the campaign of terror against Bolsheviks, which culminated in the declaration of the Red Terror in September 1918, all contributed to a siege mentality. To "hold on" until the world revolution Sovnarkom now began to build the Red Army and licensed the Cheka to grow into a body interfering in every aspect of life. At the same time the Executive Committee of the Soviets, elected by the Congresses, gradually ceased to meet. Congresses went from being quarterly to being annual. Election was often replaced by appointment and the practice of soviet executives meeting without reference to the full soviet expanded throughout the civil war.

In short, a state apparatus which was only nominally based on the soviets began to take shape. From 1919, when the Politburo of five was created, the Party was in the ascendant even over Sovnarkom, which had been, until then, the government. In 1920, after two or more years of brutal civil war the RCP(B) militarily came out on top. At this point a space opened up which might have led to a review of the need for "emergency" bodies like the Cheka, as well as a chance to revive soviet democracy. The various oppositions, from the Military Opposition and the Democratic Centralists to the Workers' Opposition and Myasnikov's Workers' Group, all continued to call for a revival of worker initiative. But they called in vain.

And at Kronstadt and in the Makhnovshchina the RCP(B) demonstrated that "holding on" until world revolution had gone beyond the military defeat of the Whites to end up extinguishing any force the Party did not directly control. And once the external enemies had been vanquished the heat turned on the internal oppositions, and as we saw in the last chapter they too were either expelled (like Myasnikov's Workers' Group) or, in the face of the ban on factions, were forced to reduce their aim of defending the original principles of the revolution based on the activity of the working class, to simply trying to insist on intra-party democracy. This too was doomed to failure as the appointment system gradually fell into the hands of Stalin and his cohorts. The latter's 1924 announcement that "socialism in one country" was now possible was not only abandonment of the internationalist premise on which the overthrow of the Provisional Government had been based. It was also the announcement of the shape the Stalinist counter-revolution would take.

In the first version of *The Foundations of Leninism* Stalin had repeated the generally accepted view that building socialism in a single country was impossible.

> *The overthrow of the power of the bourgeoisie and the establishment of a proletarian government in one country does not yet guarantee the complete victory of socialism. The main task of socialism – the organisation of socialist production – remains ahead. Can this task be accomplished, can the final victory of socialism in one country be attained, without the joint efforts of the proletariat of several advanced countries? No, this is impossible.[5]*

Deutscher tells us though that before the year was out, Stalin "corrected himself". In November he withdrew *The Foundations of Leninism* and replaced it with his *Problems of Leninism.* For this new version Stalin further ripped some of Lenin's remarks about the possibility of "socialism" out of context from such articles as "On the Slogan for a United States of Europe"[6]. Whereas Lenin had used the term to refer only to the immediate victory over the capitalist state[7], Stalin deliberately misinterpreted Lenin's position to mean the actual creation of a new society. In a deliberate challenge to Trotsky, whose theory of "permanent revolution" was well known, Stalin now argued that "socialism in one country" was possible in Russia even if a later international communist revolution would be needed to add the finishing touches. A year later he went even further:

Aftermath: Party, Class and Soviets

One can only wonder why we took power in October 1917 if we did not count on ***completely*** *building Socialism?[8]*

By the beginning of 1926 "socialism in one country" had been adopted as the official Party line and the counter-revolution announced so dramatically in 1921 was now complete. The lie that the USSR represented "real socialism" would now be peddled for the next 65 years (and is still peddled more than 30 years after its demise). Millions still believe it to have been the case, despite the fact that it shared nothing with Marx's vision of a society of "freely associated producers", one where there would be no exploitation, no money and no state.

For communists who share Marx's original vision, there is no question that Stalinism[9] is the consequence of the counter-revolution that destroyed the revolution itself. Whatever his positive contributions in 1905, and even 1917-18, Trotsky, and subsequently Trotskyism,[10] can also be ruled out as the basis for any alternative to what became a new form of state capitalism in the USSR. As this account shows he was foremost in building the very state that would run roughshod over working class initiative. In 1928, many of Trotsky's erstwhile supporters went over to Stalin when he adopted the Five Year Plans, since they had been calling for such industrialisation for years. Trotsky cannot be blamed for not seeing that he had helped to create a new form of state capitalism, but he can be blamed for his absurd attempts to justify it later. He would end up in the ridiculous position for a "Marxist" of asserting that the relations of production in the USSR were socialist, but politically "deformed" by Stalin's leadership of the Party. In short Trotsky who, as we saw, had been as responsible as anyone for the creation of a state not based on workers' democracy, held a vision of socialism which was just as state capitalist as Stalin's. The counter-revolution also took its toll on those who had a clearer idea of communism, and drove them to despair altogether. Vladimir Smirnov, who belonged to three different opposition groups of the Communist Left between 1918-22, and even signed (with reservations) the Declaration of the 46 (which is regarded as the founding document of the Trotskyist Left Opposition in 1923) because it called for inner-party democracy, allegedly ended up concluding:

> There has never been a proletarian revolution, nor a dictatorship of the proletariat in Russia, there has simply been a 'popular revolution' from below and a dictatorship from above. Lenin was never an ideologist of the proletariat. From beginning to end he was an ideologist of the intelligentsia.[11]

By this time (1929) he was debating what had gone wrong in the revolution with other "oppositionists" in the "isolator" of Verkhne-Uralsk. His despair is understandable, even if his conclusion was mistaken. He was released from confinement in 1935, only to be re-arrested and shot by Stalin's henchmen two years later. This was part of the process of wiping out the Bolshevik Old Guard of 1917. The process, though, had begun with a wave of suicides of many leading Bolsheviks in the 1920s despairing at the outcome of the revolution.[12]

Legacies of the Revolution – Councilism

The "dejection" that Sorin spoke about above was not confined to Russia. In 1918, in exhorting the world working class to complete the Russian Revolution, Herman Gorter had written:

> *The workers of the world have a brilliant example to guide them. That example is the Russian Revolution ... It has discovered the form by which the proletariat can achieve victory: Workers' Councils (Soviets). These it has set up in every village and every province in the country. These Councils have all economic and political power. The Workers' Councils, which will destroy Capitalism and establish Socialism; which will expropriate Capitalism and transfer all power and wealth to Socialism; which will build up Socialism politically and economically: these Councils are the form and expression of the New Society, of the New Humanity.[13]*

Whilst what he said was true for 1918, by 1923 he was reflecting the bitterness of the defeat of the revolution in the following terms.

> *The party dictatorship of the Bolshevists was in the highest degree bourgeois. Party dictatorship will always become so. In leader-dictatorship lies the kernel of the bourgeois capitalist revolution, and in it is the greatest proof that the Russian revolution was chiefly, and in its origin, a bourgeois capitalist one[14].*

This was echoed by Otto Rühle but he went even further. Whilst Gorter accepted the need for an international party to politically unite the class before capitalism could be overthrown, Rühle concluded that "all parties are bourgeois" and that thus they had no part to play in the revolution or, as he trenchantly put it, "the revolution is not a party affair"[15]. The notion of "councils good, party bad" thus led to the Dutch-German left eventually giving birth to "council communism". Gorter had at least the merit of understanding the Russian Revolution was at the outset a proletarian revolution, and only with its evolution in isolation, had become a new form of state capitalism. Rühle, who arrived in Russia at the nadir of soviet power in 1920, starts from the premise that parties are only vehicles of bourgeois revolutions. The Bolshevik Party was a useful vehicle for overthrowing a "semi-feudal" order like Tsarism he maintained, but not for leading a workers' revolution.

Rühle was historically wrong[16]. Even under the bourgeoisie, the notion of "party" has taken many different forms. A "man of party" in eighteenth century England was the parliamentary client of some powerful aristocrat who bought his seat. This was an entirely different concept to the purely bourgeois vote catching machines of the nineteenth century even though they evolved from the earlier loose groupings. The problem was that the Social Democratic Parties of the later nineteenth century, which started out outside the system, gradually adopted the vote catching model too. It is to this that Rühle, who was a Social Democratic deputy in the Reichstag for many years and so is speaking from experience, is referring.

Aftermath: Party, Class and Soviets

But in arguing that any form of political association in advance of the revolution can only be bourgeois, Rühle was robbing the working class of one of its main weapons. Workers by definition have no form of property to defend, that's what makes the working class a class with "radical chains". They cannot simply advance economically, and by stealth, until they have amassed sufficient power to overthrow the existing state power, as the bourgeoisie did. The revolution of the working class is always a conscious act, and depends on workers coming together to realise the latent power they possess as a collective. However, workers at different times and in various places experience capitalism differently. Circumstances thus force some down a radical road faster than others. The friction of class war throws up sparks of consciousness, but if these are not gathered they will never burst into revolutionary flame. The only way they can develop that class consciousness is for them to form some association which unites those who have seen that the real issue is not to be "fairly" exploited, but to end the system of exploitation once and for all. The formation of an international political instrument is thus an essential part of the process of developing the revolution. It was after all what Marx had tried to form as early as 1864. In 1879 he reminded the leaders of the Social Democratic Party, who were just beginning a fight against the reformism of Bernstein et al., that the First International was a revolutionary party independent of other class interests.

At the founding of the International, we expressly formulated the battle cry: The emancipation of the working class must be the work of the working class itself.[17]

This is today sometimes quoted out of context as if the class and its party were somehow not connected. After Marx's death, the Second International came into being, but it contained worse elements than Bernstein. As we saw in Chapter 2, it fell apart in 1914 as only the Bolsheviks, along with the smaller Serbian, Bulgarian and Polish parties, supported the fight against imperialist war. The Bolsheviks were thus the last defenders of proletarian internationalism, and it was because of this, as we explained earlier, that they became the vehicle which the Russian working class made its own to overthrow the capitalist state in 1917. Rühle, and the councilists, though focus only on the later abandonment of working class principles by the RCP(B) and make no allowances that these errors were committed in the face of imperialist encirclement, and the failure of the post-war revolutionary wave to make a world revolution. They thus refuse to recognise that the creation and rise of a political organisation of the class is a natural expression of the rising revolutionary consciousness of the class itself. In denying the unevenness of how class consciousness emerges, councilism thus became a curiously self-denying cult which, unsurprisingly, has prevented it from forming any significant political organisation. In some ways it too is a reflection of the counter-revolution, and it certainly spreads confusion amongst the working class.

Ironically Makhno and Arshinov, and the *Dyelo Truda* (Workers' Cause) anarchist group in their French exile, drew the opposite lesson about the Russian revolution to the councilists. They argued that, not only should the anarchist movement base its agitation primarily on the class struggle, but that they would also need to have some principled

226

political basis for working together, and so drew up their Organisational Platform of the Libertarian Communists in 1926[18]. It was rejected by many anarchists then and now, but it is notable for its recognition that if you leave the question of class political organisation to chance, the only beneficiaries are the Stalinist and Trotskyist enemies of the working class, disguised as "socialists" or "Marxists".

The councilists are right though when they argue that the soviets or workers' councils are, so far, the best historically created form for the great mass of the working class to exercise its dictatorship. Councils remain the form of the future, as they are representative of the entire working class, through the election and recall of delegates. However these councils have to control everything from the militia to any emergency bodies set up to deal with sabotage, etc., and they have to have supreme authority. They do not need a separate executive from that elected by the Soviet Congress. This was the first error of the October Revolution. The creation of Sovnarkom as an executive power appointed by its constituent parties (Bolsheviks and Left SRs), though nominally under the control of the soviet, always had the potential to escape that control. This is exactly what happened in the civil war. As we saw in Chapter 8, the Bolsheviks had no agreed idea what the role of the party would be once soviet power was established. Thanks to the Russian experience we now know that the revolutionary party is not a government in waiting for any territory. Indeed for any party to take sole responsibility for any decisions forced by circumstance on the workers' power would be to deny its real mission. This is to continue the fight, both internationally for the world revolution, and within any soviets for those measures which tend towards the abolition of the rule of the capitalist law of value, so that the mode of production can move from a commodity-based economy to one which satisfies real human needs for all. The speed with which it is able to do so will be related to the speed with which more and more of the planet comes under working class control.

The party will always be a minority of the class and thus, as Lenin himself recognised in 1918, socialism cannot be built by the party, but only by the working class majority actively creating it. Indeed the problems facing any proletarian power are bound to be extremely difficult to tackle. Revolution will emerge from some deep crisis of capitalism. In the Russian case three years of war were not ideal material preparations for any workers' power to deal with. To both retain working class initiative and ensure the decisions have the widest support of the class, the delegates of the councils are the only ones who can take decisions. The communist minority will certainly have delegates in the councils, but their role will be to defend the communist programme at all times even when the councils decide that this programme may only be applied piecemeal or have to be deferred. The Party's role is to remain in the class wide bodies to fight for measures which tend towards communism, but the decisions have to be made by the class-wide bodies. In practice, as long as capitalism still exists anywhere, the councils will remain an arena of continuing struggle for communism.

We summed up this problem of the relationship between the revolutionary minority and the wider working class elsewhere:

Aftermath: Party, Class and Soviets

> *Whilst the party has an important guiding role in the actual process of insurrection, and will have to lead in that insurrection, in the last resort it has to be this mass of the class not the party which finally overthrows the old order by drawing an even greater mass into the process which begins to build a new one. The precise relationship between class party and mass of the class cannot be decided in advance since it is only in the process of revolution that the working class shakes off "the muck of ages" (Marx, The German Ideology) but historical logic cannot be turned on its head. First, class consciousness takes a minority form, and then this minority points the way forward to the whole class in a revolutionary situation. Only once the capitalist order has been overthrown does the working class set up the required new material conditions for the development of a mass communist/class consciousness.[19]*

Legacies of the Revolution – Bordigism

Rühle was not the only one to go as a delegate to the Second Comintern Congress in 1920. Amadeo Bordiga was part of the delegation of the Italian Socialist Party, and along with the soon-to-become-Fascist Bombacci, was recognised as a delegate of the "left" of the party. He arrived in Moscow after Rühle, who thought the Congress would start in June, so turned up a month early. During that time Rühle was not only treated to some arrogant behaviour from Radek (who at this time was charged with relations with German communists) but managed to get around the Moscow gubernia to see for himself something of what was going on in reality. Unfortunately he arrived when the soviets were no longer really representative of workers. This coloured his assessment of the whole revolution[20]. Bordiga appears to have seen the same things as Rühle but, far from criticising it, concludes that this was just as it should be.

> *... the Russian Soviet Republic is led by the Soviets, which represent ten million workers out of a total population of about eighty million. But essentially, appointments to the executive committees of the local and central Soviets are settled in the sections and congresses of the great Communist Party which has mastery over the Soviets. This corresponds to the stirring defence by Radek of the revolutionary role of minorities. It would be as well not to create a majoritarian-workerist fetishism which could only be to the advantage of reformism and the bourgeoisie. The party is in the front line of the revolution in so far as it is potentially composed of men [sic] who think and act like members of the future working humanity in which all will be producers harmoniously inserted into a marvellous mechanism of functions and representation.[21]*

A few things need unpicking here. Bordiga was, of course, looking to the situation in Italy where he was trying to lead the left in forging a Communist Party out of the confused swamp that was the Italian Socialist Party. Additionally, the experience of the factory occupations in Italy in the so-called *Biennio Rosso*[22] only confirmed the need for the working class to politically overthrow the capitalist state **before** it could institute its own forms of the dictatorship of the proletariat. The weapon for doing this was the class party.

> *Revolution requires an organisation of active and positive forces united by a doctrine and a final aim. Important strata and innumerable individuals will remain outside this organisation even though they materially belong to the class in whose interest the revolution will triumph. But the class lives, struggles, progresses and wins thanks to the action of the forces it has engendered from its womb in the pains of history. The class originates from an immediate homogeneity of economic conditions which appear to us as the primary motive force of the tendency to destroy and go beyond the present mode of production. But in order to assume this great task, the class must have its own thought, its own critical method, its own will bent on the precise ends defined by research and criticism, and its own organisation of struggle channelling and utilising with the utmost efficiency its collective efforts and sacrifices. All this constitutes the Party.[23]*

This is Bordiga at the peak of his power in 1921, explaining the precise and essential role of a class political force in advance of the revolution. However, like Rühle, whilst he is extolling one organisation required by the working class to make its revolution, he does not see the real significance of the other. In Bordiga's case it is the soviet or workers' council. No-one can disagree with Bordiga that "the Soviets are the form, not the cause, of the revolution"[24], but his denunciation in the quote above of "a majoritarian-workerist fetishism" is not only consistent with his distaste for any form of voting, but also reflects the mechanical thinking of his engineering profession, rather than a dialectical appreciation of the nature of the class struggle after the bourgeois state has been overthrown. In *Party and Class* Bordiga himself gave us a brilliant way to understand how dialectical thinking is about seeing social interaction as a process.

> *The Marxist critique sees human society in its movement, in its development in time; it utilises a fundamentally historical and dialectical criterion, that is to say, it studies the connection of events in their reciprocal interaction. Instead of taking a snapshot of society at a given moment (like the old metaphysical method) and then studying it in order to distinguish the different categories into which the individuals composing it must be classified, the dialectical method sees history as a film unrolling its successive scenes; the class must be looked for and distinguished in the striking features of this movement.[25]*

But when it comes to looking at the role of the soviets in 1920 Bordiga himself does not apply the method. As we saw in 1917, the soviet was an arena of class war. The legacy of capitalism will not be overthrown in an instant. The soviets may be the form of the dictatorship of the proletariat, but they not only have to combat the actual capitalists, but also the remnants of capitalist ideology that exist in the wider working class. As we saw in the Russian Revolution, for the mass of the class this only begins, as Marx predicted, once the revolutionary process begins. Workers still steeped in the old way of thinking will have to be won over by the communists in the working class (both inside and outside the political organisation). If socialism can only be built by the mass of the class (as Bordiga also recognised) then it cannot be simply imposed on it by the revolutionary minority. Whether Bordiga likes it or not, the only alternative to workers choosing their own delegates to the councils, is what existed by 1920 in Russia – a party dictatorship where many candidates are appointed rather than elected (or rather were "proposed" by the Party, but it was the same thing, as there were no other candidates).

Given time, and the experience of Stalinism, it might reasonably be assumed that Bordiga would have had the chance to reflect on this. However he withdrew from all political contact for nearly 20 years and seemed to have remained stuck in the situation of 1920. If anything he became more fixated on the role of the party. It was one of the issues which would lead him to break with the Internationalist Communist Party (which he never formally joined) that had been founded in 1943 by his former comrades, who had founded the Communist Party of Italy with him in 1921. Failing to see that the soviets were really a potential answer to the problem of how the working class could exercise its dictatorship without establishing a permanent state, he now became a fervent defender of the Party-state. In 1951 he concluded that:

> The proletarian state can only be "animated" by a single party and it would be senseless to require that this party organise in its ranks a statistical majority and be supported by such a majority in "popular elections" — that old bourgeois trap. One of the historical possibilities is the existence of political parties composed in appearance by proletarians, but in reality influenced by counter-revolutionary traditions or by foreign capitalisms. This contradiction, the most dangerous of all, cannot be resolved through the recognition of formal rights nor through the process of voting within the framework of an abstract "class democracy". This too will be a crisis to be liquidated in terms of relationships of force.

And just in case anyone still doubted what he meant he finished with these words:

> In conclusion the communist party will rule alone, and will never give up power without a physical struggle. [26]

If history has to be seen as a movie, then Bordiga froze the frame at the point where the counter-revolution was victorious. What the Russian Revolution definitively proved was that whilst a political body is needed to unite class conscious workers (or to put it the correct way round, the class conscious workers will be compelled to come together internationally to find each other to give a guide to other workers) this world party is not equipped to be an instrument of government. It will be involved in any insurrection, and may even be the instigator of it. But the overthrow of the bourgeois order is only the first act of any real revolution. The building of a new society, as we frequently heard in the Russian Revolution, is not the work of a minority, but of the class wide bodies. The world party of the proletariat remains an instrument of world wide revolution. Its leading bodies will not be tied to one geographical area but focussed on spreading any revolution as quickly and as widely as possible. Its individual members may accept delegation to the class-wide bodies but will have to fight in them for the communist programme.

This was the lesson learned and expressed in the 1952 Platform of the Internationalist Communist Party.

> *It would be a gross and dangerous error for the future to believe that the moment the working class creates their party, then they somehow relinquish – totally or even partially – those attributes which make them the gravedigger of capitalism, as if others could act as an alternative and have the same consciousness of the need to struggle against the class enemy and to overthrow it in revolution. At no time and for no reason does the proletariat abandon its combative role. It does not delegate to others its historical mission, and it does not give power away to anyone, not even to its political party.[27]*

An international political body fighting for the communist programme (that is, all the acquisitions of all previous workers' struggles, including the ones detailed in this study) and a whole series of class-wide bodies through which the workers can reshape society are necessary conditions for the future triumph of socialism. Throughout the Russian revolutionary process from 1905 onwards Russian workers enthusiastically rallied to the soviet form. They called for their revival in February 1917 and continued to struggle to bring them to power in October by giving massive support to the one significant force with deep roots in the working class which supported soviet power as the form to begin a new epoch of workers' rule. And when under all the pressures of economic crisis, civil war and isolation from the rest of the world working class, the Bolsheviks failed, the desire for bodies to express the will of the workers burst out in Petersburg, Moscow, Kronstadt and elsewhere in 1921. This is their legacy to us and, despite living in a different historical epoch, nothing better has yet been created anywhere to surpass that achievement.

A Brief Chronological Guide

1861 Tsar Alexander II passes the Emancipation Edict, ending serfdom in Russia (but keeps peasants tied to the land through the payment of redemption dues which were supposed to last 57 years – they are ended as a response to the 1905 Revolution).

1881 Tsar Alexander II is assassinated by a member of the radical group People's Will. His son and grandson increase the power of the autocracy and adopt a reactionary agenda based on Russification of minority languages, the Orthodox Church and the secret police.

1882 Pogroms against Jews spread across the Russian Empire, leading to mass emigration of the Jewish population.

1883 Emancipation of Labour group founded in Geneva by Plekhanov.

1891–1892 Famine in Russia kills at least 500,000 and affects millions more (Vyshnegradsky the Finance Minister exported grain during it to earn foreign currency, and was eventually replaced by Witte).

1894 Nicholas II becomes the last Tsar of the Romanov dynasty.

1895 St Petersburg Union of Struggle members, including Lenin and Martov, arrested and kept in solitary confinement for 13 months.

1897 Lenin sentenced to 3 years in Siberia. Krupskaya married Lenin to join him there.

1898 First Congress of the Russian Social Democratic Labour Party held in Minsk with 9 delegates.

1899 Lenin's *The Development of Capitalism in Russia* argues that Russia was now a capitalist country. This dominates his perspectives until 1916 when *Imperialism – the Highest Stage of Capitalism* becomes the bedrock of his thinking that the time is ripe for the working class to rise against the world capitalist order.

1902 Lenin's *What is to be Done?* published.

1903 Second Congress of the Russian Social Democratic Labour Party.

1904 Russia, faced with increasing social unrest needs "a short victorious war" (Plehve) for nationalist mobilisation and declares war on Japan. It led to a humiliating defeat.

1905 First revolution against the privations caused by the Russo-Japanese War. Began on

"Bloody Sunday" **(9/22 January 1905)**. In the course of the year councils (soviets) were elected by workers in many places starting in Ivanovo-Vosnesensk.

December 1905 The army remained loyal to the system and thus the revolution comes to an end with the crushing of the Moscow workers.

1906-11 Period of reaction presided over by Prime Minister Stolypin until his assassination in 1911.

1912 Lena Goldfield strikes and killing of 200 workers spark off a wave of strikes which reach a crescendo in 1914. Sixth RSDLP Party Congress in Prague dominated by Bolsheviks who are able to form a nucleus of a separate organisation from the Mensheviks.

August 1914 Patriotic fervour drowns workers' resistance as Germany declares war on Russia. Russian Army massively defeated at the battles of Tannenberg and Masurian Lakes. Lenin calls for "the imperialist war to be turned into a civil war", and this was taken up by the Bolsheviks inside Russia.

1915 Zimmerwald (Switzerland) meeting of anti-war socialists sees the secession of the Zimmerwald Left headed by Lenin from the pacifist majority and issuing of their own Manifesto.

1916 Second anti-war conference at Kienthal. Lenin (basing himself on Bukharin's work of the previous year *Imperialism and World Economy*) writes his *Imperialism* in which he concludes that the era of "parasitism and decay of capitalism" has put world proletarian revolution on the agenda.

1917

24 February/8 March International Women's Day. Leads to strikes for bread and an end to the war in Petersburg. After almost a week and about 1,300 deaths the Tsar abdicates. The first Provisional Government is set up by members of the Tsarist Duma. In the same Tauride Palace the Petersburg Soviet is formed. It issues Soviet Order No 1 which makes the troops responsible to the Soviet and not the Provisional Government.

April Lenin returns from Switzerland. His *Letters from Afar* and *April Theses* eventually persuade the Bolsheviks to endorse his vision that the revolution is not just Russian, not just "democratic", but the first step in the world revolution. The Bolsheviks adopt the slogans "Bread, peace and land" and "All Power to the Soviets".

May Foreign Minister Milyukov (Kadet) issues his Note which says that the Provisional Government will stand by the imperialist treaties of the Tsar. Mass protests force him to resign and the Mensheviks and Socialist Revolutionaries (SRs) join the Provisional Government.

A Brief Chronological Guide

June After an initial success the Brusilov offensive fails. This increases opposition to the war both in the trenches and back home which leads to a mass demonstration, where 90% of the banners carried Bolshevik slogans, in a slap in the face to the Mensheviks and SRs. Soldiers' committees now debate orders and encourage soldiers to disobey officers. Many soldiers return home to take part in redistribution of land (which the Provisional Government is trying to resist).

July The First Machine Gun regiment aided by anarchist and Bolshevik sailors think the time has come for the Soviets to take over and organise an armed demonstration. Lenin returns from holiday to try to calm the movement, but when the demonstration is fired upon, several are killed. The Bolsheviks are blamed and outlawed. Some are killed, some arrested and Lenin, in the face of a press campaign that he is a "German spy" goes into hiding until November, during which he completes *The State and Revolution*. Kerensky, who has been in the two previous Provisional Governments, now becomes Prime Minister of the third. The gulf between the working class in the soviets and the Provisional Government becomes wider.

August Against a background of increasing class polarisation, the new Commander in Chief Kornilov leads his troops towards Petersburg with the aim of ending soviet rule. He fails due to the workers' and soldiers' fraternisation with his troops who simply melt away. The Bolsheviks now are *de facto* legalised.

September The Bolsheviks win majorities in the soviets and in some Dumas but the Menshevik/SR dominated VTsIK delays calling the new Congress to keep the Bolsheviks from taking over. Instead they declare Russia a Republic.

October Trotsky however becomes head of a new Revolutionary Military Committee of the Petersburg Soviet which the Mensheviks and Right SRs boycott.

November The "October Revolution" triumphs almost bloodlessly and the Second All-Russian Soviet Congress endorses the setting up of the "provisional" Council of Peoples' Commissars (Sovnarkom) which is boycotted by the SRs and Mensheviks. Decrees on Peace and Land are issued within days. Subsequent workers' decrees outline measures for an eight-hour working day, minimum wage and the workers' control of factories. The death penalty is abolished once again. Elections to Constituent Assembly go ahead.

December The VCheka (All-Russian Extraordinary Commission for Combating Counter-revolution and Sabotage) set up. Vesenkha (National Council of the Economy) set up. Negotiations begin at Brest-Litovsk with the German High Command. Peasant soviet elects Left SR majority. Revolutionary tribunals set up.

1918

January The Constituent Assembly refuses to endorse soviet power and is shut down after one day. This was approved by the Third All-Russian Congress of Soviets as was the dropping of the qualification "provisional" from Sovnarkom. Third All-Russian Congress of Workers' and Soldiers' Deputies. Beginning of the formation of the Red Army. Trotsky refuses to sign the treaty of Brest-Litovsk. First attempt on Lenin's life.

February Calendar changed from Julian to Gregorian. 1 February becomes 14 February. German Army occupies all the Baltic states and Sovnarkom sends a message to say they will sign a peace.

March Treaty of Brest-Litovsk signed. Russia loses one-third of the old empire's population, one-third of its railway network, half its industry, three-quarters of its supplies of iron ore, nine-tenths of its coal resources and much of its food supplies. Capital moved from Petersburg to Moscow.
At the Seventh Congress of the RSDLP, the Bolsheviks change the name of their party to the Russian Communist Party (Bolshevik). Trotsky becomes People's Commissar for War. Fourth All-Russian Congress of Soviets ratifies Brest-Litovsk. Left SRs and Left Communists resign from Sovnarkom in protest. Foreign intervention in the revolution begins as British troops land in Murmansk.

April Cheka raid anarchist premises in Moscow accused of harbouring criminals. Those who prove they are *bona fide* anarchists later released. Food crisis worsens leading to anti-Bolshevik demonstrations and the postponing/rigging of soviet elections in some places. First issue of the Left Communist journal *Kommunist* issued (in all 4 would appear until it folded in June)

May Unrest over drastic food shortages reaches new highs among Petersburg workers. Food requisitioning detachments instituted. Czech Legion revolts, sparking off a wider civil war. Final defeat of the Finnish Red Guards.

June Decree on Nationalisation of large industry. Committees of Poor Peasants (*Kombedy*) established to help in identifying grain stores of richer peasants (*Kulaks*). Right SR campaign of terror and assassination against Bolsheviks. Volodarsky killed by SR terrorists in Petersburg. The death penalty reintroduced. Mensheviks and Right SRs excluded from the All-Russian Soviet Executive Committe (VTsIK). The Czechs capture Samara thus aiding the formation of the Committee of the Members of the Constituent Assembly (*Komuch*) to form a government there.

July Fifth All-Russian Congress of Soviets. Left SR members of the Cheka murder the German Ambassador, Count Mirbach, to try to re-ignite the war. First political executions of the Cheka. Tsar Nicholas II and his family executed near Ekaterinburg. The first constitution of the Russian Socialist Federated Soviet Republic grants equal rights to men and women. Cholera epidemic in Petersburg. Bolshevik Party Petersburg Committee demands introduction of Red Terror

August Lenin seriously wounded by SR Fanny Kaplan in Moscow, and Uritsky assassinated in Petersburg. Red Terror begins.

September Sovnarkom authorises shooting of all those belonging to counter-revolutionary organisations with decree giving more power to the Cheka. 26 Bolshevik commissars shot in Baku. Cheka start to execute people before informing Sovnarkom.

October Lenin calls for a 3 million man Red Army. Revolt of sailors in Kiel presages German Revolution. Red Army captured Samara and the *Komuch* flees to Ufa. Beginning of the disintegration of the SR party. Denikin assumes main command of the White Armies.

November Revolution in Germany overthrows the Kaiser and brings the German High Command to surrender. Soviets set up in Germany. Treaty of Brest-Litovsk annulled. Sixth All-Russian Congress of Soviets. Denikin's (White) Volunteer Army captured Stavropol. Substantial British and French aid now flowed to Denikin.

December The ineffectual Committees of Poor Peasants (*Kombedy*) disbanded as the appeal was now made to middle peasants for support. Makhno begins cooperating with the Red Army against Denikin.

1919

January Defeat of the Spartakist Revolt in Germany and murder of Liebknecht and Luxemburg.

March First Congress of the Third International in Moscow. Death of Sverdlov (due to "Spanish flu"). Eighth Congress of the Russian Communist Party (Bolshevik) sets up the Political (Politburo) and Organisational (Orgburo) Bureaus of the Party. The Military Opposition demanded an end to the use of ex-Tsarist officers, and return to a democratic partisan force. The Democratic Centralists also opposed the lack of democracy in both soviets and party. Both outvoted. Hungarian Soviet Republic established.

April Soviet Republic established in Munich but was defeated by the end of the month.

May Grigoriev revolts against the Bolsheviks and carries out massive anti-semitic pogrom at Elizavetgrad. This allows Denikin to advance in South Russia and Makhno's partisans withdraw in face of his cavalry. Makhno resigned from the Red Army and had a short-lived alliance with Grigoriev.

June Two of Kronstadt's forts, Krasnaya Gorka and Seraia Loshad, revolt against the Bolsheviks in support of the advancing Yudenich, but were defeated by Soviet forces.

July Grigoriev urges Makhno to join him in going over to the Whites. Makhno rejects both this and Grigoriev's anti-semitism. In the ensuing exchange of fire Grigoriev is shot dead.

August Makhno issued his Order No. 1 condemning all rich bourgeois whatever their origin, as well as the unjust social order of Bolshevik commissars and the Cheka. The Polish Army take Minsk. Cheka expose plot by National Centre (a Kadet front) and thousands arrested.

September Last British troops evacuated from Archangel. Many of those arrested as a result of the National Centre plot in August executed by the Cheka.

October Yudenich advances on Petersburg but is defeated on its outskirts and his Army is forced to retreat to Estonia where it is disarmed. Denikin retreats from Orel as his lines are overstretched. The retreat harassed by partisan forces from minor nationalities as well as Makhno's 25,000 strong peasant force.

December Eighth RCP(B) Conference calls for more discipline in carrying out decisions but the right to internally contest decisions remain. Party fractions were to be set up in all non-Party bodies. Seventh Soviet Congress (the first for a year) held. Lenin defended the Terror against Menshevik attacks. The Mensheviks also attack the decline of soviet power.

1920

January Red Army occupies Krasnoyarsk and Kolchak's army surrendered. Makhno declared an outlaw after a failed attempt by the Fourteenth Red Army under Voroshilov to force him towards the Polish border. The subsequent harassment of Makhno depletes his forces.

March Last of the Czech Legion leave Irkutsk handing the Russian gold reserve over to the local Revolutionary Committee. RCP(B) Ninth Party Congress. Trotsky calls for the militarisation of labour and is attacked by those who would later form the Workers' Opposition. Lenin's report calls for "iron discipline" and is denounced by the Decists for its stress on "vertical centralism" or that decision-making was now the preserve of a small clique. Red Army capture Ekaterinodar and Novorossisk forcing Denikin to retreat to the Crimea.

April Last US troops under General Graves exit Russia via Vladivostok. Polish Government headed by Pilsudski attacks Russia but is driven back to Warsaw by the Red Army.

June Wrangel, having reorganised what remained of Denikin's Army, breaks out of the Crimea. Lenin publishes *Left-Wing Communism – An Infantile Disorder.*

July Wrangel sends emissaries to Makhno to ask him to cooperate against the Reds. Makhno kills the emissaries and twice suggests joint actions against Wrangel to Moscow. The US raises the trade embargo on Soviet Russia but denies recognition of its government. Second Comintern Congress decides to adopt the 21 Conditions and at this point envisages itself as one world party. It also adopts a resolution (despite opposition from Sultanzadeh and M N Roy) to support some "bourgeois democratic" national liberation struggles against imperialist domination.

August Defeat of Red Army outside Warsaw.

December Final Communist victory in the civil war as Wrangel evacuates the last White force from the Crimea. Eighth All-Russian Congress of Soviets decides to set up "sowing committees" to combat the falling area planted due to requisitioning. It agrees to let all sections of the Party produce "platforms" on the trade union question. Eight produced in all with Trotsky and Lenin openly disagreeing with each other and the Workers' Opposition.

1921

January Acute food shortages continue. Peasant rising of 50,000 in Siberia. Workers' Opposition platform published in *Pravda*.

February Pravda announces that 64 factories in Petersburg closed for lack of fuel. A Central Commission for Famine Relief set up by the Soviet government to deal with the consequences of the 1920 drought. State Central Planning Commission (*Gosplan*) set up. Strike wave breaks out in factories of Petersburg.

March The crushing of the Kronstadt Revolt. Banning of factions (and publication of their platforms) in the Bolshevik Party at the 10th Party Congress. Adoption of the New Economic Policy ended requisitioning and replaced it with a "tax in kind". Defeat of the March Action in Germany. Treaty of Riga establishes Soviet Russian-Polish border. Anglo-Soviet Trade Agreement signed.

June Famine in the Volga region where grain requisitioning was still continuing despite NEP.

June-July Third Comintern Congress. The Communist International recognises that the revolutionary wave is in retreat and adopts the policy of "going to the masses" which in December would become the United Front with social democracy.

July American Relief Administration's (headed by Herbert Hoover) offer of aid against the famine accepted by the Soviet government.

August Nestor Makhno, along with 83 followers, retreats into Romania after the defeat of his forces.

December Ninth Soviet Congress formalises the already established fact that they would meet once rather than twice a year. Stalin given charge of the Workers' and Peasants' Inspectorate (*Rabkrin*). The Executive Committee of the Comintern adopts the policy of the "united front" with social democracy despite the fact that most Communist Parties affiliated to the international had only just broken away from Social Democracy in the previous twelve months.

1922

January First Congress of the Toilers of the Far East meets in Moscow.

February Cheka replaced by the State Political Administration (GPU) with Dzerzhinsky still its head.

March-April Eleventh Party Congress. Lenin's illness means he only attends the opening and closing session but again calls for tighter discipline in the face of the retreat forced on the Party. The Workers' Opposition is condemned for their appeal to the Comintern Executive for support in their fight inside Russia and threatened with expulsion from the Party. Two Oppositionists are expelled but Shlyapnikov and Kollontai are warned against future conduct. Myasnikov's Workers Group is expelled.

April Stalin elected General Secretary of the Communist Party by the Central Committee – this makes him the only member of the top 4 Party institutions. Genoa Conference meets where Soviet Foreign Minister Chicherin calls for disarmament and world peace and offers to contribute towards world economic recovery. No agreement reached on the payment of the former regime's international debts. Treaty of Rapallo signed with Germany resumes diplomatic relations.

May Lenin suffers first stroke.

July Secretly a period of cooperation between the German military and the future USSR begins.

December Fourth Comintern Congress confirms the adoption of the policy of the "united front" with Social Democracy. Lenin only attends one session where he makes his last speech to the International. Within a few days he suffers a second stroke and dictates his "testament" followed by a memorandum condemning Stalin and his acolytes for their Russian national chauvinism in Georgia. The Russian Soviet Federative Socialist Republic to take the name Union of Soviet Socialist Republics (USSR) from the beginning of 1923.

1923

January Lenin adds postscript to his "testament" calling for Stalin to be removed as General Secretary. Later he attacks the *Rabkrin* which Stalin headed.

March Lenin sends telegram to Georgian leaders saying he supported them against Stalin, Ordzhonikidze and Dzerzhinsky.

A Brief Chronological Guide

April Twelfth Party Congress which Lenin does not attend and the main report is presented by Zinoviev. Beginning of triumvirate of Zinoviev, Kamenev and Stalin against Trotsky.

July New Constitution of the USSR adopted but no acknowledgement that power resides in the Party.

July-September Wave of workers' strikes against unemployment and low wages as a result of NEP.

October Platform of the 46 supports Trotsky's criticism of the Central Committee over the direction of economic policy and in particular the "scissors" crisis but what disturbs most of them is Dzerzhinsky's proposal that Party members should inform on each other to the OGPU (successor to the GPU a month earlier).

1924

January Thirteenth Party Conference. Trotsky and Lenin both absent due to illness and Stalin uses the opportunity to attack Trotsky as leader of the "opposition bloc". The decisions against factionalism of the 1921 Tenth Party Congress confirmed. Three days later Lenin dies.

April-May *Pravda* publishes Stalin's lectures *On the Foundations of Leninism* to aspiring bureaucrats at the Sverdlov Communist University.

May The Central Committee discuss Lenin's "testament" but against Krupskaya's protests, refuse to put it before a Party Congress. Stalin is saved by the interventions of Zinoviev and Kamenev. Trotsky remains silent. The Thirteenth Party Congress would be known as the "bolshevisation" congress. The new Lenin levy swells the number of Party members to 600,000 and further dilute the influence of the revolutionaries of the Tsarist period.

June-July Fifth Comintern Congress formally announces the policy of the "bolshevisation" of all the constituent parties of the Comintern enforcing strict discipline and centralised control by the Russian party. This was a *de jure* recognition of what had been *de facto* for some time.

December In *Pravda* Stalin openly poses the possibility of "socialism in one country" against Trotsky's theory of "permanent revolution".

Selected Reading List of Works Cited

General Histories

E. Acton *Rethinking the Russian Revolution* (Edward Arnold 1990)
J. Carmichael *A Short History of the Russian Revolution* (Sphere 1967)
E.H Carr *The Bolshevik Revolution* (3 Volumes, Penguin 1973)
E.H. Carr *The Interregnum 1923-4* (Macmillan 1954)
E.H.Carr *Socialism in One Country* (3 Volumes, Penguin, 1970)
W.H.Chamberlin *The Russian Revolution* (2 Volumes, Macmillan, 1965)
O. Figes *A People's Tragedy* (Pimlico 1996)
L. Kochan *The Making of Modern Russia* (Pelican 1963)
S.A. de Mowbray *Key Facts in Soviet History* (London 1990)
C. Read *From Tsar to Soviets* (UCL 1996)
L. Schapiro *The Communist Party of the Soviet Union* (Methuen 1963)
L. Schapiro *The Origins of the Communist Autocracy* (Palgrave Macmillan 1987)
S.A. Smith *Russia in Revolution – An Empire in Crisis 1890-1928* (Oxford, 2017)

Documentary Sources and Reminiscences

Yuri Akhapkin (ed.) *First Decrees of Soviet Power* (Lawrence and Wishart 1970)
J. Bunyan and H. Fisher *The Bolshevik Revolution 1917-18* (Stanford 1934)
R.V. Daniels *A Documentary History of Communism in Russia* (Vermont 1993)
Florence Flamborough *A Nurse at the Russian Front* (Constable 1974)
F.A. Golder *Documents of Russian History 1914-1917* (Appleton, Century Crofts 1927, reprinted Peter Smith, Gloucester, Mass. 1964)
Maurice Paleologue *An Ambassador's Memoirs* (New York 1925)
M. Philips *Price Dispatches from the Revolution – Russia 1916-18* (Pluto Press 1997)
Arthur Ransome *Six Weeks in Russia 1919* (Redwords 1992)
Arthur Ransome *The Crisis in Russia 1920* (Redwords 1992)
F.F. Raskolnikov *Kronstadt and Petrograd* (New Park 1982)
A. Rosmer *Lenin's Moscow* (Pluto Press 1971)
J. Sadoul *Notes sur la révolution bolchévique octobre 1917- janvier 1919* (Hachette Livre 2018)
Victor Serge *Memoirs of a Revolutionary 1901-41* (OUP 1963)
N. Sukhanov *The Russian Revolution 1917 – A Personal Record* (Princeton 1984)
L. Trotsky *How the Revolution Armed: The Military Writings and Speeches of Leon Trotsky.* (New Park Publications 1981)

Economic and Social Histories

Janet M. Campbell *Is there a Case for a Socialist Jurisprudence?* (PhD. thesis, University

Selected Reading List of Works Cited

of Glasgow 1997 at *http://theses.gla.ac.uk/4247/*)

M.E. Falkus *The Industrialisation of Russia* (Macmillan 1983)

M. Ferro *The Bolshevik Revolution — A Social History* (Routledge, Kegan Paul 1980)

D. Healey *Homosexual Desire in Revolutionary Russia* (Chicago, 2001)

A. F. Ilyin-Zhenevsky *The Bolsheviks in Power – Reminiscences of the Year 1918* (New Park 1984)

Ekaterina Khaustova, *Pre-revolution living standards: Russia 1888-1917* (Russian State Social University, Kursk 2013)

F. Lorimer, *The Population of the Soviet Union, History and Prospects* (Geneva, 1948)

Silvana Malle *The Economic Organisation of War Communism* (Cambridge, 1985)

Nikolai V. Mikhailov *Non-Party Workers' Organizations in St Petersburg and the Provinces before and during the First Russian Revolution in A Dream Deferred: New Studies in Russian and Soviet Labor History* (ed Kessler, Pirani et al., Verlag Peter Lang 2008)

Alec Nove, *An Economic History of the USSR 1917-91* Third edition (Pelican 1992)

R. Stites *Revolutionary Dreams* (OUP 1989)

A. Willimott *Living the Revolution* (OUP 2017)

Before 1917

Oskar Anweiler *The Soviets* (Merlin 1974)

Abraham Ascher *The Revolution of 1905: A Short History*, (Stanford 2004)

A.Y. Badayev *Bolsheviks in the Tsarist Duma* (Bookmarks 1997)

N. Bukharin *Imperialism and World Economy* (Merlin 1972)

P Frölich *Rosa Luxemburg* (Pluto Press 1972)

Rosa Luxemburg *The Mass Strike, the Political Party and the Trade Unions* in *Rosa Luxemburg Speaks* (Pathfinder 1970)

John Maclean *The War After the War*, (Socialist Reproductions 1973)

Alexander Shlyapnikov, *On the Eve of 1917: Reminiscences from the Revolutionary Underground* (Allison and Busby, 1982)

L. Trotsky *1905* (Pelican 1971)

February to October 1917

E.N Burdzhalov *Russia's Second Revolution*, (English translation by Donald J Raleigh, Indiana University Press, 1986)

J.S. Curtis *The Russian Revolutions of 1917* (van Nostrand 1957)

Tsuyoshi Hasegawa *The February Revolution Petrograd 1917* (Brill 1981)

D. Kaiser (ed) *The Workers' Revolution in Russia* (Cambridge University Press 1987)

Diane Koenker *and* William Rosenberg *Strikes and Revolution in Russia 1917* (Princeton 1989)

Donald J. Raleigh *Revolution on the Volga* (Cornell 1986)

S.A. Smith *Red Petrograd* (Cambridge 1983)

L. Trotsky *The History of the Russian Revolution* (Pluto Press 1977)

October 1917

Roy Medvedev *The October Revolution* (Constable 1979)
China Mieville *October* (Verso 2017)
A. Rabinowitch *Prelude to Revolution* (Bloomington 1968)
A. Rabinowitch *The Bolsheviks Come to Power* (New Left Books 1979)
John Reed *Ten Days that Shook the World* (Sutton Publishing 1997)

The Bolsheviks in Power

Paul Avrich *Kronstadt 1921* (Princeton 1970)
P. Binns, T Cliff and C. Harman *Russia – from Workers State to State Capitalism* (Bookmarks 1987)
C.Bettelheim *Class Struggles in the USSR 1917-23* (Harvester 1976)
M. Brinton *The Bolsheviks and Workers' Control* (London 1971)
N. Bukharin and E.Preobrazhensky *The ABC of Communism* (originally published October 1919 – Pelican edition 1970)
N. Bukharin *Economics of the Transformation Period* (Bergman 1971)
T. Cliff *Trotsky, The Sword of the Revolution* (Bookmarks 1990)
W.P. and Z.K. Coates *Armed Intervention in Russia 1918-22* (London 1935)
Lara Douds *Inside Lenin's Government: Ideology, Power and Practice in the Early Soviet State* (Bloomsbury 2019)
S.F.Cohen *Bukharin and the Bolshevik Revolution* (OUP 1981)
I. Getzler *Kronstadt 1917-21 The Fate of a Soviet Democracy (Cambridge, 1983)*
D. Koenker, W, Rosenberg and R G Suny (eds) *Party, State and Society in the Russian Civil War* (Indiana 1989)
G. Leggett *The Cheka: Lenin's Political Police* (OUP 1981)
Rosa Luxemburg *The Russian Revolution* (Ann Arbor 1972)
Robert Mair *Inside the Beleaguered Fortress: Intra-Bolshevik Struggles and the Degeneration of the October Revolution by 1921* undergraduate dissertation for MA History University of Glasgow (March 2021)
D. Mandel *The Petrograd Workers in the Russian Revolution* (Historical Materialism 2018)
Evan Mawdsley *The Russian Civil War* (Birlinn 2000)
Mary McAuley *Bread and Justice* (Oxford 1991)
Kevin Murphy *Revolution and Counter-revolution: Class Struggle in a Moscow Metal Factory* (Haymarket 2007)
Simon Pirani *The Russian Revolution in Retreat 1920-4* (Routledge, 2008)
A. Rabinowitch *The Bolsheviks in Power* (Indiana, 2007)
Oliver Radkey *The Sickle under the Hammer* (Columbia University Press 2020)
V. Serge *Year One of the Russian Revolution* (Bookmarks 1992)
T.H. Rigby *Lenin's Government: Sovnarkom 1917-1922* (Cambridge 1979)
J. Wheeler-Bennett *Brest-Litovsk – the Forgotten Peace* (Macmillan 1966)

Selected Reading List of Works Cited

Bolshevik Oppositions

Barbara C. Allen *Alexander Shlyapnikov – Life of an Old Bolshevik* (Haymarket 2015)
R.V. Daniels *Conscience of the Revolution* (Simon and Shuster/Clarion 1960)
A. Kollontai *The Workers Opposition (*Solidarity North London Pamphlet No.7, 1968)
R. Kowalski *The Bolshevik Party in Conflict* (Macmillan 1991)
R. Sakwa *Soviet Communists in Power* (New York 1988)

Anarchism

P. Avrich *Anarchists in the Russian Revolution* (New York 1973)
Colin Darch *Nestor Makhno and Rural Anarchism in Ukraine 1917-21* (Pluto Press 2020)
Michael Malet *Nestor Makhno in the Russian Civil War* (Macmillan 1982)

Lenin

Neil Harding *Lenin's Political Thought* (Macmillan 1983)
M. Liebman *Leninism under Lenin* (Merlin 1975)
Robert Service *Lenin* (Macmillan 2000)
L. Trotsky *Lenin* (London 1925)
D. Volkogonov *Lenin: A New Biography* (Free Press 1994)

International

Robert Blobaum *Feliks Dzierzynski and the SDKPiL: a study of the origins of Polish Communism (*Columbia University Press 1984)
Friedrich von Rabenau *Hans Von Seeckt Aus seinem Leben* (Leipzig 1946)
John Riddell (ed) *German Revolution and the Debate on Soviet Power* (Pathfinder Press, New York 1986)
Richard M. Watt *The King's Depart* (Pelican 1972)
G. Williams *Proletarian Order* (Pluto Press 1975)

After 1921

Anton Antonov-Ovseyenko *The Time of Stalin: Portrait of Tyranny* (Harper 1981)
Ante Ciliga *The Russian Enigma* (Pluto Press 1987)
Isaac Deutscher *The Prophet Armed* (OUP 1954)
Isaac Deutscher *Stalin* (Pelican 1966)
Roy Medvedev *Let History Judge* (Columbia 1989)
J. V. Stalin *The Foundations of Leninism* (Moscow 1924)
J. V. Stalin *Problems of Leninism* (Moscow: Foreign Language Publishers, 1934)
L. Trotsky *The Challenge of the Left Opposition 1923-5* (New York 1975)
L. Trotsky *The Revolution Betrayed* (Pathfinder 1972)

Endnotes

Chapter 1

1. See, for example, Alec Nove, *An Economic History of the USSR 1917-91* Third edition (London 1992) p.2 and M.E. Falkus *The Industrialisation of Russia* p.69. Another problem was the way Tsarist bureaucrats hid the fact that there was a class of industrial proletariat as they only recognised "estates of the realm" (*sosloviye*). There was no category for worker so that they were defined in official statistics as "peasants". According to the 1910 census 68.7% of the population of Petersburg were classed as such but there were no workers! [See S.A. Smith *Red Petrograd* p.6]

2. See *http://www.era.anthropology.ac.uk/Era_Resources/Era/Peasants/russia.html*
   "*Pre-revolutionary Russian agrarian structure was, however, diverse, varying from region to region:*
   1. European Russia: Early emancipation of serfs in Baltic (1817) without land allotments led to wage-labour based big capitalist estates, exporting to Western Europe. Western Ukraine: Sugar-beet and other agro-industry renting peasant allotments;
   2. Southeast and Siberia: Commercial small-holder farming, small capitalist farms. Because Siberia was a zone of colonisation, there were no obshchina;
   3. North/Lakes/Central Industrial Province: Commercial agriculture only profitable near big cities. The nobles sold off their land. Peasants became seasonal migrants to cities (migration becoming more permanent when Stolypin reforms cut imposed ties to obshchina);
   4. Central Black Earth/Middle Volga ('core' of old agrarian Russia): Uncommercialised peasant subsistence agriculture, obshchina general, rental of estate land to subsistence peasantry — sometimes to communities as collectivities, sometimes to household." Some writers compared the black earth provinces to Bengal whilst Siberia looked at one time like being a second Canada."

3. In the 1908 Second Edition of *The Development of Capitalism in Russia* he also calculated that 63.7 million were proletarian or semi-proletarian out of a population of 125.6 million but most sources point to much lower figures by using much narrower criteria.

4. GDP growth was said to be 6.25% per annum 1906-13 and "even higher" in the two years before the First World War largely due to the influx of foreign (mainly French) investment. See Diane Koenker and William Rosenberg *Strikes and Revolution in Russia 1917* (Princeton 1989) p.27

5. Overall it was 4.1% but in the richer agricultural areas, such as the 16 "black earth" provinces in Ukraine it was 23.3% and 30.8%. See M.E. Falkus *The Industrialisation of Russia* pp. 47-8. Little wonder in the rural violence that erupted against the landowners in 1905 and again in 1917.

6. The Russian word *mir* has several meanings including "village" or "world" which in

itself speaks volumes for the dominance of the social form over the peasantry right up to the October Revolution.

7. M.E. Falkus *The Industrialisation of Russia* p.25

8. Abraham Ascher, *The Revolution of 1905: A Short History*, (Stanford 2004) p.5. A pood equals 16.11 kilograms or 38.8 pounds.

9. Figures for Petersburg from S.A. Smith *Red Petrograd* pp 12-13

10. C. Read *From Tsar to Soviets* (UCL 1996) p.21

11. See Falkus *op. cit.* p.81

12. *Strikes and Revolution in Russia 1917* (Princeton 1989) p.p. 36-7 For more on how the Tsarist state dominated capital investment see "Banking Under the Tsars and the Soviets" by George Garvy in *The Journal of Economic History Vol. 32, No. 4* (Dec., 1972), pp. 869-893 at *https://www.jstor.org/stable/2117258?*

13. Abraham Ascher, *The Revolution of 1905: A Short History*, (Stanford 2004) p.6

14. Leon Trotsky *1905* (Pelican 1971) p. 21. The term "majestic prologue" also comes from the Preface to this seminal work

15. See E.H Carr *The Bolshevik Revolution* Volume 1 (Penguin 1973) p.75. It occurred at a time of low ebb in the workers' movement in Russia but this was soon to be revived after the massacres of striking Siberian gold field workers on the River Lena in the same year.

16. Called for by both Polish socialist parties, the PSP and the SDPKPiL. See Robert Blobaum, *Feliks Dzierzynski and the SDKPiL: a study of the origins of Polish Communism*, p. 123

17. L. Trotsky *1905* (Pelican 1971) p.98

18. *Red Petrograd* p.57

19. Oskar Anweiler *The Soviets* p.40. Although two pages earlier he tells us that the title of "soviet of workers deputies" was used by a factory strike committee at the Nadezdinskij factory in the Urals. The Ivanovo-Vosenesensk soviet lasted two months and "left a lasting impression" due to its "unprecedented solidarity and its long duration" (Anweiler p. 42). It was also a rarity in that women participated in it in significant numbers, as the photographs of the time show.

20. List based on W.H.Chamberlin *The Russian Revolution* Volume 1 (Macmillan, 1965) p. 53

21. Anweiler p.46

22. Local municipal councils set up by Alexander II in the wake of the emancipation of the serfs. They were still viewed with hostility by the Tsar and his supporters since they might demand real power one day.

23. Although general strikes and isolated uprisings continued even into 1907, e.g. the Kronstadt uprising of 1906, Chita Republic, Sveaborg rebellion of 1906, Vladivostok uprising of 1907, the mass (and soviet) movement was defeated by the beginning of 1906.

24. The most notorious of which were those in Odessa (which had a large Jewish population) and Tomsk where many people were burned alive in a building. Estimates of such deaths vary between 3000 and 4000. See W.H.Chamberlin *loc cit.* The Black Hundreds counted nobility in their ranks as well as on sponsorship by the government.

25. *https://www.marxists.org/archive/lenin/works/1906/ucong/5.htm#v10pp65-299*

26. *The Mass Strike, the Political Party and the Trade Unions* in *Rosa Luxemburg Speaks* (Pathfinder 1970) p. 179

27. L. Trotsky *1905* (Pelican 1971) p.266

28. This was in 1907. See https://www.marxists.org/archive/trotsky/1918/ourrevo/ch05. htm

29. This and the preceding quote are from *Our Tasks and the Soviet of Workers Deputies: A Letter to the Editor* in V I Lenin *Collected Works* Volume 10 (Moscow 1965) p.19-20 and p. 23

30. M. Liebman Leninism under Lenin (Merlin 1975) p. 54

31. In "Should we boycott the State Duma" in Lenin *Collected Works* Volume 10 p. 99

32. Lenin, *Collected Works* Volume 13 p.85

33. Lenin, *Collected Works* Volume 10 p.503

34. Lenin, *Collected Works* Volume 10 p. 45

35. Lenin, *Collected Works* Volume 10 p. 46

36. Lenin, *Collected Works* Volume 10 p. 47-8

37. The differences appeared both between Mensheviks (some of whom Lenin denounced as "liquidators" for wanting to devote themselves exclusively to legal work, and "liquidate" clandestine organisation) and within Bolshevism, where Lenin criticised his own supporters, like Bogdanov and Lunacharsky, for wanting to boycott the powerless Duma. They wanted the elected Bolshevik deputies to withdraw from the Duma so were called Recallists (Otzovists) whereas Lenin insisted that the Bolshevik faction could use the Duma as a tribune for revolutionary propaganda. As we shall see in the next chapter, Lenin was to be sorely disappointed by the performance of the Bolshevik faction in the Duma when it came to opposing the war.

38. The number of strikes in 1910 was 222, but in 1912 it leapt to 2,032 and in the first six months of 1914 there were 4,098 strikes. L. Kochan *The Making of Modern Russia* (Pelican 1963) p. 240

Chapter 2

1. This and the previous quote are in Neil Harding *Lenin's Political Thought* (Macmillan 1983) Volume II p.6

2. Haase, reading the German Social Democratic Party statement in the Reichstag (August 4 1914). Quoted in Harding *loc cit*. Haase was one of 14 deputies who voted against support for the war but none broke ranks then. Karl Liebknecht was the first to break "Party discipline" on 2 December 1914 when the second vote for war credits took place. For more on the German situation see *http://www.leftcom.org/en/articles/2018-11-23/ the-significance-of-the-german-revolution*

3. The story (repeated even by us in the past) that Lenin in Switzerland thought the copy of *Vorwärts* he received was a forgery appears to be a case of Chinese whispers launched by Trotsky in his *My Life,* where he wrote:

"When the issue of the Vorwaerts that contained the report of the meeting of the Reichstag on August 4 arrived in Switzerland, Lenin decided that it was a faked number published by the German general staff to deceive and frighten their enemies. For, despite his critical mind, Lenin's faith in the German Social Democracy was still as strong as that." Trotsky My Life https://www.marxists.org/archive/trotsky/1930/ mylife/ch18.htm

The only problem with this account is that Lenin was not in Switzerland. He was in in

Nowy Targ in Galicia (in the Austro-Hungarian Empire) and was more worried about his impending arrest as an enemy alien. He was arrested on 7/8 August and held until 19 August (where he distinguished himself with the other prisoners when "*he used his legal training to help them prepare their defences. He was a popular figure, despite his slender grasp of Polish, being known in the prison as a 'real bull of a fellow'.*" Robert Service *Lenin* (Macmillan 2000) pp. 224-5. Lenin and Krupskaya did not leave Vienna for Switzerland until 3 September and by this time there could be no doubt about the infamy of the German party. It seems that Deutscher relayed Trotsky's story in his biography of Stalin (but not in the later biography of Trotsky) and then it has been retold (mainly by Trotskyists) without anyone giving a source.

4. P Frölich *Rosa Luxemburg* (Pluto Press 1972) p. 202. It says "besieged" in the book but this looks like an error in a dictated translation.

5. *Tasks of Revolutionary Social Democracy in the War* in Lenin *Collected Works Vol. 21* (Moscow 1965) p.15-16 (written not later than 6 September 1914 and the first public statement of "members of the Russian Social-Democratic Labour Party").

6. *Dead Chauvinism and Living Socialism* in *Collected Works, Vol. XVIII* (1930 edition) p. 96

7. *op. cit.* p. 87, emphasis in the original

8. *Ibid.* November 1st 1914.

9. Lenin, *Collected Works Volume 21* p. 16. For a wider discussion of the international implications of Lenin's stance, see *http://www.leftcom.org/en/articles/2015-09-08/ zimmerwald-lenin-leads-the-struggle-of-the-revolutionary-left-for-a-new*

10. John Maclean *The War After the War*, Socialist Reproductions, p.iv

11. S.A. Smith *Red Petrograd* (Cambridge 1983) p.49

12. D. Koenker and W. Rosenberg. *Strikes and Revolution in Russia 1917* (Princeton 1989) p.44

13. S.A. Smith *op. cit.* p.46

14. D. Koenker and W. Rosenberg. *Loc cit.*

15. In November 1916 Paul Milyukov, the leader of the liberal Kadet party, and a believer in constitutional monarchy, gave a famous speech which criticised all the failures of the regime ending each with the rhetorical question "Is this folly or is it treason". See O. Figes *A People's Tragedy* (Pimlico 1996) p. 287

16. The words come from the first page of S.A. Smith's *Red Petrograd* quoted earlier where he contrasts the bourgeois parts of the city with the "*eery squalor*" of the proletarian districts. His Chapter One provides as good a description of working and living conditions in Petersburg in 1917 to be found anywhere.

17. Quoted in Alexander Shlyapnikov, *On the Eve of 1917*, pp. 20-1

18. *Op.cit.* p.91

19. *Ibid.*

20. Harding *op. cit.* p. 10

21. Lenin *Collected Works Vol. 21.*p.402

22. This is often unthinkingly repeated even by revolutionaries e.g. by the now defunct German "workerist" group, Kolinko (see h*ttps://libcom.org/library/discussion-paper-class-composition*) but in fact as early as 1900 70% of the population over 6 years old in St Petersburg was literate and by the end of the war was 80%. See Smith *op.cit* p.34.

23. "…welfare ratios for unskilled workers in Moscow and St.Petersburg were higher than

in Milan. Italian cities had the lowest standard of living in Europe. (Allen)." From *Pre-revolution living standards: Russia 1888-1917* Ekaterina Khaustova, Russian State Social University (Kursk, 2013).

24. Sukhanov *The Russian Revolution 1917 – A Personal Record* p. 11. In Italy the Socialist Party's position of "neither support nor sabotage" for the imperialist war (hoping, like Kautsky, that it would go away) was hardly as positive as Sukhanov makes out here.

25. *Non-Party Workers' Organizations in St Petersburg and the Provinces before and during the First Russian Revolution* Nikolai V. Mikhailov in *A Dream Deferred: New Studies in Russian and Soviet Labor History* p.43

26. One of the leading industrialists who became a minister in the Provisional Government, Guchkov (leading member of the Octobrist Party) was still trying to save the monarchy 3 days after the Provisional Government had been formed! He had plotted earlier to overthrow Nicholas II but only to replace him with his son, under the regency of his brother Michael. The other industrialists followed Guchkov though, when he finally threw in his lot with the February Revolution, they all now suddenly found a taste for constitutional government.

27. Shlyapnikov *op. cit.* p.4

28. Shlyapnikov *op. cit.* p.3

29. *loc.cit.*

30. S.A. Smith *op. cit.* p. 38

31. S.A. Smith *op. cit.* pp. 40-1

32. S.A. Smith *op. cit.* p. 50 (Table 10). The "political" and "economic" distinction was one made by the police.

Chapter 3

1. Lenin, *Collected Works Volume 31* (Moscow 1964) p 95.

2. See *https://www.leftcom.org/en/articles/2017-03-07/celebrating-international-women%E2%80%99s-day-100-years-on* for its origins.

3. The traditional figure is put at 1300 (following the estimates in J.S. Curtis *The Russian Revolutions of 1917* (van Nostrand 1957). More detailed and more recent research suggests the following: "*According to Leiberov's study, the February Revolution claimed the lives of 433 persons in Petrograd, 313 of whom were insurgents and 120 of whom were police, gendarmes, officers and loyal soldiers. An additional 1,214 were wounded, of whom 1,136 were insurgents, and 300 were crippled, of whom 291 were insurgents. Of the total of 1,740 killed, wounded and crippled insurgents, 535 or 30 percent were workers and 832 or 48 percent were soldiers. These figures show that, contrary to popular belief, the February Revolution in Petrograd was by no means bloodless.*" Tsuyoshi Hasegawa *The February Revolution Petrograd 1917* (Brill 1981) p.661

4. *Russia's Second Revolution*, E.N Burdzhalov (English translation by Donald J Raleigh, Indiana University Press, 1986) p.106. This "*may well be the best book in any language on Russia's February Revolution of 1917 in Petrograd*" (Donald J. Raleigh). Burdzhalov, like Anna M. Pankratova was a new breed of Soviet historians who after Khruschev's secret speech on Stalin's crimes in1956 broke the mould of Soviet historiography by investigating all the "heroic" claims about the role of the Bolsheviks (and Stalin). He was

sacked as editor of *Voprosy Istorii* (Problems of History) but never recanted and carried on working to give a more accurate picture of the revolution from below. He died from Parkinson's in 1985. His story is told in the translator's introduction. In using quotations from it Raleigh's US spelling has been retained.

5. Burdzhalov p.105. The Okhrana were the Tsar's secret police.

6. The foregoing is from Tsuyoshi Hasegawa *The February Revolution Petrograd 1917* (Brill 1981) p. 206 Alongside Burdzhalov, this is essential reading for those trying to make sense of the events of February/March 1917 without necessarily agreeing to all the judgements of either author. In places Hasegawa's account is written almost from the perspective of how the regime might have been saved if only the Army had sent more troops from the front in time. All the evidence suggests though that these troops would have behaved no more loyally than the ones who went over to the revolution.

7. Burdzhalov p.113 This paragraph including the "stormy" description also comes from p.106

8. Burdzhalov p.110

9. Hasegawa p.207

10. Hasegawa p.209

11. Hasegawa p.207

12. Women's Day started as an idea of the Socialist Party of America in 1908-9 to celebrate a women workers' strike and became "International" after Luise Zeitz and Clara Zetkin proposed such a day at the 1911 second International Conference of Working Women in Copenhagen. Russian women first celebrated it as a demonstration against war in 1913 (so the next year the Tsarist police arrested the organisers to prevent a repeat). It thus entered into the special days of celebration of the Russian working class like May Day and 9/22 January (anniversary of Bloody Sunday 1905).

13. Quoted in Burdzhalov *op. cit.* p.106 Kaiurov's memoirs are a key source used not only by Burdzhalov but also by Trotsky and Hasegawa.

14. Alexander Shlyapnikov, *On the Eve of 1917: Reminiscences from the Revolutionary Underground* (Allison and Busby, 1982) pp.189-90. Lenin shared the views of the Kharkov comrades. On 9 January 1917 he told a meeting of young workers in Zurich *"We must not be deceived by the present grave-like stillness in Europe. Europe is pregnant with revolution. The monstrous horrors of the imperialist war, the suffering caused by the high cost of living everywhere engender a revolutionary mood; and the ruling classes, the bourgeoisie and its servitors, the governments, are more and more moving into a blind alley which they can never extricate themselves without tremendous upheavals"*. This after he said "*... the Russian revolution – precisely because of its proletarian character ... – is the prologue to the coming European revolution*" ("Lecture on the 1905 Revolution" in *Collected Works Volume 23* (Moscow 1964) pp.252-3

15. S.A. Smith *Red Petrograd*, (Cambridge 1983) p.51

16. Smith p.51

17. Smith p.52

18. Maurice Paleologue *An Ambassador's Memoirs* (1923)

19. According to Hasegawa p.201

20. Burdzhalov p.105 (the Russian original is in a documentary source produced by Shlyapnikov himself).

21. Burdzhalov p.117

22. Hasegawa p. 207

23. Quoted in Burdzhalov p.120

24. L. Trotsky *The History of the Russian Revolution* (Pluto Press, 1977) p.171

25. Burdzhalov p.123

26. Burdzhalov p.124

27. Burdzhalov p.131

28. W.H Chamberlin, *The Russian Revolution Volume One* (New York 1965) p. 77. Chamberlin originally published what was regarded as a classic work in 1935. It is a tremendous achievement for its time and he clearly consulted many of the sources used by Burdzhalov and Hasegawa. At the time critically sympathetic to the revolution he turned against it after Stalin's forced collectivisation created famine in Ukraine. He had a low opinion of Khabalov's abilities but it is difficult to see how anyone else in the same place would have fared better. It is typical of bourgeois historical method that individuals rather than material circumstances are seen as the prime movers in history. Khabalov may have been weak but his problem was that Tsarism was lost as soon as the Petersburg garrison went over to the working class. The suggestion by Balk (the Governor of Petersburg) that if Khabalov had started shooting workers on the Thursday or Friday rather than Sunday then the revolution would have been beaten down is wishful thinking. Once the shooting started the very weakness of the state was on the line – as events on the Sunday showed. Hasegawa p. 233 is also critical of Khabalov.

29. Hasegawa p.330

30. Sukhanov *The Russian Revolution 1917 – A Personal Record* p. 25

31. Chamberlin p.78

32. Chamberlin p.78 "Pavlovsk" is given as "Pavlovsky" in other sources.

33. The Duma or Parliament was conceded by Nicholas II to split the liberals from the workers and peasants in an effort to put an end to the 1905 Revolution. The first two Dumas lasted only months, before the voting system was changed. Landowners got one third of the seats and the urban population also one third of the seats. Unsurprisingly there were few representatives of the workers (Bolsheviks and Mensheviks) in the Fourth Duma elected in 1912. The small Bolshevik faction had been arrested and deported to Siberia on account of the Party's revolutionary defeatist position (which Kamenev, the Bolshevik Duma leader shamefully failed to defend at his trial) in 1915. Golitsyn, although only 67 years old, often fell asleep at Cabinet meetings due, it is often written, to his "advanced years"!

34. Chamberlin *op. cit* p.78

35. *Loc.cit.*

36. L. Trotsky *The History of the Russian Revolution* (Pluto Press 1977) p.167

37. Burdzhalov *op. cit.* p.170

38. Burdzhalov p.223

39. Predictably Orlando Figes in his lament over the failure of the bourgeoisie and "democratic socialists" to really take the lead in the revolution tell us that many workers did not make it to the first soviet meeting because they were "drunk" *A People's Tragedy* (Pimlico 1997) p. 324

40. Chamberlin *op. cit.* p. 85 says 1315 people died in the February Revolution. 53 were officers, 602 soldiers, 73 police and 587 "citizens". For other estimates see footnote 3.

41. The words are Kerensky's quoted in Hasegawa p.232. *Stikhiia* is almost untranslatable

but "natural element" is regarded as the most accurate. An associated word "*stikhiinost*" is often translated inaccurately as "spontaneous" but it too means "elemental".

42. Hasegawa p.364
43. Trotsky p.179
44. Burdzhalov p.185
45. B.O. Bogdanov was a Menshevik and not to be confused with the more famous scientist, science fiction writer, and one time Bolshevik, Alexander Bogdanov (given name Malinovsky).
46. Ferro p.37
47. In *Leninism under Lenin*, (Merlin, 1975) p.117
48. Hasegawa p.339-40

Chapter 4

1. Burdzhalov p.274
2. *A Short History of the Russian Revolution*, J. Carmichael, p.69
3. *Documents of Russian History 1914-1917* F. A. Golder (Appleton, Century Crofts 1927 reprinted Peter Smith, Gloucester, Mass. 1964) p.387. In the Russian original the passage in bold is emphasised but not in Golder's translation.
4. Hasegawa p.450
5. Burdzhalov p.324
6. Barbara C Allen refers to this in *Alexander Shlyapnikov - Life of an Old Bolshevik* (Haymarket 2015) p.81 but the actual quotation is in L. Trotsky *The History of the Russian Revolution* (Pluto Press, 1977) p.306
7. Golder p.310
8. Sukhanov p.103 maintains that even in March "*Bolshevik and [Left?] SR members*" of the Petersburg Soviet held "*a belief that the World War would result in an absolutely inevitable worldwide revolution and that the national revolt in Russia would lay its foundations blazing a trail not only towards the liquidation of the Tsarist autocracy but also towards the annihilation of the power of capital*". Emphasis in the original.
9. Lenin, *Collected Works* (1964) Vol. 24 p.38
10. Quoted in Sukhanov p..273
11. Sukhanov p.287-8
12. "Letter on Tactics" in *Collected Works* Vol. 24 p.50
13. Sukhanov p. 289
14. Lenin "The Dual Power" *Collected Works* (1964) Vol. 24 p.40
15. S.A. Smith *Red Petrograd* p.57-9
16. Quoted in Smith p.63
17. This and the information for the preceding paragraphs from S.A. Smith *Red Petrograd* p.116
18. In Golder p.333-4
19. Lenin "The Dual Power" *Collected Works* (1964) Vol. 24 p.40
20. "Resolution on the Soviets of Workers' and Soldiers' Deputies" in Lenin *Collected Works* Vol. 24 p.296

Chapter 5

1. As Trotsky put it in Chapter XVI of *The History of the Russian Revolution.*
2. According to O. Figes *A People's Tragedy* (Pimlico 1996) p.457 who claims to base his figures on the work of S.A, Smith and Diane Koenker.
3. S.A. Smith *Russia in Revolution – An Empire in Crisis 1890-1928* (Oxford, 2017) p. 118
4. Lenin, *Collected Works*, Vol. 24 p.146
5. *loc. cit* p.237
6. Smith *loc. cit* p.113
7. Figes *loc.cit.*
8. S.A. Smith *Red Petrograd* p.119 – all figures here stem from this source or from M. Ferro *The Bolshevik Revolution – A Social History* p.160ff
9. In "Letters on Tactics" (April 1917) in *Collected Works* Vol. 24 p.46
10. See E.H. Carr, *The Bolshevik Revolution*, Vol. 1 p.100
11. Sukhanov p.419
12. Sukhanov p.417
13. A. Rabinowitch *The Bolsheviks Come to Power* (NLB 1979) p.10
14. Lenin, *Collected Works* Volume 29, p.396
15. Quoted by Rabinowitch *Prelude to Revolution* (Bloomington 1968), p.122
16. *Kronstadt and Petrograd* (New Park 1982) p.150
17. Rabinowitch (1979) p.47. On July 6 Voinov was killed by a sabre blow to the head whilst under arrest.
18. The campaign against Lenin as "a German spy" in the right wing press called for his death so the prospect of a getting to trial, let alone a fair one, looked decidedly slim.
19. "On Slogans", Lenin *Collected Works,* Vol. 25, p.184
20. *op. cit.* p.189
21. *op.cit.* p.186

Chapter 6

1. Christopher Read, *From Tsar to Soviets* (UCL 1996) p.141
2. *The History of the Russian Revolution* (Pluto Press 1977) p.711
3. Marc Ferro, *The Bolshevik Revolution — A Social History* (1980), p.56
4. A. Rabinowitch, *The Bolsheviks Come to Power* p.139
5. *The Russian Revolution 1917*, p. 505
6. Lenin, *Collected Works,* Vol. 25, p.222 The subsequent citation is on p.221
7. Lenin, *Collected Works,* Vol. 25, pp. 285-6
8. A. Rabinowitch, *The Bolsheviks Come to Power* p.166
9. Lenin, *Collected Works* Vol 25 p. 184
10. *op.cit.* p.190
11. Donald J Raleigh *Revolution on the Volga* (Cornell 1986) p. 327
12. "On Compromises" in *Collected Works* Vol. 25 p. 206 (emphasis in the original)
13. *Conscience of the Revolution* (Clarion 1960) p.56
14. "One of the Fundamental Questions of the Revolution" in Lenin *Collected Works* Vol. 25 pp 373, (emphases in the original)

Endnotes

15. *op.cit* pp 367-8
16. Ferro p.58

Chapter 7

1. *The October Revolution* (Columbia University Press 1979) p.49
2. *The Russian Revolution*, [Pluto Press] p.1138
3. S A Smith *Russia in Revolution* (Oxford, 2017) p.151
4. China Mieville *October* (Verso 2017) p.139
5. https://www.marxists.org/archive/luxemburg/1918/russian-revolution/ch01.htm
6. Quoted in John Reed *Ten Days that Shook the World* (Sutton Press) p.18
7. Lenin, *Collected Works,* Vol. 26, p.58. The reference to "parliamentary leaders" is a direct dig at Kamenev whose performance in the trial of Bolshevik Duma deputies in 1915 hardly covered him in glory (as we saw in Chapter 2)
8. Rabinowitch, *The Bolsheviks Come to Power*, p.193
9. Lenin, *Collected Works,* Vol. 26, pp.74-7
10. As quoted in Rabinowitch, p.227
11. Quoted in Rabinowitch, p.253
12. Rabinowitch p.261
13. Sukhanov *The Russian Revolution 1917* p.647
14. Sukhanov *The Russian Revolution 1917* p.646
15. Quoted in Donald J Raleigh *Revolution on the Volga* p. 282

Chapter 8

1. *Revolution on the Volga: 1917 in Saratov* (Cornell 1986) p.311
2. Quoted in S.A Smith *Russia in Revolution* p.137
3. Quoted in R Stites *Revolutionary Dreams* p.42
4. S.A. Smith *Red Petrograd* p.223
5. *To the Citizens of Russia – Appeal of the Petrograd Military Revolutionary Committee* in *First Decrees of Soviet Power* (Lawrence and Wishart,1970) p.17
6. *First Decrees of Soviet Power* p.22
7. *First Decrees of Soviet Power* p.53
8. *First Decrees of Soviet Power* p.31
9. This was the only legal area of settlement for Jews and other minorities (like Polish Catholics) in the Tsarist Empire and covered most of the Western borders of the Empire. Today it would include much of Poland Moldova and Belarus as well as parts of Ukraine, Latvia and Western Russia. Only those with special skills or education could live outside it, and Jews were often barred from towns in the Pale. It was abolished with the October Revolution.
10. Or, as she wrote in The National Question (1909) *"The Polish bourgeois-capitalistic development fettered Poland to Russia and condemned the idea of national independence to utopianism and to defeat." https://www.marxists.org/archive/luxemburg/1909/national-question/ch02.htm*
11. The "official" line of the Stalinists on this can be found here: *https://www.marxists. org/glossary/periodicals/k/o.htm*

12. For more on this disgraceful episode see *https://www.leftcom.org/en/articles/2008-09-01/georgia-on-his-mind-lenin%E2%80%99s-final-fight-against-%E2%80%9Cgreat-russian-chauvinism%E2%80%9D*

13. *http://libcom.org/history/unknown-revolution-1917-1921-voline*

14. Silvana Malle *The Economic Organisation of War Communism (Cambridge, 1985)* p.164

15. Malle's transliteration, but sometimes also written *prodrazvyorstka*

16. Smith *Red Petrograd* p. 210

17. Smith *loc cit*

18. Lenin, *Collected Works* Vol. 26 p.288

19. Published by Solidarity (North London 1971) and can be found at *https://libcom.org/library/the-bolsheviks-and-workers-control-solidarity -group*

20. R.V Daniels *The Conscience of the Revolution* p.84

21. For more on Ossinsky see *http://www.leftcom.org/en/articles/2017-09-08/n-ossinsky%E2%80%99s-critique-of-state-capitalism-in-russia*

22. Lenin, *Collected Works* (Moscow 1964) Volume 26 pp.365-6

23. Smith *Red Petrograd* p.239

24. Quoted in J. Bunyan and H. Fisher *The Bolshevik Revolution 1917-18* (Documents)

25. Roy Medvedev *The October Revolution* (Constable,1979) p.119

26. *First Decrees of Soviet Power* p.147

27. This is a complex argument which we go into in various documents to be found on our website here: *http://www.leftcom.org/en/articles/russian-communist-left*

28. On 20 January (new calendar now in operation) 1918. See *First Decrees of Soviet Power* p.88

29. On 30 May 1918 *First Decrees of Soviet Power* p.140

30. *https://www.marxists.org/archive/kollonta/1918/steps-motherhood.htm*

31. *https://www.marxists.org/archive/kollonta/1918/congress.htm*

32. *On the History of the Movement of Women Workers in Russia* by Alexandra Kollontai: *https://www.marxists.org/archive/kollonta/1919/history.htm*

33. See Alexander Rabinowitch *The Bolsheviks in Power* (2007) p.253

34. *Decree of the All-Russia Central Executive Committee and Council of People's Commissars on Civil Marriage, on Children and on the keeping of Registers* (December 18 (31 NS) 1917 in *First Decrees of Soviet Power* pp.69-70

35. *https://www.bbc.co.uk/news/world-europe-41737330*

36. A debt of gratitude owed to CWO comrades Dyjbas and Tinkotka who found the pamphlet in German in Berlin. An English translation can be found here: *https://www.marxist.com/the-sexual-revolution-in-russia.htm*

37. *https://www.bbc.co.uk/news/world-europe-41737330*

38. Some of the Revolution's detractors when faced with the legalisation of homosexuality try to say that Lenin was himself as backward on the issue as Stalin but again the evidence suggests otherwise. He went to considerable lengths to have Georgii Chicherin released from a British gaol in order to become Commissar of Foreign Affairs. Lenin seemed to know of Chicherin's private life."*Chicherin is an amazing worker, the most scrupulous, clever, competent. Such people must be appreciated. And as for his weakness — the lack of 'commandership' — so what? There are lots of people with reverse weakness in this world!*". Whatever Lenin's actual views, it seems Lenin was a lot

more tolerant than many of his time, and only interested in political competence. *https://www.calvertjournal.com/features/show/11872/lgbt-russian-cultural-figures-russia-z*

39. For more on this, see Dan Healey, *Homosexual Desire in Revolutionary Russia* (Chicago, 2001)

40. Quoted in R, Stites *Revolutionary Dreams* p.39

41. Karl Marx *Selected Writings* D. MacLellan p.179

42. R, Stites *Revolutionary Dreams* p.205

43. *Op.cit* p.200

44. *Op.cit* p.55

45. 22 November by the old calendar, 5 December by the new. *First Decrees of Soviet Power* p.44

46. See Lenin, *Collected Works* Vol. 26 p.261

47. In *Lenin's Political Thought* p.172

48. E.H. Carr *The Bolshevik Revolution* Vol 1 pp. l94-5.
For more on Lomov see *http://www.leftcom.org/en/articles/2018-09-27/two-articles-from-kommunist-april-1918*

49. Lenin, *Collected Works* Vol 27 p. 135

Chapter 9

1. Lenin, *Collected Works* (1928 edition) Vol. 21, p.259

2. Quoted in J. Wheeler-Bennett *Brest-Litovsk - the Forgotten Peace* p.116

3. Quoted in E H Carr *The Bolshevik Revolution* Volume 3 p. 29

4. L. Trotsky *Lenin* (London 1925) p.128

5. Quoted in Wheeler-Bennett *Brest-Litovsk – The Forgotten Peace* p. 170

6. Quoted in Carr *op. cit.* p.45

7. *The Bolsheviks in Power – Reminiscences of the Year 1918* (New Park 1984) p.22

8. Quoted in Wheeler-Bennett p.280

9. Quoted in Wheeler-Bennett p.276

10. In *Theses of the Left Communists*, published by Critique, Glasgow 1977, available online http://libcom.org/library/theses-left-communists-russia-1918

11. Wheeler-Bennett p. 347

12. Rosa Luxemburg *The Russian Tragedy* September 1918 *https://www.marxists.org/archive/luxemburg/1918/09/11.htm*

Chapter 10

1. Lenin, *Collected Works* Vol. 25 p.463

2. *https://www.marxists.org/archive/lenin/works/1907/sep/pref1907.htm* Both quotations are taken from a publication entitled "Twelve Years" written in September 1907. It was looking back on the history and controversies in the establishment of social democratic politics in Russia before 1907.

3. To give just a couple of example he wrote "*in our opinion ... the principal cause of the present crisis in Russian Social-Democracy is the lag of the leaders ("ideologists", revolutionaries, Social-Democrats) behind the spontaneous upsurge of the masses.*" Or

"As the spontaneous rise of their movement becomes broader and deeper, the working-class masses promote from their ranks not only an increasing number of talented agitators, but also talented organisers, propagandists, and "practical workers" in the best sense of the term (of whom there are so few among our intellectuals who, for the most part, in the Russian manner, are somewhat careless and sluggish in their habits)." Lenin, *Collected Works* Vol 5 pp. 446 and 473

4. Although the doyen of them is the ex-Stalinist Bertram D Wolfe in his various writings. He not only made the discovery that Lenin's *What is to be Done* carried the master plan for the Bolsheviks actions but reprinted Rosa Luxemburg's 1904 *Neue Zeit* article *Organisational Questions of Russian Social Democracy* as "Leninism or Marxism" (Ann Arbor 1961) coyly telling us that it had "later" appeared also as a pamphlet called "Marxism or Leninism" omitting the inconvenient fact that this was produced by the Anti-Parliamentary Communist Federation of Guy Aldred in 1935.

5. *Lenin's Political Thought* (Macmillan 1977) In particular the first three chapters of the second part.

6. Lenin, *Collected Works* Vol.21 p.146

7. Lenin, *Collected Works* Vol.22 p.193

8. Lenin, *Collected Works* Vol.26 p.288

9. *First Decrees of Soviet Power* p.42

10. Quoted in V. Serge *Year One of the Russian Revolution* p.103

11. Quoted in Serge p.119

12. Quoted in Serge p.199

13. See Oliver Radkey *The Sickle under the Hammer* p.103

14. *The Russian Revolution 1917 – A Personal Memoir* p.646

15. Radkey p.34

16. Smith *Russia in Revolution* p.204

17. See *http://www.leftcom.org/en/articles/2017-12-30/bukharin-on-the-%E2%80%9Csocialist%E2%80%9D-opposition-to-soviet-power*

18. Radkey p. 94

19. E.H.Carr *The Bolshevik Revolution* Vol 1 p.190

20. Carr p.100

21. *Bread and Justice* p.172

22. *Bread and Justice* p.173

23. Both quotes from *Bread and Justice* p.174

24. *Bread and Justice* p.183

25. See D. Volkogonov, *Lenin: A New Biography,* 1994. p.229. and Wheeler- Bennett p. 178. Platten had also been the one who organised Lenin's return to Russia in 1917. Despite, or perhaps because of, these services, Platten, who founded an agricultural commune near Lenin's birthplace Simbirsk (then called Ulyanovsk), was arrested in 1938, put in the Kargopol camp, and shot by Stalin in 1942. See Anton Antonov-Ovseyenko *The Time of Stalin: Portrait of Tyranny* (Harper 1981) pp.138-9

26. E.H.Carr *The Bolshevik Revolution* Vol. 1 p.130

27. From *First Decrees Of Soviet Power* p.76

28. Michael Malet *Nestor Makhno in the Russian Civil War* (Macmillan 1982) p.102

Endnotes

Chapter 11

1. China Miéville *October* p.307
2. Evan Mawdsley *The Russian Civil War* p.18
3. *Op.cit* p.19
4. The term was invented as a criticism of the behaviour of Russian troops by the Provisional Government but it encapsulates a lot of the initiative shown by workers and soldiers during this period.
5. Quoted in Mawdsley p.22
6. http://www.leftcom.org/en/articles/2017-09-08/n-ossinsky%E2%80%99s -critique-of-state-capitalism-in-russia
7. *Left Wing Childishness and the Petty Bourgeois Mentality* in Lenin, *Collected Works* Vol. 27 p.353-4
8. D. Kaiser (ed) *The Workers' Revolution in Russia* p.110
9. Lenin *Collected Works* Vol.25 p.463
10. *Year One of the Russian Revolution.* pp.275-6
11. Quoted by D.N. Collins in *Soviet Studies* (Vol. 24) No. 2, October 1972.
12. *First Decrees of Soviet Power*, pp.86-7
13. *From How the Revolution Armed Itself*, quoted in C.Bettelheim, *Class Struggles in the USSR 1917-23*, p.275
14. R.V. Daniels *The Conscience of the Revolution Simon and Schuster, 1969* p. 105
15. *The Challenge of the Left Opposition 1923-5* (New York 1975) p.197.
16. Quoted in R.V Daniels *The Conscience of the Revolution* p.105
17. Daniels p. 106
18. Mawdsley p. 242
19. Smith (2017) p.178
20. Rosa Luxemburg's position on the national question was more farsighted than Lenin's (and was shared by Bolsheviks like Piatakov, Bosch and Bukharin) as she clearly saw it as pandering only to the capitalist class. In this view, underdog nationalism was still anti-working class as in the epoch of imperialism there was no such thing as a progressive national struggle led by the bourgeoisie. However when (in her *The Russian Revolution*) she blamed Lenin's position on the national question for the loss of Finland and Ukraine, she was ignoring the fact that, materially, there was nothing the Bolsheviks could do in 1918 to assist the proletariat in either place, as the local bourgeoisie received military support from German imperialism at a time when the revolution in Russia could barely defend itself.
21. Quoted in Carr Vol.1 p.357
22. *The Challenge of the Left Opposition 1923-5* (New York 1975) p.92
23. All the above quotes from *op.cit* pp.151 and 155-6
24. *op. cit* p.172
25. https://www.leftcom.org/en/articles/2019-03-13/ossinsky-s-demand -for-clear-answers-april-1918
26. Quoted in T. Cliff *Trotsky, Volume 2 The Sword of the Revolution* (Bookmarks 1990)
27. "*The foundations of militarization are those forms of state compulsion without which the replacement of capitalist economy by the socialist will forever remain an empty sound*" Trotsky at the Eighth Party Congress. Quoted in Daniels p.121-2

28. *From Terrorism and Communism https://www.marxists.org/archive/trotsky/1920/terrcomm/ch08.htm*

29. Quoted in Cliff *op.cit* p.167

30. *From Terrorism and Communism https://www.marxists.org/archive/trotsky/1920/terrcomm/ch08.htm*

31. *From Terrorism and Communism https://www.marxists.org/archive/trotsky/1920/terrcomm/ch08.htm*

32. Quoted in Daniels p.123

33. The summary is by Daniels, *loc cit.*

34. The introduction to Miasnikov's document contains a more detailed discussion of the Ninth Party Congress.
http://www.leftcom.org/en/articles/2019-12-06/miasnikov-s-draft-platform-for-the-communist-workers-international-1930

35. Richard M Watt *The King's Depart* (Pelican 1972) p. 194

36. Sukhanov p. 273

37. "Our Isolation has Ended" in *Krasnaya Nov* (1926) reproduced in *The German Revolution and the Debate on Soviet Power* (ed. John Riddell, Pathfinder Press, New York 1986) p.33.

38. Lenin *Collected Works* Vol. 28 p.137

39. See Lenin *Collected Works* Vol. 28 p.434-6

40. For a deeper understanding of this episode see *http://www.leftcom.org/en/articles/2020-08-18/the-battle-of-warsaw-and-the-defeat-of-the-revolutionary-wave-in-europe*

41. Lenin *Collected Works* Vol. 30 p.228

42. F. Lorimer, *The Population of the Soviet Union, History and Prospects*, Geneva, 1948, p. 41. pdf download from marxists.org

43. R. Sakwa *Soviet Communists in Power* (New York 1988) p.104

Chapter 12

1. Lenin *Collected Works* Vol. 25 p.389

2. See Lenin *Collected Works* Vol. 25 p.63

3. Quoted in E.H. Carr *The Bolshevik Revolution* Vol. 1 p.161

4. *loc. cit.*

5. *First Decrees of Soviet Power* p.46

6. Smith (2017) p.35

7. The first meaning of the Russian word *chrezvychaynaya* is "emergency" but most books repeat the "Extraordinary" tag. Semantically the difference indicates that the commission was originally set up as a temporary body until "the emergency" had passed.

8. Lenin *Collected Works* Vol. 27 pp. 0-33

9. *http://www.revkom.com/index.htm?/biblioteka/marxism/trotckii/1924_oktyabr.htm*

10. Mary McAuley *Bread and Justice* p. 2

11. *Year One of the Russian Revolution* p. 4

12. *The Bolshevik Revolution* Vol.1 p.162

13. Lenin *Collected Works* Vol. 25 p.456 (emphasis in original)

14. Janet M. Campbell *Is there a Case for a Socialist Jurisprudence?*, PhD. thesis,

Endnotes

University of Glasgow 1997 at *http://theses.gla.ac.uk/4247/* p. 2

15. Campbell p.73

16. See M Liebman *Leninism under Lenin* pp.26-7

17. Figures from Smith (2017) p.35

18. Dzerzhinsky had been a founder member of the Social Democratic Party of the Kingdom of Poland aand Lithuania (both were part of the Russian Empire then) alongside Rosa Luxemburg and Leo Jogiches. He shared Luxemburg's position on the national question crossing swords with Lenin several times on the issue. He kept a photograph of Luxemburg on his office wall in the Lubianka headquarters of the Cheka. A complex ascetic (he was a teetotaller) and personally honest. The leader of the rival Polish Socialist Party Josef Piłsudski once wrote "he could tell no lie" he was arrested more than a dozen times and spent years in gaol or internal exile before 1917. He saw the Cheka as fighting a class war, and initially its operations were concentrated against the former privileged classes, but as the civil war became more brutal its operations widened to almost every aspect of society. Curiously the Cheka was also responsible for building orphanages, a project in which Dzerzhinsky took a particular personal interest. He remained head of the Cheka, the GPU, then OGPU until 1926 when he died of a heart attack after a three hour speech denouncing the Left Opposition.

19. Quoted in Anton Antonov-Ovseyenko *The Time of Stalin: Portrait of Tyranny* (Harper Row, 1981) p.160

20. *loc cit* p.151.

21. Carr *op. cit.* p.168

22. This speech is in V. I. Lenin *Collected Works* Volume 26 p.75 but the better translation here is by Peter Sedgwick in V. Serge *Year One of the Russian Revolution* p.197

23. From *Anarchists in the Russian Revolution* (New York 1973) p. 12

24. Carr *op.cit.* p.178

25. *Brevestnik* (Petrograd 13 April 1918 quoted in P. Avrich *Anarchists in the Russian Revolution* (New York 1973)) p.13

26. From *Anarchists in the Russian Revolution* (New York 1973) p.14

27. Richard Sakwa *Soviet Communists in Power* (New York 1988) p.171

28. Sakwa *loc cit*

29. Lenin *Collected Works* Vol. 29 pp.561-2

30. Smith (2017) p.205

31. 14 July 1918 *https://spartacus-educational.com/RUSterror.htm*

32. Lenin *Collected Works* Vol. 27 p. 19

33. Liebman p.229

34. Carr *op.cit.* p.178

35. You can get an idea of the class nature of the Cheka in such records as "*Decision: because he belongs to the proletarian class, Shustov to be released from arrest*" Quoted in Liebman p.314

36. Quoted in W.P. and Z.K. Coates *Armed Intervention in Russia 1918-22* (London, 1935) p. 29

37. Smith (2017) p. 98

38. Some of these appeared early on and the Left SR Commissar for Justice, Isaac Steinberg, instigated an enquiry into the criminal behaviour of a leading Chekist, Pyotr Krasikov who was roundly hated as a thug, even by those Bolsheviks who came across

him.

39. Victor Serge, *Memoirs of a Revolutionary 1901-41* (OUP 1963) p.80

40. For one example see Serge *op.cit.* p.82

41. Serge *op. cit.* pp.80-1

42. Alexander Rabinowitch *The Bolsheviks in Power* (Indiana, 2007 pp.222-3. The same author has also written an article (in Russian) on "*Moisei Uritskii: The Robespierre of Revolutionary Petrograd*" in *Otechestvennaiai istoriia* (National History) 2003 No 1:3-21

43. *op. cit*, p.224

44. *op. cit*, pp. 24-9

45. Lenin *Collected Works* Vol. 35 p.349

46. Lenin *Collected Works* Vol. 30 pp.327-8

47. *https://www.loc.gov/exhibits/archives/secr.html*

48. Even the meandacious and hostile Nicholas Werth had to admit this in *The Black Book of Communism https://ia800500.us.archive.org/26/items/TheBlackBookofCommunism10/the-black-book-of-communism-jean-louis-margolin-1999-communism.pdf* See p. 134

49. *https://www.dailymail.co.uk/news/article-3738277/Horrific-punishments-dreamt-Tsars-sent-millions-Siberia.html*

50. Antonov-Ovseyenko pp. 210-11

51. Anton Antonov-Ovseyenko *The Time of Stalin: Portrait of Tyranny* (already referred to above) gives a graphic account of Stalin's machinations. The author was the son of Vladimir Antonov-Ovseyenko, a leading Bolshevik who was obliterated by Stalin in 1938. His mother committed suicide in the gulag and he himself was arrested age 18. He spent 13 years in the camps. He founded a museum of the gulag in Moscow in 2001 and died age 93 in 2013.

52. See *The Russian Revolution* at *https://www.marxists.org/archive/luxemburg/1918/russian-revolution/ch01.htm*. It should also be noted that Luxemburg criticised using the terror to root out corruption as it became itself a source of corruption.

53. Serge o. 1

Chapter 13

1. *https://www.marxists.org/archive/luxemburg/1918/russian-revolution/ch08.htm*

2. Lenin *Selected Works* Vol. 2 p.505

3. Lenin *Collected Works* Vol. 33 p.98

4. Quoted in *The German Revolution and the Debate on Soviet Power*, ed. John Riddell (Pathfinder Press New York, 1986) p.33

5. The Bolshevik Party officially became the All-Russian Communist Party (Bolshevik) at it Seventh Congress on March 6-8 1918. Henceforth we will refer to them as "Communists" except when referring to earlier events.

6. Quoted in E. H. Carr *The Bolshevik Revolution* Vol. 3 p.133

7. Carr p.133 The British decided to withdraw their troops in March 1919 but it would be another six months before they left, and not before London dockers had refused to load the Jolly George supply ship bound for Archangel and Murmansk.

8. Carr p.138

9. L. Kritsman's history of the "war communism" period translates as *The Heroic Period of the Great October Revolution* (1926) p.166

Endnotes

10. Edward Acton *Rethinking the Russian Revolution* (1990) p.204

11. Diane Koenker "Urbanisation and Deurbanisation in the Russian Revolution and Civil War" in *Party, State and Society in the Russian Civil War* (ed. D. Koenker, W, Rosenberg and R G Suny) Indiana 1989 p.98

12. Figures compiled by Koenker *op.cit.* pp.81-2

13. See "The Social Background to Tsektran" by William Rosenberg in Koenker et al.

14. Koenker p.84

15. Florence Flamborough *A Nurse at the Russian Front*

16. *Notes sur la révolution bolchévique octobre 1917- janvier 1919* (Hachette Livre 2018)

17. Daniel R. Brower "The City in Danger" in Koenker et al. p.62

18. S.A. Smith *Red Petrograd* p.242

19. Smith p.244

20. Acton p.204

21. Chamberlin *The Russian Revolution* (New York 1935) Vol. 2 p.420

22. *Bread and Justice* p.94

23. Lenin *Collected Works* Vol. 27 p.241

24. All quotes from Lenin *Collected Works* Vol. 27 p.242

25. *Loc. cit.* p.258. The Taylor system was named after the mechanical engineer F.W. Taylor who, in 1909, proposed his system of extracting more work from the workforce by paying for measurable work done (akin to piece work). Lenin had previously denounced it in a 1914 article entitled *The Taylor System – Man's Enslavement by the Machine.*

26. Lenin *Collected Works* Vol. 27 p.269

27. *Loc.cit.* p. 271

28. *Loc.cit.* p. 265 And Trotsky had already called for "labour discipline and order" in a speech to the Party's Moscow City Conference on 28 March 1918. See W.H. Chamberlin *The Russian Revolution* Vol. 2 p.415

29. *Loc.cit.* p. 268. Emphasis in the original

30. *Loc.cit.* p. 272. Emphasis in the original

31. *https://www.marxists.org/history/ussr/government/constitution/1918/article4.htm* Chapter 14 is concerned with elections.

32. This and all preceding comments in quotation marks from A. Rabinowitch "The Petrograd First City District Soviet During the Civil War" in Koenker et al p.133

33. *Loc. cit.*

34. *Loc. cit.* p.138

35. W.H. Chamberlin *op. cit* Vol. 2 p.416

36. Mary McAuley *Bread and Justice* (1991) pp.91-2

37. *https://www.gutenberg.org/files/51594/51594-0.txt*

38. See Sarah Badcock, "Politics, Parties, and Power: Sormovo Workers in 1917" in *A Dream Deferred: New Studies in Russian and Soviet Labour History*, ed. D.Filtzer et al.(Peter Lang, 2008).

39. Koenker op. cit. p.84. Her source is David Mandel's *Petrograd Workers and the Soviet Seizure of Power* (London, 1984) pp. 390-413

40. *https://brill.com/view/book/9789004440395/BP000004.xml*

41. M. Liebman *Leninism under Lenin* (Merlin, 1980) p.229

42. A. Rabinowitch "The Petrograd First City District Soviet During the Civil War" in Koenker et al, p.148

43. A. Rabinowitch *op. cit.* p.145

44. S.A de Mowbray *Key Facts in Soviet History* (London 1990) p.63

45. A. Rabinowitch *op. cit.* p.150

46. A. Rabinowitch *op. cit.* p.150

47. Smith (2017) p.208. The phrase in quotations is the description of VTsIK's role in the Soviet Constitution of June 1918.

48. Marcel Liebman *Leninism under Lenin* (Merlin, 1980) p.230

49. Lenin *Collected Works* Vol.29 p.183 (emphasis in original)

50. *Loc. cit.* p.181

51. Quoted in Christopher Read *From Tsar to Soviets* (UCL, 1996) p.214

52. *Loc. cit.* p.214

53. N. Bukharin and E.Preobrazhensky *The ABC of Communism* (originally published October 1919 – Pelican edition 1970) p. 240

54. Lenin, "Speech to the First All-Russia Congress of Workers in Education and Socialist Culture" (30 July 1919) *Collected Works* Vol. 29 p.535

55. Quoted in Oskar Anweiler *The Soviets* (Merlin 1974) p.235

56. Quoted in Smith (2017) p.251

57. See Oskar Anweiler p.218 "...*the masses regarded them as "their" organs and could not be mobilised against them."*

58. Not to be confused with the Populist organisation from the 1880s called Black Repartition. This had included amongst its founders Georgi Plekhanov, Vera Zasulich and Pavel Axelrod who would go on to later found the Emancipation of Labour group, Russia's first Marxist organisation. "Chorni peredel", black repartition, meant for the peasantry "universal repartition".

59. Quoted in Smith (2017) p. 226. Tsiurupa, an agronomist by trade, despite being Commissar for Food, fainted during an early 1918 Sovnarkom meeting in the Kremlin due to lack of it. See Lara Douds *Inside Lenin's Government* p.81

60. Smith (2017) p.225

61. Kevin Murphy *Revolution and Counter-revolution: Class Struggle in a Moscow Metal Factory* (Haymarket 2007) p.64

62. Smith (2017) p.226

63. *Novaya Zhizn* 19 April 1918 (in J. Bunyan and H,H. Fisher (eds) *The Bolshevik Revolution* (Stanford, 1934)

64. Liebman p.257

65. The figure is Medvedev's *The October Revolution* (Constable, 1979) but Smith (1917) p.228 says the area "put to seed" was 15 to 24% of 1913

66. Medvedev p.152

67. Sometimes as much as three quarters of people's needs, according to Kritsman, as summarised in Alec Nove *An Economic History of the USSR*(Penguin 1982) p.54

68. Paul Avrich *Kronstadt* p.26 (based on Alexander Berkman's *The Kronstadt Rebellion* (Berlin 1922) p.10)

69. Quoted in Smith (2017) pp.227-8

70. Smith, (2017) p.218.

71. Lenin *Collected Works* Vol. 30 p.441

72. Lenin *Collected Works* Vol. 30 p.446

73. Lenin *Collected Works* Vol. 30 p.453

74. R.V. Daniels *The Conscience of the Revolution* (New York 1960) p.93
75. *http://www.leftcom.org/en/articles/2017-09-08/n-ossinsky%E2%80%99s-critique-of-state-capitalism-in-russia*
76. Quoted in Carr Vol. 1 p.182
77. As summarised by Paul Avrich from the official proceedings in his *Kronstadt 1921* (Princeton 1970) p.33

Chapter 14

1. Mary McAuley *Bread and Justice* (Oxford 1991) p.404
2. More than 380,000 workers had left the factories of Petersburg since 1917. See Sheila Fitzpatrick "The Legacy of the Civil War" in Diane Koenker et al (eds) *Party, State and Society in the Russian Civil War* (Indiana 1989) p.404
3. McAuley p. 405
4. McAuley p. 406 According to Paul Avrich the same anti-semitic calls were made in the Moscow strikes. *Kronstadt – the 1921 Uprising of the Sailors in the Context of the Political Development of the New Soviet State* (1970) p.36
5. McAuley p. 408
6. I. Getzler Kronstadt 1917-21 *The Fate of a Soviet Democracy* (Cambridge, 1983) p.213 Getzler, the biographer of Martov, tells us that the Petropavlovsk resolution may have been influenced by the thousand Menshevik posters posted up on February 27 (twenty days after the Petersburg strikes began) but the same demands were being made everywhere, even in plants in which the Communists still miraculously enjoyed majority support.
7. Avrich *Kronstadt* p.44
8. McAuley p. 406
9. McAuley p. 409
10. McAuley p. 410
11. Avrich p.57
12. Getzler p.189
13. Getzler p.191
14. *Loc. cit.*
15. *Loc. cit.*
16. Avrich p.104. Avrich has a long forensic discussion of this and other issues in his chapter "Kronstadt and the Russian Emigration" The counter-revolution hovered around the Kronstadt rebels (whose aims it did not share) and raised a fortune in cash to buy supplies to aid it (using the Russian Red Cross as a front) but these never came to fruition. However, such facts like the news of an uprising in Kronstadt had been printed in an SR newspaper in Prague and in the French press a full two weeks before the real rising, can only have underlined the case for a "White Guard plot" at the time.
17. Taken from Avrich pp.72-3
18. Getzler p.250
19. See P. Binns, T Cliff and C. Harman *Russia – from Workers State to State Capitalism* (Bookmarks 1987) p.20 . The *Kronstadt Izvestia*, edited by the SR Maximalist Lamanov, and circulated only in Kronstadt at that time, contained an article with this slogan in it but this was not a resolution of the sailors' movement. The slogan though did appear in many

of the peasant revolts around Russia at this time.

20. "Hue and Cry over Kronstadt" in *Kronstadt* a collection of writings of V.I .Lenin and Leon Trotsky (Monad Press) p.89

21. In February 1920 see Smith (2017) p. 232. *op.cit.* p.91 as prompt from Victor Serge for Trotsky to "remember" it, see *op.cit.* p.91. Trotsky is also "economical with the truth" when he sees that the suppression of Kronstadt was Dzerzhinsky's doing, when as head of the Military Revolutionary Committee in fact he ordered Tukhachevsky to carry it out (as even the introduction to the volume cited here, written by a Trotskyist tells us. See p.7).

22. Both quotes in W.H Chamberlin *The Russian Revolution* p.4. Soltz would support Stalin (who had been in the underground with him before the First World War until the Purges started to get out of hand and he denounced Vyshinsky. Stalin, presumably due to their past comradeship, did not have him arrested but when he persisted in his pursuit of Vyshinsky he lost his job and was eventually dragged off to a mental asylum. He died in 1945. See Roy Medvedev *Let History Judge* (Columbia 1989) pp.429-30

23. Avrich p.69

24. *Memoirs of a Revolutionary* (Oxford,1963) p.12

25. Avrich p.80

26. Quoted in Avrich p.84

27. *Memoirs of a Revolutionary* p.126

28. Kevin Murphy *Revolution and Counter-Revolution: Class Struggle in a Moscow Metal Factory* (Haymarket 2005) p.73

29. *Op. cit.* pp.128-9

30. Lenin *Collected Works* Vol.32 pp.441-2

31. Lenin *Collected Works* Vol. 32 p.206

32. Barbara C Allen *Alexander Shlyapnikov 1885-1937* (Haymarket 2015) p. 180

33. Allen *loc cit.*

34. Alexandra Kollontai *The Workers' Opposition* Solidarity London Pamphlet No.7 ((19) p.33 In the original it says "treated" (which makes no sense) rather than "built" but Allen (p.182) quotes the latter version. Emphasis in the original.

35. Quoted in O. Anweiler *The Soviets* (Merlin 1974) p.243

36. Allen p.183. Lenin often used such verbal violence to comrades which was figurative but given what was then happening at Kronstadt what he said in the Tenth Party Congress to Kollontai and Shlyapnikov underlines just how serious the crisis of the regime was in 1921.

37. Lenin *Collected Works* Vol. 34 p.24. Emphasis in original.

38. R.V.Daniels *The Conscience of the Revolution* (Simon and Schuster 1960) p.114

39. Lenin *Collected Works* Vol. 32 p.43

40. Both quotes from Lenin *Collected Works* Vol. 32 p.53 Emphasis in original.

41. Quoted in Daniels p.148

42. Quoted in Daniels pp.148-9

43. Quoted in Daniels p.148

44. *https://www.leftcom.org/en/articles/2019-12-06/miasnikov-s-draft-platform-for-the-communist-workers-international-1930*

45. *http://www.leftcom.org/en/articles/2017-02-17/an-epitaph-for-the-october-revolution*

46. Silvana Malle *The Economic Organisation of War Communism 1918-21* (Cambridge

Endnotes

1985) p.25 She wrote *"Some readers may find inconvenient the fact that, interrupting a well established tradition, the author provides no definition of war communism. An explanation is due for what could be interpreted as a lack of boldness. The belief acquired by the author is that no definition can encompass in a meaningful way the main attributes of the revolutionary phase of a transition from one system into another which aims at its negation, without compromising a genuine full description."*

47. Quoted in R. Sakwa *Soviet Communists in Power* (New York 1988) p.27
48. Smith (2017) p.232
49. Murphy p.64
50. *Memoirs of a Revolutionary* p.147
51. The figure is from Smith (2017) p.232
52. Quoted in Carr Vol. 2 p.291
53. Carr Vol. 2 p.320
54. Quoted in E.H. Carr *The Interregnum 1923-4* (Macmillan 1954) p.24
55. Daniels p.200
56. "Appeal of the Workers' Truth Group" published in the Berlin-based Menshevik journal *Sotsialisticheskii Vestnik* (Socialist Herald) quoted in R.V. Daniels *A Documentary History of Communism in Russia* (Vermont 1993) p.116. The Workers's Truth Group is often associated with Alexander Bogdanov, but at this point, although he shared some of its views he was not a member, and demanded an audience with Dzerzhinsky to tell him so in 1923.
57. See Simon Pirani *The Russian Revolution in Retreat 1920-4* (Routledge, 2008) p.156 There had been campaigns (literacy etc) throughout the civil war but after the Tenth Party Congress these "mobilisations" became a more conscious policy for building both the state and industrial production.
58. Carr Vol. 3 p.355
59. At least according to the not always reliable Alfred Rosmer. See A. Rosmer *Lenin's Moscow* (Pluto Press 1971) p.127
60. Serge p.140
61. See Carr Vol. 3 p.386
62. Quoted in G. Williams *Proletarian Order* (Pluto Press) p. 213
63. See *https://www.leftcom.org/en/articles/2011-11-01/platform-of-the-committee-of-intesa-1925*
64. *Platform of the Committee of Intesa* (1925) p.18 *https://www.leftcom.org/en/articles/2011-11-01/platform-of-the-committee-of-intesa-1925*
65. Fiedrich von Rabenau, *Hans Von Seeckt Aus seinem Leben* (Leipzig 1941) as translated by Ian Johnson. See *https://warontherocks.com/2016/06/sowing-the-wind-the-first-soviet-german-military-pact-and-the-origins-of-world-war-ii/*
66. E.H Carr *The Interregnum 1923-4* (Macmillan 1954) pp. 214-23

Chapter 15

1. C. Read *From Tsar to Soviets* (UCL 1996) p.270
2. Arshinov's account of Makhno's time in prison modestly omits his own role in his education. *"In 1908 he fell into the hands of the Czarist authorities, who condemned him to be hanged for anarchist associations and for taking part in terrorist acts. Because of*

his youth, the death penalty was commuted to life imprisonment at hard labor. Makhno
served his sentence in the Butyrki central prison of Moscow. Although prison life was
without hope and very difficult for him to bear, Makhno used it to educate himself.
He showed great perseverance and learned Russian grammar, mathematics, Russian
literature, the history of culture, and political economy. In fact, prison was the only school
in which Makhno acquired that historical and political knowledge which was a great help
to him in his subsequent revolutionary activity. (see *http://www.revoltlib.com/anarchism/*
history-of-the-makhnovist-movement-19181921/)

3. The transliteration of names becomes an even bigger nightmare as the Ukrainian sounds
can be rendered quite differently from the Russian. The Russian has been used here given
its greater simplicity in English (e.g. 'Grigoriev' instead of 'Hryhoriyiv') but there are
plenty of alternatives in both languages in various publications.

4. Or the Eastern side of the River Don.

5. Colin Darch *Nestor Makhno and Rural Anarchism in Ukraine 1917-21* (Pluto Press
2020) p.29. Other details of the meeting are in Michael Malet *Nestor Makhno in the*
Russian Civil War (Macmillan 1982) p.12. It is also in Paul Avrich's *The Russian*
Anarchists (Princeton, 1967) p.211. In his account of the Moscow trip, Arshinov does
not mention the meeting with Lenin, and even omits to say that the Communists gave
Makhno assistance to return to Ukraine. (see *http://www.revoltlib.com/anarchism/*
history-of-the-makhnovist-movement-19181921/)

6. Marcel Liebman *Leninism under Lenin* (Merlin 1975) p.262

7. Malet p.12

8. Darch p.102 quotes Antonov-Ovseyenko's report: "*... children's communes and*
schools are being established, and Guliaipole is and important cultural centre with ...
three secondary schools ... up to ten hospitals for the wounded and workshop organised
to repair guns". Liebman, p.263, tells us that Kamenev and Alfred Rosmer both tried to
reach an agreement with anarchists but, quoting Victor Serge, the majority of anarchists
gave a horrified refusal.

9. Darch p.61

10. Darch p.61

11. A tachanka was a sprung horse drawn cart with a mounted heavy machine gun
pointing from the rear. For all his contempt of irregular forces, Trotsky was not above
copying from them. L. Trotsky, *How the Revolution Armed: The Military Writings and*
Speeches of Leon Trotsky. (New Park Publications 1981) p.295

12. Darch p.124

13. Murphy p.61. The extreme brutality of the civil war in Russia can be better understood
if we compare it with the likes of the contemporaneous, and equally brutal, Irish Civil
War. It is no coincidence that both wars arose on the back of four years of imperialist
slaughter.

14. Azarov makes the point that the Kontrrazvedka were more subject to control by
the local committees than the Cheka, but it is clearly one of degree, as the Cheka was a
law unto itself. See Azarov's pamphlet *https://libcom.org/files/Kontrrazvedka%20-%20*
The%20Story%20of%20the%20Makhnovist%20Intelligence%20Service%20-%20V.%20
Azarov.pdf 15.

15. He returned to Russia in 1924 and was arrested by the OGPU who decided that he
(and his brother Daniel) had useful skills. He became one of the most effective OGPU

agents until 1937 when he perished like so many others in Stalin's purges.

16. Darch p.103

17. Darch p.118

18. Darch p.129

19. Avrich (1967) p.211

20. Quoted in Darch p.127 For more on the Makhnovschina and his subsequent legacy see the articles by Dyjbas at *http://www.leftcom.org/en/articles/2021-07-05/platformism-part-i* and *http://www.leftcom.org/en/articles/2021-07-09/platformism-part-ii*

21. Richard Sakwa *Soviet Communists in Power* (New York 1988) p.237

22. S.F.Cohen *Bukharin and the Bolshevik Revolution* (OUP 1981) pp.74-5 Cohen claims his quotations from Bukharin can be found in his review of Lenin's *State and Revolution* in *Kommunist* No.1 but this very short text can be found at *http://www.leftcom.org/en/articles/2019-02-21/bukharin-s-review-of-lenin-s-the-state-and-revolution* and does not contain the words he cites.

23. See N. Bukharin *Economics of the Transformation Period* (Bergman 1971) p.155

24. Quoted in Cohen p.155

25. This passage is based on Simon Pirani *The Russian Revolution in Retreat 1920-24* (Routledge 2008) pp.88-9

26. Allen p.245. See also Murphy p.73 for a longer quote from Shlyapnikov. What Lenin actually was doing was justifying the NEP. His actual words were: "*The capitalists will gain from our policy and will create an industrial proletariat, which in our country, owing to the war and the desperate poverty and ruin, has become declassed, i.e. dislodged from its class groove, and has ceased to exist as a proletariat.*" Lenin *Collected Works* Vol.33 p.65

27. Lenin *Collected Works* Vol. 33 p.288

28. "*Over half of the central commissariat officials, and around 90 per cent of upper echelon officials, had worked in some administrative position before October 1917.*" Douds p.73

29. *Loc.cit* p.290

30. Lenin told the Fourth Comintern Congress that that at the top we have "*at the outside several tens of thousands of our own people.*" However "*Down below, however there are thousands of old officials whom we got from the tsar and from bourgeois society and who, partly deliberately and partly unwittingly, work against us.*" *Collected Works* Vol. 33 p.428

31. See Pirani pp.93-6

32. *http://www.leftcom.org/en/articles/2017-09-08/n-ossinsky%E2%80%99 s-critique-of-state-capitalism-in-russia*

33. *http://www.leftcom.org/en/articles/2019-03-13/ossinsky-s-demand-for-clear-answers-april-1918*

34. See R. Kowalski *The Bolshevik Party in Conflict* (Macmillan 1991) p. 8 "*Left Communism in fact was a popular, broadly-based movement with considerable support at lower levels within the party*".

35. Bukharin when asked why he and his comrades had not moved against Lenin, he replied "*Am I of sufficient stature to become leader of a party and to declare war on Lenin... no, don't let us deceive ourselves*" Quoted in Cohen p.65. Daniels p.80. Afanasi Lomov was the only "Left" Communist on the Central Committee prepared to ditch

Lenin. Alexander Rabinowitch *The Bolsheviks in Power: The First Year of Soviet Rule in Petrograd*, p.174 quotes the *Protokoly tsentral'nogo komiteta RSDRP (b)* where Lomov is recorded as saying, *"there is no reason to be frightened by Lenin's threat to resign. We [Left Communists] must take power without V. I. [Lenin]."*

36. See Robert Mair *Inside the Beleaguered Fortress: Intra-Bolshevik Struggles and the Degeneration of the October Revolution by 1921* undergraduate dissertation for MA History University of Glasgow (March 2021)

37. Quoted in Pirani p.91

38. Sakwa p. 257

39. After this Ossinsky held several important posts in the state. He was Deputy Commissar for Agriculture from 1921 to 1923 (his views on the issue were highly respected by Lenin) and was a member of the State Planning Commission (Gosplan) as well as head of the Central Statistical Bureau. There is some irony that Ossinsky, once the arch-enemy of Taylorism, would be sent to the USA to find out how Henry Ford's factory had developed Taylorist methods and he returned to set up the first USSR car factory under licence from Ford in Gorky. He also returned with a present of a Ford car which attracted some attention in 1920s Moscow. See A. Antonov-Ovseyenko *The Time of Stalin – Portrait of a Tyranny* (Harper Row 1981) p.206

40. Mary McAuley's *Bread and Justice* p.183 was quoted earlier but the same conclusion is in Sakwa p.182

41. Taken from a Moscow regional party document and quoted in Sakwa p.182

42. *Loc. cit* p.290, and for the next ten or so pages!

43. *Loc. cit* p.302

44. See *https://www.marxists.org/archive/gorter/1920/historical-materialism.htm*. For some reason marxists.org places the pamphlet in 1920 when Kautsky and Gorter had long moved in opposite directions.

45. In *Lenin's Political Thought* (Macmillan 1977) Vol. 2 Chapter 3

46. Lenin *Collected Works* Vol. 32 p.330

47. *Loc. cit* p.333

48. *Loc. cit* p.334

49. *Loc. cit* p.350

50. *Imperialism and World Economy* (1915). For a fuller critique of Bukharin's work in this field see *http://www.leftcom.org/en/articles/2020-08-21/bukharin-on-state-capitalism-and-imperialism*

51. *Imperialism and World Economy* (Merlin 1972) p.169

52. *Economics of the Transformation Period* (Pluto Press 1971) p.158

53. See Pirani *loc. cit.* "*Chapter 6 Mass mobilization versus mass participation: Workers in 1922*"

54. See Andy Willimott *Living the Dream Urban Communes and Soviet Socialism 1917-32* (Oxford, 2017)

55. Sakwa p.186

56. This is Sakwa's summary. *Loc. cit.* p.187

57. L. Trotsky *The Revolution Betrayed* (Pathfinder 1972) p. 89-90

58. Isaac Deutscher *Stalin* (Pelican 1966) p.234-5

59. Lenin "Better Fewer, But Better" *Collected Works* Vol. 33 p.490

60. Sakwa p.274. Daniels p.116 and Liebman p.297 both also point to the liveliness of

debate at this time

61. Lara Douds *Inside Lenin's Government: Ideology, Power and Practice in the Early Soviet State* (Bloomsbury 2019) p.125 and thereafter. The People's Commissars were also not ministers but heads of a collegium. This apparently cooperative system of government, which was widely supported by the Party, had the defect of making the commissariats focus on just the work of their department rather than act as a government looking at the situation as a whole. After 1919 it was increasingly sidelined by the emerging Politburo. The Decists were still arguing in favour of collegial working at the Ninth Party Congress in 1920.

62. Quoted in I. Deutscher *The Prophet Armed* (OUP 1954) p.509

63. *The Cambridge Companion to Brecht*, Cambridge University Press, 2006, p. 239

64. Lenin *Collected Works* Vol. 31 p.23

65. Quoted in Daniels p.169, translating Stalin's article "Lenin as the Organiser and Leader of the Russian Communist Party"

66. Daniels p.165

67. Daniels p.169

68. Drabkina (1901-74) was a secretary to Sverdlov. Her memoirs were only published in edited form in the USSR but her *Gli ultimi giorni di Lenin* (Lenin's Final Days) was published in Italian (translated by Giovanna Carullo) by Tindalo (Rome 1970). She took part in the suppression of Kronstadt in 1921 and as a member of the Trotskyist opposition spent years in the gulags suffering severe beatings which damaged her hearing. Despite this she remained a supporter of "socialism" à la Stalin until she died.

69. Roy Medvedev *Let History Judge* (Columbia 1989) p.77

70. E.H. Carr *The Interregnum* (Macmillan 1954) p.340

71. The references which follow are taken from the version on marxists.org *https://www.marxists.org/reference/archive/stalin/works/1924/foundations-leninism/index.htm*

Chapter 16

1. 20,000 Communards were killed in the so-called "Bloody Week" (Semaine sanglante) in May 1871. For a starting guide to more on the Paris Commune see *http://www.leftcom.org/en/articles/2021-03-18/1871 -2021-vive-la-commune*

2. Engels in the 1891 introduction to Marx's Civil War in France wrote; *the Commune was compelled to recognise that the working class, once come to power, could not go on managing with the old state machine; that in order not to lose again its only just conquered supremacy, the working class must, on the one hand, do away with all the old repressive machinery previously used against itself, and, on the other, safeguard itself against its own deputies and officials, by declaring them all, without exception, subject to recall at any moment.*

3. A trick which the Social Democrats in Germany managed to pull off in setting up the bourgeois Weimar Republic in 1919 - an important factor in the isolation of the revolution to Russia.

4. *http://www.leftcom.org/en/articles/2021-01-04/party-and-class-in-1918 -vladimir-sorin-on-soviet-power*

5. *https://www.marxists.org/reference/archive/stalin/works/1924/foundations-leninism/*

ch04.htm

6. *https://www.marxists.org/archive/lenin/works/1915/aug/23.htm*

7. E.H. Carr discusses the controversy in *Socialism in One Country* Volume 2 (Penguin, 1970) pp.48-51

8. "October Revolution and the Tactics of the Russian Communists" 17 December 1925 in J. V. Stalin *Problems of Leninism* (Moscow: Foreign Language Publishers, 1934), pp. 162. Our emphasis.

9. For a longer comment see *https://www.leftcom.org/en/articles/2003-08 -01/stalin-and-stalinism*

10. For more on this see the pamphlet *Trotsky, Trotskyism, Trotskyists http://www.leftcom. org/en/articles/2000-10-01/trotsky-and-trotskyism*

11. The quote comes from *The Russian Enigma*, [pp.280-1] of Ante Ciliga and may be based on recall. Ciliga was not always reliable as a witness hence our use of "allegedly" about the quote. For Smirnov's own contribution to the Left Communist journal *Kommunist* see *https://www.leftcom.org/en/articles/2020-12-14/vladimir-smirnov-s -contribution-to-the-debate-on-the-soviet-economy*

12. See Carr (1970) p.236

13. H. Gorter World Revolution *https://www.marxists.org/archive/gorter/ 1918/world-revolution.htm#chapter4*

14. *https://www.marxists.org/archive/gorter/1923/world-revolution.htm*

15. See *https://www.marxists.org/archive/ruhle/1920/ruhle02.htm*

16. In this history we don't want to dwell too much on the theoretical issues but a fuller discussion of how the Russian Revolution affects our understanding of class consciousness can be found in our pamphlet *Class Consciousness and Revolutionary Organisation.* See *https://www.leftcom.org/en/ articles/2018-06-30/class-consciousness-and-revolutionary -organisation*

17. Circular Letter to Wilhelm Liebknecht et al *https://www.marxists.org/archive/marx/ works/1879/09/17.htm*

18. According to Nick Heath *"The Platform was an analysis of the disorganisation of the anarchist movement at the time, and was an attempt to push it in a more organised, class struggle direction. The Platform was not an attempt at writing an anarchist manifesto. It was a discussion document and the authors never claimed to have all the answers."* Nevertheless it was rejected by most of the famous anarchists of the epoch like Berneri, Malatesta and Volin. *http://libcom.org/thought/platformism-an-introduction*

19. *Class Consciousness and Revolutionary Organisation.* p.34

20. All taken from Rühle's own account: *https://www.marxists.org/archive/ruhle/1920/ ruhle01.htm*

21. A. Bordiga *Towards the Establishment of Workers' Councils in Italy. https://www. marxists.org/archive/bordiga/works/1920/workers-councils.htm*

22. The Red Two Years

23. A. Bordiga *Party and Class* (1921) *https://www.marxists.org/archive/bordiga/ works/1921/party-class.htm*

24. A. Bordiga *Towards the Establishment of Workers' Councils in Italy. https://www. marxists.org/archive/bordiga/works/1920/workers-councils.htm*

Endnotes

25. *Loc. cit. https://www.marxists.org/archive/bordiga/works/1921/party-class.htm*
26. Both quotes from A. Bordiga *Proletarian Dictatorship and Class Party* (1951) *https:// www.marxists.org/archive/bordiga/works/1951/class-party.htm*
27. *https://www.leftcom.org/en/articles/2020-03-16/political-platform-of -the-internationalist-communist-party-1952*

Index of Names

Alexander II (Romanov)
12, 14.
Alexandrovich, Peter
118.
Antonov, Alexander
155, 199-201.
Antonov-Ovseyenko, Vladimir
88, 125, 127, 199, 201.
Armand, Inessa
97.
Arshinov, Peter
200, 226
Avksentiev, Nikolai
116.
Bakunin, Mikhail
55, 200.
Balk, Alexander
39.
Berkman, Alexander
173, 184, 202.
Bernstein, Eduard
32, 112, 159, 226.
Bogdanov, Alexander
47.
Bordiga, Amadeo
197, 228-230.
Bosch, Yevgenia
92.
Bukharin, Nikolai
24, 55, 91-92, 95, 106-108, 113, 117, 120,
126, 133-135, 190, 203-204, 206-208, 211,
214, 221
Chernov, Viktor
54, 65, 72-73, 88, 117, 122.
Chicherin, Georgy
196.
Chkheidze, Nikolai
55.
Czernin, Ottokar
105.

Dan, Fyodor
66, 175-176, 178.
Dutov, Alexander
124-125.
Dzerzhinsky, Felix
146-147, 149-150, 152, 155-156.
Eberlein, Hugo
195.
Engels, Friedrich
13, 32, 111, 145.
Godunov, Boris
12.
Golitsyn, Nikolai
44.
Gorky, Maxim
66, 80, 150, 152, 172.
Gorter, Herman
27, 208, 225.
Gotman, Iosif
202.
Gotz, Abram
116.
Gramsci, Antonio
197.
General Graves
128.
Gvozdev, Kuzma
47-48.
Hilferding, Rudolf
113.
Iarchuk, Efim
202.
Ilyin-Zhenevsky, Alexander
86-87, 106, 118.
Jaurès, Jean
23-24.
Joffe, Adolph
103, 108-109, 137.
Kaiurov, Vasilii
37-38, 42.

Index of Names

Kaledin, Alexei
84, 124-126.

Kalinin, Mikhail
45, 184.

Kamenev, Lev
29, 53, 64, 66-67, 75, 80, 82, 84-85, 88,
102, 104, 111, 121, 170, 189, 201, 203,
208, 216.

Kamkov, Boris
116-117.

Karl I (Habsburg)
105.

Kautsky, Karl
27, 33, 112-113, 159, 208.

Kerensky, Alexander
60, 67-75, 77-78, 81-86, 88, 102, 111, 116,
121, 124, 142, 155, 220.

Khabalov, Sergey
40, 43, 45.

Kolchak, Alexander
117, 130, 132, 160, 187.

Kollontai, Alexandra
56, 66-67, 96-97, 188-189.

Kornilov, Lavr
69, 71-76, 78, 80-81, 85-86, 124-125, 151.

Krasin, Leonid
196.

Krasnov, Pyotr
124-125, 142.

Krestinsky, Nikolai
153, 189.

Kritsman, Lev
100, 161, 192.

Kropotkin, Petr
200.

Krupsakaya, Nadezhda
217.

Kseshinskaya, Matilda
64.

Kun, Béla
195-196.

Kutepov, Alexander
45.

Kuznetsov, N.V
194.

Lashkevitch, Major
43, 44.

Lenin, Vladimir
6, 11, 16, 20-21, 23, 25-31, 33, 38, 41, 52,
54-59, 61-69, 72-74, 76-77, 79, 81-82,
84-86, 88-89, 91-97, 99-107, 110-118,
121, 125-128, 132-133, 136-142, 144-145,
147-150, 152-154, 156, 158-160, 163-165,
169-172, 174-175, 179, 182-184, 186-196,
199-201, 203-206, 208-218, 221, 223-224,
227.

Levi, Paul
160, 195-197.

Liebknecht, Karl
24, 27, 55, 109, 137-138, 159, 195.

Lomov, Afanasi
95, 100, 106.

Ludendorff, Erich
109.

Lunacharsky, Anatoly
54, 67, 167.

Lutovinov, Yuri
188.

Luxemburg, Rosa
19-20, 23-24, 81, 91-92, 109-110, 112,
119, 138, 156, 158-159, 195, 221.

Lvov, Georgy
70.

Macdonald, Ramsey
25

Makhno, Nestor
123, 130, 139, 148-149, 200-203, 226.

Martov, Julius
23, 54, 63, 87-88, 116, 154, 170, 175, 178.

Marx, Karl
6-7, 74, 91-92, 98, 111, 208, 212, 220,
224, 226, 229.

Maximoff, Grigori
202.

Miasnikov, Gavril
136-137, 187, 191, 194, 207.

Miller, Yevgeny
128.

Milyukov, Pavel
50, 59-60.

Milyutin, Vladimir
94.
Mirbach, Wilhelm von
118, 149, 151.
Molotov, Vyacheslav
52.
Muranov, Matvei
53.
Nicholas II (Romanov)
18, 43, 50, 71.
Ossinsky, Nikolai
95, 106, 126, 134, 170, 175, 192, 206-207, 214.
Pankhurst, Sylvia
149, 188.
Pannekoek, Anton
27, 111.
Piatakov, Georgy
92.
Platten, Fritz
121.
Plehve, Viascheslav
15.
Plekhanov, Georgi
27.
Podtelkov, Fyodor
125.
Polkovnikov, Petrovich
85, 116.
Preobrazhensky, Yevgeni
100, 118, 207, 211.
Purishkevich, Vladimir
116.
Radek, Karl
104, 107-108, 120, 138-139, 158, 191, 195, 218, 221, 228.
Raskolnikov, Fyodor
64, 66
Riazanov, David
85, 88, 121.
Roshal, Semyon
64, 67.
Roy, M.N.
197.

Rühle, Otto
27, 225-226, 228-229.
Sapronov, Timofei
175, 189-190, 207.
Serge, Victor
182-184, 186-187, 193, 196.
Shlyapnikov, Alexander
29-30, 33-34, 38-40, 44, 48, 52-53, 187-189, 204
Shulgin, Vasily
47.
Skobelev, Matvey
55.
Smirnov, Vladimir
95, 131, 136, 175, 207, 224.
Spiridonova, Maria
117, 151, 205.
Stalin, Joseph
53, 93, 98, 100, 107, 111-112, 132, 155-156, 189, 191, 198, 210-218, 223-224.
Steinberg, Isaak
98, 144.
Sukhanov, Nikolai
32-33, 43, 55, 63, 73, 87-88, 100, 116.
Sverdlov, Jakob
100, 200.
Trotsky, Leon
6, 16, 20-21, 39, 41, 44, 54, 60, 67, 71, 78-79, 81, 84-88, 103-106, 116, 127, 130-133, 135-136, 139, 141, 144, 167, 179-185, 188-190, 192, 194, 196, 198, 201, 204, 207, 211-214, 220, 223-224.
Tsereteli, Irakli
54, 63, 66, 118.
Tukhachevsky
186, 199.
Uritsky, Moisei
117, 130, 150, 152-153.
Volin (Vsevolod Mikhailovich Eikhenbaum)
93, 111, 202.
Volodarsky, V.
68, 74, 82, 84, 117, 143, 150, 152-153.
Witte, Sergei
12-13, 18.

Index of Names

Wrangel, Pyotr
131, 140, 155, 202.
Zadov, Lev
202.
Zalutsky, Pyotr
52.
Zetkin, Clara
24, 159, 195.
Zinoviev, Grigory
66-67, 80, 84, 119, 139, 178, 185, 196,
214, 216.
Zheleznyakov, Anatoli
122.